Colours, Battle Honours and Medals of a Staffordshire Regiment

80th REGIMENT OF FOOT

by

Robert Hope

Published by
CHURNET VALLEY BOOKS
43 Bath Street, Leek, Staffordshire. 01538 399033

© Robert Hope and Churnet Valley Books 1999
ISBN 1 897949 48 0

Printed in Malta by Interprint Limited

Acknowledgements

Of all the people I need to thank, firstly it must be Linda my wife and Jonathan my son for their boundless patience in coping with my zealous enthusiasm in researching and assembling the information contained in this book. They have had to endure countless hours of meetings, discussions and trips to museums, libraries, churches and the like. For their forbearance and encouragement, I thank them most dearly.

I also wish to acknowledge the generous help I have received from the staff, both past and present, at the Staffordshire Regiment Museum, Whittington Barracks near Lichfield. I must make special mention of the Regimental Secretary, Major E. Green and Major M. K. Beedle M.B.E., who have always been at hand to offer help and advice. I have received the free use of the priceless records and artefacts at the Museum and it is with the Regiment's kind permission that some of these records, drawings and photographs have been incorporated.

Many thanks to the friends and colleagues who have shown an interest and given much encouragement for the book to be completed, too many to mention by name.

It would be very difficult to produce a book of this nature without the help of the professional institutions such as the Public Records Office, Kew, and the National Army Museum at Chelsea, and I thank them for their help. Furthermore, I wish to thank the staff at the Royal Military Academy at Sandhurst, in particular Miss D Hillier, the Librarian.

The photographs of St Michael's Chapel (dedicated to the Staffordshire Regiment), and the other memorials within Lichfield Cathedral, are reproduced by the kind permission of the Dean and Chapter of Lichfield Cathedral.

Contents

Dedication

*To the active soldier whilst serving,
not knowing that one day to be remembered
from generation to generation.*

Shako Helmet Plate
Other Ranks 1878 -1881

COVER PICTURE: The illustration used for the cover of this book is a reproduction of the painting "Ferozeshah 1845'. The painting depicts the climatic action of the battle when the black Sikh standard was captured by the 80th Regiment of Foot. The artist, Peter Archer, is recognised as one of the best military painters and he is foremost in his reproductions of the 80th Regiment and its conflicts. A print of this painting, 29½" x 20½", is available from the Staffordshire Regiment R.H.Q. and Museum, Whittington Barracks, Lichfield, WS14 9PY

Preface

The 80th Regiment of Foot (Staffordshire Volunteers) came into existence during the year of 1793 when Lord Henry William Paget formed the Regiment. The 80th was to remain an 'independent regiment' for some eighty-eight years, until in 1881 it became the 2nd Battalion of the South Staffordshire Regiment. The 80th Regiment of Foot served in various parts of the British Isles, and throughout the world, acting as peacemaker or carrying out policing duties. The Regiment also served both Sovereign and Country in defence or expansion of the realm. As a 'Foot' Regiment the Staffordshire Volunteers uniquely fought both on land and on the sea and wherever they did so, they fought with distinction. Whenever the Regiment marched displaying their Sovereign's and Regimental Colours, they did so proudly. During their service abroad the Regiment came into contact with many people who had different beliefs, religions and cultures, the Regiment and its soldiers were well respected and well thought of by the public and the communities with which they associated.

In researching the history of a regiment or similar fighting force, an important reference is the battle honours that have been awarded. This gives an indication to the campaigns and battles that the regiment has participated in and in which parts of the world it has served. These battle honours can be found proudly displayed on the regimental regalia such as its colours, guidons, horse harnesses, drums, etc. Information can also be found in regimental digests and records as well as history books.

It is recorded that the 80th Regiment of Foot (Staffordshire Volunteers) was awarded a total of seven Battle Honours. The earliest honour bestowed on the Regiment was Egypt (with the Sphinx) for the epic journey the Regiment had to undergo in 1801. Soldiers of the Regiment suffered greatly in the long and arduous passage to Egypt to fight against the French during the French Revolutionary Wars 1793-1802. Only seven Military General Service medals were claimed by members of the Regiment who actually took part in this campaign.

The next three battle honours were gained for actions during the First Sikh War 1845-1846. The first of these was Moodkee (1845), the second Ferozeshah (1845) and the third Sobraon (1846). A total of eight hundred and forty Sutlej Campaign medals were issued to members of the Regiment who took part in this conflict.

The fifth Honour to be gained was that of Pegu for the Regiments' part in the second Burma War 1852-53. One thousand and twelve men were awarded the Indian General Service medal with the clasp 'PEGU'. The penultimate honour to be awarded was that of Central India for the Regiment's involvement in the latter stages of the Indian Mutiny 1857-58. A total of eight hundred and eight men were awarded the Indian Mutiny medal with one hundred and sixty-two awarded the clasp 'CENTRAL INDIA' to go with their medal.

The seventh and final battle honour to be awarded to the 80th Regiment was South Africa 1878-79. During the period 1877 to 1879 a total of one thousand two hundred and eleven men of the Regiment took part and were subsequently awarded the South Africa medal. The Zulu War of 1879 was a small but highly controversial colonial war. Two members of the Regiment were to be awarded the Victoria Cross for their outstanding bravery in this war. These were Private Samuel Wassall and Colour Sergeant Anthony Booth, at Isandhlwana on 22nd January 1879 and at the Intombi River on 12th March 1879 respectively.

This book gives details and descriptions of the five Stands of Colours that the Regiment proudly carried throughout the various periods of its existence, whilst performing duties in this country and abroad, in peace time or in battle. Information relating to the involvement of the 80th Regiment in the various campaigns and battles in which resulted in a battle honour being awarded is included. Information on the relevant medals is incorporated including various medal lists for the 80th Regiment naming all recipients of medals who were awarded for taking part in the various wars and campaigns for which battle honours resulted. All known casualties of war, whether killed in action, died of wounds, wounded, died of disease, or died as the result of the climatic conditions whilst on campaign, are also included. The names of all officers who served with the Regiment from 1793 until it became the 2nd Battalion South Staffordshire Regiment in 1881 are listed.

This book does not attempt to describe in detail the hardships, the joy or grief, or the endurance and stamina required of a soldier serving in a foreign clime. But I hope it succeeds in telling a part of the history of a typical British Infantry Regiment through its colours, battle honours and medals and that the information will prove useful to other historians and researchers in their study of military history.

Lord Henry William Paget.
(from the painting by T. Lawrence)

Foreword

by

Major (Retd.) E Green, Regimental Secretary,
The Staffordshire Regiment (The Prince of Wales's)

This is the second book on the 80th Regiment of Foot by Robert Hope and like its predecessor on the Zulu War, it is an excellent piece of research. Robert is now a leading expert on the details of the service of the 80th Regiment and its soldiers, and his knowledge and research effort has produced another book which will be useful to serious students whilst remaining accessible to general readers.

Of all the former Regiments that go to make up the present day STAFFORDS, the 80th (Staffordshire Volunteers) is the one which can trace its history most closely to Staffordshire and much of the present day West Midlands. Although its formal existence was for less than 100 years (1793-1881) it lived on as the 2nd Battalion The South Staffordshire Regiment until 1948. Indeed my distinguished predecessor Colonel Hugh Cook, who wrote the foreword to Robert's Zulu War book, always referred to the 2nd Battalion, which he commanded at the end of the Second World War, as the 80th. In its second incarnation it was proud to include Sicily and Arnhem amongst its Battle Honours.

The Staffordshire Regiment is delighted to number Robert Hope amongst its supporters. Not only does he carry out this detailed research and turn it into books of great value, he is also active as a committee member of the Lichfield and Tamworth Branch of the Friends of the Staffordshire Regiment and is a generous donor to the Regimental Museum. It is particularly fitting that this book should go to press just as we are re-opening the Museum at Whittington Barracks, Lichfield with a completely new display. I have high hopes that this book and the refurbished Museum will share equal success.

Whittington Barracks
Lichfield
Staffordshire
8th March 1999

Officer, 80th Regiment of Foot (Staffordshire Volunteers) c1816.

Chapter 1
The 80th Regiment of Foot (Staffordshire Volunteers)

In the year 1793 the French King Louis XVI and his Queen, Marie Antoinette were executed. The revolutionary people of France soon after declared war on Britain, the Nederlands and Spain. At the start of the first French Revolutionary War the Government of Britain were facing a serious threat to the nation. Never since the actual invasion of the Normans in the eleventh century or the attempt by the Spanish in the sixteenth century had these islands faced such a crisis. The decision was made that more soldiers were required to neutralise the threat of invasion and to take on the French in battle on the main land of Europe. The government through Parliament spread the word that new regiments were to be found.

A young man of only twenty-five years of age seized the opportunity to raise his own regiment. This man was Lord Henry William Paget. He had little knowledge and limited experience of military affairs, although he did come from a military family. His only experience came from serving in his father's own militia which contained people from his vast estates in Staffordshire. Undaunted, Henry William Paget set forth to raise a regiment.

Through his family connections a meeting was arranged with Prime Minister William Pitt. Paget informed Pitt of his dream and ambition to raise a cavalry regiment. The Prime Minister's response was that it was infantry regiments that the Country required and it needed them urgently. Henry's plans thus altered, he decided, *'if this is what the country needs, it shall be an Infantry Regiment that I shall thus raise'*, and in the year 1793 the 80th Regiment of Foot was formed. Henry Paget immediately tendered his resignation from his father's militia to take up a Lieutenant-Colonelcy in his new regiment.

Henry's father, a very wealthy man, greatly financed his son's venture and generously contributed all that was necessary. The new regiment was formed within the boundaries of the County of Staffordshire with many of its first soldiers being transferred from his father's militia. The regiment was designated the regimental number '80' and given the title 'Staffordshire Volunteers'. It was the third Staffordshire regiment to be formed. It should also be noted that it was the third regiment to be allocated the number '80', although the previous two regiments had no connection with Staffordshire. The soldiers of the regiment would wear the uniform of the day, red tunics and blue trousers, and to differentiate them from other regiments they would have yellow facings - their collars and cuffs.

The new 80th Regiment, with seven hundred men of all ranks, was immediately sent to Chatham in Kent. Paget was aided by two uncles who had joined the regiment with the ranks of Major. Because of the threat to the Channel Islands by the French in 1794 the regiment was ordered to Guernsey. Paget was not happy with this posting, wanting to see action against the French, and through his family's connections he eventually succeeded in obtaining a posting for the Regiment to mainland Europe, joining the Duke of York.

This expedition to the low countries, marching and fighting in Holland and Flanders took a tremendous toll on the Regiment because of the Arctic-like conditions, the poor provisions and the lack of medical support. Many of the men were reduced to wearing rags and were very poorly shod. The 80th returned to England in 1795 with less than half of its establishment fit for duty. After a very short period to recover the Regiment was sent to the Isle of Dieu off the French coast. Unfortunately very little was achieved and the regiment again lost many men.

After these first miserable experiences, the Regiment was sent in 1796 to South Africa, and at the Cape of Good Hope the Regiment was to have its first taste of success, albeit in an unusual manner. The Regiment was ordered to take part in the capture of a Dutch naval squadron, which was successful and consequently for a short period the Regiment provided members to serve on board the ships.

France in the latter eighteenth century following the French Revolution, started to expand its empire under Napoleon Bonaparte and Egypt fell under their control. Britain saw this as a threat to their power in India and decided that Napoleon and his army in Egypt must be defeated. The 80th in 1801 was stationed in Trincomalee, Ceylon and was ordered to Egypt to join Sir Ralph Abercomby. The Regiment sailed and marched countless miles, suffering greatly in the process. In the end they arrived too late to take part in the battle, but the Regiment was thought of so highly for their efforts by the governments in England and India, that it was awarded the first of its battle honours, 'Egypt' (with the Sphinx). Following this adventurous journey the Regiment was ordered back to India where it remained for many years.

In 1816 the Regiment was ordered back to England for a period of 'Home Service', but all privates 'fit for duty' remained at that station. Therefore, one of the first jobs for the Regiment was to recruit new men to fill the ranks, but it only took a few months to regain a full establishment of men. The Regiment continued normal policing duties in England and Scotland and whilst the Regiment was in Edinburgh orders were received to march to Liverpool, on route to be stationed in Ireland. 1821 saw the 80th move to Gibraltar, Malta and the Ionian Islands for the next ten years, after which they returned home again, resuming policing duties in England and Ireland.

In 1836 the Regiment was detailed to escort convicts to Australia. Small detachments acting as guards and warders were posted to numerous ships transporting the convicts. These journeys, between November 1836 and December 1838, proved very hazardous across vast oceans. The regimental headquarters were initially based in Sydney but later transferred to Paramatta. In Australia the 80th formed detachments and soldiers were posted as garrison troops to a number of out-stations throughout New South Wales and on Norfolk Island.

During the years 1840-1844 the Regiment also provided detachments in New Zealand. When Captain Hobson landed in New Zealand on the 29th January 1840 to be installed as the Lieutenant-Governor of New Zealand, a detachment consisting of four officers and eighty-three rank and file of the 80th was ordered to leave Sydney for New Zealand. This contingent under the command of Major Bunbury formed the official escort at the Waitangi ceremonies and the signing of the treaty. Only the North Island of New Zealand was under British control and this was administered from Australia. The South Island with no substantial European settlers, was not annexed to British authority. With an increase of French and American shipping around the South Island, the claim for control was under threat, consequently Major Bunbury and a detachment of the 80th travelled to the Island to raise the Union Flag. The 80th made history, and both islands of New Zealand became part of the British Empire.

Additional detachments served in New Zealand, in the 'Bay of Plenty', Auckland and Wellington, and these troops were employed on policing duties and in the construction of barracks and defence works. During 1842 it is reputed that the Regiment subdued a disturbance between two warring tribes in the 'Bay of Plenty'. Following an incident at Wairau in 1843 a further detachment of fifty men of the 80th, with a company of the 96th Regiment of Foot, was hastily ordered to the area. The situation subsided and the troops were ordered back to Sydney.

During April 1844, members of the 80th Regiment stationed in New Zealand were replaced by men of the 96th Regiment of Foot, and returned to Australia. Four rank and file members of the Regiment took their discharge whilst in New Zealand and became some of the first settlers with direct connections with Staffordshire.

From Australia the regiment was ordered to Agra in India. During the passage to India the Regiment travelled on four ships, and one of these carrying Major Bunbury, three companies and their families, altered course and ran aground on the Andaman Islands in the Bay of Bengal. Some fifty days were spent in a most inhospitable place, populated by cannibals, until they were rescued.

In 1845 the Regiment was ordered to the borders of the Punjab region and took part in the first of the Sikh Wars. In this war, also known as the Sutlej Campaign, the Regiment fought valiantly in three of the four major battles, in which the Sikhs were defeated. The 80th were subsequently awarded three battle honours; 'Moodkee' (1845), 'Ferozeshah' (1845) and 'Sabraon' (1846).

From India the Regiment was ordered to Burma to take part in the Second Burmese War. In this short war, successful actions resulted in the capture of Rangoon, Pegu and Prome. The Regiment was awarded the battle honour, 'Pegu'. At the conclusion of the war, the Regiment went back to India and then in 1854 returned to England and 'Home Duty'.

From 1856 through to 1857 the Regiment served in South Africa, based at Fort Beaufort, providing detachments in the Cape Colony. Then, with the revolt of the Indian troops in India, the 80th was ordered there and took part in the closing stages of the Indian Mutiny. For the Regiment's involvement in Central India chasing and defeating the rebels, in this scarcely mentioned part of the mutiny, the Regiment was awarded the Battle Honour, 'Central India'.

After several more years spent in India the Regiment returned home to spend time in Ireland. In 1866 the Regiment was sent back to India to join the Bhutan Field Force to subdue the Bhutanese and to put a stop to their raiding of British Territories. After this punitive exercise, the Regiment returned to England again and further policing duties in England and Ireland.

In 1872 the Regiment was back on the move, this time to Singapore with detachments being sent to Penang and Malacca. From 1872 through to 1876, the 80th served in Hong Kong. Because of the constant conflict between the Chinese and Malays, peace was constantly disturbed in the adjoining British territory known as Perak, on the west side of the Malay peninsular. The murder of a British Resident by the Ismail encouraged the Rajahs to join forces and this situation sparked the British Government into action. A British force which included the 80th Regiment was sent to sort the situation out. The Perak expedition was successful and peace was restored.

The next posting was to South Africa in 1877. The Regiment served there with much distinction, taking part in the Sekukuni Campaigns of 1878, 1879 and the Zulu War of 1879. It should be noted that as a result of the prompt actions taken by the 80th Regiment during 1879, the first Boer War was delayed, eventually occurring in 1881. For its service in South Africa, the Regiment received its final battle honour, 'South Africa 1878-1879'. This final tour of duty as an 'independent regiment', was possibly its finest era, for the 80th marched, fought and died upholding the finest standards and traditions of a British Infantry Regiment.

Lord Henry William Paget eventually inherited the title of Lord Uxbridge, following the death of his father. He became a distinguished cavalry officer and an experienced military campaigner, achieving the rank of Field Marshal, and destined to become Wellington's second in command at the Battle of Waterloo. He was later created First Marquis of Anglesey KG, GCB. For a man who at the time of raising the 80th had limited military experience, Lord Paget could be extremely proud of the 80th Regiment of Foot's (Staffordshire Volunteers) achievments.

Through the Cardwell Reforms during the 1870s, the 38th Regiment of Foot (1st Staffordshire) amalgamated with the 80th Regiment of Foot (Staffordshire Volunteers) in 1881 to form the South Staffordshire Regiment, becoming the 1st and 2nd Battalions respectively. In 1959 the South Staffordshire Regiment amalgamated with the North Staffordshire Regiment (64th Regiment of Foot - 2nd Staffordshire and the 98th Regiment of Foot - Prince of Wales's), to form the present Staffordshire Regiment.

REGIMENT POSTINGS 1793-1881

1793-1794	Chatham
1794	Guernsey
1794-1795	Campaign in the Low Counties
1795	Isle Dieu Expedition
1796-1797	Cape Town
1797-1801	Trincomalee, Ceylon
1801-1802	Egypt, Det. Malabar Coast Southern India
1802-1803	Madras, Det. Poonamalee
1803-1804	Operations in Southern Mahratta Country
1804-1807	Cannanore, Southern India
1805	Operations against Nairs of Wynaud
1807-1809	Seringapatam, Southern India
1809-1811	Cannanore, Southern India
1811-1813	Seringapatam, Southern India
1813-1817	Quilon, Southern India
1817-1818	Chatham
1818	Colchester, Det.
1818-1819	Hull, Det.
1819	Glasgow, Det.
1819-1820	Aberdeen, Det.
1820	Edinburgh, Det.
1821	Gibraltar
1822-1828	Malta
1828-1830	Corfu, Ionian Is.
1830-1831	Cephalonia, Ionian Is. Dets.
1831-1832	Lancashire and Cheshire
1832	Dublin
1832-1833	Belfast, Det.
1833-1834	Naas, County Kildare, Dets.
1834	Lancashire and Cheshire
1834-1835	Salford
1835	Liverpool, Dets.
1835-1836	Chatham
1836-1837	Sydney N.S.W. (Convict escort duty to Australia)

1837-1841	Windsor N.S.W. Dets. incl. Norfolk Is.
1840-1844	Det. in New Zealand
1841-1845	Parramatta, N.S.W. Dets.
1845	Agra, United Provinces
1845-1846	1st Sikh War
1846-1847	Lahore, Punjab
1847	Meerut, U.P.
1847-1852	Dinapore, Bihar
1852-1853	2nd Burmese War
1853-1854	Calcutta
1854-1855	Fort George, Scotland
1855	Portsmouth
1855-1856	Aldershot
1856-1857	Fort Beaufort, Cape Colony. Dets.
1858-1859	Indian Mutiny
1859	Cawnpore, U.P.
1860-1861	Saugor, Central Provinces
1862-1864	Jhansi,U.P. Dets.Gwalior & Seepree, Central India
1864-1865	Dum Dum, Bengal
1865	Bhutan Field Force
1866-1867	Devonport
1867	Portland, Det. Weymouth
1867-1868	Aldershot
1868-1869	Fleetwood, Dets. Leeds & Liverpool
1869-1870	Birr. County Tipperary Dets.
1870-1872	Belfast, Dets.
1872	Singapore, Dets. Penang & Malacca
1872-1876	Hong Kong
1875-1876	Det. Perak Operations
1876-1877	Singapore
1877	King William's Town, Cape Colony
1877-1878	Pietermaritzburg, Natal. Det. Newcastle
1878-1879	Zulu War
1880-1881	Dublin
1881	Amalgamation
	Formation of the South Staffordshire Regiment
	1st Battalion 38th Regiment of Foot
	2nd Battalion 80th Regiment of Foot

A typical scene of the dedication and presentation of new Colours to a Staffordshire regiment.

Chapter 2
The Colours

The dictionary meaning of colours is 'a pair of silk flags borne by a military unit and showing its crest and battle honours'. Another is 'a distinguishing badge or flag'. The definition of a flag is 'a piece of cloth often attached to a pole or staff, the piece of cloth being decorated with a design and used as an emblem, symbol or standard'.

The practice of carrying such flags is steeped in antiquity. It is recorded that the Trojans were possibly the first to make use of ensigns 'that they might accustom young soldiers to know their companies and facilitate their rallying when they happen to be in flight'. Prior to this the ancients had no symbol other than the simplest of things, such as bundles of hay fastened to poles. Every Roman legion had its own, 'Ensign General', which was the Roman Eagle, and each company (Manipuli) its own ensign. The Persians used eagles as symbols and the ancient Germans carried the figures of wild beasts.

In early English history the Saxon king Hengest reigned as King of Kent in the year 449 A.D. and had a white horse depicted on his standard. When England was divided into regions under the controls of barons and earls, men had to be provided for military service in times of war. The barons, earls, other ranks and vassals were recognised by the coat of arms emblazoned on their shields, with their helmets incorporated crests.

When the 'modern' English army was formed, later developing into regiments, the regiments usually took the name of the colonel who raised them. The colours bore the armorial devices of their colonel with variations for each company. During the reign of William III 1668-1702, the number of colours carried was gradually reduced from one per company to three per regiment. A royal warrant dated September 14th 1743 commanded that the colours bearing the private armorial devices of the colonels and lieutenant-colonels be replaced by completely new designs. Nowadays each regiment and/or battalion has two colours, one known as the Queen's or King's colour, the other the Regimental colour. These colours are the embodiment of the regiment, traditionally blessed when presented, and treated with utmost reverence. Finally, when replaced, they are laid up with the greatest respect. They not only display loyalty to the Crown, but record the history of the regiment, the battles and campaigns and have the battle honours embroidered upon them.

In the past these colours were carried into battle as rallying points, to instil pride and inspire brave actions. It was total and utter disgrace to lose them, in action or otherwise - men would sooner be slain protecting them from capture. On May 11th 1811 the colours of the 3rd Foot (The Buffs - East Kents) were saved by a Lieutenant Latham at the battle of Albuhera. While fellow comrades were being killed, he grabbed the fallen colours and protected them from capture. Half of his face was cut off by a sword, another blow severed his arm, but he stubbornly defended the colours, finally ripping them from the staff and concealing them in his tunic, before collapsing face down. Lieutenant Latham survived these horrific injuries and by his actions saved the colours.

To capture the colours belonging to the enemy was a great triumph and trophy. At the battle of Ferozeshah a black Sikh standard was captured by Colour-Sergeant Kirkland of the 80th Regiment. For this act of bravery he received an instant field commission and was promoted Ensign. This standard can still be seen in the Regimental Chapel of the Staffordshire Regiment in Lichfield Cathedral, and one of the Regimental Days celebrated by the Regiment is December 21st Ferozeshah Day. The Colours of the Regiment are handed over to a sergeants' Colour Party and they remain in their custody until midnight when they are handed back to an officers' Colour Party.

The last recorded event when colours were carried in action was when the 1st Battalion of the South Staffordshire (formerly 38th Regiment of Foot - 1st Staffordshire) brought theirs ashore at Alexandria in 1882. Nowadays they are only carried on parade celebrating an historical event or on special parade duties. The parading of the colours was to show them to the troops so they could identify them in the heat of battle and it is still enacted today in the famous event of 'Trooping the Colour', each year in London. When you next see a set of colours on parade, or in some museum or cathedral, reflect on what they represent. Eventually they become tattered, faded, even threadbare, but they still hold the memory of the individuals who served with the Regiment, the battles they fought in and the battle honours they gained. They represent those who served, and those who died in battle or of disease whilst on campaign. Their bodies may lie throughout the world, but here they are remembered and united.

THE COLOURS OF THE REGIMENT

Prior to the formation of the 80th Regiment of Foot (Staffordshire Volunteers), a Royal Warrant dated September 14th 1743 was issued to standardise the number and design of colours to be paraded by both cavalry and infantry regiments. There were to be two colours, the Sovereign's and the Regiments.

During the relatively short history of the 80th Regiment it had five sets of colours. The first of the Regiment's colours was presented c1793 and these were with the Regiment some 21 years. The second set were presented in 1814 and replaced thirteen years later in 1827. The fourth stand of colours was presented during 1849 and these lasted 22 years, being replaced c1872.

Throughout the history of the Regiment, the colours were transported wherever they went throughout the world. When serving at home or abroad the colours were proudly displayed and whilst on campaign they were present in battle. The descriptions of each stand of the Regiment's Colours including a brief history, are set out below. Records may be lost or inaccurate - the details are as accurate as present research allows.

1793 COLOURS

The size of each of the Colours were as follows:-
   Flying 6ft. 6ins. (1.98m)
   Deep (on the pole) 6ft. (1.82m)
   The length of the pike (spear and ferrule included) 9ft. 10ins. (2.99m)
   Thickness of the pike at the top $^5/_8$ ins. (16mm)
   Thickness of the pike at the bottom $^7/_8$ ins. (22 mm)
   Length of cords and tassels 3ft. (0.90m)
   Length of tassel 4ins. (100mm)
   Length of spear-head 4ins. (100mm)

The Regimental Colour

The main colour of this flag (background) was yellow the same as the regimental uniform 'facings'. The Union flag (without the cross of St. Patrick) was positioned in the left hand top canton abutting the pike. Positioned in the centre of the colour was a red coloured shield with the Regimental Number incorporated in Roman numerals, the word, 'REGT' positioned below, 'LXXX'. The numerals and wording were in gold. This emblem was surrounded by a wreath of roses and thistles, the wreath having a small opening at the top.

The King's Colour

The King's Colour consisted of the Union flag, which at this time did not contain the cross of St. Patrick. A red coloured shield was incorporated in the middle of the flag and this contained the Regiment's allotted number, 'LXXX', with the wording, 'REGT' positioned below, both in gold. The shield shaped emblem was surrounded by a wreath of roses and thistles as the Regimental Colour and again had a small opening at the top.

Brief History

The actual date of presentation of the Regiment's first stand of colours is unknown. It must therefore be assumed that they were presented to the Regiment during their year of formation. As was the custom, it is believed that this first set was provided and presented by Lord Henry William Paget, the man responsible for raising the Regiment in 1793.

The earliest reports of the colours with the Regiment are those at the Public Records Office at Kew. The 80th Regiment of Foot on September 20th 1794 disembarked at Flushing and carried their colours throughout the expedition to Flanders 1794-1795, (PRO-475 WO1/70). When the Regiment carried out an attack on Bommel on December 31st 1794 one of the colours carried by Ensign John Harvey was seen to be the first placed on the dyke during the attack. Considering this was the first time the Staffordshire Volunteers were engaged in battle, the colours were well and truly christened, and proudly carried through their baptism of fire. The colours were also carried in the Egyptian campaign of 1801 and later in 1803-1804 during the Mahratta campaign in India.

In 1810 a report of the condition of the colours of the 80th Regiment of Foot is held at the Public Records Office (PRO-WO 27/98) under the heading Equipment and various small headings, thus: - 'Good - 2, bad - , wanting - , compliment - 2'. It is assumed therefore that the condition and design conformed with regulations of the day.

Whilst these colours were in use there was a major change in the design of the Union Flag, for on January 1st 1801 it was proclaimed that the St. Patrick's Cross was to be incorporated. The following information dated December 23rd 1800 was issued from Dublin Castle regarding instructions for these alterations:-

> 23rd December 1800
>
> Sir: On the 1st day of January 1801 you will cause to be hoisted and displayed on the forts and fortresses within your district, the new flags and banners established by His Excellency the Lord Lieutenant's proclamation in Council, bearing date 16th inst., wherein it is ordered and directed that on the Union of Great Britain and Ireland, certain alterations should be made in the Royal ensigns, armorial flags and banners, and His Excellency's command having, on the 18th of this month, been issued to the Quartermaster-General and Principal Officers of the Ordinance, to prepare the same conformably to the alterations required; it is presumed they are now or will be in perfect readiness at the time prescribed. When these standards or flags are hoisted, as herein ordered you will direct a Royal salute to be fired by the guns of the fort or fortresses where they may be so displayed; but it is not necessary that any other ceremony should be performed.
>
> *E B Littlehales*
> Lieutenant General Craig

The result of the above order was that many old colours were dispensed with and new ones made. In the case of those recently given out or where the silk remained firm, the King's Colour was taken to pieces and the cross of St. Patrick inserted, the space occupied by the wreath in the centre not being interfered with, except to introduce the shamrock. This had to be pushed in somewhere and its intrusion was in all cases manifest. At this time the 80th Regiment was in India and shortly after left for active service in Egypt, and there is no record to be found of new colours being issued to them before 1814.

On July 6th 1802 the War Office confirmed in a letter that the 80th Regiment could display on their colours the battle honour Sphinx superscribed 'EGYPT', for their part in the Egyptian campaign of 1801. The contents of the circular are as follows:-

> HORSE GUARDS
> July 6th 1802
>
> I have the honour to transmit herewith, for the information of the Clothing Board, the accompanying pattern of a badge which by His Majesty's gracious permission is to be in future assumed, and worn on the Colours of the several Regiment's which served during the late campaign in Egypt as a distinguished mark of His Majesty's Royal approbation, and as a lasting memorial of the glory acquired to His Majesty's arms by the zeal, discipline and intrepidity of his troops in the arduous and important campaign. It is His Royal Highness's the Commander in Chief's pleasure that the pattern in question be lodged in the office of the Controllers of Army Accounts there to be had recourse to as occasion may require.
>
> Signed Harry Calvert A.G.

The design of this battle honour was a circular piece of red silk. Two curved laurel branches bearing red berries surrounded a white coloured sphinx. The word 'EGYPT' in gold was above the sphinx, joining the two laurel branches at the top. In the next few years this design was dispensed with and the sphinx, laurels and motto embroidered directly on to the main fabric of the flag and the battle honour was centrally placed below the main wreath. This battle honour was displayed in various ways by other regiments; for example the King's Colour of the 90th Regiment of Foot displayed four sphinxes.

The Regiment's first stand of colours was replaced in 1814. In those days old colours became the property of the Colonel of the Regiment and it is believed they were retained by the Hon. Sir E. Paget. To date it has not been established what happened to these colours.

1814 COLOURS

The size of each of the Colours were as follows:-

Flying 6ft. 6 ins. (1.98m)
Deep (on the pole) 6ft. (1.82m)
The length of the pike (excluding sphinx and ferrule) 9ft. 6ins. (2.89m)
Thickness of the pike at the top ⁵⁄₈ ins. (16mm)
Thickness of the pike at the bottom ⁷⁄₈ ins. (22 mm)
Length of cords and tassels 3ft. (0.90m)
Length of tassel 4ins. (100mm)
Length of metal Sphinx approximately 12ins. (300mm)

The Regimental Colour

The main colour of the material was yellow, with the Union flag positioned in the left hand canton abutting the pike. The Union flag now contained the cross of St. Patrick, the basic principle design remaining to this day. In the centre is a red coloured shield with the Regimental Number 'LXXX' displayed in gold Roman numerals. The wording, 'REGT', is displayed in gold immediately below the numerals. A green laurel wreath consisting of roses, thistles and shamrock surround the shield shaped centre. The wreath itself had a small opening at the top above the shield. The Battle Honour 'Sphinx' superscribed 'EGYPT', as previously described, was incorporated with the lettering in gold on a red scroll. A laurel wreath surrounded the white sphinx and was tied at the bottom with a pink bow.

The King's Colour

The King's Colour consisted of the Union flag and like the Regimental Colour now contained the cross of St.Patrick. A red shield was positioned in the centre and this contained the Regimental number, 'LXXX', in Roman numerals and the wording, 'REGT', immediately below, with both inscriptions in gold. A gold wreath surrounded the shield shaped centre piece and had an opening at the top, the wreath composed of roses, thistles and shamrock. The battle honour 'Sphinx' superscribed 'EGYPT', as previously described, was incorporated with the lettering, 'EGYPT', gold on a red scroll, the sphinx being surrounded by a laurel wreath that was tied at the bottom with a pink bow.

NB On top of each of the 'Colour' pikes a heavy brass sphinx was placed. Below the Sphinx was inscribed the wording, 'EGYPT', and below that was the number '80' (for further information refer to the history of the 1814 Colours).

Brief History

The 80th Regiment of Foot second stand of colours were delivered to the Regiment when they were stationed at Quilon in Southern India. The Colonel who provided these colours wanted to enhance their appearance and consequently had a metal sphinx fitted to each of the 'Colour' pikes. Although the replacement of the standard spear head with sphinx was a new innovation it did not last long, for these metal constructed symbols proved too heavy and cumbersome. The first report of these colours was an annual inspection on October 15th 1814. The Inspecting Officer reports, 'The Colours were received from England about two months ago; there is a silver sphinx on the top of each staff which are so heavy that those who carry them are under the necessity of unscrewing them when the Regiment begins to move'. Some twelve months later a further reference is made that the sphinxes were 'Gilt and too heavy'. During 1816 another reference can be found regarding these sphinx decorations as 'very handsome, but too heavy'. No more records have been found which refer to these sphinxes, so it may be that they were replaced at some time with the regulation 'spear heads'.

The second set of colours was 'retired' in Malta, being replaced in 1827. For many years the actual whereabouts of the 1814 colours was not known. However, around the year of 1893 a search revealed that an old stand of the 80th Regiment Colours had been deposited in Malta. As a result of these investigations the colours - although the fabric had moulded away, the pikes were complete with the metal sphinxes - were still recognisable. In 1906 the remnants of the 1814 stand of colours were transported from the Armoury in Malta and delivered to the 2nd Battalion South Staffordshire Regiment, (formerly the 80th Regiment of Foot). At this time Lieutenant-Colonel E.K.Daubeney D.S.O. was in command and he received them on February 22nd 1906. In 1911 the remnants were deposited in Lichfield Cathedral. The sphinxes that crowned the pikes and fragments of the pikes themselves can still be seen at the Regimental Museum, Whittington Barracks, Lichfield.

1827 COLOURS

The size of each of the Colours were as follows:-
> Flying 6ft. 6ins. (1.98m)
> Deep (on the pole) 6ft. (1.82m)
> The length of the pike (spear and ferrule included) 9ft. 10ins. (2.99m)
> Thickness of the pike at the top 5/8 ins. (16mm)
> Thickness of the pike at the bottom 7/8 ins. (22 mm)
> Length of cords and tassels 3ft. (0.90m)
> Length of tassel 4ins. (100mm)
> Length of spear-head 4ins. (100mm)

COLOURS OF THE 80TH REGIMENT
ISSUED IN 1872.?
REPLACED IN 1906.
CARRIED DURING THE ZULU AND
SEKUKUNI CAMPAIGNS OF 1878-9.

80th Regiment of Foot (Staffordshire Volunteers) 1850.

Right:
Officers' shako
helmet plate
1869 - 1878.

Below:
Shako plate other
ranks 1861 - 1869.

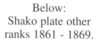

Right:
Officers' cross-belt
80th Regiment of Foot
c 1793

Former Colours of the
North and South
Staffordshire
Regiments.
Lichfield Cathedral.

The Regimental Colour

The main colour of the Regimental Colour was yellow, with a Union flag located to the top left canton next to the pike. Placed in the centre of the flag was a red silk circle that was divided into a ring and an inner circle. In the centre of the inner circle was the wording in Arabic style '80' with 'REG' positioned immediately below it. Contained in the outer circle was the wording 'STAFFORDSHIRE VOLUNTEERS', all of the inscriptions being gold. It should be noted the Arabic style print appeared around 1815-1839. The County Titles had been incorporated onto the colours as a result of a special order from Horse Guards dated 1782, although not included in the designs until about 1817. A wreath of roses, thistles and shamrock was again on the colours, but was now completely joined at the top as well as the bottom, the bottom being tied together with a pink bow. The battle honour 'EGYPT' design was the same as the 1814 colours except that the wording 'EGYPT' was gold on a blue scroll, and also two laurel branches partially surrounded the sphinx, tied at the bottom with a pink bow.

The King's Colour (later the Queen's Colour)

The King's Colour consisted of the Union flag now incorporating a red circle in the centre. This red silk circle was divided into a ring and an inner circle with the wording '80' positioned in the inner circle with the wording 'REG' immediately below. Both the inscriptions gold in colour and of Arabic style. The outer circle contained the wording 'STAFFORDSHIRE VOLUNTEERS' again in gold. A wreath of roses, thistles and shamrock surrounded the centre piece, tied at the bottom with a pink bow. As with the Regimental Colour the battle honour 'EGYPT' was gold and set onto a blue scroll. Two laurel branches partially surrounded the sphinx, tied at the bottom with a pink bow.

NB Both of the Colour Pikes had the Army regulation spear heads fitted to form the crown pieces.

Brief History

It is believed that the Regiment received their stand of colours and took them into use around March 1827. The earliest record found is a half yearly inspection report of the 80th Regiment of Foot, dated April 21st 1827, carried out by Major-General J.C.Ponsonby. The report indicates that the colours of the Regiment were in strict conformity with His Majesty's Regulations.

These colours were carried throughout the Sutlej Campaign, December 18th 1845 through to February 22nd 1846, and were carried into the battles of Moodkee, Ferozeshah and Sabraon. These colours, after they were taken out of use in December 1849, eventually had placed on them the battle honours, 'MOODKEE', 'FEROZESHAH' and 'SABRAON'. This third stand of Colours was eventually laid to rest within the walls of Lichfield Cathedral in the South Transept, although at the time of writing, the author has been unable to establish their whereabouts.

<u>1849 COLOURS</u>

The size of each of the Colours were as follows:-

     Flying 6ft. 6ins. (1.98m)
     Deep (on the pole) 6ft. (1.82m)
     The length of the pike (spear and ferrule included) 9ft. 10ins. (2.99m)
     Thickness of the pike at the top $^5/_8$ ins. (16mm)
     Thickness of the pike at the bottom $^7/_8$ ins. (22 mm)
     Length of cords and tassels 3ft. (0.90m)
     Length of tassel 4ins. (100mm)
     Length of spear-head 4ins (100mm)

The Regimental Colour

Yellow was again the main colour of the Regimental flag. The Union flag was located at the top left hand canton next to the pike. A red silk circle was positioned in the centre of the colour and was divided into a ring and an inner circle, similar to the previous 1827 Colours. The Regimental Number, depicted as Roman numerals 'LXXX', was in the centre of the inner circle. The gold 'STAFFORDSHIRE VOLUNTEERS' was positioned within the outer circle. An Imperial crown coloured gold was immediately above the red circle. A wreath of roses, thistles and shamrock surrounded the circle and at the top finished either side of the crown. At the bottom the wreath was joined together by a pink ribbon. The battle honour 'EGYPT' was in the centre immediately below the main wreath. The design was of similar design as the 1827 colours except that the laurel branches were below the sphinx and tied together in the middle with a pink bow.

    The Regiment was awarded three battle honours for their part in the 1st Sikh War; 'MOODKEE', 'FEROZESHAH' and 'SOBRAON', and they were incorporated onto the Regimental Colour. The gold wording of the battle honours was each placed on a blue scroll edged in gold 'piping'. The battle honour 'FEROZESHAH' was positioned centrally on the side nearest to the pike. The other two battle honours were positioned on the opposite side with 'SABRAON' positioned centrally and 'MOODKEE' placed above. When the Regiment was awarded two further battle honours, 'PEGU' and 'CENTRAL INDIA', these also were placed upon the colour matching the existing honours.

The Queen's Colour

The Queen's Colour consisted of the Union flag. A gold Imperial crown was placed in the middle of the colour with the Regimental Number 'LXXX' in gold Roman numerals positioned below.

Brief History

The Regiment's penultimate stand of colours was presented to them on December 31st 1849 at Dinapore, whilst they were stationed in Delhi. Lieutenant-Colonel Thomas Bunbury C.B., presented the colours on the occasion of his retiring from the Service. Brigadier-General Young and Staff were in the official party at the presentation of these new colours. The Ensigns who received the colours were Ensign Thomas William Hunt, (Queen's Colour), and Ensign James Loftus Winniett Nunn, (Regimental Colour). Ensign Hunt was later to die during the 2nd Burmese War of 1852-1853. The service was conducted by the Reverend Mr. Sterrock, who resided at Patina. At the presentation, on behalf of the 80th Regiment Lt. Colonel Charles Lewis thanked Lt. Colonel Bunbury. After the well attended ceremony, the Parade was dismissed and the spectators withdrew. In the evening the Regiment held a ball to celebrate the event, the bands of the 80th Regiment and 67th Regiment N.I. providing the music for the evening entertainment.

    When these colours were eventually replaced circa 1872, they were reverently deposited in the South Transept of Lichfield Cathedral.

N.B. Previous research has stated that, 'BHOOTAN 1864-6', was incorporated onto the Regimental Colour. However, no battle honour was given for this expedition. No sketch or drawing has been found showing this addition to the colour.

1872 COLOURS

The size of each of the Colours were as follows:
    Flying 3ft. 9ins. (1.14m)
    Deep (on the pole) 3ft. (0.90m)
    The length of the pike (Royal Crest included) 9ft. 10ins. (2.99m)
    Thickness of the pike at the top $^5/_8$ ins. (16mm)
    Thickness of the pike at the bottom $^7/_8$ ins. (22 mm)
    Length of cords and tassels 3ft. (0.90m)
    Length of tassel 4ins. (100mm)
    Length of spear-head 4ins (100mm)
    Length of fringe 2ins. (50mm)

The Regimental Colour

The design was much the same as the previous with the Union flag in the top left canton next to the pike and the main flag was yellow. The centre of the flag had a red circle that was divided as previously. The Regimental Number 'LXXX' in gold Roman numerals was in the centre with the name of the Regiment 'STAFFORDSHIRE VOLUNTEERS' incorporated in the outer circle. A wreath consisting of roses, thistles and shamrock surrounded this centre piece, at the top finishing either side of the gold Imperial crown, at the bottom joined together with pink bow. The Regiment now had a total of six battle honours. The design of the battle honour 'EGYPT' was exactly as on the previous Regimental Colours, as were the remaining five battle honours, 'MOODKEE', 'FEROZESHAH', 'SABRAON', 'PEGU', and 'CENTRAL INDIA'. The positions of the battle honours were: Nearest to the pike, 'MOODKEE' (uppermost) and 'SABRAON'. On the opposite side 'FEROZESHAH' (uppermost) and 'PEGU'. The battle honour for 'CENTRAL INDIA' was central below the main wreath, above the battle honour 'EGYPT'.

Above: The 1872 Colours of the 80th Regiment carried through the Zulu Wars 1878-79 (Artist Geoff Bell).
Below: The Sphinxes that crowned the pikes of the 1814 Colours. Regimental Museum, Whittington Barracks, Lichfield.

For the Regiment's part in the campaigns in South Africa during the years 1878 and 1879, it was awarded its final battle honour 'SOUTH AFRICA 1878/79'. This final honour was added to the colour sometime after its award in 1881, and was placed below the battle honour 'PEGU' in the style of the other honours.

The Queen's Colour

The design of the Queen's Colour was the same as the 1849 set. It incorporated the Union flag with a gold Imperial crown in the middle with Regimental Number 'LXXX' in gold Roman numerals below.

N.B. The spear-head at the tops of each of the pikes were replaced with the standardised Royal Crest of the Lion and Crown in 1855. Fringes were added to both the Regimental and Queen's Colours between the years of 1856 and 1877. On January 1st 1869 Queen's Regulations instructed that the size of the colours was to be reduced to three feet and nine inches (1.14m) flying, and three feet (0.90m) deep on the Pike. Accordingly the design of the 1872 colours included these new features.

Brief History

It is not known exactly when the Regiment received their final stand of colours. The earliest drawings available of these colours are those in the Vellum Book at the College of Arms, dated 1870. During the years 1869 to 1872 the Regiment was posted to Ireland, with various detachments serving throughout, and the headquarters at Birr in the County of Offaly. During 1871 the Regiment was ordered to go to Belfast en route to Hong Kong for December. However, on January 4th 1872 the Regiment embarked for Singapore, their posting having been changed. The Regiment arrived at Singapore on March 15th 1872 and immediately had to send two Companies to Penang. No records have been found of dates for when the Colours were consecrated, or of any presentation ceremony. Until such time as it can be proven otherwise it must be assumed that the Regiment received their new set of colours immediately prior to embarkation for service overseas.

These colours, like the others before, went with the Regiment wherever they served in the world. This set was to be carried throughout the Sekukuni and Zulu War Campaigns in South Africa during 1878 and 1879 and were present at the final battle of the Zulu War at Ulundi on July 4th 1879.

The 1872 stand of Colours was replaced in 1906, by which time the 80th Regiment of Foot (Staffordshire Volunteers) was known as the 2nd Battalion South Staffordshire Regiment. The final Colours of the old 80th Regiment were laid to rest, and can still be seen today in St. Michael's Chapel, Lichfield Cathedral.

"Ferozeshah 1845'. Artist, Peter Archer.

Above: King's Colour 1827 (later Queen's Colour)
Below: Regimental Colour 1827

Above: King's Colour 1814
Below: Regimental Colour 1814

1814

1814

Above: King's Colour 1793
Below: Regimental Colour 1793

1793

1793

Above: Queen's Colour 1872
Below: Regimental Colour 1872

Above: Queen's Colour 1849
Below: Regimental Colour 1849

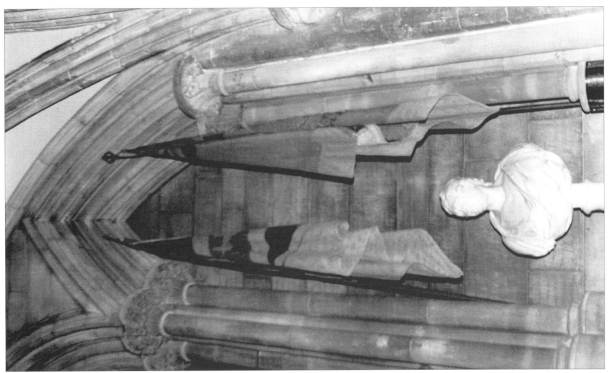

Left: Colours of the 80th Regiment of Foot carried throughout the Zulu & Sekukuni Campaigns, 1878-79

Lichfield Cathedral

Right: Colours of the 80th Regiment of Foot carried throughout the Indian Mutiny - 'Central India'

Lichfield Cathedral

Former Colours of the North and South Staffordshire Regiments, Lichfield Cathedral.

St Michael's Chapel, dedicated to the Staffordshire Regiment, 31st January 1959. Lichfield Cathedral.

Chapter 3
Battle Honours

Brief History

The reigning monarch of the day, in appreciation and recognition of services rendered, can bestow a 'battle honour' to cavalry and infantry regiments for their part in a particular battle or campaign. When battle honours are awarded, they were to be emblazoned on the colours, standards and guidons, and may also appear on regimental drums and horse regalia, etc.

The system for selection has been shrouded with anomalies since the conception of the award. Up until 1914 there appears to have been a number of unofficial rules for **not** approving such an award. These were that no battle honour shall be awarded for a defeat in battle or a lost war. Another stipulation was that the headquarters of the regiment concerned must be present in the action. These restrictions mean that in colonial history some militarily successful and notable victories are not celebrated, for example in North America during the American War of Independence. Small insignificant skirmishes have been immortalised whilst major battles and gallant fights are not recorded with an honour and are subsequently lost in the mists of time. Many years of conflict can be recorded by one single honour, whilst in some campaigns many if not all the battles are recognised with a battle honour. Over the years, battle honours have been awarded for both victory and for retreat. On rare occasions a battle honour has even been bestowed when not actually participating in the fight. Alternatively a regiment or parts of it may have been instructed to hold a position where it was expected the enemy to attack or use as a route and then not actually be engaged in the fight. In some cases if movement was made towards the enemy, it could justify the honour. No account is taken in awarding the honour to the number of men involved, be it company or regiment strength. Some colours contain a battle honour when not a single man was killed in action. A regiment could be heavily engaged in battle and suffer a great number of casualties, yet their actions may not be acknowledged with an award.

The first recorded battle honour to be awarded was sanctioned by King George III with a Royal Warrant dated 1768. This battle honour was for 'Emsdorff', which occurred on July 16th 1760 and was granted to the 15th Light Dragoon Guards. It still appears on the guidon of the 15th/19th, The King's Royal Hussars. Because the British were slow in copying their European counterparts, very few battle honours were awarded early in our military history. Over the years, as more and more honours were bestowed, some regiments who had participated in earlier battles and campaigns started to question the system and qualification for such awards. Because of the dissatisfaction and questions raised about anomalies, a committee was formed to review the whole award system. This committee was known as the Alison Committee and in 1882, following its recommendations, a number of regiments were awarded battle honours for Marlborough's four great victories, and for 'Dettington' in the War of the Austrian Succession, and 'Louisburg' and 'Quebec' in the Seven Years War. Certain regiments for their part in India during the eighteenth century were also awarded honours.

After a few years it was felt that the Alison Committee had not done complete justice and the awarding of battle honours was again reviewed. A new committee was formed and under the guidance of the Adjutant General, more awards were bestowed to various regiments in 1909; for example, 'Namur'(1695), 'Guadeloupe'(1759), 'Martinique'(1762) and 'Tangier'(1862-80).

Some honours were awarded relatively soon after the action, for example the Peninsular War (1804-1814), which were granted before 1825, although the last award for 'Busaco' was not granted until 1910. For the Battle of Waterloo that took place on June 18th 1815, the award was granted the same year. As previously stated some lesser known battles have been honoured with the award and some are still displayed on regimental colours of succeeding regiments, for example, 'Koosh-ab', (Persian War 1857), and 'Surinam'(1804), both awarded to the 64th Regiment of Foot, are still carried on the Colours of the Staffordshire Regiment.

It should be noted that during the Crimean War some militia regiments volunteered for services overseas. Recognition of their services was substantiated when some of them where granted battle honours.

There still exist anomalies in the awarding of battle honours, with some of the earlier restrictions being lifted. For in retreat or suffering a defeat, who would deny such awards to regiments whose men fought and died in actions such as Calais, Dunkirk or Arnhem?

Since the inauguration of battle honour awards, many have been awarded, with a great number being awarded during the Great War 1914-18, and later for actions during the Second World War 1939-45. Because of the number of honours awarded, in 1922 regiments were instructed not to have more than twenty-five honours incorporated into their colours, standards or guidons, and no more than ten should appertain to the Great War. This was revised in 1956 when a restriction was imposed for a limit of ten honours for the Second World War. A further amendment was issued in 1958 to have a limit of two honours relating to the Korean War. As a result of various amalgamations from 1958 onwards, regiments have been authorised to display up to forty honours maximum on each of the Sovereign's and Regimental Colours.

Battle Honours Emblazoned on the Colours
The Staffordshire Regiment (The Prince of Wales's)
The present colours of the Staffordshire Regiment were presented by Her Majesty the Queen Elizabeth II at Colchester in 1983. These colours are the symbols of the spirit of that regiment - its esprit de corps.

REGIMENTAL COLOUR
The present Regimental Colour of the Regiment has two battle honours represented by the devices of a sphinx superscibed, 'Egypt', and a dragon superscribed, 'China'. A further thirty-nine honours are emblazoned upon it as listed below:-

GUADALOUPE 1759	BUSHIRE	PENINSULA
MARTINIQUE 1794	PERSIA	MOODKEE
SURINAM	CENTRAL INDIA	SOBRAON
ROLICA	EGYPT 1882	PEGU
CORUNNA	NILE 1884-85	INKERMAN
BADAJOZ	SOUTH AFRICA 1900-02	RESHIRE
VITTORIA	MARTINIQUE 1762	KOOSH-AB
NIVE	ST LUCIA 1803	LUCKNOW
AVA	MONTE VIDEO	SOUTH AFRICA 1878-79
FEROZESHAH	VIMIERA	KIRBEKAN
PUNJAUB	BUSACO	HAFIR
ALMA	SALAMANCA	AFGHANISTAN 1919
SEVASTOPOL	ST SEBASTIAN	GULF 1991

SOVEREIGN'S COLOUR
The present Soverign's or Queen's Colour of the Regiment has a total of thirty-four battle honours emblazoned upon it. In addition to these displayed, a further fifty-five were awarded during the Great War 1914-18 and eleven for the various battles and campaigns during the Second World War 1939-45

MONS	NORTH WEST EUROPE 1940, 44	BRIEUX BRIDGEHEAD
MARNE 1914	MEDJEZ PLAIN	FALAISE
AISNE 1914, 1918	NORTH AFRICA 1940, 43	ARNHEM 1944
SOMME 1916, 18	ARMENTIERES 1914	LANDING IN SICILY
ARRAS 1917, 18	YPRES 1914, 17, 18	SICILY 1943
MESSINES 1917, 18	LOOS	ANZIO
VITTORIO VENETO	CAMBRAI 1917, 18	ROME
SULVA	ST QUENTIN CANAL	MARRADI
SARI BAIR	SELLE	CHINDITS 1944
YPRES-COMINES CANAL	KUT AL AMARA 1917	BURMA 1943, 44
CAEN	NW FRONTIER INDIA 1915	
NOYERS	DYLE	

Battle Honours of the 80th Regiment of Foot

The following seven Battle Honours were awarded to the 80th Regiment of Foot (Staffordshire Regiment)
The date of each accreditation of the award is listed below:

Egypt	6th July	1802
Moodkee	8th June	1847
Ferozeshah	8th June	1847
Sobraon	8th June	1847
Pegu	20th September	1853
Central India	3rd September	1863
South Africa 1878/79	25th July	1882

The memorial screen to the soldiers who died in
South Africa 1878-79. Lichfield Cathedral.

Sir Ralph Abercromby lands in Egypt with his troops, 8th March 1801.

Chapter 4
Battle Honours - Campaigns and Battles

1801 EGYPT

Egypt - The Background and Campaign

The French Revolutionary Wars took place between 1793 and 1802. Following the French Revolution, France was governed by the Directory (1793-1799) and the new nation was fired with patriotic fervour, the people flocking to join the colours. The large French Army, consisting of professional and part time soldiers including volunteers, threatened the boundaries of adjoining countries and the French people under Napoleon Bonaparte were to seek to conquer Europe and beyond. The First Coalition of the Austro-Prussian Alliance joined forces to stop Napoleon's advance, but the numerous battles that ensued led to victories for the French.

On the 21st January 1793, the French King Louis XVI had been executed. Britain was so outraged with this barbarous act that the French Ambassador was summoned and immediately expelled. France, at war with Austria, Prussia and the Kingdom of Sardinia (Piedmont), declared war on England, the Nederlands and Spain. Belgium was already annexed by France.

Napoleon Bonaparte was a brilliant tactician and strategist and he eventually gained French victory in the First War of Coalition (1792-1798). However, the war against Britain continued, and in January 1798 Bonaparte was in charge of an army assembled at Dunkirk. Britain still had command of the seas, so this was a very ambitious plan to invade England. During February 1798 Bonaparte placed before the French Directory the idea of advancing into Egypt, a main route to the Orient which could be used as a base for driving the British out of India. The French Directory liked the idea and with the blessing of the French politicians, Napoleon was appointed on the 12th April 1798 to command the 'Army of the East' to invade Egypt. The British fleet was out of the Mediterranean because of the impending threat of invasion to England, so Napoleon assembled his army at Toulon and on the 19th May 1798 sailed with 40,000 troops to Egypt.

The French navy under the command of Admiral Francois P. Brueys, with thirteen ships of the line, escorted the army, reaching Egypt on the 1st July 1798. En-route the island of Malta was captured by the French on 12th June. The troops reached Egypt and alighted near to Alexandria, successfully storming it on the 2nd July. They then advanced to Cairo and on the 21st July 1798 the Battle of the Pyramids took place. The French army consisting of 23,000 soldiers marched up the left bank of the Nile to face an Egyptian army of 60,000. The Egyptian forces under the command of Murad and Ibrahim were concentrated at a place called Embabeth. Although outnumbered, the French army put the Egyptian army to flight, and on the 22nd July Cairo was taken. During July and August the complete occupation of Egypt took place.

However, Napoleon's plans were soon to be spoiled. Between May and June 1798, following the news of the French navy and troop movements towards Egypt, the British Admiralty sent a small naval fleet under the command of Admiral Nelson to the Mediterranean. Nelson's fleet failed to locate the invading force. Eventually Admiral Bruey's fleet of thirteen ships were found anchored in the Bay of Aboukir. The French Admiral appears to have been unaware of the British fleet and was subsequently taken by surprise when attacked during the late afternoon of the 1st August. By dawn only three of the French ships remained, and of these only two escaped, the third having run aground and been burned by her crew. Nelson and his fleet had destroyed the French fleet at what became known as the Battle of the Nile, which meant that the French army was now stranded in Egypt. The French army was isolated and surrounded by a hostile population, and at the end of August Napoleon decided to return to France leaving Kleber in command.

On 24th December 1798 the Russo-British Alliance was formed when Emperor Paul I of Russia organised a Second Coalition. The main partners were Russia, England, Austria, Portugal, Naples, The Vatican and Turkey (Ottoman Empire). On the 9th November 1799 Napoleon Bonaparte became Dictator of France and as First Consul, he offered peace to his adversaries, but this gesture was refused. Russia left the Second Coalition, although the war continued. On the 21st of January 1800, at the convention of El Arish, the French were castigated severely by the British and the Turks.

The British Government prepared plans to enter Egypt to drive out the French and return the country to its owners the Turks. Sir Ralph Abercromby was given command of the British forces of 17,000 men and despatched to take on the French, now under the command of Jacques F. Menou. Additional forces were to be sent to Egypt from British forces around the globe, including the Cape of Good Hope, South Africa and India. Abercromby and his troops sailed from Britain with orders to reassemble at Marmorice, Asiatic Turkey. At Marmorice the troops reorganised, and somewhat refreshed, on the 2nd March 1801 proceeded to the coast of Egypt.

The invading forces, totalling 18,000 British and Turkish troops, arrived in the Bay of Aboukir during a heavy storm. On the 8th March the combined forces under the command of Sir Ralph Abercromby landed at Aboukir under intensive fire from the French, suffering casualties totalling 31 officers and 642 rank and file, killed and wounded. By evening the army was ashore. The horses were landed early next day. Horses that should have been provided by the Turkish Government at Marmorice had not arrived, so Abercromby had to content himself with less artillery and cavalry than he had originally planned.

The army advanced towards Alexandria. The French made a determined attack but were eventually driven back. Menou and the French forces retreated to Mandora to where Abercromby pursued them and attacked their positions, successfully driving them back into Alexandria itself. On the 21st March the French counter-attacked on a strip of land outside Alexandria with the sea to the North and Lake Mareotis to the South. The French were beaten back again, and were now totally besieged in Alexandria. During this battle Sir Ralph Abercromby was mortally wounded. General Hutchinson took over command and was responsible for containing Menou and the French in Alexandria.

Leaving sufficient troops to maintain the siege, Hutchinson advanced to Cairo and on the 25th June successfully took control of the city and incarcerated 13,000 French troops. He then returned to the siege of Alexandria, and because the French refused to surrender, General Coote was ordered to land with a strong force on the West side of the city to attack the fort at Marabout. On the 17th August 1801 these troops landed and attacked the French fort on an island in the harbour. The French at Marabout were eventually beaten, leaving only Menou at Alexandria. Intense fighting continued to the East and West of Alexandria. When the French commander realised his other forces at Marabout were under British control he accepted that nothing would be gained in continuing the fight, and on the 2nd September 1801, he instructed a white flag to be raised to signal the French surrender. Menou and his men were given safe passage back to France after giving their assurances that they would not take up arms against the British during the remainder of the war.

March of the 80th Regiment of Foot

Until 1801, the 80th Regiment of Foot had been stationed at Trincomalee in Ceylon for four years. During this time the Regiment had suffered the deaths of five officers and 368 rank and file due to the climate and disease. During the early part of February 1801 the regiment received sealed orders from the Governor-General of India, with instructions to proceed to Bombay without delay. The Regiment was to form part of an expedition first assembling at Trincomalee under Colonel Wellesley (later the Duke of Wellington). The 80th, with the 10th Regiment of Foot, embarked, and on the 13th February 1801 sailed for Bombay.

When the 80th arrived in Bombay, fresh provisions and water were taken on board and the sealed orders opened. The orders confirmed that the Regiment was to be part of the Indian army proceeding to Egypt to join the command of Sir Ralph Abercromby. The force, under the command of General Baird, sailed to the Red Sea, the 80th Regiment on board three ships, four companies on one, the others carrying two companies each. At departure, Colonel Wellesley did not sail due to illness.

The passage from India did not go as planned - in the days of sail, one had to rely on the weather. One of the warships, a 'seventy gunner' with Lt.Colonel Josiah Champagné and the headquarters on board, was unable to sail up the Red Sea because of the contrary winds and consequently returned to Bombay. The remaining convoy continued their journey, but a ship with two companies of the 80th on board was wrecked off the coast of Abyssinia with the loss of five lives. The crew and troops were rescued by the navy, but the regimental records and half of the 'mess plate' were lost. After their shipwreck and rescue, these two companies were amongst the first troops of General Baird's force to arrive at Suez. The two companies then marched across the Little Desert to Grand Cairo, eventually joining the other two companies of the Regiment now commanded by Lt.Colonel William Ramsay.

The four companies finally arrived at Kosseir on the 8th June 1801. Kosseir consisted of numerous mud huts served by a polluted water supply. The troops remained at this place awaiting further troops from the Cape of Good

Hope, but General Baird ultimately decided to march across the Great Desert to Keneh. The march commenced on the 16th June and it entailed a gruelling journey of 120 miles across the desert sands. The troops, carrying their arms and equipment, endured the burning sun of the day and the freezing conditions of the night. Fortunately many camels were available to transport the precious water supplies, but due to the extremities of temperature many of the water containers cracked and a substantial quantity was lost.

The strength of the 80th leaving Kosseir totalled 17 officers and 343 rank and file. The rate of march had been calculated at 2½ miles per hour and the troops were ordered to take shelter in their tents at the staging encampments. This record march across the desert was achieved in just fifteen days. The soldiers suffered greatly from the tiring sand, the climate, the poor water supply and dysentery. Many died en-route, others suffered with opthalmia, some going totally blind. The returns issued at Rosetta on the 5th October show that the 80th had lost three men, and 100 were sick, with six hospitalised.

After the fifteen days of hard marching, the force reached Keneh on the banks of the Nile. The force then took to boats and sailed down the Nile to Giza and Rhoda were they camped at El Hamed near to Rosetta. At this station the Regiment learned that the French had surrendered. The 80th would not participate in the fighting! They were ordered to Alexandria, arriving there on the 10th December 1801, where they remained stationed, or at Damietta, for the next five months.

In May 1802, the 80th were ordered to return to India, and so retraced their footsteps back to Grand Cairo, to Giza and across the desert to the Suez arriving there again on the 8th June. The next day they boarded ships and sailed back to Madras. History was to repeat itself. During the night of the 10th June one of the ships, the '*Calcutta*', carrying half the Regiment with Lt.Colonel William Harness on board, hit a rock off the coast of Abyssinia. One of the officers on board, Lieutenant James Cookson, and 30 men of the Regiment, volunteered to man one of the ship's boats and to row ashore to establish some sort of communication. The boat was swamped in the rough seas, and 12 of the volunteers were drowned, the remainder struggling ashore. At dawn all those on board the '*Calcutta*' were rescued by the Royal Naval Frigate, '*Romney*', and the men stranded on the shore were rescued by being dragged through the waves by ropes.

The naval commander, Sir Home Popham, the Captain of the '*Romney*', transported the 80th to the Southern end of the Sinai Peninsular landing them at a small village called Tor. Soon after, the '*Wilhelmina*' arrived and took them safely to Madras. From there, after a short time for quarantine, the Regiment continued its journey to Bengal, from where after a two months stay at Calcutta re-equipping, the Regiment again set sail for Madras arriving there on the 2nd September 1802.

Both the government at home and in Bengal were so impressed by the performance of the 80th that the Regiment was thanked publicly by Parliament and the Governor-General in Bengal. The soldiers of the Regiment were awarded 'prize money' equally with the troops who had sailed directly from England. The Grand Sultan of Turkey, Selim III, gave each of the officers a gold medal and the non-commissioned officers a silver medal.

The 80th Regiment of Foot (Staffordshire Volunteers) for their part in the Egyptian Campaign was awarded the Battle Honour, 'EGYPT' (with the Sphinx).

Officer, 80th Regiment of Foot (Staffordshire Volunteers) c1810

Night Bivouac of the British Army at Ferozeshah.
National Army Museum.

Colours of The Staffordshire Regiment 1st Battalion, presented at Colchester 1983.
Photo Jeff Elson.

The Victoria Cross.

Military General Service Medal 1793 - 1814.
Clasps: "Egypt" and "Egypt" and "Corruna".

Medals awarded to soldiers of the 80th Regiment of Foot
to be seen in the Staffordshire Regimental Museum, Whittington Barracks, Lichfield.

Sutlej Campaign Medal.
Right: Medal Moodke, clasps "Ferozeshuhuh" and "Sabraon".
Left: Medal Moodke, clasp "Ferozeshuhuh".

Indian General Medal.
Clasps "Pegu" and "Persia".

Indian Mutiny Medal. Clasp "Central India".

South Africa Medal.
Clasps 1879.

THE SUTLEJ CAMPAIGN

Moodkee 18th December 1845 - Ferozeshah 21st-22nd December 1845 - Sobraon 10th February 1846

The skills and knowledge of the Sikh army, transformed into a well-disciplined army by foreign instructors, were a match for any European army of the period. In the early 1840s, it was well equipped and stimulated by religious fanaticism. The Sikhs had for many years had an uneasy relationship with the British, but supported them during the confrontations with Afghanistan in 1848. This congeniality ended after the death of Ranjit Singh, and there ensued a long period of unrest and internal squabbling. The Sikh army and its leaders eventually became predominant in the control of the nation.

In 1843, the British Government followed a campaign in the Scinde and annexed the region, causing consternation amongst the Sikh leaders. The Sikh forces were under the control of Tej Singh, a Sikh Sider, and Rajah Lall Singh, a favourite of Rani Jindan, the nominal Vizier. The army, known as the 'Khalsa', could call upon artillery of two hundred guns, whose calibre in some cases exceeded those of the British. There were thirty-five infantry regiments each containing one thousand soldiers and there were fifteen thousand cavalrymen, the 'Ghorchurras'. In total some fifty thousand men could be called to arms, if necessary backed by further irregular forces, in total around one hundred thousand fighting men.

For some time, political and military leaders in India voiced concern about the unrest of the Sikhs. The British military and government leaders, Sir Henry Hardinge (Governor-General) and Sir Hugh Gough (Commander-in-Chief for India) steadily increased the various garrisons, stores and equipment, and had built large numbers of special boats that could be used as 'pontoons' for crossing rivers. Whilst trying not to raise political unrest, they slowly manoeuvred their forces to bases leading to the frontier of the Sutlej region. Their concerns were justified when the Sikh army of sixty thousand men under the command of Tej and Lall Singh crossed into the Sutlej on the 11th December 1845, an act of war.

The British forces totalled over thirty thousand men, and were distributed as follows; Ferozepore - 7000, Ludhiana - 5000, Umballa, Kassauli and Subathu - 10,000 (distributed) and Meerut - 9000:

Ferozepore - Commanding Major General Sir John Littler
    Two Troops of Horse Artillery)
    Two light field Batteries   ) each containing six guns
    H.M.'s 62nd Regiment of Foot
    Native Infantry Regiments 12th, 14th, 27th, 33rd, 44th, 54th and 63rd
    8th Native Light Cavalry
    3rd Native irregular Cavalry

Ludhiana - Commanding Brigadier H. M. Wheeler
    Two Troops of Horse Artillery - twelve guns
    H.M.'s 50th Regiment of Foot
    Native Infantry Regiments 11th, 26th, 42nd, 48th and 73rd
    Native Cavalry one regiment

Umballa - Commanding Major General W. R. Gilbert
    H.M.'s 9th Regiment of Foot
    H.M.'s 31st Regiment of Foot
    H.M.'s 80th Regiment of Foot
    Native Infantry Regiments 16th, 24th, 41st, 45th and 47th
    Cavalry 3rd Dragoons
    4th and 5th Native Light Cavalry

Kassauli
    H.M.'s 29th Regiment of Foot

Sabathu
    1st Bengal European Regiment

Meerut
    Artillery - twenty-six guns
    H.M.'s 10th Regiment of Foot
    Cavalry 9th and 16th Lancers
    3rd Native Light cavalry
    Detachments Native Infantry Regiments &
    Sappers and Miners detachments

In December 1845 the Governor-General Sir Henry Hardinge was near Ludhiana, some 25 miles from the Commander-in-Chief Sir Hugh Gough at Umballa. On the 8th, information was received that the invasion of the Sutlej was inevitable. The invasion started on the 11th, and on the following day the British plans were implemented

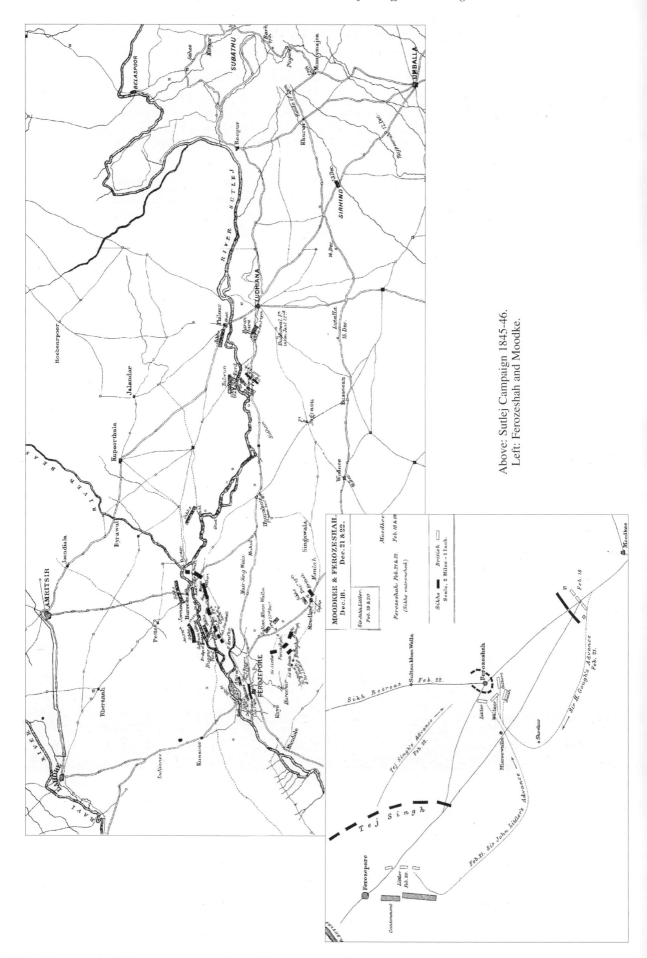

Above: Sutlej Campaign 1845-46.
Left: Ferozeshah and Moodke.

with war being declared on the 13th. On the 12th, knowing that war was inevitable, and having previously planned for troops to be moved at short notice, Sir Hugh Gough left Umballa with a military force for Ferozepore.

The troops leaving Umballa were faced with an arduous march of one hundred and sixty miles. On the 12th December, Gough and his troops also marched sixteen miles to Rajpura, then on the 13th, eighteen miles to Sirhind, twenty miles to Isru on the 14th, thirty miles to Lattala on the 15th, and thirty miles to Wadhi on the 16th December. Sir Henry Hardinge advanced towards Ferozepore with the objective of securing Bussean on the way. Bussean was an important supply depot and the stores held there were necessary for the fight against the Sikhs. Gough on his advance towards Ferozepore overtook Hardinge's force, and both columns combined on the 17th and marched to Charrak. On the 18th December the whole force proceeded to Moodkee, a distance of twenty-one miles. The combined forces amounted to between eleven and twelve thousand troops, comprising one cavalry division of five cavalry regiments, and three infantry divisions, with Generals Gilbert, McCaskill and Smith each having command of a division. Only one division was at full strength, the other two being barely at brigade strength. Of the thirteen battalions involved, only four were British, the remainder belonging to the honourable East India Company.

The opening battle of the Sutlej Campaign at Moodkee came on the 18th December 1845. The Sikh army crossed into the Sutlej confident of victory. After two months of hard fighting and four major battles at Moodkee, Ferozeshah, Aliwal and Sabraon, the Sikh army was finally defeated, with their political and military leaders either dead, captured or in flight.

The British Army crossing the River Sutlej.

Moodkee - 18th December 1845

The 80th Regiment of Foot (Staffordshire Volunteers) whilst stationed at Agra, an unhealthy cantonment, suffered greatly from sickness. At times no less than one third of its members were in hospital. Because of the conditions and his own ill health, Lieutenant-Colonel Narborough Baker sold his commission and retired from the army. On the 5th October 1845, Lieutenant-Colonel Thomas Bunbury purchased the 'rank' and became the new Commanding Officer of the Regiment. In preparation for the impending war, the 80th Regiment was ordered to move from Agra to

Umballa. On the 20th October, the Regiment, totalling 895 men, left Agra to form part of the army of the Sutlej. Following an arduous journey, they reached Umballa during the early part of December.

On the 11th December 1845 the Sikh army crossed the river Sutlej with sixty thousand troops, 12 miles from Ferozapore, where 7000 British troops were garrisoned. On the 12th the bulk of the British forces moved towards the isolated Ferozapore. The 80th Regiment had left Umballa two days earlier, with their families accompanying them on the march. After a few miles the Regiment received orders to halt and await the main force, and the soldiers' families and the sick were taken back to the relative safety of Umballa.

The march was 150 miles to Ferozapore and was done in record time, seven days. The troops had to contend with the Northern Indian winter, extremely hot during the day and very cold at night. There were no roads, the soldiers had to cross ploughed land, thorny jungles and heavy sand, and to contend with plagues of flies and incessant clouds of dust raised by the pounding feet. On the 11th December the forces of Sir Henry Hardinge and Sir Hugh Gough combined and marched to Charrack. On the 18th, the now Army of the Sutlej, marched to Moodkee, another 21 miles, where the troops enjoyed a well-earned rest. Poor organisation meant that the troops went without food some days, either because the meat rations had not arrived or no cooking facilities were available.

The topography around Moodkee was a plain with occasional slight rises. The ground conditions were a heavy sandy soil, with the hillocks covered with low thorny jungle. The British encampment enjoyed an uninterrupted view of about a mile around. When, at about four o'clock in the afternoon of the 18th, messages were received that the Sikh army was advancing on the British camp, orders were immediately issued for troops to 'fall in'. The advancing Sikh army consisted of 20-30,000 men, with artillery totalling forty guns. It appears the Sikh army had caught the British commanders by surprise and speed was now of the essence in forming a line of battle to take on the Sikhs. Men raced to their positions - some turned out in their shirt sleeves, whilst some officers drew their swords, leaving their sword belts behind.

The line of battle was hastily formed as follows: the cavalry and artillery advanced under the personal command of Sir Hugh Gough and formed the front line. The artillery of thirty artillery guns and twelve field guns was positioned in the centre. Brigadier W. McTier with the 9th Bengal Irregular Cavalry and a portion of the 4th Lancers was positioned on the left flank. Brigadiers J.A. Gough and M. White commanded the right flank with the 3rd Light Dragoons, the 5th and part of the 4th, Bengal Light Cavalry. The infantry hurriedly formed the second line: on the right flank was Smith's Division of Bolton's Brigade - HM's 31st Regiment of Foot - and the 24th and 47th Bengal Native Infantry, and Wheeler's Division - HM's 50th Regiment of Foot - and the 42nd and 48th Bengal Native Infantry. The centre was Major General W.R. Gilbert with the 2nd and 16th Bengal Grenadiers.

The left flank was commanded by Brigadier J. McCaskill, with Brigadier Wallace, second in command. McCaskill had command of HM's 80th Regiment of Foot and the 9th, 26th and 73rd Bengal Native Infantry. Some historians argue that this battle was, for the British, one of the most disorganised. Because of the lack of time to issue orders, few people actually knew what was happening. It was down to the good discipline of the soldiers that a major defeat was prevented - with the loss of a large area of the Empire. Some historians also consider that Sir Hugh Gough should have stayed where he was and allowed the Sikhs to advance upon the British, knowing that the Sikhs would have to cross a mile of open ground. Others argue that the swift and courageous decision to meet the Sikhs head on was a decisive piece of strategy.

The 80th Regiment under the command of Lt. Colonel Bunbury formed part of McCaskill's division, and was positioned on the extreme left of the left flank. They moved to a strong position on a ridge of sandhills protected both front and rear by thick masses of dense thorny scrub, but shortly had to vacate it to advance towards the enemy and again have a good 'field of fire'. The movements of the 80th were slow because of the continued forming of 'squares' of the adjacent Native Infantry regiment who kept expecting cavalry charges by the Sikhs. The 80th had to advance in column at quarter distances eventually covering the extreme left of the British lines. To the rear and a little to the left was the 45th Native Infantry, the 9th Native Infantry to the right. The 80th at times also had to form 'squares' when any enemy cavalry came into sight, again delaying their movement against the line of the British to their right.

The battle commenced with exchanges of artillery fire, the custom in those days. The Sikhs whose guns were heavier and of larger calibre soon gained the upper hand. The British commanders became concerned when the enemy started to extend their lines beyond those of their own. Frightened of being outflanked on both sides, Sir Hugh Gough ordered the cavalry to advance on both of the Sikhs' flanks. On the right, the 3rd Dragoons charged,

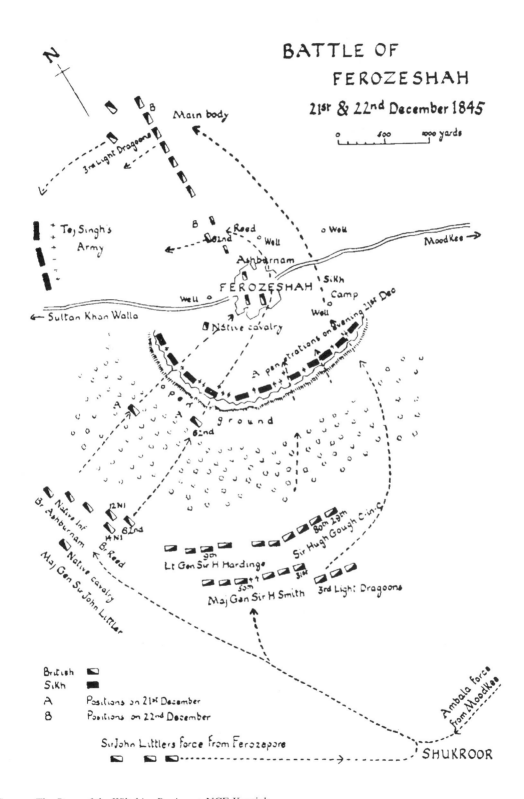

Source: *The Story of the Wiltshire Regiment*, NCE Kenrick
Drawing by Major GWM Kenrick
Published Gale and Polden 1963

causing the Sikh cavalry to withdraw, exposing the rear of their own artillery. Taking advantage of this the 3rd Dragoons wheeled left and charged along the rear attacking the guns as they went. The gunners were either killed, or left in utter confusion, and the majority of the Sikh guns were silenced.

The 3rd Dragoons were eventually recalled, and they retraced their path carrying with them a captured Sikh standard. For these actions the 3rd Dragoons were to earn the sobriquet title of 'The Moodkee Wallahs'. However, the Sikhs referred to them as the 'Shaitan ke Bachhi' meaning, 'Children of Satan'. On the left flank the cavalry under the command of Brigadier McTier advanced and chased the remaining enemy cavalry back into the jungle to the rear of the Sikh lines. Now that the Sikh cavalry had withdrawn, and the Sikh guns mainly silenced, it was the turn of the infantry to inflict the coup de grace.

Through the enemy gunfire, Bunbury had ordered his men to lie flat. This no doubt saved countless lives, although he himself remained seated in the saddle. The infantry, with the 80th, were now called upon to advance upon the enemy. Firing as they advanced, each regiment moved towards the Sikhs in an echelon of brigades starting from the right flank. Because of the clouds of dust raised and the smoke of the muskets, visibility soon became a major problem, being reduced to twenty yards. The Sikhs did their best to stand firm, but with the heavy musket fire, supplemented by artillery, they started to waver, then lost heart, broke ranks and fled in great disorder. Darkness now fell, aiding them in their retreat and forcing the pursuit to cease. The British forces formed encampments. The wounded were helped by their friends or where possible by the overworked surgeons. Those who could be transported were moved to the fort at Moodkee. The dead were mainly left on the battlefield. Some were buried, but the vast majority were to remain were they had fallen. It was reported later that, even after a month, the bodies of the fallen British soldiers still remained unburied.

During the advance Lt. Colonel Bunbury was wounded, being shot through the knee. Bunbury was convinced and believed to his dying day that the bullet came from his own side - today referred to as 'friendly fire'. After the battle ceased, a surgeon was called and the wound was examined on the battlefield. The Colonel and two wounded soldiers decided to try to rejoin their encampment some three miles to the rear. In the darkness they stumbled along and just escaped capture when they found themselves amongst a Sikh picket. Soon after the two soldiers became parted from their Commanding Officer who was still on his horse. The two men on foot eventually reached the British lines, but poor Bunbury, suffering greatly with his wounded leg, was forced to rest until daylight, when he teamed up with a friendly Sepoy patrol and reached camp safely.

So the British defeated the numerically superior Sikh army at Moodkee, the first action of the Sutlej campaign. The Sikh losses were never fully ascertained, although it is known that 15 of their guns were captured and a further four disabled. British casualties amounted to 13 officers, 2 native officers and 200 men killed, and 39 officers, 9 native officers and 600 men wounded. All ranks, killed and wounded, totalled 872. The 80th Regiment of Foot had 5 killed and 16 wounded.

The 80th Regiment of Foot (Staffordshire Volunteers) for their part in this battle was awarded the battle honour, 'Moodkee'.

Ferozeshah - 21st-22nd December 1845

Following the victory at Moodkee, the British forces remained there for a number of days to regain their strength. The British commanders knew that the Sikh forces were divided into two armies. Tej Singh was still encamped near the village of Ferozapore keeping a vigil on the place, and Sir John Littler's force that was stationed near there. Intelligence indicated that the defeated Lall Singh had regrouped and started to fortify the village of Ferozeshah. With experience now of how well the Sikhs fought, Hardinge and Gough did not want to fight the combined forces of Tej and Lall Singh, lest the unthinkable might happen. The march to Moodkee and the battle had told on the British forces and Gough required urgent reinforcements to replenish the casualties sustained on the 18th December.

The first of these reinforcements was the 29th Regiment of Foot and the 1st European Light Infantry followed by the 11th and 42nd Native Infantry. All had marched nearly two hundred miles in nine days, arriving on the 20th December. The last section of their march was helped when elephants and camels belonging to Sir Henry Hardinge were sent to give them transport and a supply of freshwater.

At Ferozapore, Major-General Sir John Littler had fortified the open cantonments. On the 13th December Littler formed up his forces to the North East of these encampments and prepared for battle, but for some reason the Sikhs did not attack. On the 15th, 16th and 17th of December when the Sikhs again manoeuvred, the defenders again reacted and formed their positions, but again no attack came. At midnight on the 20th December, Major-General

Battle of Ferozeshah, 21st December 1845, 80th Regiment of Foot in action.

Soldiers of the 80th Regiment of Foot in action - Ferozeshah, 21st December 1845.

Littler received instructions from his Commander-in-Chief to move out immediately and to march towards Ferozeshah. Preparations were hurriedly made. Lieutenant-Colonel Wilkinson and the 63rd Native Infantry and a battery of heavy guns were left to protect the cantonments, and the town of Ferozapore was protected by the 27th Native Infantry with half a field battery. Littler was faced with the very difficult task of extricating himself with the bulk of his command without letting Tej Singh know. At 8.00am, Littler and his force moved out successfully leaving the Sikhs still watching over the almost empty cantonments and town and their depleted defenders.

Back at Moodkee preparations for the advance and attack of Ferozeshah were formulated and orders issued. On the 20th December Sir Henry Hardinge as Governor-General offered to waive his position and serve as Second-in-Command to Sir Hugh Gough the Commander-in-Chief of the British Forces. This was duly acknowledged and accepted. Orders were issued and at 2.00am on the morning of the 21st December the soldiers were called to arms in perfect silence. Within the hour, the camp was struck and all of the essential equipment for the ensuing battle packed onto the backs of camels. Each man was issued with two days supply of cooked rations, a water bottle and sixty rounds of ammunition. By 4.00am the army was on the march towards Ferozeshah without the beat of drum or bugle call. The sick and wounded, the camp equipment and heavy baggage remained at Moodkee under the protection of two regiments of native infantry, one officer and a small party of men from each regiment.

Sir Hugh Gough and his force advanced slowly under the cover of darkness, in line with columns for about four miles across the rough terrain and jungle, the columns ready to be deployed if the Sikhs where met en-route. The troops again had to contend with continual dust, plagues of flies, and the coldness of the night.

The Sikhs, estimated at some 35-50,000 strong, had fortified the village of Ferozeshah forming entrenchments in the shape of a rough parallelogram with rounded corners, similar to a horse shoe. The longest of the sides faced west towards Ferozapore and eastwards towards open country in the direction of Ludhiana. The shortest sides faced north towards the Sutlej, and in the other direction, Moodkee. The village of Ferozeshah was between Moodkee and Ferozapore, some two miles to the north of the line of march.

After six hours marching, the British forces reached a position where the Sikhs entrenchments could be seen. The men were allowed to take breakfast and have a short rest. The Commander-in-Chief made a personal reconnaissance and completed his plans for an immediate assault on the Sikh stronghold with the three divisions that he had, knowing his 4th Division, Sir John Littler's force from Ferozapore, was closing in shortly and would act as reserve. Sir Hugh Gough wanted to attack with his troops relatively fresh, despite being on the march since 2.00am. The British Commanders did not want the Sikh forces to combine, and it was felt that should Tej Singh try to reinforce the attacked Lall Singh, he could be prevented from doing so by Littler's force.

Gough wanted victory before night, and the 21st December was the shortest day of the year. It was imperative that the Ferozeshah Sikh army was defeated allowing the British to concentrate on the other Sikh army under the command of Tej Singh. However, although Gough was in command, he was overruled by his chief, the Governor-General in the field, (Hardinge was an experienced soldier), who insisted their position could not be compromised or any risk of defeat taken. Too much was at stake, so he insisted that the battle would not commence by their own actions until Littler had joined them. Gough's authority was undermined, but he succumbed graciously and accepted his orders, although Commander-in-Chief. This was an historic event; no precedence had been set to cover such situations, but whatever the outcome, it would be Sir Henry Hardinge who would be ultimately responsible. The fate of India lay in this day's work.

So the battle of Ferozeshah was delayed. At about 1.00pm that afternoon, Sir John Littler joined the forces at the village of Shukur close to Misreewalla some three thousand yards south-west of the enemy's extended positions. The British forces were now increased to eighteen thousand in number. It took valuable time to organise and position these 'fresh' troops, who had also been on the march for some eight hours.

The battle of Ferozeshah was fought under the personal command of His Excellency General Sir Hugh Gough Bt., GCB At approximately 3.30pm, the line of battle was as follows: On the right flank Sir Hugh Gough in the forefront; Major-General Gilbert with Brigadier Taylor leading HM's 29th Regiment of Foot on the left; beyond them, HM's 80th Regiment of Foot, the 41st Native Infantry and Brigadier McLaran leading the 45th Native Infantry, the 1st European Light Infantry and the 16th Native Infantry; on the extreme left a troop of Horse Artillery with the 3rd Dragoon Guards and the 4th Light Cavalry under the command of Brigadier White. In the centre was the Lieutenant-General Sir Henry Hardinge GCB, with Brigadier Brookes and two troops of Horse Artillery, two 9-pounder batteries, and a troop of 8-inch Howitzers to the left of McLaran's command.

Next was Brigadier Wallace, in command of the following troops in echelon order from the right: 73rd, 2nd and the 26th Native Infantry Regiments and HM's 9th Regiment of Foot. On the left flank was Major-General Sir John Littler with Brigadier Reed and HM's 62nd Regiment of Foot and the 12th and 14th Native Infantry Regiments. To the left of Reed was Brigadier Ashburnham with the 44th, 33rd and 54th Native Infantry Regiments. To the left of HM's 62nd Regiment was positioned two troops of Horse Artillery and behind them the 5th Light Cavalry and the Governor General's Bodyguard under the command of Brigadier Gough. To the left of Ashburnham, forming the extreme left, was two 9-pounder Batteries with Brigadier Harriott and the 3rd Irregular Cavalry and the 8th Light Cavalry behind them.

The two brigades under the command of Major-General Sir Henry Smith KCB formed the reserve; Brigadier Hicks in command of the brigade on the right consisting of HM's 31st Regiment of Foot and the 24th and 47th Native Infantry; Brigadier Ryan in command of the left brigade consisting of HM's 50th Regiment of Foot and the 48th and 42nd Native Infantry.

By 4.00pm the British commanders were in a position to attack the Sikh entrenchment's and opened the battle with the usual artillery fire. As at Moodkee, the Sikhs had superior artillery, and this again quickly showed with devastating effect. On this occasion it was the left flank under the command of Littler which was the first to make a move against the Sikh entrenchment's. Reed with the HM's 62nd Regiment of Foot, and the 12th and 14th Native Infantry, made the somewhat premature move and advanced towards the enemy's positions. The Sikh's accurate artillery fire immediately started to take a toll, but the 62nd Regiment under much duress kept up the advance. To their right the 14th Native Infantry appeared to hold back, whilst to their left only a small number of the 12th Native Regiment kept pace. When they reached to within 250 yards of the entrenched positions they had to cross some open ground, and without hesitation they advanced only to be met with shot and grape. Many of the Colour party of officers were killed or seriously wounded. Casualties for all ranks were one hundred and two killed with one hundred and ninety-seven wounded, and much of the command fell onto the remaining sergeants. The 62nd having advanced almost on its own, somewhat unsupported, and with many of the soldiers now completely exhausted, could advance no further. The Sikh cavalry threatened to the left, and Reed was forced to concede most of the ground he and his troops had so bravely won. The order to retire was sounded for those who were left alive and able.

Ashburnham and his Native Indian Infantry which was not prepared for the swift advance, had stayed put and held their ground suffering no losses. The Sikhs success in repulsing this first attack soon spread, and encouraged them to believe they would be victorious against the British. The continuous fire of their more powerful artillery caused the British commanders to order their troops to lie down and again this saved many lives. When the situation had been reassessed, orders were despatched to Gilbert's Division on the right to start another attack in 'direct echelon order from the right'. Brigadier Taylor with HM's 29th Regiment of Foot immediately rose to their feet and advanced. The 80th Regiment of Foot promptly followed and with mutual support, much cheering and encouragement formed one mass of attacking infantrymen. The 41st Native Infantry was the next regiment to advance, McLaran's 45th Native Infantry, the 1st European Light Infantry and the 16th Native Infantry directly followed. Through shot and shell with smoke so thick they could hardly see their fellow troops, they eventually reached the Sikh entrenchment's. Quickly they were amongst the Sikh's guns, causing consternation and flight. The 80th and 29th Regiments of Foot paused, some to admire the guns, others to search for the 'fruits of war'. Suddenly some Sikhs clad in chain mail, who had been left for dead, sprang to their feet and attacked, claiming many lives of the soldiers who had been taken by surprise. Hand to hand combat ensued.

Beyond the artillery they found the enemy's infantry lined up in defence. The Sikhs fired a volley, McLaran's 1st European Light Infantry responded, closely followed by a charge from the rest. The Sikhs suddenly broke. Those who remained threw down their rifles, and drew their swords ready to fight to the death. A group of Sikhs suddenly started a counter attack led by a soldier carrying a large black Sikh flag. Captain's Best and Scheberras were killed at the head of the 80th when they met this attacking force. Colour Sergeant Kirkland aided by Corporal Brown and other comrades made a determined effort to capture the Black Sikh Standard. Amidst the gun fire, slashing swords and stabbing bayonets, Colour Sergeant Kirkland eventually got his hands on the Standard. Colour Sergeant Matthew Kirkland who was severely wounded later that day was rewarded with promotion to the commissioned rank of Ensign. Corporal Thomas Brown was killed in action later during the day.

Wallace's 73rd, 2nd and 26th Native Infantry Regiments and HM's 9th Regiment of Foot advanced and the enemy's guns became gradually silent. Hardinge then ordered Smith's Division into the attack, Ryan with HM's 50th

Regiment and the 48th and 42nd Native infantry, and Hicks with HM's 31st and the 24th and 47th Native infantry. Part of McLaran's force veered left and moved along the guns, spiking and disabling them as they went. McLaran was then ordered to secure the village of Ferozeshah, but on the way they received numerous casualties when a large magazine exploded. With the fires and clouds of smoke from this, and many other minor explosions, the men soon became scattered and separated.

As darkness fell, Littler regrouped his command to the West of Misreewalla. Sir Henry Smith formed up with HM's 50th Regiment of Foot on the eastern side of the village, as night brought an end to the fighting for the day. Neither Gough nor Hardinge knew the whereabouts of Sir Harry Smith and Brigadier Littler. In the pitch darkness Gough ordered all of his troops to take up positions some three hundred yards from the entrenchments, thus surrendering the ground that had been won with the loss of so many lives. The Sikhs re-occupied these positions and whatever guns were still operational were soon brought to bear on the British encampments. Throughout the bitterly cold night no camp fires were lit in the British camps for they brought the attention of the Sikh guns. The men were unable to see, totally exhausted, cold, hungry and suffering from thirst. In the darkness confusion lay all about; soldiers who in the midst of battle had become separated from their companies searched for their comrades. The sounds of the wounded and dying, were only outdone by the buglers sending out their calls. It seemed and was most certainly voiced that, *'that night the fate of India trembled in the balance'*.

However, the Commander-in-Chief never wavered, *'that on the morrow the battle would be re-commenced, ...'be it in victory or defeat, ...and better that our bones should bleach honourably on the field of battle than retire.'* The Sikh guns fired continuously, and one gun in particular caused so much destruction, it was unnerving many of the soldiers. Sir Henry Hardinge ordered Lieutenant-Colonel Bunbury and the 80th Regiment, supported by Major Birrel and the 1st European Infantry, and aided by Lieutenant-Colonel Wood, Aide-de-Camp to the Governor-General, to *'silence that gun'*. The advance to the Sikh entrenchments was carried out in perfect silence until within seventy yards when they charged and captured the gun at bayonet point. The success of the charge was signalled by a ringing cheer, the Sikhs being driven off and the gun spiked. The rest of the night was comparative peace. This night's action proved beyond doubt to the Sikhs that the British were far from finished and still determined to continue the fight. The 80th Regiment earned the praise of the British commanders and immortal fame in the annals of British warfare.

Sir Harry Smith and his Brigade held onto the village of Ferozeshah, but he decided to move away from the village before daylight and at 3.00am his force was on the move to rejoin the rest of the British forces. This force eventually met up with those of Littler near to the village of Misreewalla. Before dawn instructions were issued for attack. Sir Hugh Gough positioned himself to the front on the right, and Sir Henry Hardinge to the left of the line. Brigadiers Gilbert and Wallace were placed at the head of their respective divisions. On the extreme right the 31st Regiment of Foot and the remnants of the Native Corps were positioned. On the flanks the guns of the Horse Artillery were placed, and in the centre the heavy guns and rocket battery werepositioned. The infantry was drawn up with fixed bayonets, the cavalry with drawn swords and lances at the ready, and all awaited the signal for attack.

The British Artillery opened fire. Unknown to the Sikhs, the British Artillery was running short of ammunition, so the infantry was ordered to advance to take the Sikh entrenchments - the same they had won at such cost the previous day. The remaining Sikh guns opened fire but most of their shot and shells were too high, and as the infantry closed in, the charge was sounded. The sight of the advancing infantrymen with there fixed bayonets was too much for the Sikhs, and they were sent pell-mell in flight. With the enemy's positions taken, the British lines halted and victorious cheers rang out. Sir John Littler with his division and Sir Harry Smith and his 2nd Brigade joined the main force now in the Sikh positions. At last the victorious but exhausted soldiers could rest and eat, for the first time in more than 24 hours.

The joys of victory did not last for long. Reports started to spread that the other Sikh army, consisting of 30,000 fresh troops under the command of Tej Singh, was heading towards them from the west. The British forces with reduced numbers and low on ammunition, were faced with another battle. Bugles sounded calling the soldiers to action, but having formed up lines they were then ordered to form squares as the Sikh cavalry was sighted on both flanks. The Tej Singh artillery then opened fire causing further casualties, and the infantry were ordered to lie on the ground. The British artillery was ordered forward and brought into action.

At this point, some unauthorised movement of British troops and cannon towards Ferozeshah, led Tej Singh to assume that this was the prelude to being attacked from the rear. Having seen what had happened to the Lall Singh forces, he was so alarmed that he suddenly started to withdraw his forces. The Sikh artillery kept up its relentless fire, but the whole of the Sikh cavalry was put to flight when the 3rd Light Dragoons supported by a portion of the 4th Bengal Lancers charged. Tej Singh seeing the determination of the British and with the knowledge of the carnage of Lall Singh's forces, ordered a hasty retreat towards the Sutlej.

Thus the victory of Ferozeshah was assured without further fighting and loss of life. The Sikh army consisting of over 60,000 men had been driven from the field leaving some 10,000 casualties and 73 guns captured. For their part, the British had 694 killed and1715 wounded, 2415 in all. From these figures the 80th Regiment of Foot suffered 4 officers and 34 men killed, with 3 officers and 59 men wounded.

At the battle of Ferozeshah the 80th Regiment and its soldiers earned the respect of their peers and the Army's commanders. They were mentioned in various despatches in the Houses of Parliament in England. To this day the actions in this battle are remembered as one of the main Regimental days of the Staffordshire Regiment (The Prince of Wales's). On the 21st December each year, the Colours are handed over to the Sergeants Mess from midday to midnight, this unusual custom being to commemorate the action of Colour Sergeant Matthew Kirkland when he captured the Black Sikh Standard.

The 80th Regiment of Foot (Staffordshire Volunteers) for their part in this battle was awarded the battle honour, 'FEROZESHAH'.

Buddiwal and Aliwal. The Sikhs, driven from the field at Ferozeshah, returned in the middle of January 1846 with a force of 8000 troops and 70 guns and crossed the River Sutlej near to Phillaur, seven miles North of Ludhiana. Sir Harry Smith was ordered to attack this force and on the 20th January at Buddiwal was successful in this minor action, driving the Sikhs away again.

Following the defeats at Ferozeshah and Buddiwal, the Sikhs regrouped and an army, under the command of Runjour Singh, of some 20,000 men and 67 guns advanced and fortified the village of Aliwal. Sir Harry Smith with a force of 3000 cavalry, 7100 infantry and 28 field guns including two 8-inch Howitzers was ordered to take the village. On the 28th January 1846 the village of Aliwal was attacked and secured with the Sikhs being driven from that place. The Sikhs suffered many casualties and lost 52 guns captured, two guns spiked and 13 guns sunk in the river. British casualties amounted to 151 killed, 413 wounded and 25 missing. A total of 26 members of the 80th Regiment took part in this battle, but there is no record of any casualties. These are the names of the soldiers of the 80th who were present:

Captain	Anthony Ormsby		
Lieutenant	Edward Alan Holditch		
	Edward William Pincke Kingsley		
	Hamilton Clarke Smith		
Assistant Surgeon	Patrick Gammie		
Privates			
973	James Berry	1818	Archibald McGregor
852	Henry Cook	756	Thomas Nicklin
1690	Thomas Eaton	1520	George Peake
1692	John Edwards	1810	William Randle
2104	James Fairburn	1584	William Rice
2013	Owen Gilligan	2473	Charles Roberts
1144	John Hall	937	James Simpson
1994	John Harding	1965	George Stokes
2121	Ralph Holmes	2078	Edmond Thomas
1515	Michael McGinnis	2003	Patrick Toole
		768	David Turnbull

After their defeat at Aliwal, the Sikhs only had one more stronghold and this was Sobraon.

Sobraon - 10th February 1846

The Sikhs having suffered defeats at Moodkee, Ferozeshah and Aliwal, still wanted to fight the British. The Sikh commanders started to fortify the village of Sobraon. The town lay on a bend of the river Sutlej, some 45 miles south-east of Lahore and the defences were designed by a Spanish engineer officer called Huebra. To maintain communications and access between the two opposite banks of the river, the Sikhs constructed a bridge made from boats and timber, which also linked the main road from Sobraon to Lahore, the Sikh capital.

The defences consisted of three lines in an area of land that could be defended in the 'bow' of the river. The front line, centre and left hand positions consisted of a ditch and embankment some 3 metres in height that was reverted with wood. To the right, where the ground was much sandier, the embankment was only 1.8 metres high and also was fronted with a ditch. On the opposite side of the river, behind the entrenched positions, the Sikhs would position their artillery on the higher ground to protect their flanks. The two other inner lines of defences, again consisted of ditches and earthworks. Within these defences the Sikhs had constructed numerous concealed holes where upto 30 men could hide. The idea was that when the attackers had passed by, they could strike from behind. The surprise could be awesome. During the First World War these holes would be referred to as 'dug-outs'.

The British Commanders again prepared for a major battle whilst making provisions for any counter attacks that the Sikhs might make. Major-General Sir John Littler was ordered to hold Ferozepore and to keep watch over the ferry point that crossed the Sutlej. Sir John Grey, in command of the 8th Cavalry and the 41st, 45th and 68th Native Infantry Regiments, held Attaree and again watched over the fords located to the West of Sobraon. Brigadier H. W. Wheeler, in charge of a detachment of Native Troops, kept watch over the fords to protect Ludhiana.

The British reached full strength when the 'siege train' with ammunition for the artillery arrived on the 7th February, and then the next day Sir Harry Smith with his division. On the 9th February all of the Generals commanding were informed that the attack was to be on the 10th February and the necessary orders were issued.

The British forces of some 20,000 troops were to be positioned as follows: on the extreme right was posted Sir Harry Smith, his front line commanded by Brigadier Penny with HM's 31st Regiment of Foot, 47th Native Infantry and the Nusseeree Battalion (Goorkhas). The second line consisted of HM's 50th Regiment of Foot and the 42nd Native Infantry, under the command of Brigadier Hicks and on their extreme right was positioned Turton's troop of Horse Artillery. To the left of Smith's troops lay the village of Chota Sobraon and behind the village were positioned 8 guns, five 24 pounder Howitzers and three 12 pounder guns, behind which were the 9th Lancers and the 2nd Irregular Cavalry. At the centre of Gilbert's Infantry Divisions on the right, was the 1st Brigade consisting of HM's 29th Regiment of Foot, 41st and 68th Native Infantry under the command of Brigadier Taylor. On the left was the 2nd Brigade consisting of the 1st European Light Infantry, 16th Native Infantry and the Sirmoor Battalion, under the command of Brigadier McLaran. Between Taylor and McLaran was No.19 Field Battery of Artillery. The left flank was under Major-General Sir Robert Dick. His front line was controlled by Brigadier Stacey accompanied by Brigadier Orchard, and consisted of the 10th Regiment of Foot, 43rd and 59th Native Infantry and HM's 53rd Regiment of Foot. The second line consisting of HM's 80th Regiment of Foot, the 33rd and 63rd Native Infantry was under the command of Brigadier Wilkinson. The third line, under Brigadier Ashburnham, was formed by HM's 62nd and 9th Regiments of Foot and the 26th Native Infantry. The fourth line consisted of the 4th and 5th Native Infantry. Between McLaran's Brigade and Stacey's front line was positioned six 8 inch Howitzers, six 5.5 inch Howitzers, eight 8 inch Howitzers and five 18 pounder guns including Lamb's rocket battery. On Dick's left were the 3rd Light Dragoons, the 3rd and 9th Irregular Cavalry under the command of Brigadier Scott. Adjacent to HM's 63rd Regiment of Foot and to the front of Scott's Cavalry lay Fordyce's troop of Horse Artillery and on the extreme left of these was positioned a field battery. The British Artillery was commanded by Brigadier Gowan CB. To the rear of the village of Rodawalla was positioned the 73rd Native Infantry.

The Sikhs, whose forces now totalled approximately 35,000 troops, were well positioned. On the Sikhs left facing Smith was Sham Singh Attariwalla, to the left centre was Mehtab Singh facing McLaran. The left of the entrenchment's was commanded by a Frenchman called Mouton and he faced Dick's Brigade. Tej Singh was in overall command of the Sikh forces within the defensive entrenchments, whilst Lall Singh remained on the far bank in charge of majority of the Sikh cavalry. As previously stated the Sikhs positioned their artillery totalling 67 guns on the far banks, where the ground was higher, to cover both flanks.

On the morning of the 10th February at 1.00am the British troops were awakened and allowed to take breakfast for one hour. At 2.00am they 'fell in' and started to advance towards Sobraon, moving in columns to their respective positions. All this was done in complete silence. The attack was planned for first light at dawn. In the succeeding battle, Nature would have a significant bearing. Firstly, the earlier heavy rains caused the river to rise to such a degree that the fords became impassable, leaving the only way across the river at Sobraon via the constructed pontoon bridge. Secondly, the attack was planned for dawn, but fog caused the attack to be delayed for a number of hours. When the sun started to rise, the fog began to disperse, and when visibility was good enough, the battle commenced with the usual exchanges of cannon fire. For two hours both sets of artillery exchanged shot and shell. The British again could not gain the upper hand and it became a drain on ammunition. The situation became critical and the decision was made that the day would have to be won or lost through the Infantry - albeit by the bayonet.

At 9.00am, Sir Richard Dick received orders for his division to attack. Firstly, the Horse Artillery rode to the

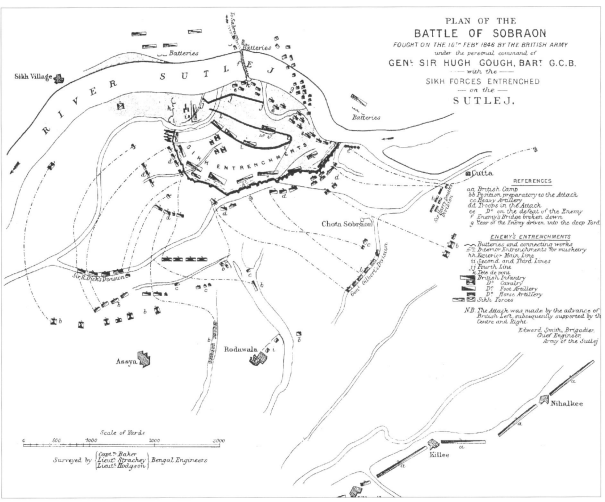

The 80th Regiment of Foot in action - Sobraon, 10th February 1846.

front to cover the advance. Stacey's command steadily advanced in a controlled movement. The 53rd Regiment of Foot positioned on the left was threatened for some time by some Sikh cavalry, but they were dispersed by well-aimed rifle and cannon fire. Stacey's advance was soon checked by the Sikhs and Dick thus ordered his second line of troops under the command of Wilkinson to move forward to reinforce Stacey's troops. The momentum of the attack, although faltering, kept going, the HM's 10th and 80th Regiment of Foot reaching the Sikh entrenchments. These two foot regiments drove the defenders to the centre of their positions.

Lieutenant-Colonel Bunbury immediately ordered three companies of the 80th to veer off to their right and to sweep along the entrenchments. Seeing the success of this attack, both Smith's and Gilbert's Divisions were ordered to attack, albeit 'feint attacks' - thus preventing the Sikhs reinforcing the areas under attack and repairing breaches in their defences. As the British advanced along the entrenchments, knowing of the 'dug-outs', they attacked from the top of the entrenchments, inflicting many casualties to those within.

The Sikh forces in the centre started a counter-attack. Orders were given for Smith's and Gilbert's divisions to throw everything into the attack on the entrenched positions. On the right, Penny's forces were repelled and had to be reinforced with Hick's troops. On the left of Dick's forces, now amongst the entrenchments, were fired upon by the Sikh cannons which had been moved to fire along their own lines. In the centre both McLaran's and Taylor's forces were met with devastating shot and shell.

But although the attacks faltered they reached the entrenchments. The height of the earthworks were such that ladders were needed, and the troops, despite the intensive and relentless fire, improvised and clambered upon the shoulders of fellow comrades to bridge the defences and get amongst the Sikhs. The British cavalry was ordered forward and a squadron of the 3rd Dragoon Guards soon created a ramp over the ramparts. They rode calmly in single file and formed up inside the entrenchments, and once assembled, charged, closely followed by other cavalrymen. The Sikhs were under attack by cavalry and infantry with such ferocity and determination that they gave way. Although the Sikhs fought stubbornly they could not withstand the onslaught and all were driven headlong towards the river - and the only means of escape because of the high water, the temporarily constructed pontoon bridge.

The British rushed their guns into position and began a heavy and destructive fire on the fleeing Sikhs. Such was the stampede that the bridge started to give way and break up, leaving the only means of escape the swift flowing river. Thus was ensured the final victory for the British at Sobraon, in this, the 'Bloodiest of Battles'. The Sikhs casualties were estimated at 10,000 and the loss of 67 guns. The British casualties amounted to 320 killed with 2063 wounded. Out of these casualties the 80th Regiment had four officers wounded, the rank and file sustained 13 killed and 47 wounded. Lieutenant-Colonel Bunbury reported that members of the Regiment had captured a total of four stands of Sikh Colours, two of which can still be seen in Lichfield Cathedral.

The 80th Regiment of Foot (Staffordshire Volunteers) for their part in this battle was awarded the battle honour, 'SOBRAON'.

Following the battle at Sobraon, the 80th Regiment entered the Sikh Capital of Lahore, ten days later, the first of Her Majesty's regiments to do so. On the 11th March 1846 the Treaty of Lahore was signed, and the Punjab became a British Protectorate.

Other ranks shako
badge
c. 1839 - 1855

The memorial to the 80th Regiment of Foot.
Lichfield Cathedral

Memorial stone to the soldiers of the 80th Regiment -
Burmah Campaign 17th March 1852 -30th November 1853.
Lichfield Cathedral

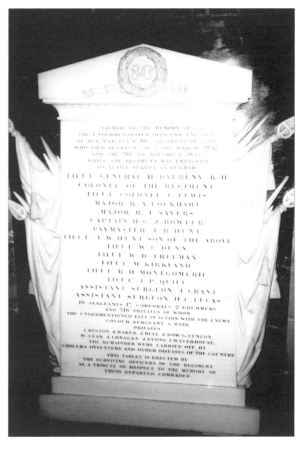

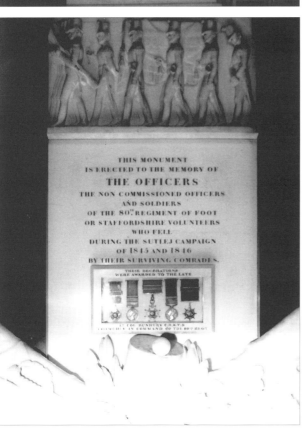

The front inscription panel of the memorial to the
80th Regiment which contains the medals of
Lt Colonel Thomas Bunbury CB.

PEGU
March 28th 1852 - June 30th 1853

Pegu is in South Burma, 17° 18" North and 96° 31" East. It is the former capital of the Mon kingdoms that dominated Burma at various times from the 6th to the 17th century. The First Burma War was from 1824 to 1826 and ended with the signing of the Treaty of Yandaboo, February 24th 1826. By this treaty Burma ceded the Arakan to Britain and renounced the claims upon Assam and other frontier regions. Trading facilities were also guaranteed in the port of Rangoon. The King of Ava signed the treaty and during his reign a period of non-conflict with the British prevailed. In 1827 the King was replaced by his brother Tharrawddi who hated the British. When Tharrawaddi's son, Pagan, succeeded him in 1846 this animosity continued. Relations between Burma and the British government finally came to breaking point with the Treaty continually being broken and the arbitrary seizure of the persons and property of British merchants, the molestation of shipping, and eventually the firing upon British warships.

Representations were made to Pagan, King of Ava by the Governor General of India. The response was contemptuous, and Lord Dalhousie, on March 15th 1852, issued an ultimatum to abide by the Treaty of Yandaboo and to stop all hostilities towards British shipping and trade, or face war. No reply was received, and the Second Burma war commenced.

Pegu - The Campaign

On April 2nd 1852, the British government declared war. The 80th Regiment of Foot had been held in readiness and on February 14th 1852 prepared to proceed to Calcutta. On February 19th, with Major R.G. Hughes in command of 2 lieutenants, 3 ensigns, 1 staff, 14 sergeants, 17 corporals, 7 drummers and 265 privates, the Regiment was ordered to Calcutta. Later, on February 25th, a further detachment of 1 lieutenant, 1 staff, 6 sergeants, 6 corporals, 5 drummers and 133 privates, under the command of Captain E. Hardinge, followed. The headquarters of the Regiment under the command of Major R.A. Lockhart, consisting of 185 rank and file, left on March 5th and arrived at Calcutta on March 15th. The following day the remaining detachment consisting of 1 captain, 1 staff and all the remaining fit and active men proceeded to Calcutta, the whole Regiment finally assembling at Fort William, Calcutta on March 16th 1852, from where they were ordered to Burma.

A military expedition with Major-General Henry Godwin in command of the military forces and Commodore G. Lambert in charge of a naval squadron was ordered out on March 28th 1852. The forces consisted of the Queen's and Sepoy Regiments from Madras and Bengal and were formed into the following Brigades:

> The Madras Brigade under the command of Brigadier-General W.H. Elliot and consisting of the 51st King's Own Light Infantry, 1st, 9th and 35th Regiments of Madras Infantry.
> The First Bengal Brigade consisting of the 18th Regiment of Foot (Royal Irish), 40th, and 60th Regiments of Bengal Infantry, commanded by Brigadier-General T.S. Reignolds
> The Second Bengal Brigade consisting of the 80th Regiment of Foot (Staffordshire Volunteers), 10th Bengal Infantry and the 54th Sikhs, with Brigadier-General T. Dickenson in command.
> The Third Bengal Brigade, with Brigadier-General H. Huishe commanding, consisting of the 1st Battalion Munster Fusiliers and the 37th Bengal Infantry.

On April 2nd 1852 the Bengal Brigade forces reached the mouth of the Rangoon River. A last attempt at peace was tried. A naval ship under a flag of truce was sent into Rangoon on April 3rd, but was fired upon. War was now unavoidable. The British commanders decided, whilst waiting for the Madras Brigade to arrive, to proceed to Moulmein and then onto Martaban where intelligence had reported strong enemy forces. This was on the 3rd and 4th of April reaching Moulmein at noon, where naval warships bombarded the Martaban fortifications. On the next day detachments totalling 1400 men from three regiments went ashore at 4.00am, and attacked the town, eventually capturing it, the Burmese forces offering little resistance. The assaulting forces included members of the 80th Regiment of Foot under the command of Captain S.T. Christie. Major R.A. Lockhart had the overall responsibility of the 80th., and was later to receive the warm approbation of the Lieutenant-General Commanding. There were only eight wounded casualties of the British forces.

After the capture of Martaban, the 18th and 80th Regiments of Foot returned to the Rangoon River leaving a force of Sepoys to defend the town. The Madras Brigade eventually arrived on April 8th and once consolidated, the whole force sailed for Rangoon on the 10th. The naval warships, on April 11th, shelled the Rangoon stockades and with accurate fire inflicted severe damage. In the early hours of the morning of the 12th at 4.00am, troops stormed ashore meeting no opposition. The defences of Rangoon had been destroyed by the naval bombardment, but the last stronghold was the mighty Shwe Dagon Pagoda. At 5.00am, the 18th and 80th Regiments of Foot along with a Native Regiment was ordered to clear the enemy from the pagoda. The Infantry had to go through thick jungle and march to the north-west about one mile. The assault commenced but because of the topography, the artillery were delayed in giving support fire and the soldiers in their advance had to keep close formation. The Infantry was subjected to accurate enemy fire all the way to the steps of the Pagoda but with a determined charge cleared the enemy from its stronghold. The 80th was led by Major Lockhart with the whole attacking force under the command of Lieutenant-Colonel Coote, 18th Regiment. The escaping enemy left in confusion via the southern and western gates of the Pagoda under the continued rifle fire of the infantry and shelling from the naval forces. Rangoon was finally secured on April 14th 1852. Records of the attack show that of the small number of casualties sustained, the 80th Regiment of Foot suffered one man killed, one officer and 25 rank and file wounded.

During May and June the 80th Regiment lost 43 men of all ranks from cholera and dysentery. It was only largely due to the experience of Major-General Godwin, with the assistance and co-operation of the Indian Government, that adequate transport, food and accommodation was provided. Wooden huts were manufactured and transported to Rangoon in sections, and a hospital was constructed at Amherst, south of Moulein.

On May 19th 1852, Bassein, about 100 miles to the west of Rangoon, was captured by two small parties of 100 men from the 80th Regiment and 67th Bengal Native Infantry, assisted by a number of Indian Sappers and Miners including members from HMS '*Fox*'. On June 3rd 1852 a party of the 80th, commanded by Captain (later Major) A.Ormsby, consisting of 2 subalterns, 1 staff, 5 sergeants, 5 corporals, 1 drummer and 91 privates embarked for Rangoon for field service.

Pegu was eventually evacuated by the numerically superior enemy. Pegu's defences were destroyed and the town was left under the control of a local friendly tribe called Tailings. The main force returned to Rangoon on June 8th 1852. The Tailings failed to hold Pegu and it again fell into enemy hands. Major-General Godwin decided to lead a counter attack and with a force that included a detachment from the 80th under the command of Captain Ormsby went forth and recaptured Pegu. It was to be held until the end of the conflict, being used as a base for the advance up the Irrawaddy River to Prome, the centre of the Burmese resistance. During August Major R.G.Hughes took temporary command of the regiment until Lieutenant-Colonel George Hutchinson arrived.

In September 1852 a force of about 2000 troops advanced by steamer from Pegu to Prome via Rangoon. On September 16th the Regiment in three divisions embarked the Bengal Marine steamships, '*Nemeses*', '*Phlegethon*', and '*Proserpine*'. The ships arrived at Yandoon on September 19th. The troops then transferred to the Company steamers, '*Fire Queen*' and '*Enterprise*', steaming on the 27th and arriving off Shenzadah on the 30th. On October 1st the force left Shenzadah. The journey was very slow but not subject to serious incident until it arrived at Prome.

When the ships arrived at Prome on October 14th the enemy opened up with cannon and rifle fire. The Navy's guns replied with accuracy. The fleet was anchored at a safe distance outside the range of the enemy's guns and Godwin ordered boats to be lowered and rowed to shore with an attacking force. The 80th Regiment under the command of Lt.Colonel Hutchinson went ashore along with artillery of two guns, to give cover for the main force. The town was held by 4000 enemy soldiers with their strongest positions 1000 yards east of the town in a range of hills and a large pagoda, both positions commanding the town. A party of two companies of the 80th under the command of Captain Christie took the large pagoda. Captain Welsh with his Grenadier Company captured a smaller pagoda with the loss of one killed, one severely wounded and five wounded slightly.

With Prome captured and under British control, the Burmese Regular forces surrendered. However, Myat Toon and his Dacoits continued the fight. Their main base was the river town of Donubyu and in November a British force under the command of a naval captain was sent to remove this troublesome rebel. Unfortunately this proved too difficult and they had to return unsuccessful. A further expedition was sent out which included a number of men equivalent to a Company from the 80th under the command of Captain (later Major) L.L.Montgomery. Another party of the 80th under the command of Captain Christie was ordered across the river to attack and capture two forts occupied by the enemy. However, the Burmese, seeing this force approaching, fled leaving three guns behind.

A small column of soldiers from the 18th and 80th Regiments and 4th Sikh Infantry was sent in pursuit of the Dacoits. Contact was not made with the enemy until March 7th 1853, who moved swiftly through the country seeking or enforcing help from the local inhabitants. The last detachment of the Regiment to leave Calcutta included Ensigns Wolseley and Wilkinson and they were involved with this column, with the Regiment's new Commanding Officer Lt.Colonel E.A. Holditch CB. A broad nullah fortified on the far side had to be cleared of the enemy bandits and this took a whole day to complete. Because of poor navigation and the jungle conditions little progress was made. Eventually the village of Kyon Tani was reached, but because of the conditions and continuous intermittent enemy sniping, progress was slow and extremely hazardous. The troops were now on half rations and due to the heat and sickness had to retrace some of their steps back to Kyon Tani. On March 14th, reinforced by troops and artillery brought by Sir John Cheape, the strengthened force again pursued the enemy. The 18th Regiment was ordered to take a stockade held by the enemy on March 18th and this was successfully completed.

The following day, approximately one mile further on, a strongly held stockade was discovered. This time it was the turn of the 80th Regiment with Sikhs in support, and the 18th Regiment in reserve, to clear the enemy positions. The position was finally taken at the point of the bayonet with the two young Ensigns, Wolseley and Wilkinson in the forefront, both being wounded. Both were later mentioned in dispatches. Heavy casualties were inflicted on the enemy. They dispersed and were no longer a threat. The detachment, now reduced in numbers, rejoined the rest of the Regiment on April 2nd 1853.

The Regiment suffered badly from cholera and dysentery. On May 9th 1853 they moved to Shildowhy some eight miles lower down the River Irrawaddy from Prome. The Regiment used rows of houses previously occupied by priests, known as Phoongie. These were large wooden structures 6 foot above the ground to escape flooding river waters. Although the Regiment soon moved to better conditions, some 32 men were to die from disease. In May a company detachment under the command of Captain Hardinge was ordered north to the river town of Tanbou, some 50 miles, and they remained at this station for four months.

During November the 80th Regiment was ordered to Rangoon. Headquarters of the Regiment, the advanced party leaving on the 4th and arriving on the 8th November, taking over the accommodation of a wooden barracks. The rest of the Regiment followed shortly afterwards. During this period the Regiment provided guards for the great Shwe Dagon Pagoda. In their last week in the country, someone of the Regiment decided a trophy was required and one small bell weighing approximately two hundred pounds went missing from the Pagoda. This bell can be seen today in the Regimental Museum at Whittington Barracks, Lichfield. It should be noted that many of the Regiment's soldiers died of diseases caught in Burma.

Extract from Division Orders by Brigadier-General Sir John Cheape KCB. Commanding the Pegu Division on the occasion of the Regiment leaving Burma en route for England.

Prome 12th November 1853

On the departure from Rangoon of Her Majesty's 18th and 80th Regiments, the Brigadier-General commanding in Pegu desires to express his approbation of the good conduct of those Regiments in the last hour of their stay in the country; they have had hard service here, and by their achievements in the field have added to their already high reputation; and the Brigadier-General begs to offer to the Officers and men his most cordial good wishes for the future welfare and prosperity and his congratulations on their return to their native land after a long period of honourable service abroad.

Between November 18th and 22nd the Regiment embarked the Indian Marine ship, '*Berenice*'. On November 29th the Regiment landed at Calcutta. After one year and seven months they returned to Fort William. The remainder of the Regiment followed the Headquarters in two detachments. On January 6th 1854, the Headquarters marched to Dum Dum, a station some 7 miles from Calcutta. The Regiment were once again assembled as a complete Regiment by the end of the month. On February 1st a total of 228 men who had volunteered for service in other Corps in India were struck off the strength of the Regiment. As a result of the loss of these soldiers and sickness reducing the number of men for active service, the Regiment was not sent to the Crimean war with the Russians.

The following highly complimentary General Order was published by His Excellency Lieutenant-General Sir William Gomm relative to the 18th and 80th Regiments on their returning home to India:

Head Quarters Simla 24 October 1853

1. Her Majesty's 18th Royal Irish and 80th Regiments of Foot, and on the point of returning home, after each completing a term of nearly 17 years Foreign Service
2. Many gallant and many arduous services mark the career of both these distinguished Corps comprised within the period above cited
3. Her Majesty's 80th contributed essentially to the success in arms of China. HM 80th assisted actively throughout the first Sikh war and conspicuously at the Battles of Moodkee, Ferozeshah and Sobraon
4. Both Corps have since maintained the high character already gained for gallantry, soldierlike steady and endurance under privation and the enervating effects of climate throughout the recent operations in Burmah.
5. The Commander in Chief cannot take leave of Corps which have so well upheld the character of the British Soldier in India, through a series of years without tendering to them severally his warmest wishes for their future welfare and for their rapid restoration to health, on their passage home
6. Neither can His Excellency forego the opportunity thus afforded him of expressing his sentiments of the recent services in the same field of HM 51st Light Infantry also about to proceed home services repeatedly brought, to his notice by the Major General Commanding the Field Force in Burmah in the course of its operations and of offering to this Regiment which will be relieved from the Madras Residency the same earned good wishes, as to Brethren in Arms, of the 18th and 80th.

The Regiment embarked at Calcutta for passage home to England in three detachments as follows:

Embarkation 80th Regiment of Foot from India to England

Date of Embarkation	Officers	Ships Names	Date of Arrival	Remarks
		1 5 6 *Lady Kernaveay*		
1854 11th Feb	Capt. C. Duperier Lieut. G. Sullivan Ensign F.B.N. Crauford Ensign W. P. Mortimer Asst. Surgeon B. Lane	6 3 144 143 *Lord Dalhousie*	16 June 1854	Invalids 1st Detachment under Command Capt. Duperier
1854 22nd Feb	Lt. Col. G Hutchison Capt. A. Ormsby Capt. E Hardinge Lieut. H.C. Smith Lieut. D.M. Fraser Lieut. J.L.W. Nunn Lt. & Adjt. E. Borrowes Surgeon J.R. Taylor Major L.L. Mongomery Capt. B.H. Boxer Lt. B.J. Hume Lt. F. Miller Lt. C HT B de Ruvignes Lt. W. Whitehead Ast. Surgeon MW Murphy 1 1 2 Pay Master G. Bodle	13 8 123 144 *Blenheim* 10 4 137 151 *Prince of Wales*	26 June 1854 1 July 1854	3rd Detachment under Comand Major L.L.Montgomery Left at Calcutta Pay Master Sgt for the purpose of adjusting accounts and then for discharge
	Total Effective at Embarkation	30 16 410 456		

In June 1855 Lieutenant-General TW Robbins presented the soldiers of the Regiment the new Indian General Service Medal with the clasp, 'PEGU', the first of the clasps to be issued with the medal. The 80th Regiment of Foot (Staffordshire Volunteers) for their service in Burma was awarded the Battle Honour 'Pegu'.

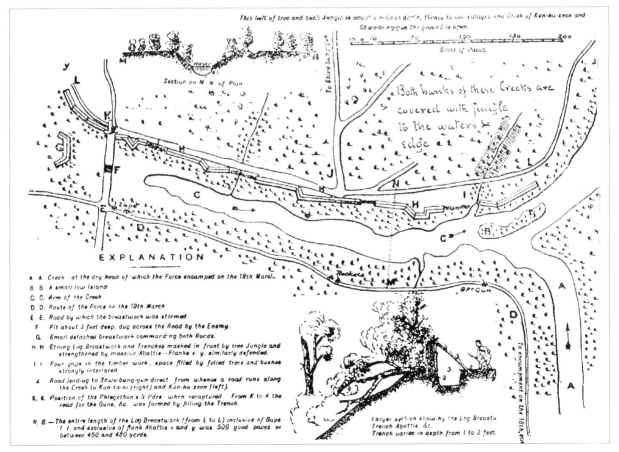

Assault on enemy posistions, 19th March 1853.

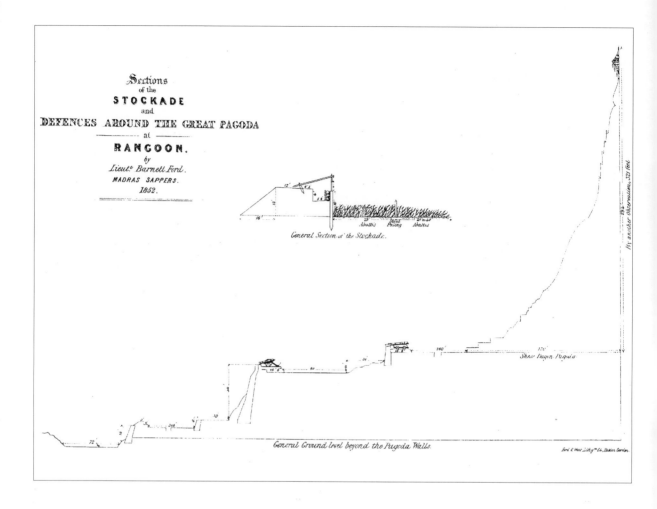

Heavy Howitzer Battery - Rangoon 14th April 1852.

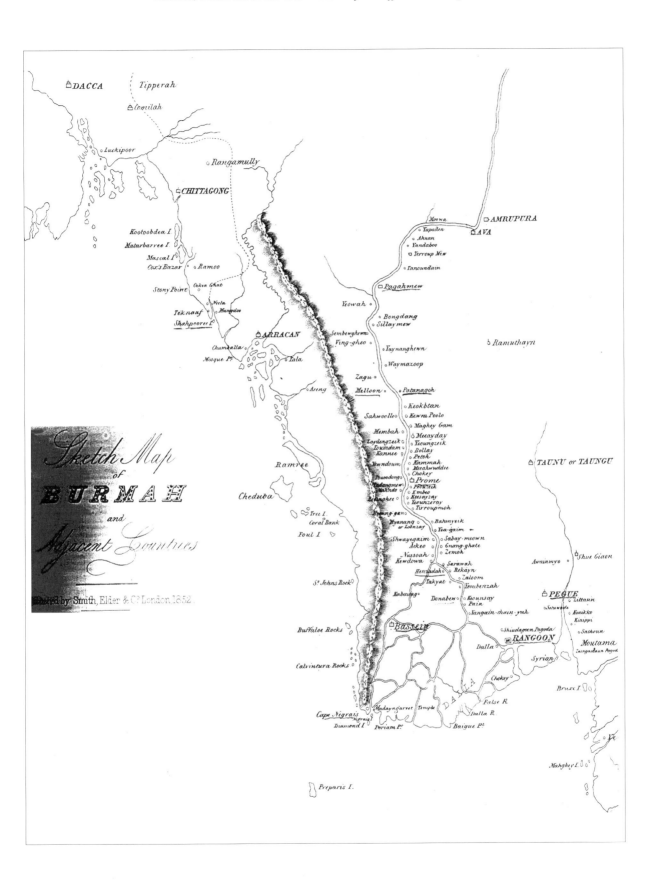

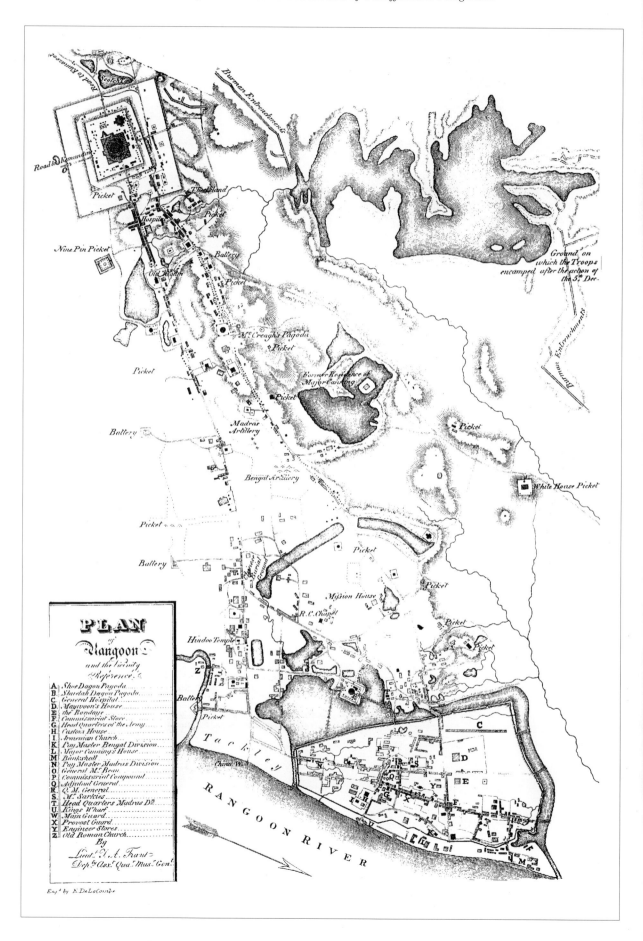

King of Ava's Ship

Hermes

H.E.I.C.S. Phlegethon

Naval ships in action: This picture shows the ships HMS '*Fox*' and the Honourable East India Company Steamer '*Phlegethon*'. Both ships carried troops of the 80th Regiment of Foot.

Below: An early sketch of the town of Rangoon

The King's Landing Place

Bazaar Godang

Great Dagon Pagoda or Royal Standard Pagota.

Custom House

House

TOWN OF RANGOON

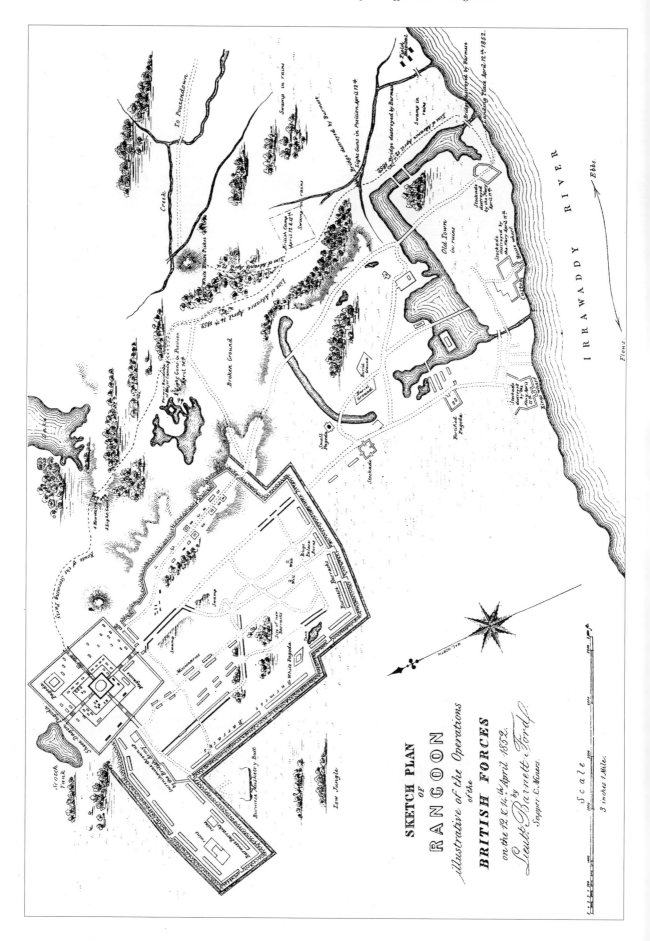

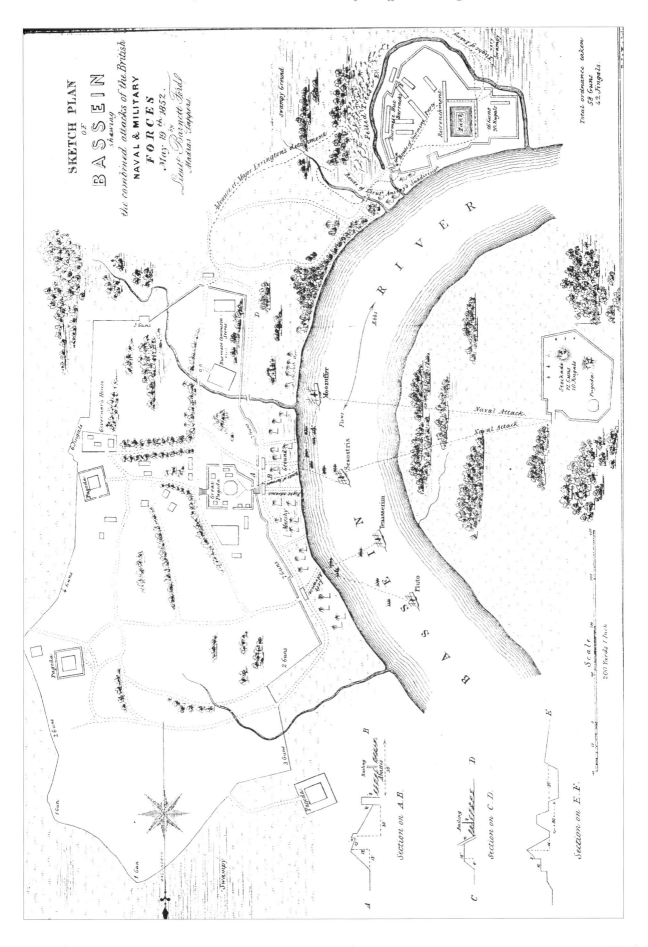

CENTRAL INDIA
January - June 1858

Central India - The background and Summary of the Mutiny

The word mutiny refers to an open rebellion against a constituted authority and is synonymous with violence. The world had not seen and hopefully will never witness again such events as those of the Indian mutiny which began in 1857. This great mutiny would have the utmost repercussions on the British presence in the sub-continent. The causes of the Indian Mutiny can at best be described as varied and complicated. One of the most contentious issues was that the men responsible for the administration and governing of this vast area of the globe did not fully understand the wants and need of their native soldiers, their faiths, beliefs and culture.

The English entered many countries as traders or merchants and India was no different. During the reign of Elizabeth I, a charter was agreed with the, 'Company of Merchants of London trading with the East Indies'. In 1613 this Company was allowed to establish a permanent trading station north of Bombay. It the early years of the 18th century squabbling began between the British interests over who should rule the vast areas of the Indian sub-continent. Foreign invaders started to enter the country and take control over various areas during this period of discontentment. The East India Company thus started to employ soldiers to protect their interests.

At the Battle of Plessey in 1757 the forces of the East India Company won a decisive victory and established British supremacy in the part of India known as Bengal. During the second half of the 18th Century the company expanded even further into the sub-continent. In 1773 the British Government passed a Parliamentary Act making the Company responsible for the territories it controlled, but a further Act was passed in 1784 that brought the East India Company under the control of the British Government. In 1833 the Company lost its monopoly of trade, and also its administrative powers with various Government Acts of 1833, 1853, and eventually 1858, with the introduction of the Indian Civil Service. The East India Company at its height was responsible for each of its Presidencies, Bengal, Bombay and Madras. The armies of each of these areas were separately maintained. At one time each of these armies consisted of one British soldier to three Indian soldiers, however, by 1856, this ratio had decreased to one British soldier to six Indian.

The occurence of mutiny in the Indian army was not new; one serious rebellion occurring at Vellore in 1806. However the 'great' Indian Mutiny that erupted in 1857 had many causes and trouble in India had been building up since 1856. It should be noted that without the loyal support of many of the Sikhs and Gurkhas, and the many reinforcements hurriedly sent out, India would not have remained part of the British Empire as long as it did.

In 1848 Earl Dalhousie became Governor-General, and started to implement the policy of annexing the Indian states when the ruler died and there was no natural heir. Two easily recognisable areas known as Jhansi and Nagpur were annexed for this reason. Families who had for generations ruled these regions were suddenly removed from power, simply because of the inability to produce a natural heir. One such ruler, named Baji Rao II was pensioned off to remove him from power. Upon his death Nana Sahib tried to obtain his pension, but to no avail. In another incident Oude was annexed on 7th February 1856, following the removal of Wajid Ali the King of Oude. The King was removed from the throne because he would not accept British dominance and openly acknowledged the fact. Even with a personal visit by both the King and Queen of Oude to England to be reinstated and to have the annexation reversed, they were refused. Oude was the home of the Bengal army and this course of action created a deep resentment. Throughout India this caused insecurity and instability amongst the Indian Princes. Another problem was the replacement of familiar customs with those of a foreign culture. The mutiny was not unexpected - Lord Dalhousie had even argued about the reduction of the presence of British soldiers because of the unrest.

The Indian troops also believed that they would be influenced and eventually forced to convert to the Christian religion. During 1856 the fear became stronger with the passing of the General Service Enlistment Act making it necessary for them to serve overseas when required to. All recruits to the 72 Battalions of the Bengal army had to accept service abroad like their counterparts in the Bombay and Madras armies. It was consideredout of the question for a faithful Hindu to go to sea, knowing it would be impossible to maintain the requirements of his religion.

It was during 1853 after successful trials, that authorisation was given to the British army to start the production of a new rifle called the, 'Enfield', at the new Royal Small Arms factory at Enfield in England. The soldiers in the Indian sub-continent were issued with various makes of rifle such as the pattern 1842 smooth bore rifle and the newly developed Enfield. Taking into account the climatic conditions in India, various trials were undertaken and it was found that the Enfield rifle musket needed a very close fitting cartridge and ball. In order for it to be loaded quickly and smoothly the cartridges were thus encased in a greased paper and to load the cartridge it required the end to be bitten off, the powder within poured down the barrel and the remainder containing the wad and ball forced home with a ramrod. Because this type of cartridge was now being used in India rumours started to be circulated that the lubricants use in their manufacture, contained fat from cows and the lard from pigs. The cow being sacred to the Hindus, and the pigs hated by the Mohammedans, this caused displeasure and bitterness throughout the native troops. The majority of historians believe that this single factor sparked off the Indian mutiny.

On 22nd January 1857, disturbances over the cartridges began at a place called Dum Dum. Other disturbances erupted at Umballa, Meerut and Lucknow, on 6th February, 26th March and 24th April 1857 respectively. On the 26th February the 19th Bengal Native Infantry rioted at Berhampore, followed by riots on the 29th March by the 34th Bengal Native Infantry at Barrackpore. Other Bengal regiments were punished, whilst others were dismissed and disbanded. The main revolt commenced on the 10th May 1857 at Meerut. At this time some 38,000 European and 200,000 Native soldiers were employed by the Honourable East India Company in India. On the 11th May troops belonging to the 38th, 54th and 74th Bengal Native Infantry Regiments mutinied at Delhi. A general extermination of Europeans began with the rebels proclaiming the great mogul Bahadur Shah as their leader. When the word spread of the rebellion, the native Bengal army resorted to open revolt.

General George Anson, the Commander-in-Chief, grouped all available troops and advanced to Delhi. Major-General Sir Henry Barnard succeeded him when the C-in-C died of cholera on 27th May 1857. Following a number of actions culminating in the battle of Badli-ke-Serai on 8th June 1857, the British reached Delhi. Shortly afterwards on 5th July Major-General Barnard also died of cholera, being briefly replaced by General Reed. Brigadier-General Archdale Wilson was placed in command shortly after on 17th July 1857. On the 14th December Delhi was laid siege, finally being taken on the 20th December. The rebels so called leader, Bahadur Shah was captured and his sons were shot.

The British garrison under the command of Sir Hugh Wheeler stubbornly held Cawnpore, but after a period of three weeks surrendered to Nana Sahib on 26th June 1857. The garrison and their families after being promised safe passage were mercilessly butchered. Some women and children did survive however and were imprisoned. Sir Henry Lawrence and his command at Lucknow defended the Residency. On the 2nd July 1857 Lawrence was killed and Brigadier Inglis took over command. On 7th July Brigadier-General Sir Henry Havelock and a small British force consisting of 1,500 men left Allahabad for Lucknow. This small force during their march to relieve Lucknow, defeated the forces of Nana Sahib at Fatehpur on 12th July, Aong on the 15th July and then at Cawnpore on the 16th July. Havelock and his command entering Cawnpore, discovered the bodies of the Europeans including women and children who had been taken prisoner.

Havelock had to wait for reinforcements because his original force had been diminished due to the heavy fighting and disease. The advance to Lucknow resumed on the 25th September following the arrival of reinforcements led by Major-General Sir James Outram. Although superior in rank, Outram allowed Havelock to retain command and 3,000 men marched to join up with the troops at Lucknow. The cost of reaching Lucknow was high, losing 535 men killed or wounded. Now not strong enough to withdraw from Lucknow, Major-General Sir James Outram resumed command of the besieged forces.

The Commander-in-Chief Sir Colin Campbell formed a second relief column of 4,500 men which advanced to Lucknow. Other forces led by General Hope Grant and Captain Peel RN all combined at Alum Bagh and the Commander-in-Chief moved forward into the city on 14th November. The strongly defended Secunda Bagh was stormed on 16th November and during the next day forces led by both Campbell and Havelock cleared the rebels. The Residency was successfully evacuated by the 23rd November but with the death of Havelock on the 24th November. Outram was ordered to remain at Alum Bagh with troops to defend it against any rebel intrusion. Campbell then left Lucknow and marched for Cawnpore. At Cawnpore on 6th December 1857 he again engaged the rebels and successfully defeated them, although the rebel leader Tantia Topi escaped. On the 2nd March 1858 Campbell with a stronger force returned to Alum Bagh and from here continued the task of reducing the rebel forces at Lucknow and by the 21st March had regained control of the city.

At the beginning of 1858, the campaign of Central India commenced with forces under the command of Major-General Sir Hugh Rose starting to flush out and destroy any remaining rebels. On the 27th January 1858 the fort of Rathghur was captured followed by a further defeat of the rebels at Barodia on 31st January 1858. The relief and securement of Saugor was completed on the 3rd February 1858. Sir Hugh Rose with 1,500 men finally defeated an enemy force of some 22,000 men led by Tantia Topi at Betwa on the 1st April. A few days later on the 5th April the rebel stronghold of Jhansi was captured. On 19th April a British force led by Major-General Whitlock defeated the rebels at Banda. Major-General Rose had further victories against Tantia Topi at Kunch on 7th May, Gowlowlee on the 22nd May, and Kalpi was finally taken on the 23rd May 1858.

Tantia Topi escaped and with the Rani of Jhansi and other rebel leaders advanced on Gwalior. A desperate fight ensued at Morar between the Maharajah and the rebels, in which the rebel forces were victorious, and Gwalior fell to the enemy. Rose again advanced upon the enemy and defeated them at Kotah-ke-Serai on the 17th June 1858 and during this battle the Rani of Jhansi was killed. Following the capture of Gwalior on the 20th June 1858, the great Indian Mutiny was virtually over, although the fighting continued against the rebel leader Tania Topi. This rebel leader was eventually captured on the 7th April and was hanged on the 18th April 1858.

NB By the time the 80th Regiment entered the war the Indian Mutiny as a whole had been quelled. However, the most exacting period was still to be played out, the flushing out, chasing and final defeat of the rebel forces.

Central India - The Campaign

The distribution of the establishment of the 80th Regiment of Foot (Staffordshire Volunteers) was sanctioned by His Royal Highness, The General Commanding-in-Chief as described in the Circular Memo, dated 'Horse Guards 29th November 1856', was 1 Lt.Colonel, 2 Majors, 12 Captains, 14 Lieutenants, 10 Ensigns, 6 Staff, 67 Sergeants (including Schoolmaster), 48 Corporals, 25 Drummers or Buglers, and 952 Privates, totalling 1000 men.

On the 1st January 1857 the total strength of the Service Companies and Headquarters at Fort Beaufort, South Africa excluding Officers was 46 Sergeants, 40 Corporals, 17 Drummers and 749 Privates, totalling 852 men. At this time the Regiment was serving in South Africa providing detachments in various places of the Cape Provinces. On the 19th October 1857 the Regiment was ordered to Ceylon and the Regiment marched out of Fort Beaufort en route to Port Elizabeth for embarkation. The Headquarters arrived on 2nd November and remained under canvas. The Regiment moved in three detachments, on the 16th November. 6 Officers and 120 men sailed on the ship, '*John Knox*'; Headquarters sailed on the '*Game Cock*' on the 20th November, with the remaining 6 Officers and 196 men sailing on the 28th November on board the '*Euphrates*'.

When the Headquarters and the rest of the Regiment, totalling 17 officers and 470 men arrived in Ceylon, orders were received to proceed to Calcutta, India without delay. On the 3rd January 1858 the whole of the Regiment was transhipped into the Honourable Company's Steamers, '*Australian*', '*Euphrates*' and '*John Knox*'. The '*Australian*' sailed on the 5th January and arrived at Calcutta on the 17th January. The troops disembarked the next day and marched to the Town Hall. The '*John Knox*' arrived on the 19th January with the second detachment and were quartered at Fort William. The remainder of the Regiment arrived on the '*Euphrates*' on the 8th February. Orders were received for the Regiment to proceed to Allahabad and a detachment of 7 Officers and 192 men left on the 22nd January. The remaining Headquarters consisting of 18 Officers and 378 men left the next day. The Regiment was transported to Raniganj by railway and then by bullock cart to Allahabad arriving on the 5th February. The detachment from the '*Euphrates*' joined Headquarters on the 22nd February and on the 23rd, three companies under the command of Field Officer Brevet Lt. Colonel Christie with 2 Captains and 5 Subalterns moved out to Khaga by railway, then by a series of marches arrived at Fatehpur some 50 miles south-east of Cawnpore.

A Column was formed, consisting of the three companies of the 80th, Madras Native Infantry (same number), a few irregular cavalry and two guns, to engage with the mutineers of the Bengal Army on the 5th March at Dhana, a village on the banks of the river Jumna. The rebels were driven out of the village and retreated to the nearby town of Sirauli. Lt.Colonel Christie ordered his guns to open fire on the town and after a few rounds the town was taken and then burnt. Unfortunately the majority of the enemy escaped across the river in boats. On the 12th March the Headquarters and the remaining five companies, leaving No. 5 Company at Fatehpur, proceeded from Allahabad to Cawnpore on the 19th March.

On its arrival in Cawnpore they occupied the Artillery Barracks to the East of that station. On the 4th April 1858 the Regiment under the command of Sir John Inglis KCB marched from Cawnpore on an expedition into Oudes, the main objective being to destroy a village called Hourah approximately 20 miles from Cawnpore, reported to be occupied by rebel forces. The village was attacked and destroyed, although the majority of the rebels escaped leaving behind them an Oude Chief and 25 dead.

On the 18th April 1878 the Headquarters now consisting of four companies, one company being at Fatehpur and three Companies in the Fatehpur District, provided an escort for His Excellency the Commander-in-Chief, Sir Colin Campbell Lord Clyde and marched from Cawnpore for Fatehpur approximately 160 miles. Lord Clyde was travelling to Bareilly with the intentions of taking this place from the rebels. The Regiment reached Fatehgarh on the 25th April and occupied the barracks. On the 26th April No. 5 Company rejoined Headquarters from Fatehpur.

The Regiment lost a number of men suffering from sun stroke and apoplexy. The temperatures reached as high as 115°F inside the tents where men sheltered from the sun. Outside it was almost impossible to walk about or march, let alone fight.

During this period Companies 2 and 3 were trained to use camels and eventually became part of the Camel Corps. This newly formed corps consisted of members from the 80th Regiment of Foot, The Rifle Brigade and loyal Sikhs, and was assigned to the Central India Field Force under the command of Sir Hugh Rose. The Camel Corps was rushed to Kalpi, an important enemy arsenal on the banks of the Jumna and controlled by a rebel army whose leader was Tantia Topi, one of the enemy's more able leaders. So far Sir Hugh Rose's forces had experienced a gruelling campaign with much fighting on the 16th and 17th May 1858. On the 18th May the Camel Corps 600 strong and under the command of Colonel Maxwell manoeuvred themselves on the opposite side of the river to Sir Hugh Rose and opened fire with their light guns.

During the night of the 20th, Maxwell crossed the river via a ford to reinforce Sir Hugh Rose. Rose's force was then attacked and he ordered his forces to the left flank. On the 22nd Tantia Topi attacked Rose's right flank where the majority of his guns had been positioned. Being numerically superior the rebels had almost reached the main batteries when the Camel Corps was ordered into action. The Camel Corps raced forward and dismounted to engage the enemy and delivered a counter-attack that eventually broke the enemy. The enemy forces on this occasion had no river to aid their escape and were pursued by the Camel Corps and some of Rose's original force. No quarter was asked and none given, hundreds being slaughtered. It should be noted that this action and decisive victory at Kalpi more or less finished the Central India campaign.

On 5th June 1858 the Headquarters of the Regiment again provided an escort for His Excellency The Commander-in-Chief and marched from Fatehgarh to Cawnpore enduring eight marches and arriving on 12th June. They remained at Cawnpore through the remainder of the hot season. Before their return to Cawnpore though, the three companies under the command of Brevet Lt.Colonel Christie left there. On the 17th May Colonel Hutchinson having been appointed Brigadier, the command of the Regiment devolved to Captain Young, (it is assumed all other senior officers were incapacitated in some way). On the 1st and 3rd October two draughts of recruits consisting of 1 Captain, 2 Subalterns, 2 Sergeants, 4 Corporals and 174 Privates joined the Headquarters of the Regiment, 2 more companies were formed and numbered 8 and 9, the old No. 8 Company becoming No. 10. The strength of the service companies of the 80th Regiment was now as follows, 2 Lt.Colonels, 2 Majors, 9 Captains, 11 Lieutenants, 4 Ensigns, 7 Staff, 49 Sergeants, 45 Corporals, 17 Drummers and 746 Privates; total 857.

On the 12th October 1858, the Headquarters, and one wing of the Regiment consisting of Companies 1, 3, 4, 6 and 7 marched from Cawnpore into Oude and joined a column at Fawahgunge on the Lucknow Road on the 13th. This column consisted of Her Majesty's 20th and 80th Regiments of Foot, Horse Artillery, Irregular Cavalry and Native Levies, the whole commanded by Brigadier Evelegh of the 20th Regiment (East Devonshire). The object of this force was to protect the road and neighbourhood from the rebels. Numerous expeditions were made into the district, but the rebels invariably fled on the approach of the force. On 1st November Colonel acting Brigadier Evelegh marched with a force consisting of the Headquarters 80th and 20th Regiments of Foot, Irregular Cavalry and Horse Artillery to Poorwah, a native village and fortifications occupied by some a newly raised Police levy and threatened by the enemy. Hearing their approach, the rebels retired.

Another small column was formed under the command of Major Bulwer 23rd Regiment (Royal Welch Fusiliers) consisting of the 23rd Regiment and some Native Levies, and they joined Brigadier Evelegh's column. On the 7th November, Evelegh hearing that a village called Simree, about 12 miles from Poorwah, was occupied by a large body of rebels, marched to Morar and from the 9th moved with the purpose of attacking the Fort of Simree. After about half an hour's march, the enemy's cavalry and infantry was observed in the jungle, and three companies of the 80th and two companies of the 20th were extended to clear the front, and the cavalry sent to turn the enemy's flank. After three hours the jungle was cleared of the enemy, and the companies returned to the column for about an hour. Due to the density of the jungle it took some time to discover the fort of Simree. The heavy guns were then brought up and two companies of the 80th and two of the 23rd were ordered down to drive the enemy through the jungle. Coming suddenly on the fort they made a rush, burst open a gate and took possession of the fort, bayoneting all the rebels that were found inside. During the advance the enemy opened fire from 2 guns in the fort, and casualties of the 80th were 1 man killed and 1 officer and 2 men wounded. The 20th Regiment lost one man killed.

The capture of Simree was on the 9th November 1858, the estimated losses of the enemy 100 men in total, all being Sepoys. In one of Brigadier Evelegh's dispatches he reports, "the advance of the 80th under Captain Young excited my warmest approbation". After remaining at Simree for a few days, during which the fort was destroyed, Brigadier Evelegh continued his march through the surrounding districts in pursuit of the rebels as information was received of their whereabouts.

On the 17th November the force was again engaged with the rebels at Berar when the enemy were thoroughly routed and a great number killed with small loss to our own forces. Brigadier Evelegh's force, on the 24th November, joined the forces under the command of the Commander-in-Chief Lord Clyde and then engaged with the enemy at Dundea Khera where the rebels led by Beni Madhu were surprised near the river Ganges 30 miles south-east of Cawnpore. The enemy lost a great number of men driven into the river and drowned. Beni Madhu escaped but lost all of his artillery. During this engagement the Regiment lost 2 men killed and 2 wounded.

After this action the Headquarters of the Regiment were ordered into Cawnpore as an escort for the sick and wounded. On the 1st December the Headquarters consisting of the Left Wing as before, again marched from Cawnpore into Oude and proceeded by regular marches to Lucknow and thence to Bahraich, near to the Nepal frontier where they joined the Commander-in-Chief on the 19th December. On the 21st Lt.Colonel Christie was detached from the Commander-in-Chief with a column consisting of a detachment of the 6th Dragoon Guards, the 80th Regiment, two companies of the 20th Regiment and some artillery and irregular cavalry. This force was engaged with the enemy at Bussingpore on the 23rd, the enemy suffering great losses. Colonel Christie, in the fore-front of the action, was shot, his horse and himself falling, the horse shot through the neck and the Colonel receiving several shots in the body. Fortunately these did not prove dangerous. Colonel Christie's Column then rejoined the Commander-in-Chief and on the 3rd January 1859 at Bara Banki, a few miles north-east of Lucknow, the rebel army was entirely destroyed, any survivors dispersing.

The Commander-in-Chief ordered his army back to quarters and announced in General Orders the termination of the Oude campaign and the almost total destruction of the rebel army. The 80th Regiment returned to Cawnpore via Lucknow. Shortly after the departure of the Left Wing from Cawnpore, the Right Wing consisting of Nos. 2, 5, 8, 9 and 10 Companies, marched from Cawnpore into the districts in pursuit of Prince Firoz Shah, a native of Delhi who had crossed the Ganges and was marching with a force. The Wing after much hard marching proved unsuccessful as a result of their inability to overtake the enemy. The enemy consisted almost entirely of cavalry - the mutinous Gwalior Horse - and consequently the Wing had to return to Cawnpore. From Cawnpore it marched to Lucknow where it remained encamped until 11th January when it was ordered back to Cawnpore. The Right Wing arrived in Cawnpore on the 14th and the Left Wing arrived on the 20th January. The whole Regiment immediately occupied its former quarters, the old Artillery barracks. The Regiment continued to be employed in India after the cessation of hostilities.

The 80th Regiment of Foot (Staffordshire Volunteers) for their services during the Indian Mutiny and especially for their part in Central India was awarded the Battle Honour 'Central India.'

Lucknow.
Indian Mutiny.

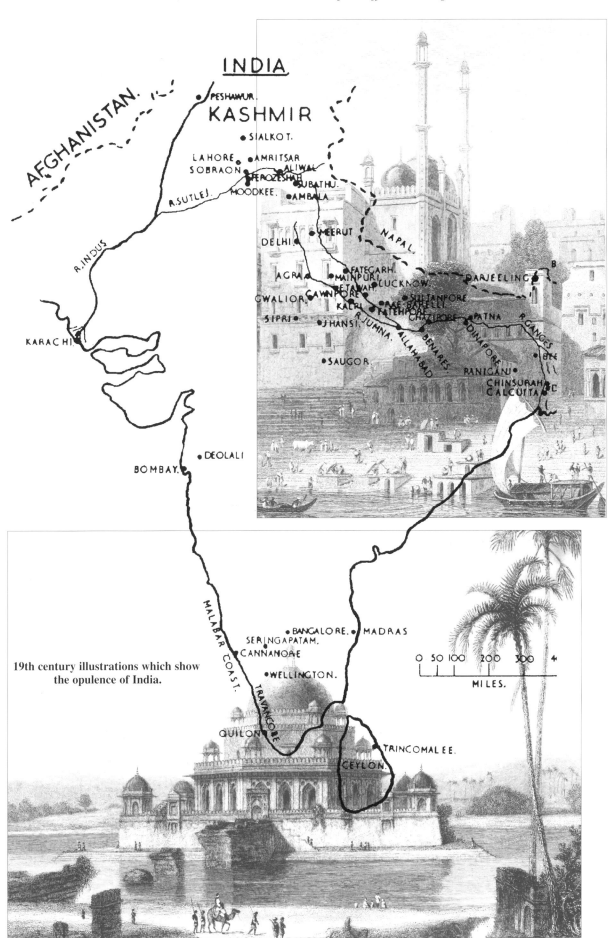

INDIA

AFGHANISTAN.

KASHMIR

PESHAWUR.
SIALKOT.
LAHORE
SOBRAON
AMRITSAR
ALIWAL
FEROZESHAH
SUBATHU.
MOODKEE.
AMBALA
R.SUTLEJ.
R.INDUS
MEERUT
DELHI
NAPAL.
AGRA
MAINPURI
FATEGARH.
GWALIOR
ETAWAH
LUCKNOW
DARJEELING
CAWNPORE
SULTANPORE
KALPI
RAE BARELLI
SIPRI
JHANSI
FATEHPORE
GHAZIPORE
PATNA
R.GANGES
R.JUMNA.
BENARES.
DINAPORE
SAUGOR
ALLAHABAD
RANIGANJ
CHINSURAH
CALCUTTA
KARACHI.

DEOLALI
BOMBAY.

MALABAR COAST.

BANGALORE.
MADRAS
SERINGAPATAM.
CANNANORE
WELLINGTON.

TRAVANCORE
QUILON
TRINCOMALEE.
CEYLON.

0 50 100   200   300   4

MILES.

19th century illustrations which show
the opulence of India.

Troops in transit - Bullock carts.

Camel Transport - note the dhoolies in the foreground.

SOUTH AFRICA 1878-79

South Africa - Background and Summary

British interest in South Africa came to ahead during the latter part of the 18th century and the beginning of the 19th. The importance of the Cape and its various harbours became apparent when the Dutch who had started to colonise the area were defeated by the French in 1794. French shipping, including warships, could find refuge and have unlimited supplies of fresh water and provisions. They thus controlled the high seas in that area. Because of this threat, the British, in 1795, set forth and seized the Cape from the French. Following the end of the French Revolutionary War, the Treaty of Amiens was signed in 1801 and as a consequence the Cape was handed back to the Dutch. However, the British were to retake the Cape in 1806 during the Napoleonic War. Because of the importance of the Cape on one of the main routes to India and the far East, they were to remain here indefinitely to ensure suitable facilities for their own shipping needs and those of other friendly nations.

The 80th Regiment of Foot first came to be in South Africa during 1856 and 1857 when they provided various detachments at Fort Beaufort, Cape Colony. During 1876 the Regiment again served in South Africa when 300 men were stationed at Newcastle. The Regiment was further strengthened, more because of circumstances than planning. On the 29th January 1877 Lt.Colonel Amiel and 300 men of the 80th Regiment set sail on board the '*Orontes*' bound for Mauritius. However, on their journey a number of cases of measles were discovered and the ship was refused entry to Mauritius. The disease was a killer, and the ship had to lie at anchor in Port Louis, Mauritius under quarantine conditions. Eventually the ship with its passengers was ordered to sail to Natal, South Africa, where it was again refused landing. The ship, after visiting various ports on the coast of South Africa, was again ordered back to Natal and upon arrival this time allowed to off load the troops. In consequence of their children having measles, nine non-commissioned officers and men, ten wives and fourteen children were not allowed to leave the ship and were eventually taken to Cape Town where they were allowed to go ashore. From this point the Regiment was to serve in various parts of South Africa until 1880.

HMS Orontes, the ship that transported the troops of the 80th Regiment to South Africa, in May 1876 and January 1877, and then transported the Regiment back to Ireland in April and May 1880.

During 1878 and 1879 there was to be two major conflicts in South Africa, the first of these, in 1878, the campaign to subdue Sekukuni and his Bapedi tribe. Sekukuni proved to be a most formidable leader and it became necessary to suspend the actions against him during the latter part of that year and to continue the campaign during the later months of 1879. The second major conflict was the war against the Zulus in 1879.

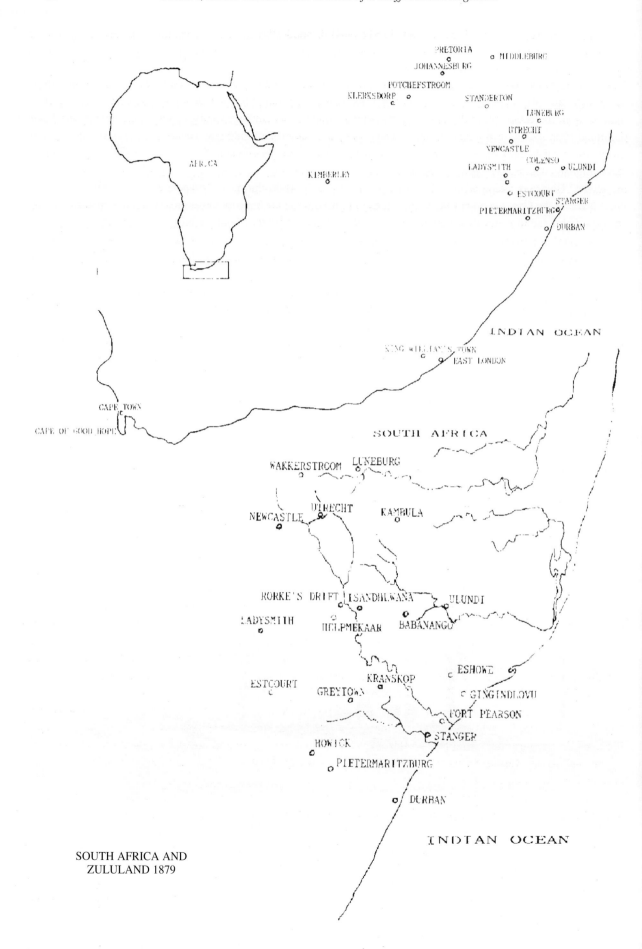

SOUTH AFRICA AND
ZULULAND 1879

In the 1870s, gold and diamonds were discovered in South Africa. Many of the minerals were found on the surface, but much more was buried below. Prospectors rushed to the area, and labour, especially cheap labour, would be required to mine these riches.

Some of the Dutch Boers, having left the Cape, started to populate the Transvaal and permanent settlements were established. In the early 1870s, when gold was discovered around Lydenburg area, it led to a great influx of miners, traders and the like. The Reverend Thomas Burger was elected President of the Transvaal in 1871. He had a scheme to make the Transvaal more independent by providing a railway from Pretoria to Delagoa Bay on the Indian Ocean. To secure the finance for the railway, areas of the Transvaal were put up as security for the loan. Chief Sekukuni and the Bapedi people originated from the Basuto and were strongly independent. Their base and stronghold lay in the Lulu Mountains located in the north eastern part of the Transvaal.

In 1876, the Boers, aided by Swazi tribesmen, began a campaign to drive Sekukuni and his tribe away. Sekukuni was defiant and refused to give up his tribal lands. The Boer campaign was a total failure and much condemned by the British Government. It left Sekukuni in a strong position and being unopposed, he struck fear into the settlers, miners and traders with continuous raiding parties. The Transvaal State soon became bankrupt. Although reluctant at first, the British Government eventually seized the opportunity to bring the Transvaal under its control. On the 12th April 1877 the bankrupt State of the Transvaal accepted British Annexation and British domination. Transvaal now became part of an overall plan of Confederation of the area in South Africa.

The British now wanted to demonstrate to the Boers how to rule and govern. The territory occupied by Sekukuni was part of the lands annexed by the British, and it was deemed necessary to remove this troublesome Chief and the Bapedi tribe, (a complete change of British policy towards Sekukuni). Shepstone, the British Government's representative, with limited resources, embarked on this first campaign against Sekukuni. With only 3 companies of the 1st Battalion of the 13th Light Infantry and a number of volunteer units, it was doomed to failure.

The newly appointed Lord Chelmsford wanted results and ordered Colonel Henry Rowlands VC, CB, with a force of 1200 British infantrymen and 600 cavalry, to proceed to the area and remove Sekukuni. This force marched 430 miles from Pietermaritzburg to Lydenburg in just 21 days. This somewhat over ambitious plan of showing unquestionable might was to backfire with much embarrassment and humiliation. Colonel Rowlands began his march, in the heat of summer. The area had suffered two years of drought and the landscape was semi-desert and this fever ridden, harsh climate soon took its toll. Many of the cavalry horses died from horse sickness, which crippled his mounted force. By the time Colonel Rowlands arrived, the four military forts nearest to Sekukuni's stronghold had been abandoned. He re-garrisoned these forts, within sight of the enemy's main base and then had to decide what to do next, and, taking into account the lack of water, the climatic conditions, the depleted cavalry force, and the sickness that prevailed, he decided to withdraw his forces and leave Sekukuni unchallenged. The dejected and tired troops began their long march back and Sekukuni would remain at large a further twelve months.

Of all the tribes, the Zulus were the strongest in the southern part of the continent at the time. The Zulus were a most self sufficient nation rearing cattle and cultivating the fertile river valleys. Zululand extended from the Pongola River in the North to the Tugela River in the South, and from the coast in the East to the Drakensberg Mountains in the West. The Father of the Zulus was Shaka, born about 1787, and assassinated in 1828. He ascended the throne in 1816 when he had approximately four hundred warriors, but by 1817 he had quadrupled his forces. At the time of his death, he could call upon some 30,000 warriors.

The principle political figures in South Africa at this time were Sir Bartle Freer, Governor of Cape Colony and High Commissioner for Native Affairs in South Africa and Sir Theophilus Shepstone, Secretary for Native Affairs in Natal and Administrator of the Transvaal from 1877. Their Military Commander was Frederic Augustus Thesiger, Lieutenant-General Commanding British Forces in South Africa. Frederic in 1878 inherited his father's title and became the 2nd Baron Chelmsford.

It is questionable whether the Zulu Nation posed a threat to the British, but the Zulu culture was based around military training and military institution and 50,000 warriors could be called upon. Sir Bartle Freer was convinced that if the Zulus could be defeated and the Zulu Nation conquered, other tribes in Africa would quickly become subdued and other states and areas would submit to British rule and become part of the British Empire. Freer wanted a war with the Zulus, although his own Government in England did not.

The war might have been earlier when a tract of land was in dispute. A court of inquiry was summoned and met at Rorke's Drift on March 7th 1878, but, to great annoyance, the land was found to legally belong to the Zulus.

But another opportunity soon came to challenge the Zulus later the same year when two married Zulu women ran away and crossed the River Tugela into Natal. Zulu warriors followed them and eventually captured them. The women were taken back to Zululand and executed. Sir Theophilus Shepstone demanded that the warriors who had entered Natal in pursuit of the women, be handed over to the Natal Police. The demands were not met, and it was just the excuse Sir Bartle Freer wanted. On December 11th 1878, on the banks of the River Tugela, an ultimatum was handed to King Cetshwayo's representatives. The ultimatum consisted of 10 demands - the first four items, relating to the border incident, had to be complied with, within 20 days:

1) Sihayo's brother and three sons were to be surrendered for trial by Natal Courts
2) A fine of five hundred head of cattle was to be paid for Mehlokazulu's outrages and for Cetshwayo's delay in acceding to Natal's previous request for surrender
3) A further fine of one hundred head of cattle was to be paid for the offence committed against a surveyor named Smith and a trader called Deighton
4) Mbilini and others to be named later, were to surrender for trial by the Transvaal Courts

The last six demands had a time limit of 30 days, and were the most difficult for the Zulu King to fulfil, for in essence they were directed to break the Zulu's traditions and way of life. The demands meant the Zulu Nation was to submit to foreign rule, British rule.

5) The observance of the Zulu King's promises he made at his Coronation
6) A British Diplomatic resident is to be stationed in Zululand to enforce these provisions
7) The Zulu Army is to be disbanded
8) Young warriors were to be free to marry
9) Missionaries were to be allowed into Zululand to carry on with preaching
10) The Zulu Nation would not be able to declare war or implement any form of retribution including expulsion etc., without the consent of the British Resident or National Council

War was wanted by the British and was manipulated until it was inevitable. It was a war without any clear authority or justification and was much against the will and desires of Her Majesty's Government in England. The Zulu War commenced on January 11th and 12th 1879 when three columns of British and Colonial troops invaded Zululand. Their main tasks were to defeat the Zulu Army, destroy the Zulu King's principal residence, Ulundi, and to capture Cetshwayo the Zulu King. The British Military leaders believed the conflict would be over in 6 weeks. The Zulu warriors were to prove no easy pushover, even though they were armed with spears and shields and old obsolete rifles. The war effectively ended when the Zulu Army was defeated at Ulundi.

Lord Chelmsford at the onset of war had at his command 17,000 men consisting of 5000 regular infantrymen, 1500 regular and irregular mounted infantry/cavalry, with the remainder made up of Native troops. Following the disaster at Isandhlwana, to protect Britain's might, reinforcements were hurriedly sent out and the British Forces increased to 34,000 men. Although the British and Colonial forces were still numerically outnumbered they were confident of victory because of their modern equipment and weapons of war.

The first of the major battles took place at Inyezance on January 22nd when Colonel Pearson's No. 1 Column was attacked by 6000 Zulus, and the attack was successfully repulsed. This small insignificant colonial war soon hit the headlines when the Zulus attacked and took the British base camp at Isandhlwana on January 22nd. Over 1000 British and Colonial soldiers were slaughtered by a so called army of savages armed only with spears and shields. British honour was restored later that same day and over night when the hospital and stores at Rorke's Drift were successfully defended by only 139 men against 4000 Zulu's. A further two reverses took place, one on March 12th when a Company of the 80th Regiment was attacked and many killed, at Myer's Drift on the Intombi River. The other setback was when nearly 2000 men were killed in the disastrous action on the Hlobane Mountain that took place on March 28th.

The battle that did most damage to the Zulus was on March 29th at Kambula when a force of 20,000 warriors was driven from the battle field. During the second invasion of Zululand, on April 2nd, Lord Chelmsford's force was attacked by 12,000 Zulus at Gingindhlovu, and this Zulu army was again driven off. A most dramatic event took place at the Ityotosi River on June 1st when an European dynasty was brought to an abrupt end with the death of the Prince Imperial, Louis Napoleon. The final battle against the Zulus took place on July 4th at Ulundi when a force of 20,000 Zulus was defeated, and Ulundi and other kraals burnt to the ground.

On August 15th the principal chiefs of the Zulus surrendered to Sir Garnet Wolseley and on August 28th Cetshwayo the Zulu King was captured. The chiefs on September 1st accepted the terms and conditions for settlement and on the next day the British and Colonial troops started to withdraw from Zululand.

South Africa - The Marching, the Fighting and the Dying

The 80th Regiment arrived in South Africa in 1876. Throughout their time in the region, until they left for Ireland and 'Home Service' in 1880, the Regiment provided detachments to serve in many districts of the area. The Regiment marched throughout the vast country and flew the British flag with pride, demonstrating to the inhabitants what a typical British Army Infantry Regiment should be like. Members of the Regiment were well received and respected wherever they were to travel. Their discipline and behaviour were acknowledged by letters and statements now in the Regimental records.

The first of the major armed conflicts the Regiment became involved with was the campaign against Sekukuni during 1878. The Boers had failed to dispel Sekukuni and although the British Government appeared to be indecisive, behind the scenes Lord Carnavon and the Foreign Office, on the 5th October 1876, instructed Shepstone to make preparations to enter the Transvaal. On the 24th March 1877 British forces of five companies of the 1/13th Light Infantry supported by an escort of twenty-five mounted policemen arrived at Newcastle. Meanwhile on the 8th April 1877 notice was given to two companies of the 2/3rd Regiment of Foot and the 80th Regiment of Foot including the remainder of the 1/3rd Regiment to march to the border of the Transvaal. On the 9th April the annexation of the Transvaal was implemented and was officially confirmed a few days later on the 12th April 1877.

As one would now expect, the British Military machine was immediately activated, Colonel Pearson moving into the Transvaal while Colonel Durnford, the senior ranking officer in Natal, took over as the Commanding Officer. Durnford had under his command 32 officers and 743 men. At Fort Napier were stationed 26 officers and 632 rank and file that included four companies of the 2/3rd Regiment of Foot and one Company of the 1/13th Light Infantry. At this time 6 officers and 289 men of the 80th Regiment were at Durban. The British High Command then ordered a field force of 300 men and two cannon to go to Newcastle.

Colonel Rowlands, with a force of 1200 infantry and 600 cavalry, marched in the heat of the African summer some 430 miles to take on Sekukuni. Colonel Rowlands not only had to contend with Sekukuni and his tribe but also had to keep a watchful eye on the Transvaal Boers and the Zulus. Although there were tons of supplies and provisions in Durban, transporting them was a logistical nightmare. Transport waggons were bought or rented including the drivers and conductors who would work them. The problem was the purchase or hire of the animals to pull the waggons. The area had had no rains for some time and the climate was unhealthy to man and the animals.

The long arduous march was achieved and even though the four nearest military forts to Sekukuni's stronghold were re-garrisoned, Rowlands decided to withdraw his forces from the area. This tactical withdrawal was total disappointment and left Sekukuni to act as he wished. However, Colonel Rowlands and his forces were soon to be required for duties in the ensuing war against the Zulus.

The 80th Regiment's Regiment Digest for the period is as follows:-

7th DECEMBER 1877 Major Charles Tucker with a command of 200 Officers and men leave Newcastle for Utrecht at twenty-four hours notice. The force included two mountain guns. The Officers who accompanied Major Tucker are as follows:- Captain D.B. Moriarty "E" Company, Captain W.T. Anderton "D" Company, Lieutenant A.W. Hast, Lieutenant A.B. Horsbrugh, Sub Lieutenant T.E. Griffin, Captain & Brigade Major R.W. Stone remains at Newcastle with "A" Company. Lt. Hast. was assigned the responsibility of the mountain gun detachment which comprised of twenty-five men of the 80th Regiment of Foot.
8th DECEMBER 1877 The Officers and men of Major Tucker's force arrives at Utrecht and makes camp. At this time His Excellency the Administrator was residing at Utrecht and consequently a portion of mounted troops were also here to act as an escort.
12th DECEMBER 1877 At Utrecht there was a stone settlers laager. An adjoining military earthwork fort is started by men of the 80th Regiment of Foot.
12th JANUARY 1878 "H" Company under the command of 2nd Lieutenant A.H. Lindop consisting of 5 Sergeants, 4 Corporals, 2 Drummers and 85 Privates leave Lydenburg to increase Brev. Major Creagh's command at Derby on the Zulu border.
16th FEBRUARY 1878 The military earthwork fort at Utrecht is completed. Water is becoming very scarce at Utrecht, several wells are sunk by the troops and water is procured.
23rd FEBRUARY 1878 Brev. Major Creagh leaves Derby.
3rd MARCH 1878 Due to the disturbed state of the Transvaal "C", "B" and "F" Companies leave Pietermaritzburg for Utrecht, Lt. Colonel Twenlow is in command of this force consisting of 260 Officers and men consisting of the following:- Captain W. Howard "F" Company, Captain A. Saunders "B" Company, Lieutenant T.J. Chamberlain, Lieutenant W. Moore, Lieutenant H.H. Harward "C" Company, 15 Sergeants, 15 Corporals, 5 Drummers, 220 Privates. This force reached Howick about 40 miles distance and were recalled as three Companies of the 90th Light Infantry are ordered to proceed instead.
4th MARCH 1878 The command of Troops in South Africa was handed over by General Sir A. Cunynghame to Lt. General The Honourable F.A. Thesiger (later Lord 2nd Baron Chelmsford) at King William's Town. The Imperial troops consisted of two Batteries Royal Artillery (N/5 and N/117), the 7th Company of Royal Engineers and the 1/24th, 88th and the 90th Regiment of Foot in the Cape Colony. The 2/3rd with the 80th Regiment of Foot being in Natal and the 1/13th in the Transvaal. This amounted to 5000 Imperial troops.

3rd JUNE 1878 Distribution of Troops - Pietermaritzburg Fort Napier 2 Field Officers 3 Captains 8 Subalterns 1 Staff 31 Sergeants 13 Buglers 547 Rank & File 5 Horses Durban 1 Subaltern 2 Sergeants 33 Rank & File Newcastle 1 Captain 1 Subaltern 6 Sergeants 2 Buglers 53 Rank & File Sent to Transvaal 1 Field Officer 2 Captain 2 Subalterns 8 Sergeants 1 Bugler 172 Rank & File Kokstaladt 1 Sergeant

8th JUNE 1878 Distribution of Troops - Transvaal Pretoria Utrecht 1 Field Officer 2 Captains 2 Subalterns 8 Sergeants 1 Buglers 172 Rank & File 2 Horses 2 Guns 39,000 Small Arms Ammunition 2 Mountain Guns 12 Mules

24th JULY 1878 Lieutenant J.O. Sherrard with 1 Sergeant, 2 Corporals and 23 Privates leave Durban for Newcastle.

26th JULY 1878 Headquarters staff leaves Pietermaritzburg for Utrecht. This force consisted of the following Officers and men:- Major C. J. R. Tyler, Captain and Brev. Major C. A. F. Creagh "H" Company, Captain W. Howard "F" Company, Captain C. E. W. Roworth "G" Company, Captain A. Saunders "B" Company, Lieutenant H. J. Johnson, Lieutenant W. Moore, Lieutenant H. H. Harward "C" Company, Lieutenant H. C. Savage, 2nd Lieutenant T. E. Griffin (Adjutant), Quarter Master J. Belt, Civil Surgeon W. I. Cobbin, 32 Sergeants, 23 Corporals, 12 Drummers, 457 Privates, Lieutenant Chamberlain remaining behind in charge of a Detail consisting of 1 Sergeant and 34 Privates including the soldiers families.

7th AUGUST 1878 The Regiment reached Newcastle and there orders were received to send out three detachments with all possible speed to relieve the 1/13 Light Infantry from Garrison duty. This was to enable them to be able to take to the field against Sekukuni the Kaffir Chief. Sekukuni's territory was in the North Eastern portion of the Zulu mountains. The detachments were sent out on the 12th and 13th August instant.

12th AUGUST 1878 "B" Company under the command of Captain A.Saunders, Lieutenant W.Moore with 3 Sergeants 3 Corporals 2 Drummers and 71 Privates to be stationed at Standerton. Lieutenant Moore is to act as Commissariat Officer there.

13th AUGUST 1878 "F" Company under the command of Captain W. Howard, 2nd Lt. H.A. Raitt with 3 Sergeants, 5 Corporals, 2 Drummers and 88 Privates to Middlesburg. Brev. C.A.F. Creagh accompanied by Captain C.E.W. Rowarth, Lt's H.H. Howard and H.C. Savage and 2nd Lieutenant F.W. Lyons with "G" and "H" companies consisting of 8 Sergeants, 9 Corporals, 3 Drummers and 176 Privates to Lydenburg. There Headquarters to march Pretoria with the least possible delay and is to be followed by the Utrecht and Newcastle detachments. All the troops, Imperial and Colonial in the Transvaal District are placed under the command of Colonel H. Rowlands VC, CB.

14th AUGUST 1878 Lieutenant J.O. Sherrard's force joins Headquarters at Newcastle.

16th AUGUST 1878 Colonel C.F. Amiel was too ill to travel. Headquarters under the command of Major C.J.R. Tyler, accompanied by Lieutenant Sherrard and 2nd Lt's T.E. Griffin and T.A. Porter, with Civil Surgeon Cobbin and 18 Sergeants, 6 Corporals, 4 Drummers and 84 Privates leave Newcastle with six Mill waggons and march to Pretoria. Lieutenant A.B. Horsbrugh and 10 men follow the convoy of ox waggons.

18th AUGUST 1878 Lieutenant A.W. Hast is directed to hand over to Lieutenant Nicholson R.A. command of the mountain gun detachment which he had commanded for some time. Lt. Hast is conveyed probation of "H" Company. The Lieutenant General Commanding the forces in South Africa was pleased in the satisfactory manner in which Lt. Hast had performed his duties with the gun detachment.

25th AUGUST 1878 A farewell address from the inhabitants of Utrecht was received by Major C. Tucker, setting forth the good behaviour and kindly feelings towards the civil population by the the men of the Detachments. A detachment of 182 Officers and men leaves Utrecht for Pretoria under the command of Major C. Tucker. The force consisting of the following:- Captain D. B. Moriarty, Captain W. T. Anderson, Lieutenant L. C. Potts, Lieutenant A. W. Hast, 7 Sergeants, 9 Corporals, 1 Drummer, 160 Privates

27th AUGUST 1878 Major C.J.R. Tyler and Headquarters reach Pretoria.

29th AUGUST 1878 Major C.J.R. Tyler remains at Pretoria being in command from the 29th August 1878, with Lieutenant L.C. Potts as District Adjutant.

4th SEPTEMBER 1878 Lieutenant A.B. Horsbrugh and his command reach Pretoria.

9th SEPTEMBER 1878 Major Tucker and his force of 182 men of all ranks arrive at Pretoria and takes command.

10th SEPTEMBER 1878 Lt. Nicholson R.A. and the mountain gun detachment consisting of 20 men march from Pretoria and accompanies the column commanded by Major Russell 12th Lancers commanding 1st Squadron Mounted Infantry.

11th SEPTEMBER 1878 Captain Roworth with 50 non commissioned Officers and men proceed to Kruger's Post. Lieutenant Harward with 50 non commissioned Officers and men go to MacDonald's Farm.

14th SEPTEMBER 1878 Captain D.B. Moriarty and "E" Company consisting of Lieutenants Hast and Horsbrugh including 4 Sergeants, 4 Corporals, 1 Drummer and 85 Privates leaves Pretoria for Lydenburg. They are stopped next day, and their destination changed to Fort Weeber. The force is increased by 26 men.

17th SEPTEMBER 1878 Captain D.B. Moriarty and "E" Company recommences the march to Ford Weeber.

18th SEPTEMBER 1878 Lieutenant H.H. Harward with a force of 50 non commissioned Officers and men leave MacDonald's Farm and proceeds to Labuseogues Farm, these movements of the 11th and 18th were intended to preserve the lines of communication between Fort Burgher and Lydenburg.

20th SEPTEMBER 1878 Captain and Brev. Major Creagh is appointed Acting Staff Officer to the Lydenburg District.

24th SEPTEMBER 1878 Major Tucker and Lieutenant Sherrard with 30 non commissioned Officers and men of "C" Company proceeds to Fort Weeber. Major Tucker is assigned the command of the Left attack against Sekukuni. Lieutenant J.O. Sherrard is appointed Adjutant.

27th SEPTEMBER 1878 2nd Lieutenant F.M.H. Marshall joins the Regiment from England on his first appointment. He proceeds from Newcastle with a force of 1 Lance Sergeant and 20 Privates to Lydenburg. Lieutenant H.J. Johnson with "A" Company consisting of 3 Sergeants, 4 Corporals, 2 Drummers and 49 Privates leaves Newcastle for Lydenburg.

28th SEPTEMBER 1878 Captain J.E.H. Prior with two 2nd Lieutenants A.H. Lindop and E.K. Daubeney including a force consisting of 1 Sergeant and 59 Privates arrive at Durban from the Depot.

30th SEPTEMBER 1878 Captain Moriarty and Lieutenant Horsbrugh with 100 non- commissioned Officers and men march from Fort Weeber for Fort Oliphant.

1st OCTOBER 1878 Captain Moriarty's force arrive at Fort Oliphant.

3rd & 4th OCTOBER 1878 The mountain gun detachment are engaged with the enemy either in supporting movements or repelling attacks.

5th OCTOBER 1878 Lieutenant H.C. Savage with a detachment of 19 men escort a convoy containing a supply of ammunition from Lydenburg to Fort Burgher. The mountain gun detachment are again engaged with the enemy either in supporting movements or repelling attacks.

6th OCTOBER 1878 The mountain gun detachment engaged with the enemy either in supporting movements or repelling attacks.

7th OCTOBER 1878 2nd Lieutenant F.W. Lyons with an escort of 19 men are employed on the same escort duty conveying ammunition from Lydenburg to Fort Burgher.

9th OCTOBER 1878 Lieutenant H.J. Johnson with "A" Company arrive at Pretoria.

15th OCTOBER 1878 "A" Company with Lieutenant Johnson leave Pretoria for Fort Weeber. The Company is made up of 4 Sergeants, 3 Corporals, 1 Drummer and 60 Privates. 2nd Lieutenant Marshall with an escort of 21 men arrive at Lydenburg. He immediately proceeds to Labuseoques Farm with a force consisting of 47 non commissioned Officers and men. He is to replace Lt. Harward, who is ordered to go to Speckboom Drift with his detachment of 50 men.

18th OCTOBER 1878 Lieutenant Savage and 2nd Lieutenant Lyons each with an equal force of 19 men return to Lydenburg.

23rd OCTOBER 1878 Captain Moriarty and Lieutenant Horsbrugh with 99 men of "E" Company, march from Fort Oliphant for Pretoria Flats.

24th OCTOBER 1878 Lieutenant Harward takes a party of men including some volunteers on patrol and succeeds in destroying a quantity of mealie belonging to the enemy. Lieutenant Harward had been reinforced by 2nd Lieutenant Lyons and 34 non commissioned Officers and men. Lieutenant S.W. Cameron and 2nd Lieutenant Daubeney arrive at Pretoria.

25th OCTOBER 1878 Lieutenant Cameron's force proceeds to join Headquarter Staff at Fort Weeber.

27th OCTOBER 1878 Lieutenant Johnson in command of "A" Company, consisting of 46 non commissioned Officers and men, accompanied by Civil Surgeon Nardop moves from Fort Weeber to Fort Morlock. The mountain gun detachment are engaged with the enemy either in supporting movements or repelling attacks.

13th NOVEMBER 1878 The District Order is issued as follows:- The following distribution of the Companies in the right and left attack were directed to be carried out , right Column under the command of Brev. Major Creagh. At Lydenburg by 1 Company "H", at Krugers Post by 1 Company "G" and at the Bieg, 1 Company "A". The left advance under the command of Major Tucker at Fort Weeber 1 Company "C", at Middleburg 1 Company "F" and at Whitport 1 Company "E". The movements of "A" and "E" Companies aforementioned took place in consequence.

15th NOVEMBER 1878 "E" Company with Captain Moriarty, Lieutenant Horsbrugh and 82 non commissioned Officers and men are directed to march to Whitport a station on the road to Fort Weeber and Middleburg.

16th NOVEMBER 1878 "A" Company returns to Fort Weeber.

18th NOVEMBER 1878 "A" Company marches to Lydenburg.

26th NOVEMBER 1878 By instructions from Army Headquarters, South Africa dated 26th November 1878, The detachments at Krugers Post and the Bieg were directed to become concentrated up on Lydenburg and the detachment at Fort Weeber to march to Middleburg on being relieved by Raaff's Volunteers.

27th NOVEMBER 1878 The latter portion of the Order of Distribution was cancelled and the company of the 80th Regiment at Fort Weeber and Whitport are ordered to be concentrated at Middleburg. Major Tucker takes Command of the Regiment and Headquarters is situated at Middleburg.

3rd DECEMBER 1878 Lieutenant H.H. Harward and 2nd Lieutenant F.W. Lyons with 5 Sergeants, 5 Corporals and 70 Privates move to Lydenburg from the fort on the Burg to join Brev. Major Creagh's force.

4th DECEMBER 1878 Captain C.E.W. Roworth with 2 Sergeants, 2 Corporals, 1 Drummer and 45 Privates join Brev. Major Creagh's force from Kruger's Post.

9th DECEMBER 1878 Captain J.E.H. Prior proceeds to Newcastle from Pretoria for service with the Frontier Light Horse, under the command of Major Redvers Buller C.B. in the impending war with the Zulu Nation.

17th DECEMBER 1878 Major Tucker, Lieutenants J.C. Sherrard and A.W. Hast including Headquarter staff at Fort Weeber consisting of 3 Sergeants, 4 Corporals, 3 Drummers and 72 Privates march for Middleburg.

22nd DECEMBER 1878 Major Tucker's force arrive at Middleburg.

31st DECEMBER 1878 Major C. Tucker proceeds to Middleburg from Lydenburg in accordance with orders received from Colonel Rowlands VC, CB, Commandant, to assume command of the troops at that station. "C" and "E" Companies under the Command of Brev. Major Creagh march from Middleburg to Derby, New Scotland so to relieve the Detachment of the 1/13 Light Infantry who proceeds to Utrecht to take part in any operation against the Zulu King. The Officers who accompanied Brev. Major Creagh being Captain D.B. Moriarty, Lieutenants J.O. Sherrard, T.J. Chamberlain, A.W. Hast and 2nd Lieutenant B.W.R. Ussher. The strength of the two Companies being 7 Sergeants, 7 Corporals, 3 Drummers and 37 Privates.

1st JANUARY 1879 "B" Company under the command of Captain A. Saunders accompanied by Lieutenant W. Moore with a force consisting of 2 Sergeants, 2 Corporals and 69 Privates march for Pretoria. "H" Company whose strength is compiled of 5 Sergeants, 4 Corporals, 2 Drummers and 85 Privates under the command of 2nd Lieutenant A.H. Lindop leaves Lydenburg to increase the strength of Brev. Major Creagh's force on the Zulu border at Derby. Lieutenant J.O. Sherrard is appointed as the commissariat Officer to the troops under the command of Colonel Rowlands VC CB.

8th JANUARY 1879 Captain Saunders and "B" Company arrives at Pretoria.

Following the suspension of hostilities against Sekukuni, the majority of the regiment was stationed at Luneburg, part of No. 5 Column for the war against the Zulus.

Because of the fragmented politics in the southern part of Africa, in particular around the Cape region, the British representatives, Sir Bartle Frere and Sir Theophilus Shepstone thought that the best thing for South Africa was to establish a confederation and unite all the areas under one rule, British rule. Land was at a premium, cheap labour was required and confederation was necessary for the organisation of labour migration and the development of the new mineral discoveries. The Zulus, amongst others, could provide the labour once conquered. It was also felt that once the strongest tribe in the area had been subdued other smaller and weaker tribes would succumb to British rule. The Honourable Frederic Augustus Thesiger (later 2nd Baron Chelmsford) Lieutenant-General commanding British forces in South Africa 1878-79, devised the plan of conquest, the objects being a) To defeat the Zulu army, b) To destroy the Zulu King's principal residence, Ulundi, c) To capture the Zulu King, Cetshwayo.

The British military commanders knew that the Zulus were highly mobile- the warriors carried only what they immediately required including all their weaponry. They lived off the land or obtained food from kraals en-route. But the Zulu people could not afford a lengthy war, the populace would need to maintain the food chain or otherwise the Zulu Nation would starve. Lord Chelmsford estimated that the campaign would last six weeks or at the most two months. Because of the mobility of the Zulu forces it was decided not to invade Zululand in one single column. It was thought that the Zulus would not attempt to attack one column and might sweep round it and attack Natal.

The date of invasion was set for January 1879. The Zulu border stretched for approximately 200 miles and was impossible for the British to defend against attack. During the dry season the rivers that bordered Zululand were easily passable, but when the rains came they could only be crossed in flat iron-bottomed ponts at certain points - 'drifts'. It was at these crossing points that a watch could be maintained, thus restricting the risk of Zulu forces crossing the border undetected.

The British and Colonial forces were distributed into five columns. Columns 1, 2 and 4 would invade Zululand at three differing points on the Zulu border, thus reducing the risk of an outflanking movement. Column No. 2 was to be held in reserve and No. 5 Column was positioned on the Northern Borders to keep surveillance.

No. 1 Column Eastern (Right) would cross the border at Fort Pearson at the lower drift of the Tugela River. No. 3 Column Central would cross into Zululand at Rorke's Drift. No. 4 Column Northern (Left) would cross the disputed territories around the headwaters of the Blood River. The three columns would proceed to Ulundi, some 70 miles from each of the points of invasion, destroy it and hopefully capture the Zulu King, Cetshwayo. It was hoped that one of these columns would be attacked by the Zulu army and accordingly be so convincingly defeated that Cetshwayo would sue for peace. With every day that passed during the invasion each of the columns, as they proceeded, would come closer and would be able to march to each others aid in the event of attack. The British forces were a modern army with modern weapons and without doubt would defeat a foe armed only with spears, shields and antiquated rifles.

At the beginning of the war Lord Chelmsford had approximately 17,000 men. At the various depots there were adequate ammunition and food stores to keep the columns supplied and the army on the move. The military establishment had the use of 977 waggons and 123 two wheeled carts including 5955 oxen, 803 horses and 713 mules. The soldiers were equipped with the most modern weapons available. The lines of communication were as follows:- No. 1 Column Eastern (Right). The Column obtained supplies from Stanger and Durban, crossing the border at Fort Pearson at the lower drift of the Tugela River. The route for the Column would then be towards Eshowe. No. 3 Column Central. The lines of supplies being Helpmakaar, Greytown, Ladysmith, Pietermaritzburg and Durban. The Column would then cross into Zululand via Rorkes Drift. No. 4 Column Northern (Left). The assembly point for this Column was at Balte Spruit. The column drew supplies from Newcastle and Utrecht, whilst advancing to Conference Hill and then onto Bemba's Kop. No. 2 Column Reserve. This Column was kept in reserve at the Middle Drift of the Tugela River below Kranz Kop. Column No. 5 was located at Luneburg in the Transvaal, to protect the border and to keep an eye on the Transvaal Boers. The three invading columns had use of 4895 oxen, 185 horses and 311 mules to pull 645 waggons and 111 carts.

On the 11th January 1879 Lord Chelmsford had organised and distributed his forces, (1st invasion) as follows:
General Commanding Lieutenant General Lord Chelmsford KCB.
No. 1 Column Eastern (Right) Colonel Commanding Colonel Charles Pearson, 3rd. Foot Totalling 4750 men
No. 3 Column Central Commanding Brev.Colonel Richard Glyn, CB, 24th. Foot Totalling 4709 men
No. 4 Column Northern (Left) Commanding Brev.Colonel Evelyn Wood, VC CB. 90th. Foot Totalling 2278 men No. 2 Column Reserve Commanding Lt. Colonel Anthony Durnford, RE. Staff. Totalling 3871 men
No. 5 Column Colonel Commanding Colonel Hugh Rowlands, VC CB. Staff. Totalling 1565 men
The 80th Regiment of Foot (Staffordshire Volunteers) were part of No 5 Column. Staff in charge of this Column:

Colonel Commanding Colonel Hugh Rowlands, VC CB.
Staff Officers   Principal Staff Officer Captain Harvey, 71st Foot

	District Adjutant Lieutenant Potts, 80th Foot
	Senior Commissariat Officer Asst. Commissary-General Phillips Commissary of Ordnance
	Commissary Wyon Sub District Paymaster Asst.
	Paymaster Burgers
	Senior Medical Officer Surgeon Major Johnson
Troops	80th Regiment of Foot
	Schutte's Corps
	Eckersley's Contingent
	Raaff's Corps
	Ferreira's Horse Border Horse
	Transvaal Rangers Cape Mounted Rifles
Artillery	1 Krupp gun. 2 No. 6-prs Armstrong guns.

Total: 15 Staff and Departments; 834 Infantry; 553 Cavalry; 338 Native Contingent; 25 Conductors, drivers and Foreloopers; 1 Krupp gun; 2 6 prs Armstrong guns; 17 Waggons; 2 Carts; 150 Oxen; 10 Horses and 12 Mules.

On the 12th January 1879 Sihayo's Kraal was the first of the Zulu kraals to be attacked and destroyed. The attack was carried out by troops of No. 3 (Central) Column. Each of the invading columns made arrangements each afternoon to establish a safe camp each night. Suitable camp sites would be surveyed and determined in advance.

For No. 3 Column, one such camp site was on the slopes of Isandhlwana. The shape of this natural structure bore an outline not unlike a sphinx - part of the 24th Regiment's uniform regalia. Isandhlwana will remain synonymous forever with the Zulu War, for on Wednesday January 22nd 1879 the first disastrous engagement with the Zulus took place, when the Zulu army attacked and took the British encampment on its slopes. King Cetshwayo had sent one of his Impi's of some 20,000 warriors to oppose and repel this central column. It was planned that the Impi would move towards the invading army and rest in the shadows of the Nquthu mountain range, attacking after January 22nd. On January 21st Lord Chelmsford, commanding the British forces in South Africa, ordered out reconnaissance parties with the hope of finding the main Zulu army. One of the patrols of 80 men from the Natal Mounted Police and some 40 volunteers under the command of Major J. Dartnell made contact with a large number of Zulus during the late afternoon, 10 miles from the main camp. Because of the lateness of the day and the failing light he decided to stay out in the 'open' and to send a message back to Lord Chelmsford of his findings. Lord Chelmsford decided to split his forces, leaving half of his force at Isandhlwana under the command of Brevet Lieutenant Colonel H.B.Pulliene. He set off with the remainder of the men and Colonel R.Glyn, Officer Commanding No. 3 Column, to reinforce Major Dartnell, and attack what was thought to be the main Zulu army. At approximately 4.00 am on the morning of the 22nd, Lord Chelmsford and his command left Isandhlwana. Brevet Lt.Colonel Pulliene was in command until Colonel A.W.Durnford RE arrived. Durnford's and Pulliene's orders were quite clear 'defend the camp if attacked'.

At about 8.00 am, prior to the arrival of Colonel Durnford, Zulus were reported to be advancing from the North East, buglers sounded the 'fall in', and for over an hour watch was kept. Some two hours later Colonel Durnford arrived. It is assumed at this point that Col. Durnford took over command and shortly afterwards an order was given for a company of 1/24th Regiment with their officer Lieutenant C.W. Cavaye to advance to the higher ground some fifteen hundred yards north of the camp. Shortly after this order was issued, he received further information about the Zulus and decided to leave the camp himself with his original command. It is thought by some historians that this was to prevent any substantial Zulu force getting in between the camp and Lord Chelmsford's 'rear'. At approximately 12 noon mounted Basutos under the command of Lieutenant Raw on reconnoitring patrol spotted some cattle, and upon further investigation discovered the main Zulu army in a large valley that had not yet been surveyed. The Zulus had no intentions of attacking that day, but once discovered there could be no holding back - the 'die' had been cast.

Back at the camp more gun fire was heard and again the buglers summoned the troops to 'fall in'. Shortly afterwards Captain W.E.Mostyn with his company and Lieutenant Cavaye's company combined and started to engage the enemy, eventually having to withdraw slowly back towards the camp. At approximately 12.30pm, Zulus were reported to be advancing on the right of the camp. By 1.00pm all the defenders of the camp were fully occupied in fighting the Zulus. For the defenders of the camp, totalling 37 officers and 1707 non commissioned officers and men, things now went disastrously wrong. The Zulus outnumbered and out-manoeuvred the British and Colonial forces. By 2.00pm all constructive defence of the camp had ceased, the survivors endeavouring to make good their escape, and at approximately 2.30 pm the camp had been taken by the Zulus.

Estimated Zulu casualties were in excess of 1000 men killed. Only 79 European survivors escaped from the carnage of Isandhlwana, two of who belonged to the 80th Regiment, Privates 919 Samuel Wassall and 228 Thomas Westwood, both members of the 1st Squadron Mounted Infantry. The 80th Regiment of Foot lost 7 men from the Regiment in this action. Only those on horseback had any chance of escape. Samuel Wassall, riding a small Basuto pony, raced across the African veldt, and crossed the Buffalo River. At the point of safety, he heard someone shouting from the water, and was faced with the dilemma of ignoring them or attempting a rescue, with Zulus everywhere stabbing and clubbing to death any escaping 'Red Coats'. Without hesitation, Samuel Wassall stopped, rode back into the fast flowing waters, jumped off his horse swiftly tying it to a tree and waded into the river to rescue his drowning comrade. Samuel saved the life of Private Thomas Westwood, a member of his own Regiment and in doing so was later awarded the first Victoria Cross of the of the Zulu campaign.

On the battlefield at Isandhlwana the British and Colonial Forces lost a total of 52 officers and 806 non-commissioned officers and men including 471 native and non combatant troops. In the annals of British military history this was to be the most catastrophic annihilation of a modern army by a force whose warriors carried no more than spears and shields. It also meant that Chelmsford's plans had been devastated, his main Central Column now partly destroyed, his transport crippled with numerous waggons wrecked and the animals that once pulled them taken by the enemy. The Commander-in-Chief had no option but to withdraw his remnant No. 3 Column back to Rorke's Drift and instruct Pearson and No. 1 Column who was to become besieged at Eshowe to 'Hold out', and Colonel Wood with No. 4 Column to act on his own initiative. This defeat, however, immediately activated the British Parliament into action to save British prestige and honour. Reinforcements were hurriedly despatched to the Cape and ordered up to Natal and into Zululand. Lord Chelmsford began to organise his 2nd invasion of Zululand. This 2nd invasion was planned for May. He distributed his troops as follows:-

General Commanding Lieutenant General Lord Chelmsford

1st DIVISION
Major General Commanding Major General Henry Hope Crealock C.B.
1st Brigade Colonel Charles Pearson 3rd Foot, 2/3rd Regiment of Foot 8 Companies, 88th Regiment of Foot 6 Companies, 99th Regiment of Foot 8 Companies
2nd Brigade Lt. Colonel Charles Mansfield Clark 57th Foot, 57th Regiment of Foot 8 Companies, 3rd/60th Rifles 7 Companies, 91st Regiment of Foot 8 Companies, Divisional Troops Naval Brigade (inc.3 guns) 795 men, 4th Battalion N.N.C. 789 men, 5th Battalion N.N.C. 1107 men. John Dunn's Scouts 112 men, Mounted Troops 564 men, M/6 Royal Artillery (6-7 prs) 160 men, 8/7 Royal Artillery (2-7 prs) 50 men, 11/7 Royal Artillery (2-7 prs) 25 men, O/6 Royal Artillery Amn. Col. 75 men, 30th Company Royal Engineers 85 men.

11nd DIVISION
Major General Commanding Major General Edward Newdigate
1st Brigade Colonel Richard Glyn C.B. 24th Foot, 2/21st Regiment of Foot 6 Companies, 58th Regiment of Foot 6 Companies, 2nd Brigade Colonel William Pole Collingwood 1/24th Regiment of Foot 7 Companies, 94th Regiment of Foot 6 Companies, Divisional Troops N/5 Royal Artillery (6-7 prs) 150 men, N/6 Royal Artillery (6-9 prs) 150 men, O/6 Royal Artillery Amn. Col. 68 men, 2nd Company Royal Engineers 55 men, Mounted Troops 210 men, 2nd Battalion N.N.C. 900 men, Army Service Corps 150 men, Army Medical Department 46 men,
The Cavalry Brigade (attached to the 11nd Division) Major General Commanding Major General Frederick Marshall 1st Dragoon Guards 634 men 545 horses, 17th Lancers 613 men, 583 horses, Natives attached 108 men, 110 horses.

FLYING COLUMN
Brigadier General Commanding Colonel Evelyn Wood V.C. C.B., 1/13th Regiment of Foot 617men 80th Regiment of Foot 373 men, 90th Regiment of Foot 654 men, 11/7 Royal Artillery (4-7prs) 81 men, 10/7 Royal Artillery Gattlings 64 men, 5th Company Royal Engineers 82 men, Mounted Infantry 95 men, Frontier Light Horse 209 men, Transvaal Rangers 77 men, Baker's Light Horse 202 men, Natal Native Horse 117 men, Natal Native Pioneers 104 men, Natal Light Horse 84 men, Wood's Irregulars 485 men.

The revised lines of communication and the various garrisons and posts were: Durban, Stanger, Lower Tugela Forts, Pietermaritzburg, Greytown, Krantz Kop near Middledrift, Dundee, Helpmaaker Rorke's Drift, Ladysmith, Utrecht, Newcastle, Balte Spruit, Luneburg and Conference Hill.

Whilst Chelmsford and his officers were busy implementing their revised strategy plans and getting the troops to their respective stations, a second disaster was to hit them in somewhat unusual circumstances, a mini Isandhwana scenario, this time on the banks of the Intombi River. On Wednesday 12th March 1879, at a river crossing known as Myer's Drift on the Intombi River, a convoy under the protection of the 80th Regiment of Foot was attacked and the encampments taken with the Regiment suffering many casualties.

The lines of communication and transport to Luneburg where the 80th was based were a roadway that stretched some 160 miles from Lydenburg, passing the main settlements of Middlesburg and Derby. The only means of moving stores and equipment was by cattle drawn waggons. During late February a convoy of eighteen waggons was commissioned to deliver stores and provisions to Luneburg. Major Tucker the Officer Commanding at Luneburg ordered out, on March 1st, "D" Company under the command of Captain W.T. Anderson, with instructions to meet up with the waggons and escort them into Luneburg. However, because of other pressing needs Major Tucker recalled Captain Anderson on March 5th. Two days later Captain Moriarty with a detachment of Company strength was ordered out again to locate the waggon convoy and escort it safely into Luneburg. Captain Moriarty was accompanied by Lieutenant H.J. Johnson and 2nd Lieutenant A.H. Lindop.

The first of the waggons was found at a place called Myer's Drift, a crossing on the Intombi River. After the withdrawal of Captain Anderson's original escort, some zulus had attacked the waggons and driven off some of the draught cattle. Not having sufficient oxen, the waggoners decided to haul the waggons down to the river in relays. This was obviously very unsatisfactory, knowing full well that Prince Mbilini, whose stronghold was nearby, held allegiance to King Cetshwayo. Due to heavy rains the river was swift flowing and had risen to such an extent that it was approximately 45 metres across. Of the several waggons that were now on the north bank of the river, all were stranded following an attempt to get one waggon across the river, with the result that it had become marooned mid-stream. Over the next couple of days, men and animals toiled in appalling weather conditions and eventually got all the remaining waggons to the drift by March 9th. Lieutenant Lindop and some of the men in between time had managed to get two of the waggons across the river, but because of the continuous heavy rain no more were able to go across and there was no alternative but to sit it out until the waters of the river subsided.

On 11th March the convoy was now much overdue and Major Tucker accompanied by Lieutenant H.H. Harward, set out to discover its whereabouts. They soon found them, with sixteen waggons on the North bank with the other two on the South bank. Major Tucker expressed deep concern at the method of laagering the twin encampments. On the North bank waggons had been lined up to form an inverted 'V' from the river, and the waggons were too far apart, the whole scenario being very unorthordox. Captain Moriarty acknowledged the situation, but pointed out the terrain, ground conditions and weather, and the state of both the men and animals. Nothing was done to alter things, to the possible detriment of the encampment. Major Tucker left the camp taking with him the two Lieutenants, Johnson and Lindop. Lieutenant Harward remained to give assistance to the Captain. Later the same day Harward with some men went in search of stray cattle, returning just before dark. Upon his return Lieutenant Harward went to the Captain's tent and fell asleep, only to be awakened and ordered across the river, because the most senior ranking soldier on that side was only a sergeant.

Captain David Barry Moriarty,
killed in action 12th March 1879, Intombi River.

Sentries were posted to both encampments, cattle were herded inside the 'V' shaped laager, the soldiers going to their tents and the conductors and drivers going either into or underneath their waggons. All precautions appeared to have been taken, and men and animals were settled for the night. In the early hours of the next day, the 12th March, at approximately 4.00am, a single shot was heard by the sentries on the South bank. Lieutenant Harward was told and he made his men 'stand to'. A message was sent across the river to inform the Captain. It appears that the only instruction given by Captain Moriarty was for the sentries guarding his side to be on greater alert.

A mist settled over the encampments and river. Taking advantage of this, at approximately 4.40 am Prince Mbilini and his forces crept to within 90 metres of the main laager, totally undetected, and attacked. Men in various stages of undress and sleep fell out of their beds, tents and waggons to repel the enemy, but to no avail. Within minutes the Zulu warriors were amongst the tents and animals, men were being stabbed with assegais or bludgeoned to death with knobkerries. The men on the South bank opened fire, which only attracted the enemy and part of its forces started to cross the fast flowing river to attack them. Lieutenant Harward seeing his small element of command starting to disintegrate, ordered his second in command Sergeant Anthony Booth to rally as many men as he could and proceed with a fighting retreat to a remote disused farm house some three miles from the river. Harward then mounted his horse and left the field to summons help from Major Tucker at Luneburg. Sergeant Booth with great presence of mind, coolness and discipline, along with several other men, held firm, and with steady volleys held the enemy at bay. This enabled his men to retire in an orderly manner and for some to escape almost certain death.

Major Tucker was alerted at approximately 6.30 am by Lieutenant Harward, and immediately ordered as many mounted men who could be mustered to proceed with utmost speed to the Intombi River. A further 150 men followed immediately on foot. It was not long before Tucker and his mounted force were in sight of the strickened encampments, and the Zulus, spotting the advancing 'Red Coats', withdrew back to their stronghold some five kilometres to the North-East. Mbilini had taken the camps, driven off the cattle and taken most of the supplies and ammunition. Anthony Booth with his little command of bedraggled survivors were now safe. The sight that the rescuers beheld was a scene of utter carnage and horror, their fellow comrades lay dead in various postures, all slain and horrendously mutilated. Captain Moriarty had commanded 105 soldiers; he now lay dead, along with 60 other non-commissioned officers and men, 2 white waggon conductors and 15 black drivers and the Civil Surgeon Cobbin. The remainder of the day was spent collecting and burying the dead. Sergeant Anthony Clarke Booth for his coolness in battle was recommended for the Distinguished Conduct Medal. However on later reflection, for his calm bravery whilst under fire, he was awarded a most deserved Victoria Cross.

The official returns of the War Office aptly describe the events of what turned out to be one of the most notorious days in the history of the 80th Regiment of Foot. The following dispatches were received at the War Office on the 21st April 1879, from the Lieutenant-General Commanding the forces in South Africa.

Sir, It is my sad duty to report to you that on the morning of the 12th March a convoy of waggons halted on it's road from Derby to Luneburg, on the left bank of the Intombi River, was attacked by the Zulus, and with the exception of some ten men who escaped by swimming the river, the whole of the escort who were within the waggon laager on that bank are reported to have been killed. The Officer in command of the detachment on the right bank, Lieutenant Harward, 80th Regiment, appears to have done his utmost to assist his comrades in their unequal struggle, as soon as he was aware of what was occurring. I have the honour to forward the report from this officer, and that of Major Tucker, 80th Regiment, commanding at Luneburg. I have desired that Colonel Wood to make further enquiries into the matter. His report, when received, shall be forwarded. As I am leaving for the frontier at the Lower Tugela to- morrow, I have desired my Deputy Adjutant-General, pending the arrival of a general officer, to forward you any reports that may arrive during my absence. The reports enclosed are printed, as I considered it advisable to communicate the reports received to the public through the press. I have, &c.

CHELMSFORD Lieutenant-General

Luneberg, 12th March 1879
To the Officer Commanding the Troops at Luneburg:
"Sir, I have the honour to report as follows, from the camp at Intombi River, where an escort of the 80th Regiment, under Captain Moriaty, were laagered on the 12th March 1879:- Being awake during the night I heard a shot fired in the distance, I got up and ordered the sentry to rouse the detachment on the side of Intombi Drift nearest Luneberg, and to apprise Captain Moriarty of the fact, and ask for his orders; these were that the escort should remain under arms. I afterwards found that this shot was fired about 4 a.m. I retired to my tent close by, where I waited, dressed, and about an hour afterwards I heard, "Guard turn out" I instantly turned out and saw, as the fog lifted, a dense mass of Zulus about 200 yards from the waggon laager, extending all across the valley with a front of some 2 or 3 miles apparently. I immediately put my men (35 of all ranks) under a waggon near our tents, and directed their fire on the flanks of the enemy, who were endeavouring to surround our waggon laager on the other side of the river. I next observed that the enemy had gained full possession of the camp, and were driving off the cattle. Our men were retiring on the river, which was now full of human beings. On seeing this, I directed my fire entirely with a view to covering the retreat of our men. This was well sustained, and enabled many to get over the river alive. The enemy were now assegaing our men in the water, and also ascending the banks of the river close to us; for fear, therefore, of my men being stabbed under the waggon, and to enable them to retire before their ammunition should be exhausted, I ordered them to retire steadily, and only just in time to avoid a rush of Zulus to our late position. The Zulus came on in dense masses and fell upon our men, who being already broken, gave way, and a hand to hand fight ensued. I endeavoured to rally my men, but they were too much scattered, and finding re-formation impossible, I mounted my horse and galloped into Luneburg at utmost speed, and reported all that had taken place. I estimate the strength of the enemy at not less than 4000 men. I beg to draw attention to the good service rendered by Sergt. A. Booth and the men of the party on the Luneburg side of the river, whose steady fire was instrumental in saving many lives.

(Signed) H. H. HARWARD Lieut., 80th Regt.

Luneberg, 12th March 1879

From Major C. Tucker, 80th Regiment, Commanding troops to Assistant Military Secretary, Headquarters, Pietermaritzburg:

"I have to report, for the information of His Excellency the Lieutenant-General commanding, that on the 7th instant a party consisting of 104, all ranks, under command of Capt. D.B. Moriarty 80th Regiment, left Luneburg with a view of escorting and bringing into Luneburg 18 waggons, variously loaded on their way from Derby. Some of these waggons were reported as broken down on the Little Intombi River. Captain Moriarty's orders were to bring these waggons or their loads into Luneburg, but if this was impossible, owing to the fearful state of the road, he was to laager his waggons at the Intombi River and wait until he should be able to cross. During the 8th, 9th and 10th, the river was so very high from the constant rains, that nothing could be done. On the 11th the river lowered some 4 feet, but the stream was so rapid nothing could be got across. A light raft consisting of planks and empty barrels had been made, but would carry very little weight. On the morning of the 12th, about 6.30 Lieut. Harward arrived at Luneburg from the Intombi River reporting that the camp and waggons were in possession of the enemy. I enclose a copy of a report from this officer:- As I have no mounted men under my command, I at once ordered all the horses belonging to the officers of the regiment to be saddled, and proceeded to the camp at the Intombi River, leaving orders for 150 men of the 80th Regiment to follow. On approaching Myers' Mission Station we observed, extending for about two miles under the brow of Umbeline's Hill, a long thick line of Zulus making eastward. I computed the body of the enemy in view at not less than 4000; there were undoubtedly many more; as we could see no cattle being driven, these Zulus were evidently making a hurried retreat. Arriving at the Intombi River, I found the laager completely wrecked, the cattle being taken and the contents of the waggons strewn about the place, and from the bank of the river we could see the dead bodies of our men lying about on the opposite side. On the arrival of the 80th from Luneburg, the bodies were collected and interred on this side of the river. I regret to report that Captain D. B. Moriarty was killed, together with Civil Surgeon Cobbin. Out of a total of 104 Officers and men of the 80th Regt. 40 are known to be killed, 20 are missing, and 44 have escaped to Luneberg - 1 man slightly wounded. In addition to the above Mr. Whittington waggon conductor, a volunteer named Campbell, late of Ferreira's Horse and a native driver, have been killed. With regard to the 20 men reported missing of the 80th Regiment I fear most of them have been drowned or assegaid in the river, which was running swiftly, and was exceedingly high at the time. A list of the waggon employees will be sent as soon as possible.

It is impossible to ascertain the loss of the enemy, twenty-five bodies were found at the scene of the action, principally on the bank of the river, and doubtless many more were drowned. Two Zulus have been taken prisoner, both wounded severely. From one I gathered the information that the "impi" which attacked the laager was headed by Umbeline, who was instigated to bring this force by Manyanyobe. This prisoner distinctly stated twice that there were 9000 Zulus present, and that there were collected from all parts of the surrounding country; he further stated that Umnyamana was asked to assist, but refused to send his men. From all information I can gather on the subject, the camp was evidently surprised, the enemy taking advantage of the mist to approach the camp unseen. I consider the men fought well and bravely, but were completely outnumbered. The small party under Lieut. Harward, on this side of the river, rendered to a hopeless cause valuable assistance, in covering the retreat across the river of such men as were able to reach it; and I am of the opinion that but for those on this side of the Intombi River, not one man would have escaped, and that had the escort been double it's number, the result must have been the same. The river having subsided about midday, I was enabled to bring across the rockets, gun ammunition and powder untouched by the enemy.

C TUCKER, Major Commanding 80th Regiment and Troops

Return of killed and missing of 80th Regiment at Intombi river, 12th March 1879

In the following list the killed and missing are distinguished by "k" and "m"

Captain D.B. Moriarty, Company E, k; 459 Colour-Sergeant Henry Frederick, Company A, m; 544 Lance-Sergeant Ernest Johnson, Company E, k; 1726 —- George Sansam, Company C, k; 733 Corporal John McCoy, Company F, k; 1647 Drummer John Leather, Company A, m; Privates of the following Companies: 585 John Anthony, Company A, k; 203 Arthur Banks, Company A, k; 943 John Banner, Company A, m; 745 George Broughton, Company A, k; 488 Henry Brownson, Company A, k; 1797 James Christie, Company A, k; 1042 Alfred Day, Company A, k; 753 John Dodd, Company A, m; 260 Henry Dutton, Company A, k; 1028 William Farrell, Company A, m; 176 William Flyfield, Company A, m; William Fox, Company A, k; 1925 John Fourneaux, Company A, m; 500 Edward Gittings, Company A, k; 1696 Joseph Green, Company A, k; 526 George Hadley, Company A, m; 227 George Haines, Company A, k; 999 Eli Hawkes, Company A, m; 783 Thomas Healey, Company A, m; 709 Thomas Hodges, Company A, k; 902 John Ingham, Company A, k; 1865 John Luffarty, Company A, k; 1931 Henry Lodge, Company A, m; 1976 George Mitchel, Company A, k; 2048 Robert Moore, Company A, k; 1032 William Moran, Company A, k; 1926 Henry Night, Company A, k; 1770 Joseph Silcock, Company A, m; 510 Henry Smith, Company A, m; 587 Joseph Tibbett, Company A, k; 716 Joseph Weaver, Company A, k; 48 James Brown, Company C, k; 222 William Findley, Company C, k; 2008 Julien Hart, Company C, m; 1919 Henry Jacobs, Company C, k; 999 Ralph Leese, Company C, k; 2063 Arthur Middow, Company C, k; 2085 Charles Pritchard, Company C, m; 2070 Henry Ruffle, Company C, k; 546 Jonah Adey, Company E, k; 1290 John Chadwick, Company E, k; 1163 Arthur Pummell, Company E, m; 1291 Richard Tomlinson, Company E, m; 1705 George Tucker, Company E, m; 104 Thomas Tucker, Company E, k; —- John Robinson, Company E, k; 370 James Vernon, Company E, k; 1605 Herbert Woodward, Company E, m; 1021 Henry Hill, Company B, k; 1499 John Hughes, Company B, k; 1378 Bernard McSherry, Company B, k; 220 William Phipps, Company B, k; 615 Michael Sheridan, Company B, m; 520 Henry Meadous, Company F, k;

C TUCKER, Major 80th Regiment, Commanding Troops

In the aftermath of this sad episode there was an enquiry into the causes of the disaster. For the only surviving officer, Lieutenant Henry Hollingworth Harward it resulted in a court martial. On the 14th February 1880 Lieutenant Harward was placed under arrest, the charges being:-

1. Having misbehaved before the enemy, in shamefully abandoning a party of the Regiment under his command when attacked by the enemy, and in riding off at speed from his men.

2. Conduct to the prejudice of good order and military discipline in having at the place and time mentioned in the first charge, neglected to take proper precautions for the safety of a party of a Regiment under his command when attached.

The hearing was held on the 20th February 1880 at Fort Napier, Pietermaritzburg. The trial was in session from the 20th-27th February 1880. The court acquitted Lieutenant Harward on all charges. When the findings reached Sir Garnet Wolseley, he was aware that he could not alter the course of justice, but because he disagreed with the court's findings, he refused to confirm them. He remarked, *"That a Regimental Officer who is the only Officer present with a party of men actually and seriously engaged with the enemy, can, under any pretext whatever, be justified in deserting them, and by so doing, abandoning them to their fate. The more helpless a position in which an officer finds his men, the more it his bounden duty to stay and share their fortune, whether for good or ill"*. The Duke of Cambridge the Commander in

Inscription on the Memorial, Intombi River.

Chief of the Army supported Sir Garnet Wolseley's comments and instructed them to be read out in the General Order to the head of every Regiment. Lieutenant H.H. Harward was released from arrest and on the 14th March 1880 returned to duty to continue an army career now in ruins. He resigned his commission on the 11th May 1880. Allegedly his name was never to be mentioned in the mess.

Colonel Wood in command of No. 4 Column eventually established a fortified camp at Kambula providing protection from any possible Zulu advance on Utrecht and Luneberg. The position of the camp was approximately 6 miles from Zungwin Mountain, just beyond which lay the Hlobane and Itentika mountains. Some members of the 80th Regiment joined a mounted gun detachment, part of the 11th Battery 7th Brigade Royal artillery and attached to Colonel Wood's Column. Colonel Wood was eventually requested by Lord Chelmsford to create a diversion designed to keep the Zulus occupied in the North East of the country and make Cetshwayo send warriors to the area. This would hopefully help Chelmsford with his advance to relieve the besieged troops at Eshowe.

The first diversionary attack was an assault on the Hlobane mountain on the 28th March, the reputed stronghold of Mbilini and his followers. The plan was to scale the mountain plateau from two differing points and, once upon the mountain, combine forces and flush out the enemy. During the assault, both of the attacking forces at differing times spotted a Zulu army moving in five columns on the far side of the mountain. The exact whereabouts of this Impi, in the region of 20,000 warriors, was unknown, but the Impi once alerted by gun fire moved in to engage Wood's forces. Outnumbered and in danger of being cut off from the main camp at Kambula, a somewhat hasty retreat was called, and the third of Chelmsford reverses was thus enacted. With the mountain cleared of British and Colonial forces, the Zulus moved off to rest by the Umvolosi River.

Colonel Wood now knew the Zulus exact location and strength. With fresh intelligence, he realised that the Zulus were intending to attack him at Kambula - and at midday that very day, Saturday, March 29th. At 11.00 am Zulus were reported to be moving in five columns., but although they were being monitored, the actual direction of their march was unclear. At 12.45 pm, after the soldiers had eaten, tents were dropped and the final preparations for the defence were completed. King Cetshwayo had instructed his military leaders not to take on the enemy in fortified positions, but to tempt the defenders out in the open. Unconvinced of the Zulu's intentions and commitment and fearing they might bypass his fortified positions, Wood ordered out his mounted troops to provoke them into attacking. The rouse worked, and the Zulus, although well disciplined, with the success of Isandhlwana and Hlobane fresh in their minds, advanced to attack the fortified positions against the King's instructions. By 2.15 pm the attacks on Kambula were fully committed on both flanks. It all appeared uncoordinated and the defenders easily fought off the attackers. By about 5.00 pm the Zulus attacks seemed to lose momentum and enthusiasm, and Colonel Wood ordered out his mounted troops. The Zulus started to retreat, and before long, it turned into a rout. The Zulus were not accustomed to taking prisoners and asked for no quarter - and none was given.

The total number of British and Colonial troops engaged were 2086 men, of which 88 men were listed as sick. British casualties amounted to 3 officers and 26 rank and file killed in action and a further 5 officers and 49 men wounded. Of those wounded, one man belonged to the 80th Regiment, with wounds to the head. The Zulu casualties were in excess of 1000 killed and wounded. This was a fiercely fought battle and a most critical one, for it is believed that the Zulus finally realised they would not be able to drive the 'Red Coat' soldiers from their lands.

The 80th Regiment, in the second invasion, had to face many miles of marching for they were now to be part of the IInd Division and attached to the 'Flying Column'. Following reorganisation of the British and Colonial forces on the 17th June 1879, Lord Chelmsford and the IInd Division and Flying Column prepared to march on Ulundi. A few days later on the 19th June the 1st Division crossed over the Tugela River.

From the Regimental Digest:

27th MARCH 1879 "D" and "H" Companies march from Lydenburg for Utrecht. The Officers were Captain W.T. Anderson, Lieutenants L.C. Potts and H.H. Harward with 2nd Lieutenants A.H. Lindop and E.K. Daubeney. Strength, 6 Sergeants, 8 Corporals, 2 Drummers and 148 Privates.

30th MARCH 1879 "D" and "H" Companies arrive at Utrecht from Luneburg.

8th APRIL 1879 "H" Company under the command of Lieutenant L.C. Potts accompanied by 2nd Lieutenant A.H. Lindop with 4 Sergeants, 6 Corporals, 1 Drummer and 78 Privates march from Utrecht for Balte Spruit arriving on the same day.

9th APRIL 1879 Major C. Tucker Commanding 80th Regiment, "A" "C" and "E" Companies with Captain J.E.H. Prior, Lieutenants H.J. Johnson, J.O. Sherrard, T.J. Chamberlain, A.W. Hast and 2nd Lieutenant B.W.R. Ussher including 10 Sergeants, 9 Corporals, 3 Drummers and 189 Privates march from Luneburg for Utrecht.

11th APRIL 1879 Major C. Tucker with "A" "C" and "E" Companies arrive at Utrecht.

18th APRIL 1879 Major Tucker accompanied by Captain J.E.H. Prior with Lieutenants' H.J. Johnson, J.O. Sherrard, T.J.Chamberlain, A.W. Hast and 2nd Lieutenant B.W.R. Ussher with "A" "C" and "E" Companies march for Balte Spruit. "A" "C" and "E" Companies consisting of 10 Sergeants, 8 Corporals, 3 Drummers and 183 Privates. Major Tucker and his command arrive at Balte Spruit. "D" Company remain at Utrecht.

22nd APRIL 1879 Major C. Tucker in command of "C" and "H" Companies including Lieutenants' J.O. Sherrard, L.C. Potts, T.J. Chamberlain and 2nd Lieutenant B.W.R. Ussher, with a force of 5 Sergeants, 9 Corporals 2 Drummers and 131 Privates proceed from Bault Spruit to Doornburg to collect fuel for Brigadier General Wood's column.

26th APRIL 1879 Major C.Tucker in command of three Companies are ordered to cut wood for fuel at Doornburg. At the northerly point they construct an earthen fort.

27th APRIL 1879 Major C. Tucker with "C" and "H" Companies arrive at Doornburg.

1st MAY 1879 Captain W.T. Anderson and 2nd Lieutenant E.K. Daubeney with "D" Company, strength 2 Sergeants, 4 Corporals, 1 Drummers and 60 Privates leave Utrecht and march for Balte Spruit arriving on the same day. H.M.S. 'Orontes' with 2 Officers and 151 non commissioned officers and men of the 80th Regiment on board leave Portsmouth on it's voyage to South Africa.

3rd MAY 1879 Lieutenant H.J. Johnson with "A" Company reinforce Major Tucker's force at Doornburg.

10th MAY 1879 "D" Company arrive at Doornburg.

15th MAY 1879 2 Sergeants, Drum Major O. O'Day, 4 Drummers and 3 Privates left Pretoria to join their respective Companies in the field in Zululand. 1 Sergeant, 5 Corporals, 1 Drummer and 59 Privates all time expired or invalids march to Durban for passage to England. Lieutenant W. Moore proceeded in command of these details with instructions to rejoin his regiment after reaching Pietermaritzburg and handing over his charge.

17th MAY 1879 The Five Companies "A", "C", "D", "E" and H Companies are at Doornburg with "E" Company arriving this day.

26th MAY 1879 The following order was published by Colonel Hugh Rowlands VC, CB on his relinquishing the Command of the Transvaal Column dated Pretoria 26th March 1879. "District Orders. By Col. Rowlands VC, CB on leaving the command of the Transvaal to take up a Command with the army operations in Zululand, desires to thank all Officers commanding Companies and Heads of Departments for their support and assistance which they have given him. He desires particularly to record the zeal and judgement with which the Officers Commanding the principal stations, Major C.J.R. Tyler, Brevet Major C.A.F. Creagh, Captain W. Howard 80th Regiment and Brevet Major F.W. Carrington 24th Regiment of Foot, have invariably carried on their duties during the period of continued disturbance on the Northern frontier of the Transvaal. By Order Signed C.L. Harvey. Captain Staff Officer"

27th MAY 1879 Major C. Tucker with five Companies of the 80th Regiment leave Doornburg and march to join General Wood's Column via Conference Hill, to take part in the second invasion of Zululand. This force included a battery of gatling guns. The five Companies consisted of 18 Sergeants, 20 Corporals, 5 Drummers and 328 Privates. The Officers accompanying these Companies were Captains W.T. Anderton, J.E.H. Prior, Lieutenants H.J. Johnson, J.O. Sherrard, L.C. Potts, T.J. Chamberlain, A.W. Hast, 2nd Lieutenants A.H. Lindop, E.K. Daubeney and B.W.R. Ussher. Lieutenant Tovry of the Queens Tower Hamletts Militia who was attached to the 80th Regiment also accompanied Major Tucker. Colonel W.O. Lanyon CB, CMG Administrator of the Transvaal took up the appointment of Commandant Transvaal.

28th MAY 1879 Major C. Tucker with five Companies of the 80th Regiment join General Wood's Column at his encampment located between Mundla and Incanda Hills.

29th MAY 1879 The second invasion of Zululand commences.

1st JUNE 1879 Major C. Tucker's force march from Mundla and camp near the Itelzi.

2nd/3rd JUNE 1879 The five Companies with Major Tucker arrive at the Ityotyosi River near it's junction with the Tombokala and encamp at Nondwine.

4th JUNE 1879 Brevet Major J.L. Bradshaw and Lieutenant C.C. Cole including 3 Sergeants, 3 Corporals, 2 Drummers and 143 Privates are landed at Durban.

5th/6th JUNE 1879 Major C. Tucker and his command encamp at Machonchlabi.

7th JUNE 1879 Major Tucker and the five Companies marched to Fort Newdigate on the Nondweni River.

8th JUNE 1879 Major Tucker and his men march to Koppie Allein and camped.

8th/12th JUNE 1879 Encamped at Koppie Allein.

13th JUNE 1879 Major Tucker and his command reaches Isipezi Hill and encamps. Brevet Major J.L. Bradshaw force leave Durban and march to join Headquarters.

14th JUNE 1879 Major Tucker leaves the Isipezi River for Fort Newdigate.

15th JUNE 1879 Major Tucker and his force reach Fort Newdigate.

16th JUNE 1879 The five Companies with Major Tucker remain at Fort Newdigate.

17th JUNE 1879 Major Tucker with his men leave Fort Newdigate for Fort Marshall and after marching some distant encamp on the Upoki River. The London Gazette publishes the award of the Victoria Cross to Private Samuel Wassall.

18th JUNE 1879 The Five Companies with Major Tucker arrive at Fort Marshall.

19th JUNE 1879 The Companies leave Fort Marshall and march to Ibabanango Spruit.

20th JUNE 1879 The Companies continue their march and reach Itala Ridge.

21st JUNE 1879 After encamping at Itala Ridge Major Tucker and his men march to the Umhlatoosi River.

22nd JUNE 1879 Major Tucker with his five Companies arrive at Fort Evelyn.

23rd JUNE 1879 The five Companies remain at Fort Evelyn.

24th JUNE 1879 Major Tucker and his command leave fort Evelyn and reach Taikals Ridge.

25th JUNE 1879 March to Lundhla and camped. A strong reconnaissance of mounted men and Royal Artillery destroy three military Kraals, these being Ochlambedhla, Usixepi and Dugaiza.

27th-30th JUNE 1879 Marched for and reached the top of Entonjaneni Hill and remained until the 30th instant.

30th JUNE 1879 Left Entonjaneni Hill and marched for Fort Victoria.

1st JULY 1879 Reached the right hand bank of the White Umvolosi River and encamped.

3rd JULY 1879 The IInd Division spends the day making a defensive laager.

Cetshwayo, now aware of the advance of British and Colonial forces towards Ulundi and knowing he was unable to drive the 'Red Coats' from his lands, sued for peace on the 2nd July 1879. Chelmsford would have none of this, for he wanted to avenge the catastrophe at Isandhlwana. Knowing that he was to be replaced by Sir Garnet Wolseley, he wanted to defeat the Zulus and leave with his reputation intact, albeit a little blemished.

On the 3rd July the IInd Division and the Flying Column, under the direct control of Lord Chelmsford, marched to the White Umvolosi River. Negotiations for peace were in progress, but certain demands had not been fulfilled, so Chelmsford continued to move forward to take the Zulu King's principal kraal at Ulundi. On July 4th, leaving five companies of 1/24th Regiment of Foot, one company of Royal Engineers, and various detachments from differing Regiments, to defend his encampment, he ordered the advance to attack and destroy Ulundi. At 6.00am the mounted men of the Flying Column crossed the Umvolosi River, closely followed by the combined forces of the IInd Division and the Flying Column. When the attacking force reached suitable ground at about 7.30am, they were formed into one huge hollow rectangle. The 80th Regiment of Foot, of five companies, formed the vanguard of this human fighting 'square'. A pair of gattling guns were positioned in the centre of the advancing face of the 'square' with a further 12 pieces of artillery along the other sides and at the corners. The order was given to advance at 8.00am, the band of the 13th Regiment of Foot started to play, and the various Colours were unfurled and displayed.

At approximately 8.45am the Zulus forces came into contact with the mounted men Chelmsford had sent out in advance. After baiting the Zulus to attack, the mounted men soon retired within the hollow 'Square'. The Zulu force of 15-20,000 warriors manoeuvred to attack this invading force at around 9.00am. The British and Colonial soldiers were positioned four deep on each face of the 'square', the front two rows were kneeling with the rear two standing. With the use of modern rifles and the use of gattling guns and artillery, the Zulus were no match. Their attacks became uncoordinated, although some 2-3000 warriors did make a determined attempt to break the ranks at one of the corners held by the 21st and 58th Regiments of Foot. Having had the experience of the devastating effect of fire power at Kambula, the Zulus soon realised that they could not defeat or even compete with the whiteman's technology. At 9-35am noting that the momentum of the Zulu attack had lessened, Lord Chelmsford ordered out the calvalry and mounted troops to attack the retreating Zulus. It soon turned into a rout and the Zulus were pursued with no quarter asked or given. Shortly after 10.00am the artillery was ordered to shell Ulundi and then the order

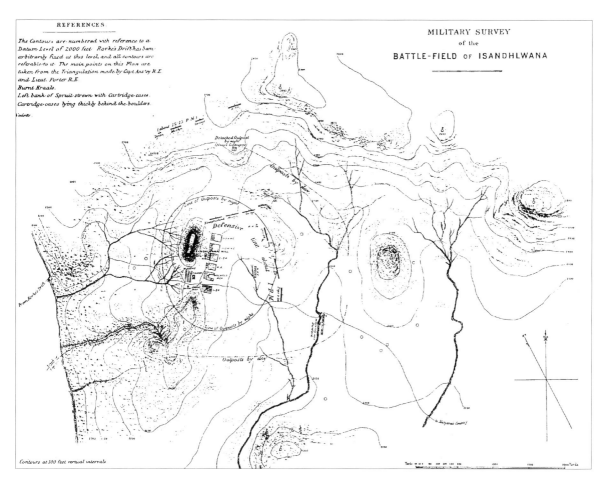

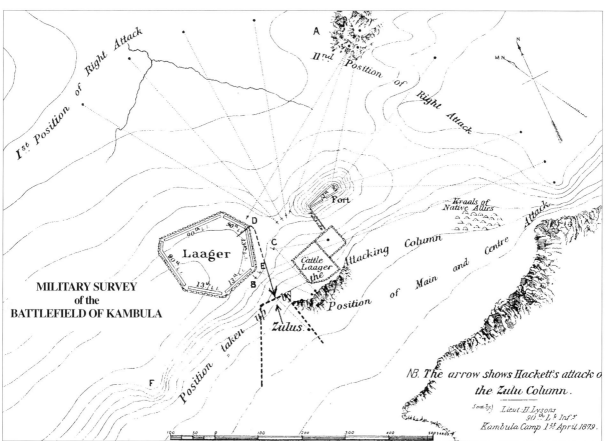

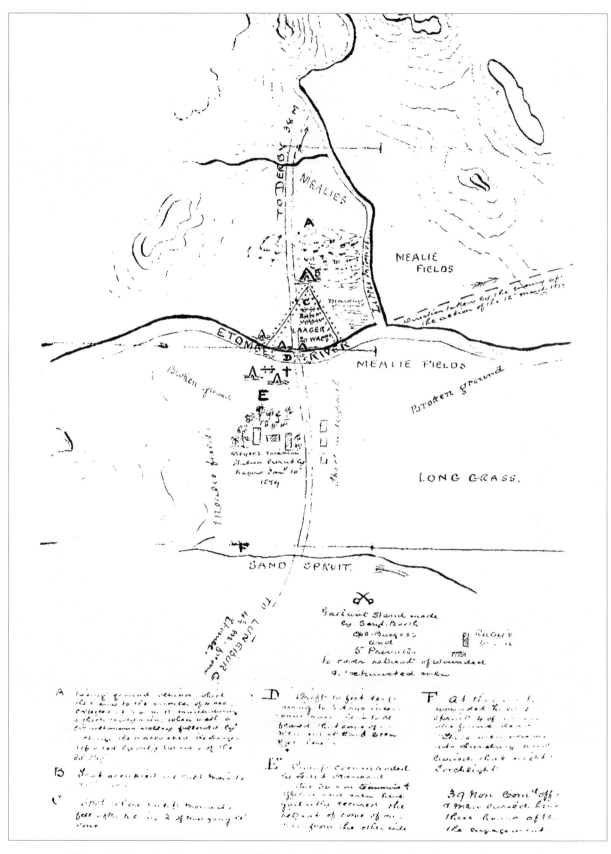

Map of the Intombe River and Mealie Fields, the original of which was found amongst the papers of
Lieutenant Colonel Charles Tucker (later Major General).

The 80th Regiment of Foot on the move.

Battle at the Intombe River, 12th March 1879.

An officer of the 80th Regiment of Foot c1879. believed to be Captain Wilfred Turner Anderson, who served with the Regiment from 4th August 1865 until his retirement on 1st July 1888.

Officers Mess - 80th Regiment Uphoko Camp June 1879.

was given to put Ulundi to the torch. Other kraals were also burned and the smoke from the Mahlabathini Plains could be seen for miles around. Following the battle and the burning of the kraals, the wounded were attended to, the dead buried and the troops were allowed to have a meal. The men were then ordered at 2.00 pm to retire to their own encampment, satisfied that the Zulus were beaten and that Isandhlwana had been avenged.

Of the 4166 Europeans and 1005 natives who took part in this battle, British and Colonial casualties amounted to 2 officers and 10 men killed including 3 natives. Two of those killed were members of the 80th Regiment. The total wounded were 19 officers and 69 men and 10 natives, and of these 5 belonged to the 80th. The casualties for the 80th were light considering the Regiment formed most of the front line of the 'British square' and, with their controlled volleys, were largely responsible for smashing the Zulu attack before they could get to close quarters.

The Zulu army was beaten and the King's principal residence was destroyed. Lord Chelmsford and his forces had now belatedly completed their objectives. The only thing that remained for complete victory was the capture of Cetshwayo, the Zulu king and this became the responsibility of Sir Garnet Wolseley.

The 80th Regiment record:

5th JULY 1879 Major C. Tucker with members of the 80th Regiment leave the White Umvolosi River and marched for Fort Victoria. "F" Company under the command of Captain W. Howard proceeded from Middleburg for Fort Weeber.
6th JULY 1879 Reached Fort Victoria.
7th JULY 1879 Left Fort Victoria and marched for Entonjaneui Hill.
8th JULY 1879 Reached Entonjaneui Hill and halted there. Brigadier General E. Wood VC, CB held a parade of the Flying Column and read out the order previously recorded and afterwards thanked the non commissioned officers and men in his own name, saying they had rendered all his work a pleasure to him more than duty.
9th JULY 1879 Five Companies of the 80th Regiment march two miles from Entonjaneui Hill in the direction of Kwamagwasa and encamp.
10th JULY 1879 The five Companies march a further ten miles and then encamp.
11th/12th JULY 1879 The force continues march and reaches the deserted Kwamagasa Mission Station. Halts there for 2 days.
13th JULY 1879 The five Companies leave Kwamagwasa and march for St. Paul's Mission. After completing seven miles the force encamps.
14th JULY 1879 After completing a further seven miles the force encamps.
15th JULY 1879 The five Companies continues march and reaches St. Paul's Mission Station. "F" Company with Captain W. Howard arrive at Fort Weeber.
16th JULY 1879 His Excellency Sir Garnet Wolseley GCMG, KCB inspected the Flying Column.
22nd JULY 1879 The IInd Division march to a new camp site approximately two miles down the Upoko and remained there till it was broken up.
26th JULY 1879 Part of the IInd Division's leave and march for Fort Newdigate.
31st JULY 1879 The Flying Column under the Command of Colonel Harrison is Broken up. Five Companies under the Command of Major C. Tucker march from St. Paul's for Ulundi and cover six miles towards Kwamagwasa. 83 time expired and reserved men having been handed over to the 1/13th Regiment of Foot proceed to England.
1st AUGUST 1879 The Regiment march a further seven miles and halt.
2nd AUGUST 1879 The Regiment remain encamped.
3rd AUGUST 1879 The march is resumed and the Regiment reach Kwamagwasa.
4th AUGUST 1879 The Regiment leave Kwamagwasa and march for Entonjaneni. A march of eight miles is completed and a halt is called. Brev. Major C.A.F. Creagh proceeds to take over the command of the Colonial Mounted Volunteers near Derby, New Scotland.
5th AUGUST 1879 The Regiment remains encamped.
6th AUGUST 1879 The march is resumed and six miles is completed.
7th AUGUST 1879 The Regiment breaks camp and marches beyond the Entonjaneni by about five miles towards Fort Victoria. The draft under the command of Brev. Major Bradshaw joins the Regiment here.
8th AUGUST 1879 The Regiment encamps at Fort Victoria.
10th AUGUST 1879 The Regiment leaves Fort Victoria and reaches the White Umvolosi River.
11th AUGUST 1879 Headquarters crossed from the right bank of the White Umvolosi River and camped about two miles north west of the ruins of Ondine kraal near to the camp of Gen. Sir Garnet Wolseley on the Hammer Alabetine Plains, Ulundi.
16th AUGUST 1879 Captains H.J. Johnson and J.O. Sherrard started out with eight other Officers under the command of Captain Herbert Stewart of the 3rd Dragoon Guards in pursuit of Cetshwayo.
18th AUGUST 1879 Brev. Major Bradshaw and Lieutenant Hast with "E" Company leave Ulundi to make a road via the Isiahlals and Inhlazatye mountains to Fort Cambridge.
19th AUGUST 1879 "E" Company camps at Langasanis kraal.
20th AUGUST 1879 Lt. Col. C. Tucker was placed in command of Headquarters personal escort of General Sir Garnet Wolseley GCMG, KCB at Ulundi. The escort consisted of Five Companies of the 80th Regiment of Foot, two Companies 2/24th Regiment of Foot, three Troops of the King's Dragoon Guards and two nine pounders guns of the Royal Artillery.
22nd AUGUST 1879 Brev. Major Bradshaw with "E" Company encamped in the Isihlals Valley on the Umhlalus River. Captains H.J. Johnson and J.O. Sherrard return from patrol after searching for King Cetshwayo.
23rd-24th AUGUST 1879 Brev. Major Bradshaw with "E" Company remain encamped in the Isihlals Valley on Umhlalus River.
25th-29th AUGUST 1879 "E" Company encamped at the Inhlazatye Mission Station.
30th AUGUST 1879 Brev. Major Bradshaw and Lieutenant Hast with "E" Company leave Inhlazatye for Fort George.

31st AUGUST 1879 "E" Company arrive at Fort George.

1st SEPTEMBER 1879 "E" Company march and reach Fort Cambridge and encamp there.

2nd SEPTEMBER 1879 "E" Company remained encamped at Fort Cambridge. Headquarters begin their march from Ulundi past Langasanis kraal, Inhazatye Mission Station, Conference Hill, Van Ruani Farm and proceeds towards Utrecht.

2nd-4th SEPTEMBER 1879 "E" company remained encamped at Fort Cambridge.

5th SEPTEMBER 1879 "E" Company remained encamped at Fort Cambridge. 2nd Lieutenant H.A. Raitt, 2 Sergeants, 1 Corporal and 32 Privates were detached at Fort Oliphant from Fort Weeber in the vicinity of Sekukuni's country.

6th SEPTEMBER 1879 "E" Company march and joins up with Headquarters.

10th SEPTEMBER 1879 Headquarters reach Utrecht.

11th SEPTEMBER 1879 Headquarters leave Utrecht and go past Doorne Kop, Parade Kop and Slang River towards Whistlestroom. Private Samuel Wassall with Private Robert Jones of the 24th Regiment receive their Victoria Cross medals from Sir Garnet Wolseley at Utrecht.

15th SEPTEMBER 1879 Headquarters encamp at Whistlestroom in the District of Wakkerstroom.

5th OCTOBER 1879 The distribution of the 80th Regiment of Foot was as followed:- Pretoria Headquarters and 1 Company Wakkertroom 5 Companies Fort Weeber 1/2 Company Fort Oliphant 1/2 Company Lydenburg 1 Company

6th OCTOBER 1879 Lt. Col. C. Tucker leaves Wakkerstroom, Pretoria and the five Companies become a Detachment.

18th OCTOBER 1879 Twenty-seven non commissioned Officers and men of the 80th Regiment of Foot accompanied General Sir Garnet Wolseley GCMG, KCB to Fort Weeber as an escort.

6th NOVEMBER 1879 Lieutenant Lindop and 50 non commissioned officers and men leave Wakkerstroom and proceed for Lydenburg.

11th NOVEMBER 1879 Lieutenants A.B. Horsbrugh and H.A. Raitt with 33 non commissioned Officers and men of "F" Company leave Fort Weeber and march for Lydenburg. Nineteen non commissioned and men of the 80th Regiment are detached for duty as Gunners with the Transvaal Artillery under the command of Captain Know Royal Artillery. The men are to be employed in operations against Sekukuni.

13th NOVEMBER 1879 Captain W. Howard is ordered to proceed to the Lydenburg District and to meet his Companies which would arrive from Fort Weeber.

16th NOVEMBER 1879 Lieutenants A.B. Horsbrugh and H.A. Raitt with 33 non commissioned Officers and men of "F" Company arrive at Lydenburg from Fort Weeber.

17th NOVEMBER 1879 In compliance with instructions the five companies at Wakkerstroom, strength 4 Captains, 2 Sub Lieutenants, 15 Sergeants, 14 Corporals, 9 Drummers and 349 Privates march for Pretoria.

18th NOVEMBER 1879 Lieutenant A.H. Lindop and an escort arrive at Middleburg from Wakkerstroom.

19th NOVEMBER 1879 The five Companies arrive at Standerton.

20th NOVEMBER 1879 The Five Companies resume the march for Pretoria. Lieutenant T.J. Chamberlain upon the departure of the five companies proceed to join the Depot Companies.

Following the defeat of the Zulus at Ulundi, King Cetshwayo was eventually captured on the 29th August 1879 at the kraal of Umhlongulu in the remote Ngome forest to the north of the Black Umfolozi River. On the 1st September prominent chiefs of the Zulu Nation surrendered and accepted the terms and conditions for settlement. British and Colonial troops then were officially withdrawn from Zululand.

Now that the Zulus had been subdued the British Goverment was able to concentrate its energies on the removal of Sekukuni. Plans for the second campaign against this chief were soon drawn up and members of the 80th Regiment were to take part as the entries in their Digest recall:

23rd NOVEMBER 1879 Major Creagh Commanding Column, Captains' Howard and Roworth with Lieutenants' Horbrugh,Lyons and Raitt with "F" and"G" Companies, strength 5 Sergeants, 4 Corporals, 2 Drummers and 83 Privates proceed from Lydenburg to Sekukuni Hill in operations against Chief Sekukuni.

27th NOVEMBER 1879 An attacking force including Major Creagh and his command leave the fort at 9.00 p.m. to attack Sekukuni Town.

28th NOVEMBER 1879 The force attacked the hills at the back of Sekukuni Town and the 80th and Eckersley's Contingent leading, and in the face of a heavy fire reached the hill and cleared the ridge as far as the back of the town, and with the Swazis succeeded in cutting off the retreat of the Makatees up the gorge at the back enabling the Swazis by dint of numbers to seize and burn the town and thus render possible this sebsequent attack upon the "Vecht Koppie" joined the Headquarters camp at the conclusion of the day and left the Sekukuni Town.

The battle that finally saw the defeat of Sekukuni was on 28th November 1879 when the chief's stronghold known as Sekukuni Town was attacked and eventually taken. The following extracts from the London Gazette No. 24802, dated 16th January 1880 graphically record the events.

War Office, January 15, 1880

Despatches, of which the following are copies, have been received by the Secretary of State for War from General Sir Garnet Wolseley, Commanding the troops South Africa:-

Army Head Quarters, Camp,
Sekukuni Town, Transvaal
South Africa, December 1, 1879

Sir

I have the honour to forward for your information the enclosed report from Lieutenant-Colonel Baker Russell, C.B., 13th Hussars, commanding the Transvaal Field Force, of the action fought here on the 28th ultimo, the successful result of which I communicated to you by telegram on that same evening.

The conduct of the troops, both regulars and volunteers, was everything that could be desired. The steadiness of Her Majesty's young soldiers in action, discipline, and the dashing manner in which they assaulted the 'Fighting Koppie' showed they were as well capable of sustaining the military reputation of the British army as any men who have ever served in it.

The skill and gallantry with which the Volunteer Corps worked over those scarped and difficult mountains was most conspicuous, and I have great pleasure in bringing especially to your notice the invaluable services performed by Commandant Ferreira's Horse.

The action began at 4.30 am and lasted until 10.00 a.m., when the 'Fighting Koppie' was stormed by a general charge of all the corps engaged, the assault being led by Colonel Russell in person.

Of Colonel Russell, who had his horse shot under him, I cannot speak too highly; the force under his command, which may be roughly estimated as consisting of 2,200 British and about 10,000 Natives, was hastily collected from all sides and where native levies are concerned, it is no easy matter to plan and carry out an extensive operation extending over some miles of a very difficult mountain country with the skill, accuracy, and success which have characterised Colonel Russell's operations here.

The Chief, Sekukuni, who did not personally take any part in the action, is now in a cave about fifteen miles from this. The cave is closely surrounded by troops, and I hope that want of water will soon compel him and those with him to surrender.

In a few days more I hope to clear out all the robber chiefs living in these Zulu mountains, when the Transvaal Field Force will be broken up.

I believe that the success which has attended this little campaign will confer lasting benefit upon the Transvaal by securing peace to a district where life nor property has been safe for many years past.

The destruction of Sekukuni's stronghold and of his power, and the breaking up of the robber clans who look up to him as their King, cannot fail to have a quieting effect upon the native mind generally in South Africa, and I will, I am sure, go far towards settling all native difficulties in the Transvaal.

In the organization and concentration of the forces engaged in these operations, and in all the many complex arrangements required for supplying them with stores, food, &c., &c., during the campaign, I have received the most efficient and able assistance from Lieutenant-Colonel H. Brackenbury, Royal Artillery, who is acting as my chief of the Staff.

Surgeon-Major Jackson, C.B., who is attached to my Head Quarters did good work during the action in attending to the wounded, many of whom he dressed under fire.

Captain Maurice, Royal Artillery, my Camp Commandant, acted as Staff officer to one of the attacking columns, and did excellent work until he was unfortunately wounded.

My Aides-de-Camp, Major McCalmont, 7th Hussars, and Lieutenant A. G. Creagh, Royal Artillery, both performed their duties to my entire satisfaction

I have, &c.,
G. J. WOLSELEY, General'

To the Chief of Staff,
Head Quarters, Fort Alexandria,
November 28, 1879
    Sir,
The Transvaal Field Force having been concentrated upon the night of the 27th instant, opposite the eastern and western faces of the spier of the Zulu mountains, upon which Sekukuni's town is situated, I have the honour to report that, in accordance with your orders, I attacked the town this morning.

The troops, as per return marked 'A' attached, were employed.

The following plan of operations was carried out:-

(1) An attack against the town itself from the western side, subdivided into a right, central, and left attack.

(2) An attack against the eastern face of the mountains, with the object of crowning the heights overlooking the town, moving down the ridges, and acting in combination with the western force.

With reference to (1), the right attack was led by Commandant Ferreira. The troops placed at his disposal consisted of his own corps, Mapoch's Native Contingent, and two Companies Rustenberg Contingent. Commandant Ferreira experienced the usual difficulties that are to be anticipated in the employment of native levies in this country, Mapoch's Contingent failing to render him any assistance. Regardless of this, he led his men to the assault, and, his volunteers promptly responding, he succeeded, without a check, in carrying out the object. I had intimated to him, namely the seizure of Sekukuni's kraal and the heights bordering the south of the town. The central force was commanded by Lieutenant-Colonel Murray, 94th Regiment, and was composed of - Detachment Royal Engineers, 2nd Battalion 21st Regiment Royal Scots Fusiliers, Detachment 80th Regiment, 94th Regiment, Transvaal Artillery and small Arm Ammunition Reserve.

The object to be held in view was the attack and seizure of the 'Fighting Koppie', an isolated mass of irregular boulder rocks, intersected with caves, and strongly defended with stone walls, opposite to the centre of the town. It was manifest, that if the right and left attacks were successful, the defenders of this position would be cut off. Consequently Lieutenant- Colonel Murray was directed to carry on a delaying action until progress made on the right and left could be ascertained. This was done with great steadiness, skirmishers having been thrown out to hold the enemy's fire in check, whilst the artillery at the same time prepared the way for the final assault. Major Carrington, 24th Regiment, commanding the left attack, was ordered to move with the Mounted Infantry, Border Horse, Transvaal Mounted Rifles, Rustenberg Contingent and Zoutspansberg Contingent against a point of the town some 800 yards to the north of the 'Fighting Koppie', and to seize the positions to the north of Sekukuni's kraal. This attack, successful in its outset, was somewhat checked by the retreat of Zoutspansberg Contingent. These men were, however, speedily rallied and the orders issued to Major Carrington successful accomplished. With regard to the eastern attack Major Bushman, 9th Lancers, commanded the entire force against the hill upon that side. Shortly after 6am this force, after considerable opposition, gained the top of the ridge. This being done, the ridge was held by the European Infantry, and the Swazies, benefiting by the previous success of the right and left attacks, pushed down the hill and through the town. By the above operations the 'Fighting Koppie', had become completely surrounded. At 10 a.m., a general assault was made against this position. After an obstinate defence, the Koppie succumbed, and thus the town, the surrounding country, and a large number of prisoners were in our hands.

A return of the casualties amongst the Europeans troops is attached, marked 'B' showing two officers killed and 6 wounded, and 5 non commissioned officers, rank and file killed, and 41 wounded. The approximate loss of native allies was 200 killed and wounded, but it is difficult to estimate this exactly, owing to their reluctance to bring forward their wounded, but all troops received the same medical attention. The enemy's loss in killed and wounded and prisoners was very heavy, the latter including amongst others the whole garrison of the 'Fighting Koppie', of which some 500 have already appeared, and others are still coming out of their caves.

I am much indebted to all ranks, both of the Regular and Colonial forces, nothing could exceed their gallantry and steadiness. I would venture to bring to your notice the names of the following officers, all of whom rendered me most valuable assistance:- Lieutenant-Colonel Murray, 94th Regiment, commanding the central column, rendered me the greatest aid, and showed a power of commanding men that was most marked. Commandant Ferreira, commanding the right column of attack upon the town, exhibited an energy and determination in leading men that I cannot too highly praise. Major Carrington, 24th Regiment, commanding the left column of attack, who maintained his position against large numbers of the enemy with the greatest coolness, when his native allies fell back. Major Carrington speaks in the highest terms of the assistance he received from his Staff Officer, Captain Maurice, Royal Artillery. Major Bushman, 9th Lancers, commanding the eastern column of attack, who though much hampered by the dilatory unpunctuality of the Swazie Contingent under his command, yet topped the mountain in good time, and did excellent service. Lieutenant Macgregor, commanding Royal Engineers. Captain Knox, Royal Artillery, commanding Transvaal Artillery, who handled his guns, manned by troops, trained to his branch of the service comparatively but a short time, with a skill that was as creditable to himself as to his men. Major Hazlerigg, commanding 2nd Battalion Royal Scots Fusiliers. Major Anstruther, commanding 94th Regiment.

The Medical arrangements were excellent, and I am deeply grateful to Surgeon-Major Kerr, Principle Medical Officer, as also to Surgeon-Major Hector, in charge of Bearer Company, and Surgeon-Major Johnston in charge of first dressing station, for the great celerity with which all wounded were removed, and for the care bestowed on them on arrival. Veterinary-Surgeon Moore, who attended to wounded horses on the field with great coolness. Lieutenant Hutchinson, 4th Kings Own Royal Regiment, in charge of small arms ammunition train, showed the greatest foresight and common sense in supplying the different attacks with ammunition, the supply of which he never allowed to slacken for a moment.

To my Staff Officer, Captain Stewart, 3rd Dragoon Guards, my thanks are most especially for. The energy and power of hard work displayed by him were marvellous, and the skill, tact, and good temper he showed in dealing with the very various and conflicting elements of which the force under my command was composed were beyond praise. I tribute, in great measure, the complete success of the battle of the 28th instant to the invaluable aid I received from Captain Stewart. My Orderly Officer, Captain Fraser, 60th Rifles, displayed great gallantry and zeal throughout the day. My acting Orderly Officers for the day Com *** Reeves, Captain Spratt, 29th Regiment, Captain Lawrell, 4th Hussars (killed), and Captain Christian, Frontier Light Horse, rendered me most valuable assistance, and carried my orders to the difficult parts of the field under a very heavy fire with the greatest coolness and accuracy. I deeply regret the death of Captain Lawrell. The Service has to deploy the loss of a most promising cavalry officer. I much regret to say that Mr Campbell attached to the Swazies, through an interpreter, states that he saw Mr Campbell shot dead in a cave on the mountain. As the Swazies never remove their killed, the body was not brought away, and I am sorry to say I have been unable to discover it, I will make further search, and I shall be successful.

I Have, &c.,

BAKER RUSSELL, Lieutenant- Colonel
Commanding Field Force.'

Chief Sekukuni fell into the hands of the British, the event being described in the same publication:

'Army Head Quarters, Pretoria Transvaal'
South Africa
December 12, 1879
Sir,
I Have the honour to inform you that on the morning of the 2nd instant the Chief Sekukuni surrendered himself to Major Clarke, R.A., Special Commissioner, the cave in which he was taking refuge having been closely surrounded by troops under Commandant Ferreira, since the morning of the 30th November. Sekukuni was brought into my camp as a prisoner ....

I have, &c.,
G. J. Wolseley, General.'

Meanwhile the remainder of the Regiment continued their march through southern Africa:

1st DECEMBER 1879 The five companies reach Pretoria as also Lieutenant Lindop's escort. At this time therefore, there were six companies concentrated at Pretoria.
9th DECEMBER 1879 The Personal escort of General Sir Garnet Wolseley G.C.M.G., K.C.B. arrived at Pretoria, and the following letter received, They had taken part in the attack on Sekukuni's stronghold and were the first British troops to reach

The site of Captain Moriarty's
encampments - Intombe River looking
towards Mbilini's stronghold.

The memorial commemorating the fallen at
the Battle of the Intombe River - the mass
grave looking North East.

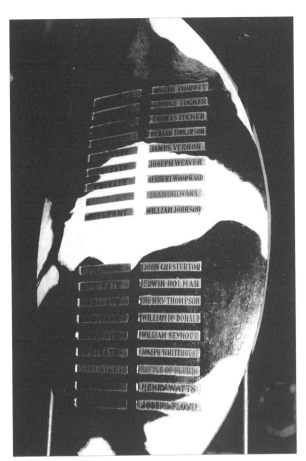

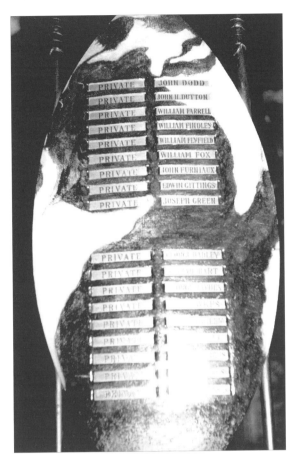

Shield memorials, St Michael's Chapel, Lichfield Cathedral.

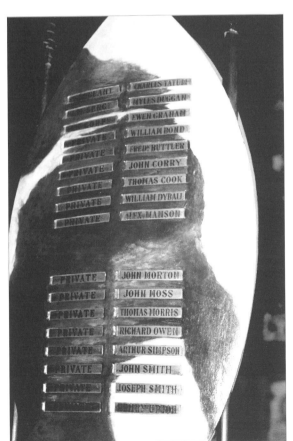

Close up of a memorial shield and the memorial screen to the soldiers who died in South Africa 1878-9.

Colour Sergeant Anthony Clarke Booth VC.

A family portrait - Colour Sergeant Anthony Booth with his wife Lucy and four of their sons, who all served with the Colours.

the summit of the Fighting Koppie, "gallantly taking at the point of the bayonet."

> Army Headquarters Pretoria 9th December 1879
> To. Lt. Col. C. Tucker Commanding Her Majesty's 80th Regiment
> Sir,
> I am directed by General Sir Garnet Wolseley to bring to your special notice the very admirable conduct of Sergeant Horton and the detachment of the 80th Regiment who formed the escort of the General Commanding during the recent operations against the chief Sekukuni. From the day when the General left Pretoria on the 18th October last and until his return today the behaviour of the Regiment has been all that could possibly be desired, it is not only that they gave any trouble or cause for reproof, but they showed a cheerfulness and willingness in their performance of their duties and was beyond praise, no soldier could have done better. Sergeant Horton and the whole of the detachment joined in the storming of the Fighting Koppie at Sekukuni's Town on the morning of the 28th November.
>> I have, re etc., etc.
>> signed Henry Brackenbury
>> Lieutenant Colonel Military Secretary and Acting Chief of Staff

"F" & "G" Companies having joined at Lydenburg on the 16th November 1879, proceeded on the 20th under the command of Captain Walter Howard to join the column under the command of Major Bushman. 9th Lancers.

"G" Company with Captain Roworth and Lieutenant Lyons "F" Company Lieutenant Horsbrugh and Raitt marched through the Waterfall Valley and joined the force under Major Bushman consisting of 2 companies 94th Regiment, Lydenburg Rifles, Eckersleys Contingent and 8000 Swazis on the 23rd November 1879. They moved on next day and on the 25th November 1879 formed the advanced laager of Fort George and opened communications with the force operating from the other side.

14th DECEMBER 1879 For the first time on the 14th December after taking part in four campaigns since November 1875 when 300 men were sent to Perak from Hong Kong the Regiment was concentrated at Pretoria, Transvaal. Many hardships and heavy marches were suffered and performed during this period.
24th DECEMBER 1879 After a well earned rest orders to proceed via Kimberley, Beaufort and Cape Town were received with welcome.
26th DECEMBER 1879 The Regiment was drawn up in close column and at 11 am with officers and colours to the front and General Sir Garnet Wolseley taking the general salute. The following General Order was then read out to the Regiment by the Chief of Staff:-

> General Order by his Excellency Sir Garnet Wolseley GCMG, KCB commanding the forces in South Africa. The 80th Regiment will march today from Pretoria by way of Potchefstroom and Kimberley to Beaufort West in the Cape Colony and will hence proceed by rail to Cape Town for England. The General commanding cannot allow this Regiment to enter upon its homeward march without expressing his high sense of its soldier like bearing and conduct. The 80th Regiment has served for three years in South Africa during which time it has taken part in the Zulu war and in two expeditions against Sekukuni and has become the fatigue of long marches over a great extent of country yet after this varied and trying service it's appearance and discipline would do credit to any Regiment in Her Majesty's army. The General Commanding is well assured that in the march now before it the 80th Regiment under command of Lt. Col. Tucker will show to the inhabitants of the Transvaal, Grigualand West and the Cape Colony an example of what a British Regiment should be, not only in marching power but in loyalty, discipline and orderly conduct. By
>> Order Signed H. Brackenbury
> Lt. Col. Acting Chief of Staff Army Headquarters Pretoria 26th December 1879'

Sir Garnet Wolseley addressed Lt. Col. Tucker, the officers and the Regiment in a few well chosen words and bade all God's speed to England. The Regiment then moved off from Pretoria, halting and encamping at Humops River, seven miles from Pretoria.

27th DECEMBER 1879 Marched to kyokesky's river some twenty and half miles.
28th DECEMBER 1879 Marched to Groblio's Farm some thirty-five and a half miles distance.
29th DECEMBER 1879 Marched to Brait Valley approximately fifty and a half miles.
30th DECEMBER 1879 Marched to Windecfintein Valley some seventy miles.
31st DECEMBER 1879 Marched to Nia Wolman's Farm covering a distance of eighty-six and a half miles.
1st JANUARY 1880 Marched and reached Potchefstroom.
2nd JANUARY 1880 At Coumigas Spruit.
3rd JANUARY 1880 Marched for Klerksdorp.
4th JANUARY 1880 Halted at Klerksdorp, in consequence of the distributed state of the district and for the purposes of arresting Mr Pretorius, President of the Peoples Committee, Boer Population. Lt. Col. Tucker, Captains Howard and Potts with Lieutenant Raitt in command of 57 non commissioned officers and men returned to Potchefstroom on mule waggons.
5th JANUARY 1880 Lt. Col. Tucker and his small command reach Potchefstroom early in the morning. During the afternoon Lt Col Tucker recalled part of the Regiment to Potchefstroom and directed that the heavy baggage remain at Klerksdorp under an escort of ten men, with Captain Anderson in command and Lieutenant Lindop and 2nd Lieutenant Marshall accompanying.
6th JANUARY 1880 In obedience to these instructions the Regiment marched from Klerksdorp lightly equipped at 8.00am and reached Potchefstroom at 9.40pm covering a distance of thirty-three miles.

8th JANUARY 1880 The Regiment encamped at Potchefstroom. Mr Pretorius was admitted to bail

13th JANUARY 1880 The Regiment moved into camp to a position outside the town. The Boers having broken up their encampment and dispersed. Under instructions by Sir Garnet Wolseley GCMG, KCB the march of the Regiment was changed from by way of Kimberley and Beaufort to by way of Heidelberg and Pietermaritzburg to Durban for embarkation.

14th JANUARY 1880 The Regiment marched for Heidelberg.

18th JANUARY 1880 The Regiment reach Heidelberg.

19th JANUARY 1880 The Regiment march for Sugar Bush River and halting and encamp.

20th JANUARY 1880 The Regiment is remain encamped.

21st JANUARY 1880 The regiment resumed it's march and arrived at Newcastle, Natal by way of Standerton, Transvaal.

28th JANUARY 1880 Lt. Col. Tucker and his force encamp at Standerton, Transvaal.

29th JANUARY 1880 The regiment remains encamped.

30th JANUARY 1880 The regiment continues its march towards Ladysmith.

3rd FEBRUARY 1880 Lt. Col. Tucker and the Regiment arrive at Ladysmith.

4th FEBRUARY 1880 The Regiment remains at Ladysmith.

5th FEBRUARY 1880 The Regiment leave Ladysmith and march for Colenso and reach it that day.

6th FEBRUARY 1880 The Regiment continues its march towards Estcourt.

7th FEBRUARY 1880 Lt. Col. Tucker and the Regiment arrive at Estcourt.

8th FEBRUARY 1880 The Regiment encamp at Griffin's Farm eight miles from Estcourt.

9th FEBRUARY 1880 The Regiment march for and reach the Western Mooi River.

10th FEBRUARY 1880 The march is resumed and reach Currie's Post.

11th FEBRUARY 1880 The Regiment march and reach Howick.

12th FEBRUARY 1880 The march is resumed and the Regiment march into Pietermaritzburg and encamp above Fort Napier.

26th MARCH 1880 The Regiment marched from Pretoria for the post of embarkation and arrive at Botha's Hill where it encamped.

27th MARCH 1880 The Regiment remains encamped at Botha's Hill.

2nd APRIL 1880 The Regiment remains at Botha's Hill.

3rd APRIL 1880 The Regiment is transported by railway in three divisions from Botha's Hill and embark on H.M.S. *"Orontes"* at Durban.

6th-9th APRIL 1880 H.M.S. *"Orontes"* called in at Simons Bay and refuelled with coal.

10th APRIL 1880 H.M.S. *"Orontes"* calls at Table's Bay, it's last port of call before finally sailing for home waters and the British Isles.

The 80th Regiment of Foot (Staffordshire Volunteers) for their services in South Africa throughout the period of 1878-79 was awarded its seventh and final battle honour, 'SOUTH AFRICA 1878-79'.

Charles Tucker commanded the 80th Regiment during the Zulu War, later becoming Sir Charles Tucker GCB, GCVO. He became one of the Regiment's outstanding Commanding Officers and later Colonel of the South Staffordshire Regiment 1911-1935.

(Officers Mess, Whittington Barracks)

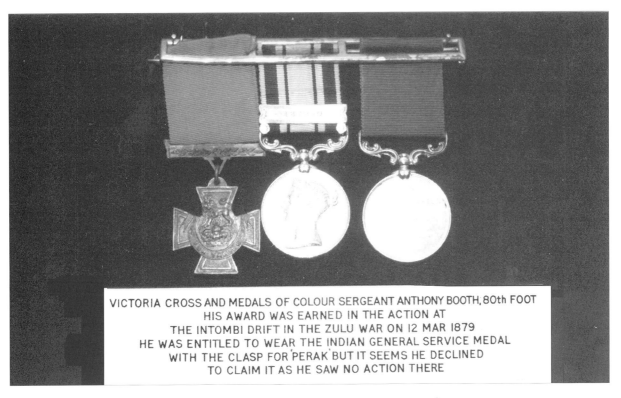

VICTORIA CROSS AND MEDALS OF COLOUR SERGEANT ANTHONY BOOTH, 80th FOOT
HIS AWARD WAS EARNED IN THE ACTION AT
THE INTOMBI DRIFT IN THE ZULU WAR ON 12 MAR 1879
HE WAS ENTITLED TO WEAR THE INDIAN GENERAL SERVICE MEDAL
WITH THE CLASP FOR 'PERAK' BUT IT SEEMS HE DECLINED
TO CLAIM IT AS HE SAW NO ACTION THERE

The medals of 919 Colour Sergeant Anthony Booth VC:
Victoria Cross, South Africa Medal with clasp 1878-79, Long Service and Good Conduct Medal.

Sergeant Anthony Booth rallying survivors - Intombi River.

The medals of 427 Private Samuel Wassall VC: Victoria Cross. South African medal 1877-8-9.

VICTORIA CROSS AND SOUTH AFRICA 1877-79
MEDAL OF PRIVATE SAMUEL WASSALL, 80th. FOOT
WHO EARNED HIS AWARD IN THE AFTERMATH OF THE
BATTLE OF ISANDHLWANA IN ZULULAND ON 22 JAN 1879
WHILE SERVING WITH A MOUNTED INFANTRY DETACHMENT
ONLY VERY FEW OF THE 80th EARNED THE 1877 CLASP TO THE MEDAL

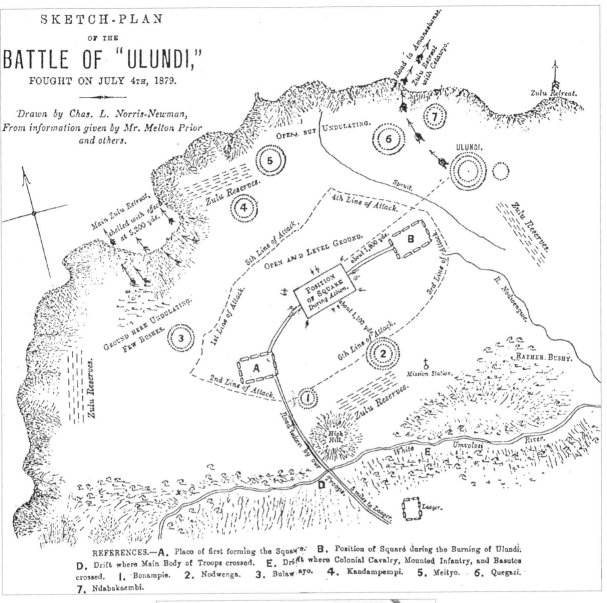

SKETCH-PLAN
OF THE
BATTLE OF "ULUNDI,"
FOUGHT ON JULY 4TH, 1879.

*Drawn by Chas. L. Norris-Newman,
From information given by Mr. Melton Prior
and others.*

REFERENCES.—A. Place of first forming the Square. B. Position of Square during the Burning of Ulundi.
D. Drift where Main Body of Troops crossed. E. Drift where Colonial Cavalry, Mounted Infantry, and Basutos
crossed. 1. Bonampie. 2. Nodwenga. 3. Bulawayo. 4. Kandampempi. 5. Meityo. 6. Quegazi.
7. Ndabakaembi.

South Africa Medal.

The final battle of the Zulu War at Ulundi, 4th July 1879, as depicted in the Illustrated London News.

Chapter 5
THE MEDALS

A medal is a small flat piece of metal incorporating an inscription or image, given either as an award for some outstanding event or for a commemorative purpose.

The award of tokens or articles such as medals in military employment goes back into the mists of time. The historian Flavius Josephus recorded in the 3rd century BC that King Alexander sent a gold button to Jonathan the High Priest in recognition of his leadership of the Jews in battle. For further brave deeds, he was sent a second gold button. In ancient Greece and Rome the commemoration was usually in the form of coins, and it is probable that the earliest designs of medals take their basic configuration from coinage. Medals primarily served as recognition and can be awarded in four basic ways: Gallantry Medals - for some single brave act or daring deed(s). Campaign Medals - to commemorate some single battle, war or campaign. Long/Meritorious Service Medals - in acknowledgement of loyal and faithful service including good conduct. Coronation & Jubilee Medals - to commemorate a royal occasion

The mass issue of medals in terms of military history is a modern phenomenon. In Europe, especially England, manufacturing and presenting medals as a reward did not really begin until the 17th century and then it was only a spasmodic occurrence. Slightly earlier during the 16th century, in the reign of Elizabeth I, some of the earliest English medals were produced and issued. These early medals served as a quasi-commemorative acknowledgement of service, one of the best known being the 'Armada Medal' of 1588.

During the English Civil War, 1642-1649, a few medals made of gold and silver were awarded to officers for distinguished service. Following the defeat of a Scottish Presbyterian army in June 1650, Parliament sanctioned a medal which was known as the 'Dunbar Medal', and it served as the basis for the criteria for awarding future medals. The Dunbar Medal was awarded to both officers and men, although no records exist to confirm that all who were due the medal received it. Further medals were also struck and distributed to admirals and captains for their services in the first war against the Dutch 1650-1653.

One of the earliest campaign medals created was the 'Naval Gold Medal' dated 1795 and was awarded to officers for naval actions 1795-1815. In 1810 the 'Army Gold Medal' was established and again awarded to officers for their part in the campaigns of the Peninsular War 1806-1814 and the War of 1812.

The first of the cross pattée design medals was commissioned in 1813, when the 'Army Gold Cross' was created and granted to generals and officers of field rank for service in four or more battles in the Peninsular War (Peninsular War and War of 1812). One of the first medals to be awarded to all ranks was the 'Waterloo Medal', commissioned in 1815 immediately following the great victory at Waterloo on the 18th June 1815. The medal was also awarded to those soldiers who had participated in the earlier battles at Ligney and Quatre Bras on the 16th June. These medals were the first to have the recipients name impressed around the edge and also the first made available for entitlement to the next of kin of those killed. The British Government was so grateful to these soldiers that a period of two years was also credited to each of the soldier's service. In 1847 two new medals were inaugurated, the 'Naval General Service Medal', for naval battles and boat actions 1793-1840, and the 'Military General Service Medal', for participation in the French Revolutionary and Napoleonic Wars 1793-1814.

It could be said that the first actual gallantry medal was the 'Forlorn Hope Medal'. This medal was instituted with a Royal warrant, dated 18th May 1643, and addressed to the Wardens of the Mint at Oxford, Sir William Parkhurst and Thomas Bushell. The word 'Forlorn' is derived from the German word 'foloren' meaning 'lost'. The medal was awarded to members of the party which led an attack on the enemy - many did not live to receive it. One of the oldest gallantry awards of the British Empire is that of the 'Indian Order of Merit', which came into existence in 1837 and was introduced by the Honourable East India Company.

During the Crimean War 1854-1856, it was first recognised that there was a need for a gallantry award to the ordinary soldier and subsequently in 1854 the 'Distinguished Conduct Medal' was introduced. In 1855 the 'Conspicuous Gallantry Medal' was established for petty officers and seamen on a par with the Army's Distinguished Conduct Medal. The Victoria Cross was introduced in 1856, and still remains the highest award that this country can bestow on an individual.

Over the years numerous medals have been initiated for long and loyal service with good conduct. The award was primarily for the rank and file, with some awards carrying an annuity of a small sum of money for life. The earliest of these were the Army 'Long Service and Good Conduct Medal' (1830), the Royal Navy 'Long Service and Good Conduct Medal' (1831), the Army 'Meritorious Service Medal' (1845) and for the Indian Army, the Indian Army 'Long Service Medal' (1848) and the Indian Army 'Meritorious Service Medal' (1848).

The first medal officially created to celebrate a royal occasion was cast by Henry Basse to commemorate the succession to the throne by King Edward VI in 1547. Since then few monarchs have failed to follow suit.

Over the years many wars and campaigns have taken place throughout the world involving members of our armed forces, in large armies or small contingents. Men and women have devoted their lives in service to their country. Many medals and honours have been implemented to recognise this service; those above are only a few.

MILITARY GENERAL SERVICE MEDAL 1793 - 1814

The Military General Service Medal 1793-1814 was authorised by a General Order dated June 1st 1847. The medal was eventually issued the following year, some 34 years after the last battle it was issued to commemorate.

The medal, which was designed by W. Wyon RA is made of silver and is 36mm in diameter. It has a 32mm wide crimson ribbon, with a 6mm wide dark blue border, attached to the medal by the use of a plain straight swivelling suspender. On the obverse is depicted the diademed head of Queen Victoria with the legend 'VICTORIA REGINA' and the date '1848'. Queen Victoria is seen on the reverse, standing on a raised dais with the Duke of Wellington kneeling on his left knee in front of her. The Queen is placing a laurel wreath on his head. To the side of the dais is a diminutive British Lion. The words 'TO THE BRITISH ARMY' are inscribed around the top part of the circumference with the dates, '1793-1814' in the exergue below. The first bar the medal was issued with was for 'EGYPT', the date for entitlement March 2nd 1801 to September 2nd 1801.

Approximately 25,650 applications were made for the medal, which commemorates battles in Egypt, the East and West Indies and the United States of America. The medal issued had a total of 29 bars that could be applied for, with the bars being fixed in multiples of three. The naming was indented in large Roman capitals. Of the 29 bars issued, a total of 21 were for actions in the Peninsular War and it is often referred to as the 'Peninsular Medal'.

Egypt	March 2nd 1801-September 2nd 1801	Java	August 14th 1811 -August 26th 1811
Maida	July 4th 1806	Ciudad Rodrigo	January 8th 1812 -January 19th 1812
Roleia	August 17th 1808	Badajoz	March 17th 1812 - March 18th 1812
Vimiera	August 21st 1808	Salamanca	July 22nd 1812
Sahagun	December 21st 1808	Fort Detroit	August 16th 1812
Benevente	December 29th 1808	Vittoria	June 21st 1813
Sahagun&Benevente	December 21st 1808-December 29th 1808	Pyrenees	July 25th 1813- August 2nd 1813
Corruna	January 16th 1809	St. Sebastian	July 17th 1813 - September 8th 1813
Martinique	January 30th 1809-Feb 24th 1809	Chateauguay	October 26th 1813
Talavera	July 27th 1809 - July 28th 1809	Nivelle	November 10th 1813
Guadaloupe	January 30th 1810-February 4th 1810	Chrystler's Farm	November 11th 1813
Busaco	September 27th 1810	Nive	December 9th 1813 - December 13th 1813
Barrosa	March 5th 1811	Orthes	February 27th 1814
Fuentes D'Onor	May 5th 1811	Toulouse	April 10th 1814
Albuhera	May 16th 1811		

MEDAL LIST
MILITARY GENERAL SERVICE MEDAL with Clasp 'EGYPT'

The 80th did not actually take part in the conflict in Egypt March 2nd to September 2nd 1801. However several members of the Regiment did eventually claim medals and 7 men were subsequently awarded the Military General Service Medal with the clasp, 'Egypt'. Lieutenant Harvey later became Lieutenant-General Sir John Harvey KCB and was awarded the clasp 'Chrystler's Farm' to the Medal for the action that occurred on November 11th 1813. The 'Army Small Gold Medal' was also awarded to Sir John Harvey for his part in this action in North America. Captain John St.George who later became ADC to Lieutenant-General Bentinck was also awarded a further clasp, 'Corruna' to his General Service Medal for the action on January 16th 1809. Three of these medals whose recipients are identified with an * can be viewed at the Regimental Museum, Whittington Barracks, Lichfield. The 'medals' issued are as follows:

St. George*,	John.	Captain	Fox,	John.	Private
Bazalgette,	John Lewis.	Lieutenant	Howard,	William.	Private
Harvey,	John.	Lieutenant	Rogers*,	Jacob.	Private
Kingdon*,	Dennis.	Lieutenant			

SUTLEJ CAMPAIGN MEDAL
18th DECEMBER 1845 - 22nd FEBRUARY 1846

The Sutlej Campaign Medal was sanctioned by a General Order dated April 17th 1846. It was awarded to those officers and men who served in Her Majesty's Armed forces in Sutlej between December 18th 1845 and February 22nd 1846, and was the first to be issued to both officers and men with 'bars', with the maximum number of bars being three - 'Ferozeshuhur', 'Aliwal' and 'Sobraon'.

The medal was designed by W. Wyon RA and is made of silver and is 36mm in diameter. It has a 32mm wide, dark blue ribbon with crimson edges 6mm in width and is attached by means of an ornamental swivelling suspender. The obsverse side of the medal shows the diademed head of Queen Victoria, with the legend 'VICTORIA REGINA'. On the reverse side can be seen the standing figure of Victory, facing left. Her outstretched right hand holds a wreath and in her left hand is an olive branch, a collection of trophies can be seen at her feet. The legend 'ARMY OF THE SUTLEJ' is inscribed around the circumference. Also on the reverse side is the exergue, of which there are four types, 'Moodkee 1845', 'Ferozeshuhur 1845', 'Aliwal 1846' and 'Sobraon 1846', the medal bearing the name of the first battle the recipient took part in. This meant that four types of medal had to be produced, the only time that this has been done in the case of a battle. There was a variant of the medal, glazed silver gilt specimens with three bars. The naming was indented in capital letters or light Roman skeleton lettering.

The following list contains 840 names of soldiers who served as officers, surgeons, non commissioned officers and men with the 80th Regiment of Foot (Staffordshire Volunteers), during the Sutlej Campaign and were awarded the Sutlej Campaign Medal. These soldiers were part of the army and served under the command of His Excellency the Right Honourable the Lord Gough GCB. The medal roll is not dated but was certified by J.W. Nunn Major, Commanding and by H.A. Helman, Lieutenant and Adjutant, 80th Regiment of Foot..

The medal was issued for the first action in which the recipient took part, incorporated in the exergue on the reverse of the medal, with 'clasps' issued for any subesequent actions. The battles in which the recipient took part can be identified by the letters after the rank of the individual, 'M' - Moodkee, 'F' - Ferozeshuhur, 'A' - Aliwal and 'S' - Sobraon. The actions were confirmed to GOCC 17th April 1846 and GOC-in-C 6th March 1846 and 23rd April 1846. The total number of varience medals issued according to the medal roll are as follows: 7 'Moodkee' Medals, 137 'Moodkee' Medals with Clasp 'Ferozeshuhur', 2 'Moodkee' Medals with Clasps 'Ferozeshuhur', 'Aliwal', and 'Sobroan', 666 'Moodkee' Medals with clasps 'Ferozeshuhur' and 'Sobraon', 2 'Moodkee' medals with clasp 'Abraon', 7 'Aliwal' Medals, 17 'Aliwal' Medals with clasp 'Sobroan', 2 'Sobraon' Medals.

N.B. Some spellings and Army Numbers are slightly different between the Medal List and the Regiment's Nominal Roll. Those differences identified have been included, the Medal List version taking precedence, the Nominal Roll format in brackets. Where an * is after the surname, refer to the Casualty List.

No.	Surname	First name	Rank	Actions
1802	**Allen***,	Alfred.	Sergeant	M-F-S
1633	Asbury,	Henry.	Sergeant	M-F-S
600	Austin,	George.	Sergeant	M-F-S
2240	Aspden*,	Benjamin.	Corporal	M-F
1591	Ainsworth,	William.	Private	M-F-S
1412	Aldridge,	Mathew.	Private	M-F-S
1019	Allen*,	Isaac.	Private	M-F-S
2144	Allen,	John.	Private	M-F-S
1625	Allpress,	John.	Private	M-F-S
1529	Allsop*,	Francis.	Private	M-F
1272	Allsworth,	John.	Private	M-F-S
1599	Arlett,	William.	Private	M-F-S
2027	Aspey,	George.	Private	M-F-S
1812	Atkins,	John.	Private	M-F-S
685	Atkinson*,	Robert.	Private	M
	Bunbury* (CB),Thomas.		Lt. Colonel	M-F-S
	Best*,	Abel Dottin William.	Captain	M-F
	Bodle,	George.	Lieutenant	M-F-S
	Bowler,	Henry George John.	Lieutenant	M-F-S
	Bythesea*,	George Charles Glossop.	Lieutenant	M-F
888	Briscoe,	Thomas.	Non-Commissioned Staff	M-F-S
545	Brown,	John.	Non-Commissioned Staff	M-F-S
690	Bailiff,	John.	Sergeant	M-F-S
1564	Barker,	John Joseph.	Sergeant	M-F-S
460	Batho,	Thomas.	Sergeant	M-F-S
801	Birks,	Joseph.	Sergeant	M-F-S
1621	Bish,	John.	Sergeant	M-F-S
920	Blackburn,	William.	Sergeant	M-F-S
1137	Brannagan,	Christopher.	Sergeant	M-S
868	Buxton,	Thomas.	Sergeant	M-F-S
1433	Billington,	William.	Corporal	M-F-S
1346	Bleack*,	Thomas.	Corporal	M-F
1958	Brown*,	Thomas.	Corporal	M-F
1715	Broad,	Thomas.	Drummer	M-F-S
1606	Bailey,	Charles.	Private	M-F-S
622	Bailey,	John.	Private	M-F-S
2096	Bailey*,	John.	Private	M-F
1073	Bailey,	Thomas.	Private	M-F-S
2051	Balderson,	James.	Private	M-F-S
2211	Banton,	Henry.	Private	M-F-S
1209	Barclay,	Hugh.	Private	M-F
1987	Barden,	George.	Private	M-F-S
1675	Barker,	Richard.	Private	M-F-S
951	Barlow*,	James.	Private	M-F-S
1530	Barnes,	Josiah.	Private	M-F-S
2248	Barnes,	Thomas.	Private	M-F
2169	Bartlett,	Samuel.	Private	M-F-S
533	Barton,	Robert.	Private	M-F-S
2071	Bates,	John.	Private	M-F-S
1696	Bates*,	Thomas.	Private	M-F-S
2171	Bates*,	Thomas.	Private	M-F
1305	Bathgate,	Robert.	Private	M-F
1273	Baxter,	Richard.	Private	M-F-S
1146	Beamish,	William.	Private	M-F-S
1695	Beardsley,	William.	Private	M-F-S
1613	Beaty,	John.	Private	M-F-S
2150	Beck,	John.	Private	M-F-S

1902	Benstead*,	James.	Private	M-F-S
1280	Bentley,	John.	Private	M-F-S
973	Berry,	James.	Private	A-S
2250	Besley*,	William.	Private	M-F-S
2256	Beswick,	John.	Private	M-F-S
1849	Biddulph,	William.	Private	M-F-S
2115	Billing,	John.	Private	M-F-S
2213	Bishop*,	John.	Private	M-F-S
1687	Blades*,	Thomas.	Private	M-F
2235	Blatchley,	Edward.	Private	M-F-S
923	Boardman*,	John.	Private	M-F-S
1878	Bobbins,	William.	Private	M-F-S
2105	Bolton,	William.	Private	M-F-S
1609	Boorman,	Edward.	Private	M-F-S
2142	Boot,	Joseph.	Private	M-F-S
2016	Boreham,	Thomas.	Private	M-F-S
2052	Bottomley,	George.	Private	M-F-S
2234	Bowen,	Jessie.	Private	M-F-S
2194	Bowler*,	Edward.	Private	M-F
1341	Boyles,	Stewart.	Private	M-F-S
2239	Brennan,	James.	Private	M-F-S
909	Brierly*,	James.	Private	M-F-S
869	Brooks,	James.	Private	M-F-S
1597	Brooks*,	James.	Private	M-F-S
2236	Brooks,	John.	Private	M-F-S
1323	Broom,	Hugh.	Private	M-F-S
2178	Broughton,	George.	Private	M-F-S
1037	Brown,	Charles.	Private	M-F-S
1970	Brown,	David.	Private	M-F-S
1215	Brown,	George.	Private	M-F-S
1590	Brown,	James.	Private	M-F-S
1548	Brown*,	William.	Private	M-F-S
1998	Brown,	William.	Private	M-F-S
2260	Brown,	William.	Private	M-F-S
1932	Bryant,	George.	Private	M-F-S
1610	Burchett,	Allan.	Private	M-F-S
1724	Burden*,	George.	Private	M
1744	Burgess,	John.	Private	M-F-S
2187	Burnes*,	James.	Private	M-F-S
2010	Bush,	Charles.	Private	M-F-S
933	Butler,	Daniel.	Private	M-F-S
1707	Butler*,	David.	Private	M-F
1665	Butler,	Henry.	Private	M-F-S
2231	Button,	John.	Private	M-F-S
1801	Bye,	John.	Private	M-F-S
1781	Byrne*,	Patrick.	Private	M-F-S
2065	Byrne,	Patrick.	Private	M-F-S
	Cookson*,	William,	Captain	M-F-S
	Coleman,	Wlm Frederick Adams.	Lieutenant	M-F-S
	Crawley*,	Richard.	Lieutenant	M-F-S
704	Crawford,	George.	Non-Commissioned Staff	M-F-S
1441	Christian*,	John.	Sergeant	M-S
764	Cleghorn,	Ralph.	Sergeant	M-F-S
1223	Connell,	John.	Sergeant	M-F-S
1358	Cooper,	John.	Sergeant	M-F-S
1586	Cromar,	William.	Sergeant	M-F-S
1501	Curtis,	Edward.	Sergeant	M-F-S
1929	Clayton*,	John.	Corporal	M-F
2147	Coghlan,	John.	Corporal	M-F-S
1445	Constable,	William.	Corporal	M-F-S
2136	Cagby,	George.	Private	M-F-S
1877	Cagby*,	William.	Private	M-F
2252	Campbell,	James.	Private	M-F-S
2258	Cavanagh,*	James.	Private	M-F
2026	Cavanagh,	William.	Private	M-F-S
1701	Cave,	Jabez.	Private	M-F-S
1768	Chalmers,	James.	Private	M-F-S
1879	Chapman,*	James.	Private	M-F-S
1732	Chenvours,	Cornelius.	Private	M-F-S
	(1732 Chevours, Cornelius)			
1817	Chippington,	George.	Private	M-F-S
1656	Christian,	John.	Private	M-F-S
1600	Christian,	Thomas.	Private	M-F-S
1760	Church,	William.	Private	M-F-S

1983	Churchman,	James.	Private	M-F-S
2141	Claringbold,	Henry.	Private	M-F-S
2181	Clarke,	James.	Private	M-F-S
2182	Clarke,	James.	Private	M-F-S
1911	Clarke*,	William.	Private	M-F
2103	Clay,	Joshua.	Private	M-F-S
1282	Clayton*,	William.	Private	M-F
1828	Clements,	Thomas.	Private	M-F-S
1909	Coadwell,	James.	Private	M-F-S
1866	Coghlan*,	John.	Private	M-F-S
1637	Collins,	James.	Private	M-F-S
1841	Conisky,	Michael.	Private	M-F-S
1688	Connell,	James.	Private	M-F-S
1622	Connolly,	John.	Private	M-F-S
1995	Connolly,	John.	Private	M-F-S
2119	Connor*,	Richard.	Private	M-F
1907	Cook,	George.	Private	M-F-S
852	Cook,	Henry.	Private	A-S
1075	Cook*,	John.	Private	M-F-S
1361	Cooke,	Henry.	Private	M-F-S
2080	Cooke,	William.	Private	M-F-S
1923	Cooper*,	Frederick.	Private	M-F-S
1776	Cox,	Frederick.	Private	M-F-S
2127	Cox*,	John.	Private	M-F
1927	Craddock,	Henry.	Private	M-F-S
2123	Crask,	William.	Private	M-F
1706	Crawford,	William.	Private	M-F-S
2227	Crowley*,	John.	Private	M-F
	De Quincey,	Paul Frederick.	Lieutenant	S
1888	Day,	John Stephen.	Non-Commissioned Staff	M-F
1009	Donagher,	William.	Corporal	M-F-S
1605	Donovan,	Timothy.	Corporal	M-F-S
1819	Dempsey,	John.	Drummer	M-F-S
1956	Daley,	Patrick.	Private	M-F-S
2242	Danton*,	William.	Private	M-F
1652	Dare,	George.	Private	M-F-S
1992	Darrant,	John.	Private	M-F-S
1832	Davis,	Isaac.	Private	M-F-S
1928	Davis,	James.	Private	M-F-S
782	Davison*,	Farrington.	Private	M-F-S
1532	Davison,	William.	Private	M-F-S
1946	Day,	William.	Private	M-F-S
1595	Deaken,	Robert.	Private	M-F-S
1705	Deakin,	John.	Private	M-F-S
1070	Dean,	Matthew Martin.	Private	M-F-S
2032	Denton*,	Ebenezer.	Private	M-F
2228	Devitt,	James.	Private	M-F-S
1996	Dickinson,	James.	Private	M-F-S
1344	Dickson*,	David.	Private	M-F-S
1861	Dison*,	Thomas.	Private	M-F-S
2207	Dixon*,	Thomas.	Private	M
2160	Doggett,	William.	Private	M-F-S
2214	Donald,	David,	Private	M-F-S
2114	Donnoly,	John.	Private	M-F-S
2002	Donohue,	Alexander.	Private	M-F-S
	(2002 Donohoe, Alexander.)			
1533	Douglas*,	James.	Private	M-F
1292	Dow*,	Joseph.	Private	M-F-S
1807	Duran*,	Robert.	Private	M-F-S
1506	Durrance,	Charles.	Private	M-F-S
1741	Dycks,	William.	Private	M-F-S
1534	**Eagan***,	Thomas.	Private	M-F-S
1931	Eagle,	John.	Private	M-F-S
2124	Eames,	William.	Private	M-F
1977	East*,	Alfred.	Private	M-F
491	Eastman*,	William.	Private	M-F
930	Eastwood,	James.	Private	M-F
1690	Eaton*,	Thomas.	Private	A-S
1565	Edis*,	Robert.	Private	M-F
1918	Edwards,	Edward.	Private	M-F-S
1716	Edwards,	George.	Private	M-F-S
1615	Edwards,	John.	Private	M-F-S
1692	Edwards,	John.	Private	A-S
1276	Edwards*,	Thomas.	Private	M-F

No.	Surname	First name	Rank	Medals
541	Eke*,	Timothy.	Private	M-F
1416	Elliot,	Michael.	Private	M-F-S
1138	Ellis*,	Ernest.	Private	M-F-S
2063	Ellis,	George.	Private	M-F-S
1421	Ellis,	William.	Private	M-F-S
1916	Emmings,	James.	Private	M-F-S
1078	Evans*,	Barton.	Private	M-F
2196	Evans,	Henry.	Private	M-F-S
2216	Evans*,	Joseph.	Private	M-F-S
1941	Everett*,	John.	Private	M-F-S
1362	Everhurst,	George.	Private	M-F-S
1492	Everitt,	Edmund.	Private	M-F-S
2005	Ewing,	John.	Private	M-F-S
1772	Eylward,	Thomas.	Private	M-F-S
2041	Eyre,	Stephen.	Private	M-F-S
	Fraser,	Simon.	Lieutenant	M-F
	Freeman*,	Mathew Deane.	Lieutenant	M-F
1894	Files,	John William.	Non-Commissioned Staff	M-F-S
637	Funney,	John.	Non-Commissioned Staff	M-F-S
2249	Freeman,	Patrick.	Sergeant	M-F-S
1640	Fagney*,	Daniel.	Corporal	M-F
1312,	Feanis,	Joseph.	Corporal	M-F-S
1194	Fleming*,	George.	Corporal	M-F-S
1717	Forsey,	John.	Corporal	M-F-S
1098	Florey*,	William.	Drummer	M-F-S
2104	Fairburn,	James.	Private	A-S
1252	Farmer,	Jabez.	Private	M-F-S
1651	Faulkes,	Benjamin.	Private	M-F-S
791	Faulkner,	William.	Private	M-F-S
1553	Faunes,	Thomas.	Private	M-F-S
1314	Ferguson,	John.	Private	M-F
1830	Field*,	Edward.	Private	M-F-S
1378	*Field,	William.	Private	M-F-S
1378	*Fielder,	William.	Private	M-F-S
1702	Fielding,	Henry.	Private	M-F-S
1581	Finnigan,	Patrick.	Private	M-F-S
1343	Fisher*,	James.	Private	M-F
1427	Flannery*,	Patrick.	Private	M-F-S
2237	Fletcher,	Francis.	Private	M-F-S
1821	Floyd,	Richard.	Private	M-F-S
1601	Foden,	Joseph.	Private	M-F-S
1010	Foot,	James.	Private	M-F-S
1498	Foote*,	Henry.	Private	M-F
1720	Foote,	John.	Private	M-F-S
1616	Foothead*,	John Norris.	Private	M-F
1793	Fordham*,	Charles.	Private	M-F-S
1507	Foreman*,	Caleb.	Private	M-F-S
1984	Foster,	William.	Private	M-F-S
2028	Fowler*,	John.	Private	M-F
891	Fox,	Thomas.	Private	M-F-S
1109	Frame,	George.	Private	M-F-S
1069	Franck*,	John.	Private	M-F
2019	Franklin,	David.	Private	M-F-S
2062	Fraser,	William.	Private	M-F-S
1270	Freeman*,	William.	Private	M-F-S
1403	French,	Charles.	Private	M-F-S
1390	French,	Francis.	Private	M-F-S
2035	French,	Mark.	Private	M-F-S
1620	French*,	Raymond.	Private	M-F
1623	Friend,	Thomas.	Private	M-F-S
1914	Frost,	John R.	Private	M-F-S
1021	Frost*,	William.	Private	M-F
1085	Fullerton,	James.	Private	M-F-S
	Gammie,	Patrick.	Assistant Surgeon.	M-F-A-S
893	Griffiths,	James.	Sergeant	M-F-S
1271	Garrick,	James.	Corporal	M-F-S
1957	Geeves,	James.	Corporal	M-F-S
1948	Giles,	Richard.	Corporal	M-F-S
970	Goodhall*,	Edmond.	Corporal	M-F-S
497	Gray,	John.	Corporal	M-F-S
1972	Gaffey,	James.	Private	M-F-S
2075	Gafney,	John.	Private	M-F-S
1027	Galvin,	James.	Private	M-F-S
1767	Gamester,*	Robert.	Private	M-F-S
1764	Gardner,	John.	Private	M-F-S
1811	Gardner,	William.	Private	M-F-S
1870	Garner,	Begley.	Private	M-F-S
1628	Gary,	William.	Private	M-F-S
1869	Geddes,	John.	Private	M-F-S
	(1869 Geddies, John.)			
1197	Gillies*,	George.	Private	M-F-S
2013	Gilligan*,	Owen.	Private	A
2153	Golher*,	John.	Private	M-F-S
2084	Goodenough,	James.	Private	M-F-S
832	Gooderhave,	William.	Private	M-F
511	Goodwin,	William.	Private	M-F-S
2158	Gordon,	John.	Private	M-F-S
2016	Gore,	Thomas.	Private	M-F-S
1864	Graham,	Cornelius.	Private	M-F-S
1329	Granger*,	John.	Private	M-F-S
1149	Greaves,	Charles.	Private	M-F-S
1626	Green,	Charles.	Private	M-F-S
1997	Green*,	Joseph.	Private	M-F
1726	Green,	Thomas.	Private	M-F-S
1751	Green*,	William.	Private	M-F-S
2198	Green,	William.	Private	M-F-S
264	Greenway,	James.	Private	M-F-S
1503	Greenwood,	James.	Private	M-F-S
794	Greer,	David.	Private	M-F-S
1068	Greer*,	John.	Private	M-F-S
1735	Gregson,	Thomas George.	Private	M-F-S
2210	Grimes,	Thomas.	Private	M-F-S
	(2210 Grime, Thomas.)			
	Haines,	Frederick Paul.	Captain	M-F
	Hardinge,	Arthur Edward.	Lieutenant	M-F-S
	Hardinge,	Edward.	Lieutenant	M-F-S
	Holditch,*	Edward Alan.	Lieutenant	M-F-A-S
	Hunter,	William.	Lieutenant	S
	Hunt,	Thomas Bloomfield.	Pay Master	M-F
	Hayes*,	Frederick.	Quarter Master	M-F-S
	Hunt,	Thomas Bloomfield.	Surgeon	M-F-S
1240	Harrison,	John.	Sergeant	M-F-S
1028	Hart*,	John.	Sergeant	M-F-S
681	Hulme,	Thomas.	Sergeant	M-F-S
1677	Heusenran*,	William.	Corporal	M-F
1804	Higgins,	James.	Corporal	M-F
1536	Hirst,	Robert.	Corporal	M-F-S
1895	Horam,	James.	Drummer	M-F-S
1738	Hale,	Ezekiel.	Private	M-F-S
1919	Hale,	William.	Private	M-F-S
1947	Hall,	George.	Private	M-F-S
1460	Hall,	James.	Private	M-F-S
587	Hall*	,James.	Private	M-F
984	Hall,	John.	Private	M-F-S
1144	Hall*,	John.	Private	A
1660	Hall,	Thomas.	Private	M-F-S
1437	Hall,	William.	Private	M-F-S
2168	Hall*,	William.	Private	M-F-S
1368	Halliday,	John.	Private	M-F-S
1784	Halligan,	John.	Private	M-F-S
2217	Hamilton,	James.	Private	M-F-S
1961	Hammond,	Joseph.	Private	M-F-S
955	Hanson,	John.	Private	M-F-S
1768	Harding*,	John.	Private	M-F
1994	Harding,	John.	Private	A-S
1872	Hardwick*,	George.	Private	M-F-S
743	Hare,	Robert.	Private	M-F-S
1313	Harp*,	Thomas.	Private	M-F-S
	(1313 Horpe, Thomas.)			
1725	Harrington*,	George.	Private	M-F-S
2088	Harrington,	James.	Private	M-F-S
1587	Harris*,	William.	Private	M-F
1867	Harrison,	James.	Private	M-F-S
2200	Harrison,	Thomas.	Private	M-F-S
755	Hart*,	John.	Private	M-F
813	Harvey*,	Thomas.	Private	M-F
1930	Hayes,	Richard.	Private	M-F-S
2074	Haywood*,	George.	Private	M-F

1732	Heathcock,	Thomas.	Private	M-F-S
2097	Henderson,	James.	Private	M-F-S
1014	Hennessy*,	Michael.	Private	M
1913	Hercock*,	George.	Private	M-F-S
1614	Herrick,	Thomas.	Private	M-F-S
1723	Herrick,	William.	Private	M-F-S
1196	Heveran*,	John.	Private	M-F-S
1025	Hewett,	George.	Private	M-F
1787	Hick,	Thomas.	Private	M-F-S
588	Highgreaves,	Francis.	Private	M-F-S
1788	Higgins,	Henry.	Private	M-F-S
1942	Hilaage,	Thomas.	Private	M-F-S
1814	Hill*,	David.	Private	M-F-S
1827	Hill,	George.	Private	M-F-S
1188	Hill*,	Nicholas.	Private	M-F
2099	Hill*,	William.	Private	M-F-S
1401	Hills*,	George.	Private	M-F-S
1034	Hillsby,	Charles.	Private	M-F-S
1698	Hinton,	Israel.	Private	M-F-S
1806	Hobbs*,	Robert.	Private	M-F-S
1700	Hodgson,	William.	Private	M-F-S
1602	Hodson,	John.	Private	M-F-S
1596	Hollowell,	George.	Private	M-F-S
2121	Holmes,	Ralph.	Private	A-S
2262	Holmes,	William.	Private	M-F-S
2102	Homan,	Richard.	Private	M-F-S
1889	Homes,	Henry.	Private	M-F-S
917	Homored*,	Henry.	Private	M-F-S
1315	Hope,	James.	Private	M-F
1118	Hough,	John.	Private	M-F-S
1151	Hough,	John.	Private	M-F-S
1160	Howard,	John.	Private	M-F-S
1926	Howard*,	John.	Private	M-F
614	Howard,	Thomas.	Private	M-F
751	Howe,	David.	Private	M-F-S
1324	Howison,	George.	Private	M-F-S
1871	Huggins,	James.	Private	M-F-S
2172	Hughes,	Richard.	Private	M-F-S
1629	Humphries	Edward.	Private	M-F
1922	Hurley,	Dennis.	Private	M-F-S
1641	Husk,	John.	Private	M-F-S
525	Hutton*,	William.	Private	M-F-S
35	**Irwin**,	James.	Sergeant	M-F-S
1309	Imphett,	William.	Drummer	M-F-S
1438	Irwin,	George.	Drummer	M-F
1040	Imeson,	William.	Private	M-F-S
1008	**Johnstone**,	Frederick.	Non-Commissioned Staff	M-F-S
822	Janaway,	John.	Sergeant	M-F-S
46	Johnson,	Thomas.	Sergeant	M-F-S
1953	Jones.	William.	Sergeant	M-F-S
1797	James,	Joshua.	Corporal	M-F-S
2202	Jenkins,	Thomas.	Corporal	M-F-S
1973	Jones,	James.	Corporal	M-F-S
1508	Jackson,	George.	Private	M-F-S
1847	Jakes,	Joseph.	Private	M-F-S
2030	James,	John.	Private	M-F-S
1645	James,	Thomas.	Private	M-F-S
1592	Jaunstone,	Frederick.	Private	M-F-S
1934	Jay,	Henry.	Private	M-F-S
864	Jennings*,	Edward.	Private	M-F-S
1989	Jinks,	Edward.	Private	M-F-S
1517	Johnson,	Edward.	Private	M-F-S
	(1517 Johnston, Edward.)			
1756	Johnson*,	John.	Private	M-F
2037	Johnson,	Joseph.	Private	M-F-S
2156	Johnsone,	Thomas.	Private	M-F-S
1038	Jones,	David.	Private	M-F-S
887	Jones,	Edward.	Private	M-F-S
1562	Jones,	James.	Private	M-F-S
1284	Jones*,	Thomas.	Private	M-F
2152	Jones,	Thomas.	Private	M-
1739	Jones	William.	Private	M-F-S
2098	Jones*,	William.	Private	M-F-S
2149	Jordan,	Patrick.	Private	M-F-S
1886	Jude,	Page.	Private	M-F-S
	Kershaw,	Stewart Alexander.	Lieutenant	M-F-S
	Kingsley*,	Edward William Pincke.	Lieutenant	A-S
1057	Kirkland*,	Matthew.	Colour Sergeant	M-F
681	Key,	William.	Sergeant	M-F-S
1745	Kilby,	John.	Corporal	M-F-S
	(1745 Kelly, John.)			
1617	King*,	David.	Corporal	M-F-S
2012	Kelly,	Charles.	Private	M-F-S
1260	Kelly*,	Edward.	Private	M-F
1015	Kelly,	John.	Private	M-F-S
2066	Kelly*,	John.	Private	M-F
1649	Kemp,	Frederick.	Private	M-F-S
1893	Kemp,	Thomas.	Private	M-F-S
1908	Kent,	James.	Private	M-F-S
1734	Kerry,	William.	Private	M-F-S
2233	Kesterson*,	Peter.	Private	M-F-S
1752	King,	George.	Private	M-F-S
1259	King,	James.	Private	M-F-S
1920	King,	John D'Catter.	Private	M-F-S
2126	Kinton,	Richard.	Private	M-F-S
2100	Kitching,	Robert.	Private	M-F-S
1990	Knott,	George.	Private	M-F-S
	Lockhart*,	Robert Alexander.	Major	M-F-S
	Leslie,	Charles Henry.	Captain	M-F-S
	Lewis,	Charles.	Captain	M-F-S
632	Loone,	Daniel.	Sergeant	M-F-S
2049	Lucas*,	Hardman.	Corporal	M-F-S
1096	Lett*,	Edward.	Drummer	M-F-S
1796	Lacey,	William.	Private	M-F-S
1838	Lackey,	James.	Private	M-F-S
2170	Lafargue,	Peter.	Private	M-F-S
2238	Laisler*,	Mark.	Private	M-F-S
1237	Lamborn*,	John.	Private	M-F-S
1528	Lancaster,	Josias.	Private	M-F-S
1035	Lang*,	Robert.	Private	M-F-S
2268	Laurence,	William.	Private	M-F-S
1604	Laurie*,	James.	Private	M-F
1885	Leadbetter,	James.	Private	M-F-S
	(1885 Leadbeater, James.)			
997	Leason,	George.	Private	M-F-S
962	Lee*,	Philip.	Private	M-F
1603	Lee,	Ralph.	Private	M-F-S
1420	Lennan,	William.	Private	M-F-S
843	Lennington,	George.	Private	M-F
799	Lett,	Charles.	Private	M-F-S
1729	Lewing,	William.	Private	M-F-S
2248	Lewington	John.	Private	M-F-S
1558	Lewis,	Daniel.	Private	M-F-S
2230	Lewis,	Henry.	Private	M-F-S
1593	Lightfoot,	William.	Private	M-F-S
1509	Lilley*,	Thomas.	Private	M-F
2113	Lloyd*,	William.	Private	M-F-S
1743	Lock,	John.	Private	M-F-S
714	Lockett*,	George.	Private	M-F-S
1094	Lockett,	Patrick.	Private	M-F-S
1298	Lockett,	Thomas.	Private	M-F-S
1114	Long,	Charles.	Private	M-F-S
1773	Long,	William.	Private	M-F-S
1588	Lovegrove*,	Levi.	Private	M-F-S
2057	Lowe,	Benjamin.	Private	M-F-S
1685	Lowe,	David.	Private	M-F-S
1519	Lunn,	John.	Private	M-F-S
	Montgomery,	Lambert Lyons.	Captain	M-F-S
1794	McAtee,	Henry.	Sergeant	M-F-S
1624	Maloney,	William.	Sergeant	M-F-S
1546	Mott*,	William.	Sergeant	M-F-S
1808	Muir,	Robert.	Sergeant	M-F-S
1689	McIntosh,	Henry.	Corporal	M-F-S
1709	Marsh,	John.	Corporal	M-F-S
1108	Millar*,	Charles.	Corporal	M-F-S
2176	Morgan,	John.	Corporal	M-F-S
1737	Morris,	Henry Edward.	Corporal	M-F-S
1836	Muir,	John.	Corporal	M-F-S

2069	Murphy,	Jeremiah.	Corporal	M-F-S
1896	McDermott*,	William.	Drummer	M-F
1206	McKean,	Thomas.	Drummer	M-F-S
1510	Madden,	John.	Drummer	M-F-S
661	Malster,	Robert.	Drummer	M-F-S
2004	McBride,	Joseph.	Private	M-F-S
2243	McCabe,	Joseph.	Private	M-F-S
1397	McCarthy,	Jeremiah.	Private	M-F-S
1627	McCauley,	Henry.	Private	M-F-S
878	McClain*,	Joseph.	Private	M-F
1195	McClaren,	James.	Private	M-F
1816	McCowan,	William.	Private	M-F-S
1611	McGary,	John.	Private	M-F-S
	(1611 McGarry, John.)			
1515	McGinnis,	Michael.	Private	A-S
1818	McGregor,	Archibald.	Private	A-S
1134	McJemeson,	William.	Private	M-F-S
2073	McKenny,	Thomas.	Private	M-F-S
	(2073 McKinny, Thomas.)			
1905	McLaughlin,	Francis.	Private	M-F-S
2014	McMahon,	John.	Private	M-F-S
	(2014 MacMahon, John.)			
2007	McMehon,	Joseph.	Private	M-F-S
2177	McNeilly*,	William.	Private	M-F
1892	McQuade*,	Peter.	Private	M-F-S
1845	MacDonald,	William John.	Private	M-F-S
1047	MacDowell,	William.	Private	M-F-S
2173	Machon,	Thomas.	Private	M-F-S
1830	Madden,	John.	Private	M-F-S
1742	Maddocks,	George.	Private	M-F-S
640	Madine*,	Patrick.	Private	M-F
1102	Magee,	Fenton.	Private	M-F-S
	(1102 Magee, Fanton.)			
1708	Magee,*	James.	Private	M-F
1538	Maguire,	George.	Private	M-F-S
	(1538 McGuire, George.)			
2025	Magvrwa,	Laurence.	Private	M-F
659	Malpas,	George.	Private	M-F-S
1578	Manning,	James.	Private	M-F-S
865	Mansbridge*,	John.	Private	M-F
	(865 Mausbridge, John.)			
766	Manson,	Robert.	Private	M-F-S
1385	Markham,	John.	Private	M-F
2193	Mason,	William.	Private	M-F-S
1968	Massey*,	Edward.	Private	M-F-S
	(1968 Massey, Edmond.)			
1126	Massey*,	Paul.	Private	M-F-S
1755	May,	Charles.	Private	M-F
1949	Meadows,	James.	Private	M-F-S
842	Membery,	John.	Private	M-F-S
1906	Middleditch,	Benjamin.	Private	M-F-S
813	Miles,	James.	Private	M-F-S
1063	Millar,	James.	Private	M-F-S
1963	Milligan*,	John.	Private	M-F-S
572	Milner*,	Thomas.	Private	M-F
1800	Mitchell,	Henry.	Private	M-F-S
1654	Mitchell*,	John.	Private	M-F-S
2046	Mitchell,	Joseph.	Private	M-F-S
1679	Moisey,	Thomas.	Private	M-F-S
1680	Moisey,	William.	Private	M-F-S
1899	Money*,	John.	Private	M
1446	Moneypenny,	John.	Private	M-F-S
1872	Moore,	James.	Private	M-F-S
2138	Moore*,	James.	Private	M-F-S
3220	Moore,	John.	Private	M-F-S
1964	Morgan,	David.	Private	M-F-S
1630	Morgan*,	Thomas.	Private	M-F-S
1951	Morris,	George.	Private	M-F-S
2257	Morris,	John.	Private	M-F-S
1500	Morris,	William.	Private	M-F-
1754	Mortimer,	Henry.	Private	M-F-S
1171	Moreton*,	Thomas.	Private	M-F
2186	Moss,	Edgar.	Private	M-F-S
1668	Mothershaw*,	Thomas.	Private	M-F-S

1366	Murdock,	Hugh.	Private	M-F-S
1839	Murphy,	John Thomas.	Private	M-F-S
2067	Murphy,	Joseph.	Private	M-F-S
2143	Murphy*,	Michael.	Private	M-F-S
1833	Murray,	Robert.	Private	M-F-S
1579	Murtagh,	Patrick.	Private	M-F-S
1992	Myers,	John.	Private	M-F-S
	Nunn,	James Loftus Winniett,	Major	M-F-S
1607	Neaves,	William.	Sergeant	M-F-S
1608	Neaves,	William.	Sergeant	M-F-S
1061	Nixon,	James.	Corporal	M-F-S
1706	Nash,	James.	Private	M-F-S
1682	Neaves,	Thomas.	Drummer	M-F-S
1561	Newell*,	John.	Private	M
2225	Newlan,	William.	Private	M-F-S
2111	Nicholls,	Alfred.	Private	M-F-S
756	Nicklin*,	Thomas.	Private	A-S
1819	Nicol,	John.	Private	M-F-S
1750	Nichols,	James.	Private	M-F
	(1750 Nicholls, James.)			
1596	Nixon,	Edward.	Private	M-F
1662	Nixon*,	John.	Private	M-F
2196	Norbury,	Peter.	Private	M-F-S
2246	Norris*,	James.	Private	M-F-S
2026	Noyes*,	John.	Private	M-F-S
1945	Nunn*,	Jonathan.	Private	M-F
	Ormsby,	Anthony.	Captain	A-S
935	Oddey*,	Benjamin.	Private	M-F
1975	O'Dowd,	James.	Private	M-F-S
2159	Oldfield,	Simeon.	Private	M-F-S
938	Ormrod*,	George.	Private	M-F-S
867	O'Riley,	Philip.	Private	M-F-S
1218	Orr*,	Edward.	Private	M-F
2087	**Purchase**,	Nicholas.	Sergeant	M-F-S
1526	Parrott,	Frederick.	Drummer	M-F-S
1704	Pendry,	Edmond.	Drummer	M-F-S
	(1704 Pendery, Edmund.)			
1511	Padgett,	Luke.	Private	M-F-S
1954	Page*,	William.	Private	M-F-S
1639	Paice,	Charles.	Private	M-F-S
1301	Palmer*,	William.	Private	M-F
1901	Parcel,	Richard.	Private	M-F-S
833	Parker,	John.	Private	M-F-S
1805	Parkes*,	William.	Private	M-F-S
1944	Parsons,	Allan.	Private	M-F-S
1225	Partridge,	Thomas.	Private	M-F-S
2166	Patten*,	Edward.	Private	M-F
1520	Peake*,	George.	Private	A-S
2148	Peppard,	William Standish.	Private	M-F-S
2212	Peto,	Edward.	Private	M-F-S
1107	Phelan*,	John.	Private	M-F
2223	Philips,	James.	Private	M-F-S
	(2223 Phillips, James.)			
1205	Philips,	John.	Private	M-F-S
	(1205 Phillips, John.)			
1619	Piercey*,	Thomas.	Private	M-F-S
	(1619 Purcy, Thomas.)			
946	Porter*,	James.	Private	M-F-S
1568	Porter,	James.	Private	M-F-S
1676	Powell*,	Thomas.	Private	M-F-S
1898	Pratchett,	Thomas.	Private	M-F-S
2079	Price*,	Henry.	Private	M-F-S
1916	Purdie,	James.	Private	M-F-S
1825	Purdy,	Edwin.	Private	M-F-S
1727	Purseglove,	Francis.	Private	M-F-S
1660	Pye,	Thomas.	Private	M-F-S
1786	**Quinn***,	Alexander.	Private	M-F
1091	Quinn*,	Edward.	Private	M-F-S
	Riley,	Alexander William.	Captain	M-F-S
1295	Reed,	Robert.	Sergeant	M-F-S
1567	Roberts,	Joseph.	Sergeant	M-F-S
1666	Robinson,	James.	Sergeant	M-F-S
1299	Rodmore,	George.	Sergeant	M-F-S
1442	Rudkin,	Daniel.	Sergeant	M-F-S

No.	Surname	Forename	Rank	Medals
547	Robinson,	Isaac.	Corporal	M-F-S
1809	Rickards,	Charles.	Drummer	M-F-S
	(1809 Richards, Charles.)			
1220	Rae*,	David.	Private	M-F
2009	Rafter,	Thomas.	Private	M-F
2064	Rahilly,	Dennis.	Private	M-F-S
	(2064 Rahilley, Dennis.)			
1810	Randle*,	William.	Private	A-S
2056	Ranton,	William.	Private	M-F-S
1382	Ratcliffe,	James.	Private	M-F-S
2146	Ratcliffe,	Robert.	Private	M-F-S
1119	Rathbone*,	James.	Private	M-F
1238	Rawley,	John.	Private	M-F-S
	(1238 Rowley, John.)			
2024	Redican*,	Thomas.	Private	M-F-S
1890	Reeve*,	William.	Private	M-F
1122	Reeves,	William.	Private	M-F-S
1254	Reid,	James.	Private	M-F-S
1999	Reid,	Mark.	Private	M-F-S
2244	Reynolds,	George.	Private	M-F-S
830	Reynolds*,	John.	Private	M-F
1584	Rice*,	William.	Private	A
2029	Richards*,	James.	Private	M-F-S
1831	Richardson,	Henry.	Private	M-F
2043	Rix,	Samuel.	Private	M-F-S
2437	Roberts*,	Charles.	Private	A
2192	Roberts,	James.	Private	M-F-S
2188	Roberts,	Thomas.	Private	M-F-S
2085	Robinson*,	John.	Private	M-F
1921	Rodgers*,	Thomas.	Private	M-F
	(1921 Rogers, Thomas.)			
1789	Rolfe*,	Thomas.	Private	M-F
1181	Ross,	John.	Private	M-F-S
1900	Rusby,	William.	Private	M-F-S
1319	Russell,	Richard.	Private	M-F-S
2165	Ryan,	Augustin.	Private	M-F-S
	(2165 Ryan, Augustine.)			
1928	Ryan,	Timothy.	Private	M-F-S
	Sayers,	Richard Talbot.	Captain	M-F-S
	Scheberras*,	Rinaldo.	Captain	M-F
	Smith,	Hamilton Charles.	Lieutenant	A
722	Stanfield*,	Thomas.	Sergeant	M-F-S
1179	Storey*,	Thomas.	Sergeant	M
2251	Stokes,	James.	Corporal	M-F-S
2258	Simmonds*,	Thomas.	Drummer	M-F
1917	Sale*,	James.	Private	M-F-S
1388	Sanderson,	George.	Private	M-F-S
862	Sawyer,	Samuel.	Private	M-F-S
2032	Scott,	John.	Private	M-F-S
1555	Scott*,	William.	Private	M-F-S
1663	Seppings*,	Alfred.	Private	M-F
1265	Shanks,	William.	Private	M-F-S
1848	Shaw,	Hugh.	Private	M-F
2107	Shaw,	John.	Private	M-F
1350	Shearing*,	John.	Private	M-F-S
2161	Shephard*,	William.	Private	M-F-S
1884	Sherratt,	Robert.	Private	M-F-S
2137	Shields,	David.	Private	M-F
793	Shilton,	William.	Private	M-F-S
890	Shore*,	Edward.	Private	M-F
924	Shore,	John.	Private	M-F-S
1417	Shouk,	Thomas.	Private	M-F-S
1274	Silvey,	Edward.	Private	M-F
1746	Simmonds,	Isaac.	Private	M-F-S
937	Simpson*,	James.	Private	A
1785	Sims,	Daniel.	Private	M-F-S
2140	Skinner,	John.	Private	M-F-S
2042	Skinner*,	Thomas.	Private	M-F
829	Slade*,	Isaac.	Private	M-F-S
740	Smalwood,	Stephen.	Private	M-F-S
1232	Smeaton,	Charles.	Private	M-F-S
1369	Smith*,	Andrew.	Private	M-F
1671	Smith*,	Charles.	Private	M-F-S
2000	Smith,	Edward.	Private	M-F-S
1393	Smith*,	George.	Private	M-F-S
2059	Smith,	George.	Private	M-F
1980	Smith,	James.	Private	M-F-S
1962	Smith,	John.	Private	M-F-S
2107	Smith,	John.	Private	M-F-S
2118	Smith,	John. (Alias John Duffett)	Private	M-F-S
2205	Smith	John.	Private	M-F-S
691	Smith,	Joseph.	Private	M-F-S
2201	Smith,	Robert.	Private	M-F-S
1527	Smith,	Thomas.	Private	M-F-S
1306	Smyth,	William.	Private	M-F-S
1758	Snell,	William.	Private	M-F-S
915	Spakman,	Thomas.	Private	M-F-S
2022	Spenceby,	William.	Private	M-F-S
	(2022 Spenceley, William.)			
2195	Spicer,	George.	Private	M-F-S
1128	Sproson*,	Charles.	Private	M-F-S
1230	Stanha*,	Thomas.	Private	M-F
	(1230 Stanbra, Thomas.)			
2108	Starton,	Thomas.	Private	M-F-S
1883	Stearnes,	Alfred.	Private	M-F-S
623	Steele,	Aaron.	Private	M-F-S
2189	Steele,	Thomas,	Private	M-F-S
2088	Stewart,	Charles.	Private	M-F-S
2157	Stewart,	Thomas.	Private	M-F-S
2175	Stiles,	William.	Private	M-F-S
1965	Stokes*,	George.	Private	A-S
2072	Stokes,	Joseph.	Private	M-F-S
2162	Stroud,	Henry.	Private	M-F-S
2677	Sullivan,	Arthur.	Private	M-F-S
1351	Sunderland,	John.	Private	M-F-S
2006	Sutcliffe*,	Samuel.	Private	M-F-S
2017	Suttinstall,	Ellis.	Private	M-F-S
	(2017 Sattinstall, Ellis.)			
1582	Swan,	John.	Private	M-F-S
753	**Turner***,	Charles.	Sergeant	M-F-S
2163	Tudor,	Richard.	Corporal	M-F-S
940	Taylor,	William.	Drummer	M-F-S
2044	Talbot*,	James.	Private	M-F
1730	Talrar,	William.	Private	M-F-S
	(1730 Tabrar, William.)			
2264	Tate,	Thomas.	Private	M-F-S
1598	Tate*,	William.	Private	M-F-S
465	Taylor,	George.	Private	M-F-S
713	Taylor,	George.	Private	M-F-S
1673	Taylor,	George.	Private	M-F-S
1775	Taylor,	George.	Private	M-F-S
918	Taylor,	James.	Private	M-F-S
1965	Taylor,	James.	Private	M-F-S
1834	Terner,	Robert.	Private	M-F-S
2078	Thomas*,	Edmond.	Private	A
2148	Thomas*,	Richard.	Private	M-F-S
2048	Thomas*,	William.	Private	M-F-S
1543	Thompson,	John.	Private	M-F-S
1105	Thompson,	Philip.	Private	M-F-S
746	Thompson,	William.	Private	M-F-S
757	Thompson,	William.	Private	M-F-S
1549	Thorndicraft,	John.	Private	M-F-S
	(1549 Thorndycroft, John.)			
1516	Thrift*,	James.	Private	M-F-S
1798	Tigwell,	John.	Private	M-F-S
2106	Tiley*,	James.	Private	M-F-S
803	Tomkinson,	Thomas.	Private	M-F-S
1570	Toole*,	John.	Private	M-F
2003	Toole,	Patrick.	Private	A-S
2095	Topney*,	Robert.	Private	M-F-S
768	Turnbull,	David.	Private	A-S
1342	Turnbull,	Walter.	Private	M-F-S
1792	Turner,	Henry.	Private	M-F-S
2092	Tyler,	John.	Private	M-F-S
1771	Tyrell,	John.	Private	M-F-S
1002	**Veadon**,	John.	Corporal	M-F-S
1142	Vernon,	David.	Private	M-F-S
	Wood* (C.B.),	Robert Blucher.	Lt.Colonel	M-F-S

	Warren*,	Robert Boyle.	Lieutenant	M-F
	Welman,	Hercules Atkin.	Lieutenat and Adjutant	M-F-S
518	Walpole,	William.	Sergeant	M-F-S
1055	Watson,	Richard.	Sergeant	M-F-S
1545	Wynn,	William.	Sergeant	M-F-S
1903	Williams,	William.	Corporal	M-F
1780	Wood,	Anthony.	Corporal	M-F-S
1573	Wade,	John.	Private	M-F-S
1248	Walker*,	William.	Private	M-F
1310	Walley*,	James.	Private	M-F
1311	Walley,	Thomas.	Private	M-F-
1712	Walton,	Thomas.	Private	M-F-S
1315	Warburton,	William.	Private	M-F-S
1665	Ward*,	James.	Private	M-F
2221	Waters,	John.	Private	M-F-S
847	Waters,	William.	Private	M-F-S
682	Waterson,	John.	Private	M-F-S
1969	Watson*,	John.	Private	M-F-S
2167	Watts,	George.	Private	M-F-S
2120	Watts*,	John.	Private	M-F-S
1840	Watts,	John Wren.	Private	M-F-S
1243	Watts,	William.	Private	M-F-S
2101	Webb,	James.	Private	M-F-S
942	Webb*,	Joseph.	Private	M-F
1938	Webb,	William.	Private	M-F-S
2259	Wedderspoon*,	David.	Private	M-F-S
2197	Weldon*,	Henry.	Private	M-F
1496	Wellstead,	Edward.	Private	M-F
2252	Welton*,	John.	Private	M-F-S
1612	West,	John.	Private	M-F-S
1250	Weston,	Joseph.	Private	M-F-S
2183	White,	Charles.	Private	M-F-S
1943	White,	James.	Private	M-F-S
2034	White,	John.	Private	M-F-S
981	Whitfield,	John.	Private	M-F-S
708	Whitfield,	Wallace.	Private	M-F-S
1713	Whitwell,	William.	Private	M-F-S
988	Whitworth,	John.	Private	M-F-S

2201	Whitworth,	Thomas.	Private	M-F-S
2070	Whybrow,	William.	Private	M-F-S
788	Wilcox,	Stowe.	Private	M-F-S
1936	Williams,	Bulkely.	Private	M-F-S
	(1936 Williams, Balkeley.)			
1693	Williams,	George.	Private	M-F-S
846	Williams*,	James.	Private	M-F-S
1554	Williams,	John.	Private	M-F-S
2060	Williams*,	John.	Private	M-F-S
2191	Williams,	John.	Private	M-F
1776	Williams,	Robert.	Private	M-F-S
1560	Williamson*,	John.	Private	M-F
2241	Williamson,	William.	Private	M-F-S
1392	Wilson*,	Peter.	Private	M-F
1904	Wilson*,	Thomas.	Private	M-F
1648	Wise,	George.	Private	M-F-S
1646	Wise,	Joseph.	Private	M-F-S
1199	Wolfenden,	Thomas.	Private	M-F-S
1699	Wood*,	Elijah.	Private	M-F-S
1330	Woodall,	Joseph.	Private	M-F-S
1589	Woods,	James.	Private	M-F-S
2151	Woodward*,	James.	Private	M-F
1547	Woodward,	Samuel.	Private	M-F-S
1710	Wooger*,	Jessie.	Private	M-F
1862	Worster,	James.	Private	M-F-S
1563	Wright*,	James.	Private	M-F
828	Wright,	John.	Private	M-F
1842	Wright,	John.	Private	M-F-S
1999	Wright,	Patrick.	Private	M-F-S
2068	Wright,	Richard.	Private	M-F-S
	Young*,	George Samuel.	Lieutenant	M-F-S
1513	Yates*,	Joseph.	Private	M-F
1504	Yates*,	Richard.	Private	M-F-S
1209	Yorston,	James.	Private	M-F-S
1803	Young,	James.	Private	M-F-S
1556	Young,	John.	Private	M-F-S

1378	*Field,	William. }	This may be the the same person
1378	*Fielder,	William. }	

CASUALTIES SUTLEJ CAMPAIGN

A total of 244 names are included in the following list of casualties for the Sutlej campaign. At the battle at Moodkee on December 18th 1845 the Regiment's only officer casualty was their own Commanding Officer, Lieutenant-Colonel Bunbury who was wounded in the knee, the other ranks sustaining 5 men killed, 17 wounded and one died of wounds. At the Battle of Ferozeshah on December 21st 1845, four officers were killed, three wounded and one died of wounds; a total of 34 men were also killed and 59 wounded. On the following day one officer and four men were wounded, the total for the Regiment for this battle being 100 casualties. On February 10th 1846 at the Battle of Sobraon, four officers were wounded, and 13 men killed and 47 wounded. Two men were wounded twice, in consecutive battles. These were 1427 Private Patrick Flannery, wounded on December 18th and 21st December 1845 and 714 Private John Lockett, wounded on December 21st 1845 and February 10th 1846.

In addition to the casualty figures listed above, one officer and 8 men died later of wounds received. A total of two officers and 5 men were killed, and three men wounded, in other minor skirmishes. One officer and 40 men died, whose cause of death has not been established.

Officers

Killed	Wounded	Died of Wounds	Died	Total
4	8	2	1	15

Non Commissioned Officers and Men

Killed	Wounded	Died of Wounds	Died	Total
57	123	9	40	229

Totals

Killed	Wounded	Died of Wounds	Died	Total
61	131	11	41	244

No.	Surname	Forename	Rank	Fate	Date		
1802	Allen,	Alfred.	Sergeant	Died	11th July	1846	
1019	Allen,	Isaac.	Private	Wounded	10th Feb.	1846	
1529	Allsop,	Francis.	Private	Wounded	21st Dec.	1845	
2240	Aspden,	Benjamin.	Corporal	Slightly Wounded	22nd Dec.	1845	
685	Atkinson,	Robert.	Private	Killed	18th Dec.	1845	
2096	Bailey,	John.	Private	Died	13th Jan.	1846	
951	Barlow,	James.	Private	Died	24th June	1846	
1696	Bates,	Thomas.	Private	Wounded	10th Feb.	1846	
2171	Bates,	Thomas.	Private	Killed	21st Dec.	1845	
1902	Benstead,	James.	Private	Wounded	10th Feb.	1846	
2250	Besley,	William.	Private	Died of Wounds	17th Feb.	1846	
	Best,	Abel Dottin William.	Captain	Killed	21st Dec.	1845	
2213	Bishop,	John.	Private	Killed	10th Feb.	1846	
1687	Blades,	Thomas.	Private	Wounded	21st Dec.	1845 (invalid sent to England)	
1346	Bleack,	Thomas.	Corporal	Wounded	22nd Dec.	1845	
923	Boardman,	John.	Private	Killed	10th Feb.	1846	
2194	Bowler,	Edward.	Private	Wounded	21st Dec.	1845	
909	Brierly,	James.	Private	Died	11th June	1846	
1597	Brooks,	James.	Private	Wounded	11th Feb.	1846 (Burnt by explosion of mine)	
1958	Brown,	Thomas.	Corporal	Killed	21st Dec.	1845	
1548	Brown,	William.	Private	Wounded	21st Feb.	1846	
	Bunbury (CB)	Thomas.	Lt. Colonel	Wounded	18th Dec.	1845 (Leave to England)	
1724	Burden,	George.	Private	Died	20th Dec.	1845	
2187	Burnes,	James.	Private	Died	16th May	1846	
1707	Butler,	David.	Private	Killed	21st Dec.	1845	
1781	Byrne,	Patrick.	Private	Wounded	10th Feb.	1846 (invalid sent to England)	
	Bythesea,	George Chas Glossop.	Lieutenant	Killed	22nd Dec.	1845	
1877	Cagby,	William.	Private	Killed	21st Dec.	1845	
2258	Cavanagh,	James.	Private	Died	15th July	1846	
1879	Chapman,	James.	Private	Died of Wounds	2nd March	1846	
1441	Christian,	John.	Sergeant	Severely Wounded	21st Dec.	1845	
1911	Clarke,	William.	Private	Wounded	18th Dec.	1845	
1929	Clayton,	John.	Corporal	Wounded	18th Dec.	1845	
1282	Clayton,	William.	Private	Killed	21st Dec.	1845	
1866	Coghlan,	John.	Private	Killed	10th Feb.	1846	
2119	Connor,	Richard.	Private	Wounded	21st Dec.	1845	
1075	Cook,	John.	Private	Wounded	18th Dec.	1845	
	Cookson,	William,	Captain	Wounded	10th Feb.	1846	
1923	Cooper,	Frederick.	Private	Wounded	10th Feb.	1846	
2127	Cox,	John.	Private	Killed	21st Dec.	1845	
	Crawley,	Richard.	Lieutenant	Died of Wounds	20th Feb.	1846	
2227	Crowley,	John.	Private	Wounded	21st Dec.	1845	
2242	Danton,	William.	Private	Wounded	22nd Dec.	1845	
782	Davison,	Farrington.	Private	Wounded	18th Dec.	1845	

2032	Denton,	Ebenezer.	Private	Killed	21st Dec.	1845
1344	Dickson,	David.	Private	Wounded	21st Dec.	1845 (invalid sent to England)
1861	Dison,	Thomas.	Private	Died	19th June	1846
2207	Dixon,	Thomas.	Private	Killed	18th Dec.	1845
1533	Douglas,	James.	Private	Killed	21st Dec.	1845
1292	Dow,	Joseph.	Private	Wounded	10th Feb.	1846
1807	Duran,	Robert.	Private	Died	4th May	1846
1534	Eagan,	Thomas.	Private	Died	26th July	1846
1977	East,	Alfred.	Private	Wounded	18th Dec.	1845
491	Eastman,	William.	Private	Wounded	21st Dec.	1845
1690	Eaton,	Thomas.	Private	Wounded	10th Feb.	1846
1565	Edis,	Robert.	Private	Wounded	21st Dec.	1845
1276	Edwards,	Thomas.	Private	Wounded	21st Dec.	1845
541	Eke,	Timothy.	Private	Wounded	21st Dec.	1845 (invalid sent to England)
1138	Ellis,	Ernest.	Private	Wounded	21st Dec.	1845
1078	Evans,	Barton.	Private	Wounded	21st Dec.	1845
2216	Evans,	Joseph.	Private	Wounded	21st Dec.	1845
1941	Everett,	John.	Private	Died	13th May	1846
1640	Fagney,	Daniel.	Corporal	Wounded	21st Dec.	1845
1830	Field,	Edward.	Private	Killed	10th Feb.	1846
1343	Fisher,	James.	Private	Wounded	21st Dec.	1845
1427	Flannery,	Patrick.	Private	Wounded	18th&21st Dec.1845	
1194	Fleming,	George.	Corporal	Died	31st July	1846
1098	Florey,	William.	Drummer	Wounded	10th Feb.	1846
1498	Foote,	Henry.	Private	Died of Wounds	29th Dec.	1845
1616	Foothead,	John Norris.	Private	Wounded	18th Dec.	1845 (invalid sent to England)
1793	Fordham,	Charles.	Private	Wounded	10th Feb.	1846 (Burnt by explosion of mine)
1507	Foreman,	Caleb.	Private	Wounded	10th Feb.	1846
2028	Fowler,	John.	Private	Died	11th April	1846
1069	Franck,	John.	Private	Wounded	18th Dec.	1845
	Fraser,	Simon.	Lieutenant	Severely Wounded	21st Dec.	1845, Died of Wounds 24th Dec. 1845
	Freeman,	Mathew Deane.	Lieutenant	Severely Wounded	21st Dec.	1845 (Leave to England)
1270	Freeman,	William.	Private	Wounded	21st Dec.	1845
1620	French,	Raymond.	Private	Died of Wounds	21st July	1846
1021	Frost,	William.	Private	Killed	21st Dec.	1845
1767	Gamester,	Robert.	Private	Wounded	10th Feb.	1846
1197	Gillies,	George.	Private	Died	8th June	1846
2013	Gilligan,	Owen.	Private	Killed in the affair	21st Jan.	1846
2153	Golher,	John.	Private	Wounded	10th Feb.	1846
970	Goodhall,	Edmond.	Corporal	Wounded	10th Feb.	1846
1329	Granger,	John.	Private	Wounded	21st Dec.	1845
1997	Green,	Joseph.	Private	Killed	21st Dec.	1845
1751	Green,	William.	Private	Killed	10th Feb.	1846
1068	Greer,	John.	Private	Wounded	21st Dec.	1845
	Haines,	Frederick Paul.	Captain	Wounded	21st Dec.	1845
587	Hall,	James.	Private	Died	22nd Feb.	1846
1144	Hall,	John.	Private	Killed in the affair	21st Jan.	1846
2168	Hall,	William.	Private	Died	5th June	1846
1768	Harding,	John.	Private	Wounded	21st Dec.	1845
1872	Hardwick,	George.	Private	Wounded	10th Feb.	1846
1313	Harp,	Thomas.	Private	Wounded	10th Feb.	1846
	(1313 Horpe, Thomas.)					
1725	Harrington,	George.	Private	Wounded	10th Feb.	1846
2088	Harrington,	James.	Private	Wounded	21st Dec.	1845
1587	Harris,	William.	Private	Wounded	21st Dec.	1845 (invalid sent to England)
755	Hart,	John.	Private	Wounded	21st Dec.	1845
1028	Hart,	John.	Sergeant	Died	30th July	1846
813	Harvey,	Thomas.	Private	Killed	21st Dec.	1845
	Hayes,	Frederick.	Quarter Master	Died	19th June	1846
2074	Haywood,	George.	Private	Wounded	21st Dec.	1845 (invalid sent to England)
1014	Hennessy,	Michael.	Private	Killed	18th Dec.	1845
1913	Hercock,	George.	Private	Wounded	10th Feb.	1846
1677	Heusenran,	William.	Corporal	Severely Wounded	18th Dec.	1845 (invalid sent to England)
1196	Heveran,	John.	Private	Wounded	10th Feb.	1846
1814	Hill,	David.	Private	Wounded	21st Dec.	1845
1188	Hill,	Nicholas.	Private	Killed	21st Dec.	1845
2099	Hill,	William.	Private	Died	26th April	1846
1401	Hills,	George.	Private	Died	31st July	1846
1806	Hobbs,	Robert.	Private	Died of Wounds	16th April	1846
	Holditch,	Edward Alan.	Lieutenant	Wounded	10th Feb.	1845
917	Homored,	Henry.	Private	Wounded	10th Feb.	1846 (Invalid sent to England)
1926	Howard,	John.	Private	Killed	21st Dec.	1845
525	Hutton,	William.	Private	Wounded	10th Feb.	1846
864	Jennings,	Edward.	Private	Died	30th July	1846

1756	Johnson,	John.	Private	Wounded	10th Feb.	1845 (invalid sent to England)
1284	Jones,	Thomas.	Private	Died	20th Jan.	1846
2098	Jones,	William.	Private	Died	12th June	1846
1260	Kelly,	Edward.	Private	Died	12th June	1846
2066	Kelly,	John.	Private	Killed	21st Dec.	1845
2233	Kesterson,	Peter.	Private	Wounded	21st Dec.	1845
1617	King,	David.	Corporal	Wounded	10th Feb.	1846
	Kingsley,	Edward William Pincke. Lieutenant		Wounded	10th Feb.	1846
1057	Kirkland,	Matthew.	Colour Sergeant	Severly Wounded	21st Dec.	1845
2238	Laisler,	Mark.	Private	Died	12th July	1846
1237	Lamborn,	John.	Private	Wounded	10th Feb.	1845
1035	Lang,	Robert.	Private	Wounded	21st Dec.	1845
1604	Laurie,	James.	Private	Killed	21st Dec.	1845
962	Lee,	Philip.	Private	Killed	21st Dec.	1845
1096	Lett,	Edward.	Drummer	Killed	10th Feb.	1846
1509	Lilley,	Thomas.	Private	Wounded	18th Dec.	1845
2113	Lloyd,	William.	Private	Died	29th June	1846
714	Lockett,	George.	Private	Wounded	21st Dec.1845 & 10th Feb. 1846	
	Lockhart,	Robert Alexander.	Major	Severe Combustion	21st Dec.	1845
1588	Lovegrove,	Levi.	Private	Wounded	21st Dec.	1845
2049	Lucas,	Hardman.	Corporal	Died	22nd Feb.	1846
640	Madine,	Patrick.	Private	Killed	21st Dec.	1845
1708	Magee,	James.	Private	Wounded	21st Dec.	1845
865	Mansbridge,	John.	Private	Killed	21st Dec.	1845
	(865	Mausbridge, John.)				
1968	Massey,	Edward.	Private	Wounded	10th Feb.	1846
	(1968	Massey, Edmond)				
1126	Massey,	Paul.	Private	Wounded	21st Dec.	1845
878	McClain,	Joseph.	Private	Died	23rd Jan.	1846
1896	McDermott,	William.	Drummer	Killed	21st Dec.	1845
2177	McNeilly,	William.	Private	Wounded	21st Dec.	1845 (invalid sent to England)
1892	McQuade,	Peter.	Private	Died	25th July	1846
1108	Millar,	Charles.	Corporal	Died	8th Aug.	1846
1963	Milligan,	John.	Private	Died of Wounds	15th March	1846
572	Milner,	Thomas.	Private	Killed	21st Dec.	1845
1654	Mitchell,	John.	Private	Killed	10th Feb.	1846
1899	Money,	John.	Private	Died of Wounds	20th Dec.	1845
2138	Moore,	James.	Private	Wounded	10th Feb.	1845
1171	Moreton,	Thomas.	Private	Killed	21st Dec.	1845
1630	Morgan,	Thomas.	Private	Wounded	10th Feb.	1846
1668	Mothershaw,	Thomas.	Private	Wounded	10th Feb.	1846
1546	Mott,	William.	Sergeant	Wounded	10th Feb.	1846
2143	Murphy,	Michael.	Private	Died	26th May	1846
1561	Newell,	John.	Private	Killed	18th Dec.	1845
756	Nicklin,	Thomas.	Private	Died	30th June	1846
1662	Nixon,	John.	Private	Killed	21st Dec.	1845
2246	Norris,	James.	Private	Wounded	18th Dec.	1845
2026	Noyes,	John.	Private	Wounded	21st Dec.	1845
1945	Nunn,	Jonathan.	Private	Wounded	21st Dec.	1845 (invalid sent to England)
935	Oddey,	Benjamin.	Private	Wounded	21st Dec.	1845 (Invalid sent to England)
938	Ormrod,	George.	Private	Killed	10th Feb.	1846
1218	Orr,	Edward.	Private	Died of Wounds	3rd Feb.	1846
1954	Page,	William.	Private	Died	24th May	1846
1301	Palmer,	William.	Private	Killed	21st Dec.	1845
1805	Parkes,	William.	Private	Died	17th July	1846
2166	Patten,	Edward.	Private	Wounded	21st Dec.	1845
1520	Peake,	George.	Private	Wounded	10th Feb.	1846
1107	Phelan,	John.	Private	Wounded	21st Dec.	1845
1619	Piercey,	Thomas.	Private	Wounded	10th Feb.	1846
	(1619	Purcy, Thomas.)				
946	Porter,	James.	Private	Died of Wounds	15th March	1846
1676	Powell,	Thomas.	Private	Wounded	21st Dec.	1845
2079	Price,	Henry.	Private	Wounded	10th Feb.	1846
1786	Quinn,	Alexander.	Private	Wounded	21st Dec.	1845
1091	Quinn,	Edward.	Private	Wounded	10th Feb.	1846
1220	Rae,	David.	Private	Killed	21st Dec.	1845
1810	Randle,	William.	Private	Wounded	10th Feb.	1846
1119	Rathbone,	James.	Private	Killed	21st Dec.	1845
2024	Redican,	Thomas.	Private	Wounded	10th Feb.	1846
1890	Reeve,	William.	Private	Wounded	21st Dec. 1845, Died 14th Feb. 1846	
830	Reynolds,	John.	Private	Wounded	18th Dec.	1845
1584	Rice,	William.	Private	Killed in the affair	21st Jan.	1846
2029	Richards,	James.	Private	Killed	10th Feb.	1846
2437	Roberts,	Charles.	Private	Killed in the affair	21st Jan.	1846

2085	Robinson,	John.	Private	Killed	21st Dec.	1845
1921	Rodgers,	Thomas.	Private	Wounded	21st Dec.	1845
	(1921 Rogers, Thomas.)					
1789	Rolfe,	Thomas.	Private	Killed	21st Dec.	1845
1917	Sale,	James.	Private	Wounded	10th Feb.	1846
	Scheberras,	Rinaldo.	Captain	Killed	21st Dec.	1845
1555	Scott,	William.	Private	Killed	10th Feb.	1846
1663	Seppings,	Alfred.	Private	Died	29th Mar.	1846
1350	Shearing,	John.	Private	Killed	10th Feb.	1846
2161	Shephard,	William.	Private	Died	6th July	1846
890	Shore,	Edward.	Private	Wounded	21st Dec.	1845
2258	Simmonds,	Thomas.	Drummer	Wounded	22nd Dec.	1845 (invalid sent to England)
937	Simpson,	James.	Private	Killed in the affair	21st Jan.	1846
2042	Skinner,	Thomas.	Private	Killed	21st Dec.	1845
829	Slade,	Isaac.	Private	Died	13th June	1846
1369	Smith,	Andrew.	Private	Wounded	18th Dec.	1845 (invalid sent to England)
1671	Smith,	Charles.	Private	Wounded	10th Feb.	1846
1393	Smith,	George.	Private	Died	25th July	1846
1128	Sproson,	Charles.	Private	Wounded	10th Feb.	1846
722	Stanfield,	Thomas.	Sergeant	Wounded	10th Feb.	1846
1230	Stanha,	Thomas.	Private	Wounded	21st Dec.	1845
	(1230 Stanbra, Thomas.)					
1965	Stokes,	George.	Private	Wounded	10th Feb.	1846
1179	Storey,	Thomas.	Sergeant	Killed	18th Dec.	1845
2006	Sutcliffe,	Samuel.	Private	Killed	10th Feb.	1846
2044	Talbot,	James.	Private	Wounded	21st Dec.	1845
1598	Tate,	William.	Private	Wounded	21st Dec.	1845
2078	Thomas,	Edmond.	Private	Killed in the affair	21st Jan.	1846
2148	Thomas,	Richard.	Private	Wounded	10th Feb.	1846
2048	Thomas,	William.	Private	Wounded	10th Feb.	1845 (invalid sent to England)
1516	Thrift,	James.	Private	Died	(Date not Known)	
2106	Tiley,	James.	Private	Wounded	21st Dec.	1845
1570	Toole,	John.	Private	Killed	21st Dec.	1845
2095	Topney,	Robert.	Private	Wounded	18th Dec.	1845
753	Turner,	Charles.	Sergeant	Wounded	10th Feb.	1846
1248	Walker,	William.	Private	Wounded	18th Feb.	1846 (invalid sent to England)
1310	Walley,	James.	Private	Wounded	21st Dec.	1845
1665	Ward,	James.	Private	Wounded	21st Dec.	1845
	Warren,	Robert Boyle.	Lieutenant	Killed	23rd Dec.	1845 (explosion of mine)
1969	Watson,	John.	Private	Wounded	10th Feb.	1846
2120	Watts,	John.	Private	Died	5th Aug.	1846
942	Webb,	Joseph.	Private	Wounded	21st Dec.	1845
2259	Wedderspoon,	David.	Private	Wounded	10th Feb.	1846
2197	Weldon,	Henry.	Private	Wounded	21st Dec.	1845
2252	Welton,	John.	Private	Killed	10th Feb.	1846
846	Williams,	James.	Private	Wounded	10th Feb.	1846
2060	Williams,	John.	Private	Wounded	10th Feb.	1846
1560	Williamson,	John.	Private	Killed	21st Dec.	1845
1392	Wilson,	Peter.	Private	Killed	21st Dec.	1845
1904	Wilson,	Thomas.	Private	Killed	21st Dec.	1845
1699	Wood,	Elijah.	Private	Died	7th May	1846
	Wood (C.B.),	Robert Blucher.	Lt.Colonel	Severely Wounded, Broken Leg	21st Dec.	1845
2151	Woodward,	James.	Private	Killed	21st Dec.	1845
1710	Wooger,	Jessie.	Private	Wounded	18th Dec.	1845
1563	Wright,	James.	Private	Wounded	21st Dec.	1845
1513	Yates,	Joseph.	Private	Killed	21st Dec.	1845
1504	Yates,	Richard.	Private	Wounded	21st Dec.	1845
	Young,	George Samuel.	Lieutenant	Slightly Wounded in hand	10th Feb. 1846	

INDIAN GENERAL SERVICE MEDAL 1854-1895

The Indian General Service Medal with the bar, 'PEGU', was proclaimed on December 22nd 1853. The medal was eventually authorised by a General Order of the Governor-General and finally approved on March 1st 1854. It was agreed to issue one single medal with 'bar' and thereafter an additional 'bar' to show further service rendered, to avoid confusion and the need to produce further medals. The first, 'bar', was for, 'Pegu' for services rendered in Burma between March 28th 1852 and June 30th 1853. This medal could not be awarded without the issue of a 'bar'.

The medal was of silver and bronze, 36mm in diameter. The designers were W.Wyon RA (obverse) and L.C.Wyon (reverse). A ribbon 32mm wide, red with two blue stripes, each 6mm wide, was attached by the use of a florated swivelling suspender. The obverse is the diademed head of Queen Victoria with the legend, 'VICTORIA REGINA'. On the reverse is the winged, standing figure of Victory, crowning a seated warrior. Also on the reverse is the exergue, which contains a Lotus flower and four leaves, denoting the connection with the East. The naming of the medals varies on the time of issue and the relevant 'bar'. The total number of 'bars' issued was 24 as follows:-

Pegu	March 28th	1852 -	June 30th	1853
Persia	December 5th	1856 -	February 8th	1857
NorthWest Frontier	December 3rd	1849 -	October 22nd	1868
Umbeyla	October 20th	1863 -	December 23rd	1863
Bhootan	December	1864 -	February	1866
Looshai	December 9th	1871 -	February 20th	1872
Perak	November 2nd	1875 -	March 20th	1876
Naga 1879-80	1875 & Dec	1879 -	January	1880
Jowaki 1877-8	November 9th	1877 -	January	1878
Burma 1885-7	November 14th	1885 -	April 30th	1887
Sikkim 1888	March 15th	1888 -	September 27th	1888
Hazara 1888	October 3rd	1888 -	November 9th	1888
Burma 1887-89	May 1st	1887 -	March 31st	1892
Burma 1887-9	May 1st	1887 -	March 31st	1892
Chin Lushai 1889-90	November 13th	1889 -	April 30th	1890
Samana 1891	April 5th	1891 -	May 25th	1891
Hazara 1891	March 12th	1891 -	May 16th	1891
NE Frontier 1891	March 28th	1891 -	May 7th	1891
Hunza 1891	December 1st	1891 -	December 22nd	1891
Burma 1889-92	April16th	1889 -	April 18th	1892
Lushai 1889-92	January11th	1889 -	June 8th	1892
Chin Hills 1892-93	October19th	1892 -	March 10th	1893
Kachin Hills 1892-93	December 3rd	1892 -	March 3rd	1893
Waziristan 1894-95	October22nd	1894 -	March 13th	1895

MEDAL LIST
INDIAN GENERAL SERVICE MEDAL 1854-1895 with Clasp 'PEGU'

The following list contains the names of 1012 men who served as officers, surgeons, non-commissioned officers and men with the 80th Regiment of Foot (Staffordshire Volunteers), who were awarded the Indian General Service Medal with the clasp, 'Pegu'. The list is from the Roll dated Fort George (Inverness), January 9th 1855 and certified by Lieutenant-Colonel George Hutchison, Commanding.

A total of 400 medals were sent to the Headquarters of the Regiment at Manchester, (reference to a letter to Colonel Hutchison dated June 1st 1855). The list includes the names of 341 men who had since died and 28 men who had either retired, been discharged or invalided out of the army. The names of some 239 men are also included who volunteered to serve with other regiments of her Majesty's Army, namely the 8th, 10th, 24th, 32nd, 52nd, 53rd, 60th, 70th, 75th, 81st and 87th. Four men have been included in the list but no medals were forwarded to them. Three of them had deserted, whilst the remaining soldier had been discharged with ignominy.

N.B. Some spellings and Army Numbers are slightly different between the Medal List and the Regiment's Nominal Roll. The differences identified have been included, the Medal List version taking precedence, the Nominal Roll in brackets. Where an * is after the surname, refer to the Casualty List.

Amiel,	Charles Frederick.	Lieutenant	
Appleyard,	Frederick Ernest.	Lieutenant	
Auchinleck,	Grahame.	Assistant Surgeon	
2144 Allen,	John.	Sergeant	
2278 Armer*,	Samuel.	Sergeant	

2413	Allitt,	Thomas.	Corporal
2480	Abrahams*,	John.	Private
2315	Acton,	Benjamin.	Private
3110	Acton*,	Thomas.	Private
1591	Ainsworth*,	William.	Private
2590	Allard,	William.	Private
3118	Allen*,	Stephen.	Private
1829	Allsop,	Francis.	Private
	(1529 Alsop,	Francis.)	
2694	Allsop,	Joseph.	Private
1599	Arlett*,	William.	Private

2154	Arnold*,	Joseph.	Private
2027	Aspey,	George.	Private
2997	Atkinson*,	William.	Private
2315	Ayrton,	Benjamin.	Private
	Boxer,	Benjamin Hallowell.	Captain
	Bodle,	George.	Lieutenant
	Borrowes,	Erasmus.	Lieutenant and Adjutant
	Bowler*,	Henry George John.	Lieutenant
	Batchelor,	Horatio Pettus.	Ensign
1346	Blake*,	Thomas.	Colour Sergeant
	(1346 Bleack, Thomas.)		
2345	Burke,	James.	Colour Sergeant
1606	Bailey,	Charles.	Sergeant
1613	Beaty,	John.	Sergeant
2417	Biddle,	Samuel.	Sergeant
2804	Bradshaw*,	George.	Sergeant
1564	Barker,	John Joseph.	Corporal
2962	Blackall*,	Alexander John.	Corporal
	(2962 Blackhall, Alexander John.)		
2762	Butterworth*,	James.	Corporal
2943	Butterworth,	Joseph.	Corporal
1530	Barnes*,	Josiah.	Drummer
1715	Broad,	Thomas.	Drummer
2498	Bailey,	John.	Private
2547	Baker*,	Alfred.	Private
	(2549 Baker, Alfred)		
2510	Baker*,	John.	Private
2051	Balderson*,	James.	Private
2696	Banning*,	John.	Private
1675	Barker,	Richard.	Private
3052	Barnes,	Christopher.	Private
1096	Bates,	Thomas.	Private
2082	Bates,	William.	Private
1305	Bathgate*,	Robert.	Private
2728	Bayley*,	John.	Private
1778	Beaumont*,	Joseph.	Private
2150	Beck*,	John.	Private
2624	Bell,	John.	Private
1902	Banstead,	James.	Private
	(1902 Benstead, James.)		
973	Berry*,	James.	Private
3038	Bierne*,	John.	Private
2430	Biggs,	Charles.	Private
2292	Billinge,	James.	Private
2978	Birchall,	John.	Private
1850	Bird,	John.	Private
2971	Bird,	Philip.	Private
2199	Bird*,	William.	Private
2793	Bishop,	John.	Private
2889	Blake*,	Frederick.	Private
	(2289 Blake, Frederick.)		
2476	Blake,	William.	Private
2742	Blake,	William.	Private
2279	Blunt,	Robert.	Private
1878	Bobbins,	Williams.	Private
2976	Boghan,	John.	Private
3060	Bolkin*,	John.	Private
2761	Bomd,	William.	Private
2881	Booker,	Arnold.	Private
1607	Boorman,	Edward.	Private
2443	Booth*,	John.	Private
3008	Booton*,	George.	Private
2086	Borham,	Thomas.	Private
2052	Bottomley,	George.	Private
2639	Bowen,	John.	Private
2802	Bowler,	George.	Private
2803	Bowler,	Robert.	Private
1341	Boyes,	Stewart.	Private
1037	Brannagan*,	Christopher.	Private
	(1137 Brannagan*, Christopher.		
2612	Brenchley,	William.	Private
2656	Brennan*,	Patrick.	Private
3022	Briggs*,	Benjamin.	Private
	(3026 Briggs, Benjamin.)		

2414	Bright*,	John.	Private
2960	Brock*,	John Clear.	Private
	(2960 Brook, John Clear.)		
3106	Brooke,	Jacob.	Private
1597	Brooks,	John.	Private
2236	Brooks*,	John.	Private
2442	Brophy*,	Patrick.	Private
2187	Broughton*,	George.	Private
	(2178 Broughton, George.)		
1970	Brown,	David.	Private
1590	Brown,	James.	Private
2599	Brown,	Robert.	Private
1548	Brown*,	William.	Private
1998	Brown,	William.	Private
2853	Brown*,	William.	Private
2552	Bryson,	James.	Private
2776	Bull*,	Josiah.	Private
1610	Burchett*,	Allan.	Private
2596	Burgess,	James.	Private
1776	Burgess*,	John.	Private
3082	Burgess*,	William.	Private
3042	Burke,	Peter.	Private
2093	Burrell*,	Stephen.	Private
2010	Bush,	Charles.	Private
2800	Bush,	George.	Private
2481	Bush,	Samuel.	Private
2808	Bush,	Thomas.	Private
2856	Butler,	Edward.	Private
2616	Butler,	George.	Private
1655	Butler,	Henry.	Private
2365	Butler,	Thomas.	Private
2209	Butterworth,	William.	Private
2231	Button,	John.	Private
1804	Bye*,	John.	Private
	(1801 Bye, John)		
2655	Byrne,	Dennis.	Private
3077	Byrne*,	Mark.	Private
2065	Byrnes,	Patrick.	Private
	(2065 Byrne, Patrick.)		
	Christie,	Samuel Tolfrey.	Major
	Craufurd,	Frederick Brown Numa.	Ensign
2875	Carthy,	Edward.	Sergeant
2419	Casey,	Thomas.	Sergeant
1637	Collins,	James.	Sergeant
2911	Collins,	William.	Sergeant
2321	Coulter,	William.	Sergeant
1054	Crook*,	William.	Sergeant
1501	Curtis,	Edmund.	Sergeant
2820	Chamberlain,	James.	Corporal
2408	Clarke*,	Abraham.	Corporal
2123	Crask,	William.	Corporal
1703	Crawford,	William.	Corporal
2857	Collins,	James.	Drummer
2780	Connolly,	Michael.	Drummer
2886	Caffrey,	Thomas.	Private
2136	Cagby,	George.	Private
2499	Campbell,	Neil.	Private
2277	Cannon,	James.	Private
2991	Carbray,	Patrick.	Private
1960	Carey,	Owen.	Private
1844	Carr,	Samuel.	Private
2465	Carroll,	John.	Private
2923	Carroll,	John.	Private
2373	Carroll,	Patrick.	Private
2592	Carroll,	Patrick.	Private
2663	Carroll,	Timothy.	Private
2305	Catterell,	Joseph.	Private
2020	Cavanagh*,	William.	Private
1701	Cave,	Jabez.	Private
2051	Cawley*,	Patrick.	Private
2650	Chadwick,	William.	Private
2650	Chandler,	James.	Private
1732	Cheveours,	Cornelius.	Private
	(1732 Chevours, Cornelius.)		

1781	Chippington*, George.	Private
1600	Christian, Thomas.	Private
1760	Church, William.	Private
1983	Churchman*, James.	Private
2855	Clarke, Charles.	Private
2555	Clarke, Patrick.	Private
2193	Clay, Joshua.	Private
2116	Clayson*, Thomas.	Private
2453	Clinnon*, John.	Private
	(2453 Clinnan, John.)	
2393	Clyde, Samuel.	Private
2185	Clydesdale*, John.	Private
1909	Coadwell*, James.	Private
2147	Coghlan, John.	Private
2589	Colclough, James.	Private
2375	Colligan, Cornelius.	Private
2903	Collins, John.	Private
2341	Commacks, James.	Private
1841	Commisky*, Michael.	Private
2882	Condon, John.	Private
2332	Conlan*, Michael.	Private
	(2332 Conlon, Michael.)	
1688	Connell*, James.	Private
1223	Connell*, John.	Private
2918	Connell, Owen.	Private
1995	Connolley, John.	Private
	(1995 Connolly, John.)	
2985	Connolley, Joseph.	Private
2344	Connolley, William.	Private
2979	Connors*, Michael.	Private
3067	Connors, Patrick.	Private
2934	Connors, Peter.	Private
2635	Connors*, Thomas.	Private
2812	Conway*, George.	Private
1907	Cook*, George.	Private
852	Cook*, Henry.	Private
2556	Cook, John.	Private
2217	Cook, Thomas.	Private
2280	Corr, James.	Private
2720	Cover, Samuel.	Private
1779	Cox, Frederick.	Private
2227	Crawley*, John.	Private
	(2227 Crowley, John.)	
1880	Creek, Thomas.	Private
1586	Cromar*, William.	Private
2441	Crott, Dennis.	Private
2887	Crowe*, John.	Private
	(2887 Crow, John.)	
2563	Cubbage, Edward.	Private
2741	Cuddy, Martin.	Private
2647	Curtis*, James.	Private
2623	Cussens, John.	Private
2351	Cutts*, Thomas James.	Private
	Duperier, Charles.	Captain
	De Ruvignes, Charles Henry Theodore Bruce.	Lieutenant
1888	Day*, John Stephen.	Pay Master Sergeant
2378	Dowling, John.	Colour Sergeant
2706	Denby*, Jarvis.	Sergeant
2215	Duigan*, John.	Corporal
1891	Dempsey, John.	Drummer
1935	Dorran, Mathew.	Drummer
2500	Daily, John.	Private
2862	Daley*, John.	Private
	(2862 Daly, John.)	
2244	Danton, William.	Private
1652	Dare*, George.	Private
2614	Darling, Hugh.	Private
2893	Darmody, James.	Private
1993	Darrant, John.	Private
1832	Davis, Isaac.	Private
1738	Davis, James.	Private
2317	Davis, Jonah.	Private
2858	Davis*, Samuel.	Private
	(2854 Davis, Samuel.)	
3112	Davis*, Thomas.	Private
2998	Davis. William.	Private
3116	Davis*, William.	Private
1946	Day, William.	Private
3099	Dean*, James.	Private
1070	Dean*, Matthew Martin.	Private
2956	Deardon, William.	Private
2719	Deegan, James.	Private
3087	Delany*, Cornelius.	Private
	(3078 Delany, Cornelius.)	
2754	Dennison*, William.	Private
2705	Depledge, William.	Private
2357	Derry, Edward.	Private
2838	Derry, James.	Private
2511	Devine, Bryan.	Private
2228	Devitt, James.	Private
2622	Dewest*, James.	Private
	(2621 Dewest, James.)	
3098	Dickenson*, Joseph.	Private
1990	Dickinson, James.	Private
3002	Doig, John.	Private
1009	Donagher, William.	Private
2114	Donald, David.	Private
2926	Donoghue*, Michael.	Private
2002	Donohoe*, Alexander.	Private
2312	Donovan*, Daniel.	Private
2646	Doran, James.	Private
2483	Dorcey, Anthony.	Private
2877	Dordon*, Michael.	Private
	(2877 Dordow, Michael.)	
1292	Dow*, Joseph.	Private
2241	Dowling*, Richard.	Private
3117	Down*, Samuel.	Private
	(3119 Down, Samuel.)	
3039	Downey, John.	Private
3099	Doyle*, John.	Private
	(3079 Doyle, John.)	
2377	Drew, Robert.	Private
2320	Drewitt*, Jacob.	Private
	(2320 Drewett, Jacob.)	
3074	Drury*, John.	Private
3501	Duff, John.	Private
3083	Duffy, James.	Private
2521	Dwyer*, Michael.	Private
1741	Dycks*, William.	Private
	(1741 Dicks, William.)	
1715	Dyson*, Richard.	Private
2608	**Edwards**, John.	Sergeant
2063	Ellis, George.	Sergeant
2951	Edwards*, Arthur.	Corporal
	(2957 Edwards, Arthur.)	
2462	Eagle*, Francis.	Private
	(2463 Eagar, Francis.)	
1931	Eagle, John.	Private
2124	Eames, William.	Private
1777	East. Alfred.	Private
1690	Eaton. Thomas.	Private
2749	Edwards*, Henry.	Private
2457	Edwards, Joseph.	Private
1416	Elliott, Michael.	Private
1421	Ellis, William.	Private
3115	Emmett*, Robert.	Private
1910	Emmings, James.	Private
2382	Ennis, John.	Private
2522	Evans, George.	Private
2911	Evans*, John.	Private
1362	Everhurst, George.	Private
2005	Ewing, John.	Private
2279	Eyles, William.	Private
2040	Eyre*, Stephen.	Private
	Fraser, Donald MacLean.	Lieutenant
1623	Friend*, Thomas.	Colour Sergeant
1959	Faulkner, Benjamin.	Sergeant
1343	Fisher*, James.	Sergeant

1098	Florey,	William.	Drummer
2699	Fallon,	Michael.	Private
2378	Fannon*,	William.	Private
3068	Fawcett*,	Mathew.	Private
	(3084 Fawcett, Mathew.)		
2567	Feeney,	John.	Private
3058	Fenlon*,	George.	Private
2883	Ferguson,	Martin.	Private
1795	Field,	William.	Private
1702	Fielding*,	Henry.	Private
2711	Finney,	Daniel.	Private
1581	Finnigan,	Patrick.	Private
2955	Finnigan*,	Patrick.	Private
2420	Fisher,	Daniel.	Private
2817	Fitch,	John.	Private
2451	Fitton,	George.	Private
2821	Fitzgerald*,	John.	Private
2418	Fitzpatrick*,	James.	Private
3031	Flannigan,	Edward.	Private
3070	Flannigan*,	John.	Private
	(3070 Flannagan, John.)		
2237	Fletcher*,	Francis.	Private
1821	Floyd,	Richard.	Private
2275	Foden*,	Jeffrey.	Private
2980	Fogarty,	Edmund.	Private
2485	Fogarty,	Thomas.	Private
2330	Foley,	Jeremiah.	Private
2302	Foley,	Timothy.	Private
2846	Foley,	William.	Private
1010	Foot*,	James.	Private
2440	Foot*,	James.	Private
1721	Foot*,	William.	Private
	(1721 Foote, William)		
2810	Foot,	William.	Privare
1984	Forster,	William.	Private
2006	Forster,	William.	Private
2370	Foryth,	John.	Private
2486	Foster,	James.	Private
2698	Fox,	Joseph.	Private
2999	Fox*,	Michael.	Private
2942	Fox,	Patrick.	Private
2952	Fox,	Patrick.	Private
2799	Fox*,	Robert.	Private
891	Fox*,	Thomas.	Private
1109	Frame*,	George.	Private
2249	Freeman,	Patrick.	Private
1406	French,	Charles.	Private
1390	French*,	Francis Thomas.	Private
2879	Fulcher*,	Alfred.	Private
2361	Fulham*,	James.	Private
1634	Furness,	James.	Private
2198	**Green**,	William.	Sergeant
2786	Guise*,	Charles.	Sergeant
	(2756 Guise, Charles.)		
1811	Gardner*,	William.	Corporal
1271	Garrick*,	James.	Corporal
2084	Goodenough,	James.	Corporal
2412	Gunn,	Henry.	Drummer
2075	Gaffney,	John.	Private
	(2075 Gafney, John.)		
2996	Gaffney,	Michael.	Private
2942	Gallagher,	John.	Private
3094	Gallagher,	John.	Private
2989	Galligher,	Patrick.	Private
1027	Galvin*,	James.	Private
2941	Galvin*,	James.	Private
1764	Gardner*,	John.	Private
1870	Garner,	Begley.	Private
3001	Garrett,	James.	Private
1628	Geary*,	William.	Private
	(1628 Gary, William.)		
1869	Geddes*,	John.	Private
	(1869 Geddies, John.)		
2661	Gheen,	Patrick.	Private
2899	Gilday,	John.	Private
1948	Giles*,	Richard.	Private
2554	Gilham*,	Edward.	Private
2884	Gill*,	Henry.	Private
2947	Gill,	Patrick.	Private
2904	Gilligan,	Bernard.	Private
2571	Gittings*,	Richard.	Private
3068	Gleeson,	James.	Private
3009	Gleeson,	Martin.	Private
2544	Glover,	John.	Private
3062	Goggins,	John.	Private
3029	Goldsmith*,	David.	Private
970	Goldhall,	Edmund.	Private
	(970 Goldhall, Edmond.)		
2158	Gordon,	John.	Private
2016	Gore*,	Thomas.	Private
2411	Gready,	John.	Private
1726	Green*,	Thomas.	Private
2164	Greenway*,	James.	Private
2964	Gregory,	John.	Private
1735	Gregson*,	Henry.	Private
	(1735 Gregson, Thomas George)		
2354	Gresham*,	George.	Private
	(2364 Gresham, George.)		
2888	Griffin,	John.	Private
2210	Grimes*,	Thomas.	Private
	(2210 Grime, Thomas.)		
2974	Grogan,	John.	Private
2913	Gubbins,	Patrick J.	Private
	Hutchison,	George.	Lt. Colonel
	Holdich (C.B.),	Edward Alan.	Brevet Lt. Colonel
	Hughes,	Robert George.	Major
	Hardinge,	Edward.	Captain
	Hawkes,	Robert.	Captain
	Hume,	Bliss John.	Lieutenant
	Hunt*,	Thomas William.	Lieutenant
	Hurford,	Henry.	Ensign
	Hunt*,	Thomas Bloomfield.	Pay Master
1196	Heveran,	John.	Sergeant
2102	Homan,	Richard.	Sergeant
1875	Huggins*,	James.	Sergeant
2937	Hand*,	James.	Corporal
2488	Hardbattle,*	James.	Corporal
1722	Heathcock,	Thomas.	Corporal
1536	Hirst,	Robert.	Corporal
1595	Hollowell,	George.	Corporal
	(1596 Hollowell, George.)		
1355	Hope,	James.	Corporal
1151	Hough,	John.	Corporal
2851	Humphries,	Frederick.	Corporal
3027	Hennessey,	Nicholas.	Drummer
2487	Hague,	Thomas.	Private
1738	Hale,	Ezekiel.	Private
1919	Hale*,	William.	Private
1947	Hall*,	George.	Private
1460	Hall,	James.	Private
1660	Hall,	Thomas.	Private
1386	Halliday,	John.	Private
1784	Halligan,	John.	Private
1950	Hamilton*,	Joseph.	Private
2283	Hamilton,	Richard.	Private
1152	Hancock*,	Edward.	Private
2951	Handley,	Charles.	Private
3084	Hanlon,	Edward.	Private
3024	Hardgrove,	John.	Private
1766	Harding,	John.	Private
1994	Harding,	John.	Private
2139	Hargreaves,	Joseph.	Private
2815	Hargrove,	Henry.	Private
1725	Harrington,	George.	Private
1867	Harrison,	James.	Private
2200	Harrison,	Thomas.	Private
2755	Harrison*,	Thomas.	Private
1204	Harrison,	William.	Private

2268	Harrison,	William.	Private
3040	Harrison*,	William.	Private
3090	Hart,	John.	Private
2496	Hayes,	Daniel.	Private
3017	Hayes,	Isaac.	Private
1930	Hayes,	Richard.	Private
3051	Hayes*,	Robert.	Private
2789	Haylings*,	John.	Private
2649	Heagarty*,	Thomas.	Private
2594	Healey,	Charles.	Private
2285	Healy*,	Michael.	Private
2294	Heavy,	William.	Private
2927	Heckett*,	Patrick.	Private
2673	Hemmings*,	Thomas.	Private
2097	Henderson,	James.	Private
2837	Hennessey,	William.	Private
2460	Hennessy,	Thomas.	Private
2503	Henry*,	Robert.	Private
2825	Henry,	William.	Private
1930	Hercott*,	George.	Private
	(1913 Hercott, George.)		
1025	Hewitt*,	George.	Private
1787	Hick*,	Thomas.	Private
1788	Higgins*,	Henry.	Private
1814	Hill*,	David.	Private
3050	Hindle,	John.	Private
1698	Hinton*,	Israel.	Private
2970	Hirst,	Charles.	Private
3014	Hodgskins*,	Benjamin.	Private
2841	Hogan*,	Alexander.	Private
3049	Hoggarth,	Joseph.	Private
2620	Holingshead*,	George.	Private
2778	Holland,	George.	Private
1889	Holmes*,	Henry.	Private
	(1889 Homes, Henry.)		
2121	Holmes,	Ralph.	Private
2912	Holmes,	Thomas.	Private
2262	Holmes,	William.	Private
3097	Honald,	John.	Private
2768	Hook,	Charles.	Private
2504	Hopkins,	John.	Private
2381	Horan*,	James.	Private
2786	Horan,	Martin.	Private
1313	Horpe,	Thomas.	Private
1160	Howard,	John.	Private
2558	Hulme*,	James.	Private
3113	Humston*,	Mark.	Private
1922	Hurley,	Dennis.	Private
2973	Hutton*,	Thomas.	Private
1307	**Impitt**ature*,	William.	Drummer
	(1307 Impett, William.)		
1140	Imeson*,	William.	Private
	(1040 Imeson, William.)		
3004	Ireland,	Peter.	Private
1438	Irwin,	George.	Private
1011	Irwin,	James.	Private
2626	Irwin,	Jeremiah.	Private
2174	Irwin,	Samuel.	Private
2771	Ison*,	Henry.	Private
2921	Ivers,	John.	Private
972	**Johnstone***,	Frederick.	Sergeant
	(972 Johnston, Frederick.)		
2542	James,	Thomas.	Corporal
2870	Jones,	Thomas.	Drummer
2030	James,	John.	Private
1930	Jay*,	Henry.	Private
	(1934 Jay, Henry.)		
1989	Jinks,	Edward.	Private
1517	Johnstone*,	Edward.	Private
	(1517 Johnson, Edward.)		
2659	Johnstone*,	Robert.	Private
	(2659 Johnson, Robert.)		
1582	Jones*,	James.	Private
	(1562 Jones, James.)		

1973	Jones*,	James.	Private
2575	Jones*,	John.	Private
2752	Jones,	John.	Private
2076	Jones,	Robert.	Private
2142	Jones*,	Thomas.	Private
	(2152 Jones, Thomas.)		
2642	Jones,	Thomas.	Private
2753	Jones,	Thomas.	Private
2792	Jones,	Thomas.	Private
1739	Jones,	William.	Private
2938	Jordan*,	Patrick.	Private
2972	Joseph,	Patrick.	Private
1886	Jude*,	Page.	Private
2100	**Kitching**,	Robert.	Colour Sergeant
1617	King*,	David.	Sergeant
1259	King,	James.	Sergeant
1745	Kelly,	John.	Corporal
1752	King,	George.	Corporal
3021	Knowles,	George.	Drummer
2651	Keefe,	Daniel.	Private
2012	Kelly*,	Charles.	Private
2359	Kelly,	Henry.	Private
1015	Kelly,	John.	Private
2518	Kelly,	John.	Private
3003	Kelly*,	John.	Private
2506	Kelly,	Richard.	Private
3091	Kelly*,	William.	Private
2891	Kemp*,	George.	Private
1893	Kemp,	Thomas.	Private
2388	Kenny,	James.	Private
2832	Kenny,	John.	Private
2446	Kenny,	William.	Private
2569	Kenny,	William.	Private
2977	Kershaw,	Joseph.	Private
2233	Kesterton,	Peter.	Private
2507	King,	Henry.	Private
2126	Kinton,	Richard.	Private
2933	Kirby,	John.	Private
2535	Kirk,	David.	Private
3061	Kyrne*,	Patrick.	Private
	(3061 Kyne, Patrick.)		
	Lockhart*,	Robert Alexander.	Major
	Lane,	Benjamin.	Assistant Surgeon
2940	Leppard,	John.	Sergeant
1114	Long,	Charles.	Sergeant
1237	Lambourne*,	John.	Corporal
	(1237 Lamborn, John.)		
2806	Leech*,	Alfred.	Corporal
2903	Lacey,	James.	Private
2628	Lacey*,	John.	Private
1796	Lacey*,	William.	Private
2170	Lafargue*,	Peter.	Private
2757	Lamb,	James.	Private
1528	Lancaster,	Josias.	Private
2925	Laughlin,	John.	Private
2987	Lawler*,	Christopher.	Private
	(2987 Lawlor, Christopher.)		
2396	Lawler*,	John.	Private
2845	Lawler,	John.	Private
3053	Lawless,	John.	Private
2406	Lawrence,	James.	Private
2410	Lawson*,	James.	Private
1885	Leadbeater*,	James.	Private
2432	Leadbeater,	Jessie.	Private
2179	Lear,	Thomas.	Private
2501	Lear*,	William.	Private
	(2508 Lear, William.)		
2470	Ledward*,	Thomas.	Private
	(2470 Ledwards, Thomas.)		
1603	Lee*,	Ralph.	Private
2919	Lees,	Charles.	Private
2830	Leeson,	Thomas.	Private
1420	Lennam,	William.	Private
	(1420 Lennan, William.)		

1509	Lilley*,	Thomas.	Private
2277	Lloyd,	John.	Private
1743	Lock,	John.	Private
1298	Lockett,	Thomas.	Private
3114	Loncester*,	Peter.	Private
	(3114 Longcester, Peter.)		
2929	Lonergan*,	John.	Private
	(**NB**. Monument Lichfield Cathedral - Lonagan, John. -		
	Nominal Roll Lonugan, John.)		
1035	Long*,	Robert.	Private.
2553	Longmore*,	John.	Private
3111	Longstant,	Thomas.	Private
2836	Looney,	John.	Private
1588	Lovegrove*,	Levi.	Private
2159	Lowe,	Benjamin.	Private
3117	Lowrey,	Michael.	Private
1519	Lunn,	John.	Private
2849	Lyons*,	John.	Private
3043	Lyvison,	Robert.	Private
	Montgomery,	Lambert Lyons.	Major
	Miller,	Frederick.	Lieutenant
	Montgomery,	Robert Hamilton.	Lieutenant
	Mortimer,	William Picton.	Ensign
	Murphy,	Miah William.	Assistant Surgeon
1737	Morris,	Henry Edward	Pay Master Sergeant
1624	Maloney,	William.	Quarter Master Sergeant
1134	McPamison,	William.	Colour Sergeant
2384	McKay,	William.	Sergeant
2909	Mayow,	Charles.	Sergeant
1446	Moneypenny,	John.	Sergeant
2423	Moore,	William.	Sergeant
2695	Mullins,	James.	Sergeant
2642	Murphy,	John.	Sergeant
1538	McGuire,	George.	Corporal
2914	Mack,	Joseph.	Corporal
1708	Magee,	James.	Corporal
1385	Markham,	John.	Corporal
2775	Marshall,	James.	Corporal
2818	Mills,	Joshua.	Corporal
2186	Moss,	Edgar.	Corporal
2343	Mullin,	Patrick.	Corporal
3033	McInerey,	Thomas.	Drummer
1206	McKean,	Thomas.	Drummer
2813	McKeown,	Thomas.	Drummer
3095	McAndrew,	Joseph.	Private
2243	McCabe,	Joseph.	Private
2640	McCann*,	John.	Private
2610	McCarthy,	John.	Private
1627	McCauley,	Henry.	Private
2564	McCluskey,	James.	Private
2869	McCrate,	Michael.	Private
2455	McDermott,	Bryan.	Private
2984	McDermott*,	John.	Private
3055	McDermott,	John.	Private
2953	McDonald,	Edward.	Private
1148	McDonald,	James.	Private
3056	McElra,	James.	Private
1611	McGarry,	John.	Private
2691	McGinn,	John.	Private
2873	McGinn,*	Peter.	Private
2550	McGlynn,	William.	Private
2922	McGrath,	Mathew.	Private
2809	McGregor*,	Archibald.	Private
2305	McGregor,	John.	Private
2363	McGuckin*,	Thomas.	Private
	(2362 McGuckin, Thomas.)		
2604	McGuinness,	Patrick.	Private
2842	McGuire*,	Edward.	Private
2725	McKay,	George.	Private
2073	McKenny*,	Thomas.	Private
	(2073 McKinny, Thomas.)		
3025	McKernan,	William.	Private
1134	McLaren*,	James.	Private
2880	McMahon,	Francis.	Private
2014	McMahon*,	John.	Private
	(2014 MacMahon, John.)		
2963	McMahon*,	Michael.	Private
2354	McMahon*,	Samuel.	Private
2992	McMullion,	George.	Private
1593	McMullion,	John.	Private
3018	McNamara*,	John.	Private
3049	McQuilkin,	Archibald.	Private
1380	Madden*,	John.	Private
1102	Magee,	Fantin.	Private
	(1102 Magee, Fanton.)		
2509	Magovern,	James.	Private
2731	Mahoney*,	Daniel.	Private
3071	Malcolm*,	John.	Private
	(3071 Malcolm, James.)		
2860	Maley*,	Philip.	Private
3027	Mann*,	John.	Private
2988	Manners,	James.	Private
2854	Mansfield,	William.	Private
2974	Marriott,	Benjamin.	Private
1709	Marsh,	John.	Private
2400	Mason,	George.	Private
2436	Mason*,	John.	Private
2193	Mason*,	William.	Private
1968	Massey,	Edmund.	Private
2307	Massey,	John.	Private
2944	Masterson,	Patrick.	Private
1791	Mathews*,	James.	Private
1755	May*,	Charles.	Private
3089	Maycock,	George.	Private
1949	Meadows,	James.	Private
2593	Meale*,	James.	Private
	(2593 Male, James)		
3064	Meanigan,	Michael.	Private
3057	Medicroft*,	John.	Private
2785	Meeson*,	Edward.	Private
2660	Merrick,	Thomas.	Private
2871	Mewbury,	Thomas.	Private
2801	Miles,	Henry.	Private
3109	Milner*,	John.	Private
2404	Mingey*,	William.	Private
	(2405 Mingey, William.)		
1784	Mitchell,	Edmund.	Private
3081	Mitchell,	Michael.	Private
1679	Moisey,	Thomas.	Private
3007	Montgomery*,	Archibald.	Private
2879	Mooney*,	John.	Private
2968	Mooney*,	John.	Private
2701	Mooney,	Luke.	Private
2449	Moore,	Charles.	Private
3000	Moore*,	Isaac.	Private
1872	Moore,	James.	Private
2609	Moore*,	Michael.	Private
2822	Moran,	Edward.	Private
3075	Moran,	John.	Private
3011	Moran*,	Patrick.	Private
1764	Morgan,	David	Private
2709	Morgan*,	Michael.	Private
2288	Morley*,	William.	Private
1951	Morris*,	George.	Private
2557	Morris*,	John.	Private
	(2257 Morris, John.)		
1050	Morris*,	William.	Private
	(1500 Morris, William.)		
2617	Morris,	William.	Private
2403	Morrison,	William.	Private
1546	Mott,	William.	Private
2446	Moyes,	James.	Private
2337	Munrott,	James.	Private
1366	Murdock,	Hugh.	Private
2712	Murphy,	James.	Private
2750	Murphy,	James.	Private
2069	Murphy*,	Jeremiah.	Private
1839	Murphy,	John Thomas. Private	

2067	Murphy,	Joseph.	Private	3016	Pott,	Thomas.	Private
3037	Murphy,	Martin.	Private	2527	Potts,	John.	Private
2721	Murray,	Andrew.	Private	2741	Powell,	Robert.	Private
3013	Murray*,	John.	Private	2920	Power,	Thomas.	Private
3027	Murray*,	John.	Private	1898	Pratchett,	Thomas.	Private
1833	Murray*,	Robert.	Private	2795	Preece,	John.	Private
1579	Murtagh,	Patrick.	Private	2766	Price,	Thomas.	Private
1992	Myers*,	John.	Private	2429	Prime,	Samuel.	Private
	Nunn*,	James Loftus Winniett.Lieutenant		2769	Prime,	William.	Private
2225	Newlan*,	William.	Sergeant	2655	Ptolomey,	Andrew.	Private
1706	Nash*,	James.	Corporal	1619	Purcey,	Thomas.	Private
1750	Nicholls,	James.	Corporal		(1619 Purcy, Thomas.)		
3028	Naughton,	John.	Private	1786	**Quinn**,	Alexander.	Colour Sergeant
2930	Neagle*,	John.	Private	2666	Quinn*,	Thomas.	Corporal
2560	Neil,	Lawrence.	Private	3045	Queensborough,	Henry.	Private
2434	Neil*,	Stephen.	Private	1091	Quinn*,	Edward.	Private
3005	Nelson,	Mathew.	Private	3001	Quinn,	James.	Private
2350	Nelson,	Thomas.	Private	2568	Quinn,	John.	Private
2543	Newcome,	Richard.	Private	2335	Quirke*,	James.	Private
2746	Newitt,	James.	Private	1567	**Roberts***,	Joseph.	Sergeant Major
2474	Newman*,	Thomas.	Private	2165	Ryan,	Augustine.	Corporal
	(2474 Newmans, Thomas.)			1809	Richards,	Charles.	Drummer
2111	Nicholls,	Alfred.	Private	2064	Rahilley,	Dennis.	Private
1061	Nixon*,	James.	Private	2024	Ramsden,	George.	Private
2006	Nocton*,	Lawrence.	Private	2754	Randall*,	Richard.	Private
2363	Noonan,	William.	Private	1382	Ratcliffe*,	James.	Private
2246	Norris,	James.	Private	2146	Ratcliffe*,	Robert.	Private
2710	Nuttall*,	Henry.	Private	3092	Rawlinson,	James.	Private
	Ormsby,	Anthony.	Major	1915	Ray,	Joseph.	Private
1952	O'Hara,	Daniel.	Sergeant	2630	Reader*,	Henry.	Private
2843	O'Kane,	Patrick.	Corporal		(2636 Reader, Henry.)		
1975	O'Dowd,	James.	Private	2904	Reddington,	Malachi.	Private
2159	Oldfield*,	Simeon.	Private	2545	Reeves,	Charles.	Private
3019	O'Niel,	John.	Private	1254	Reid,	James.	Private
867	O'Rielly*,	Philip.	Private	1790	Reid*,	John.	Private
2447	Orr,	Robert.	Private		(1790 Reed, John.)		
2864	Owens,	James.	Private	2244	Reynolds,	George.	Private
	Paterson,	William.	Lieutenant	2730	Reynolds,	Thomas.	Private
2087	Purchase,	Nicholas.	Hospital Sergeant	3076	Reynolds,	Thomas.	Private
2792	Probert,	James.	Sergeant	2545	Richards,	John.	Private
1901	Parcel*,	Richard.	Corporal	2577	Richards,	Price.	Private
2824	Park*,	George.	Corporal	2309	Richardson,	James.	Private
2797	Peel,	John.	Corporal	2512	Rielley,	John.	Private
1678	Powell,	Thomas.	Corporal	3108	Rielley,	Edward.	Private
2310	Prescott,	George.	Corporal	3015	Rielley*,	John.	Private
1526	Parrot,	Frederick.	Drummer		(3015 Reiley, John.)		
	(1526 Parrott, Frederick.)			2353	Rielley*,	Luke.	Private
1704	Pendrey,	Edmund.	Drummer		(2353 Riley, Luke.)		
	(1704 Pendery, Edmund.)			3063	Rielley,	Thomas.	Private
1511	Padgett*,	Luke.	Private	3020	Rishworth,	John.	Private
2892	Page*,	James.	Private	2047	Rix,	Samuel.	Private
2777	Painter,	John.	Private	2491	Roache,	John.	Private
2779	Palmer,	John R.	Private	2932	Roache,	Patrick.	Private
2745	Palmer*,	William.	Private	2188	Roberts*,	Thomas.	Private
833	Parker*,	John.	Private	3100	Robinson*,	George.	Private
2885	Parker*,	William.	Private	1666	Robinson*,	James.	Private
3093	Payton,	John.	Private	2299	Robinson,	Joseph.	Private
2490	Payton,	Michael.	Private	2524	Rogers,	Richard.	Private
1520	Peake*,	George.	Private	1921	Rogers,	Thomas.	Private
2247	Pearce,	Jacob.	Private	3096	Rogers*,	William.	Private
2852	Peart,	Joseph.	Private	2831	Rooney,	Michael.	Private
2796	Peel,	George.	Private	2863	Ross,	David.	Private
2878	Petch,	Frederick William.	Private	1238	Rowley.	John.	Private
2212	Peto,	Edward.	Private	2659	Rowlinson,	Charles.	Private
2223	Phillips*,	James.	Private	3008	Ryan,	Edward.	Private
1205	Phillips,	John.	Private	2944	Ryan*,	James.	Private
2125	Phillips,	John.	Private		(2946 Ryan, James.)		
3092	Phillips,	Mathew.	Private	3030	Ryan*,	Mathew.	Private
3044	Pierce,	Joseph.	Private	2356	Ryan*,	Patrick.	Private
2318	Pike,	James.	Private	2928	Ryan,	Patrick.	Private
2722	Pitchford*,	Mark.	Private	1928	Ryan,	Timothy.	Private
2433	Plumpton,	William.	Private	2471	Ryan,	Timothy.	Private
3035	Polwarth,	William.	Private		**Sayers***,	Richard Talbot.	Major
1568	Porter,	James.	Private		Smith,	Hamilton Charles.	Captain

	Sullivan,	George.	Lieutenant
	Swift,	Richard.	Ensign
2401	Smith,	William.	Drum Major
1962	Smith,	John.	Sergeant
1417	Shank,	Thomas.	Corporal
	(1417 Shouk, Thomas.)		
2969	Starr*,	Archibald.	Corporal
2942	St. John*,	Patrick.	Private
2001	Salter*,	John.	Private
2907	Sammon*,	Thomas.	Private
1388	Sanderson*,	George.	Private
2017	Satinstall,	Ellis.	Private
	(2017 Sattinstall, Ellis.)		
2513	Saunders,	William.	Private
1868	Savage,	Joseph.	Private
3032	Scott*,	John.	Private
1848	Shaw,	Hugh.	Private
2372	Sheeran,	William.	Private
2137	Shields,	David.	Private
1559	Shepherd,	Hereas.	Private
1884	Sherratt,	Robert.	Private
2576	Shoreland*,	James.	Private
	(2576 Shorlain, James.)		
2908	Sida,	John.	Private
1274	Silvey*,	Edward.	Private
2786	Silvey*,	George.	Private
	(2783 Silvey, George.)		
2763	Simon,	Charles.	Private
1785	Sims,	Daniel.	Private
2905	Skeehan,	Luke.	Private
2738	Slade,	John.	Private
1232	Smeaton*,	Charles.	Private
2000	Smith*,	Edward.	Private
2750	Smith,	George.	Private
3054	Smith,	George.	Private
1980	Smith,	James.	Private
2826	Smith,	James.	Private
3049	Smith*,	James.	Private
1661	Smith,	Job.	Private
2205	Smith*,	John.	Private
2668	Smith*,	John.	Private
2717	Smith*,	Richard.	Private
2201	Smith,	Robert.	Private
2758	Smith*,	Thomas.	Private
2894	Smith,	Thomas.	Private
2844	Smith*,	Thomas.	Private
3085	Smith*,	Thomas.	Private
1758	Snell,	William.	Private
2022	Spencley,	William.	Private
	(2022 Spenceley, William.)		
2195	Spicer,	George.	Private
1991	Spronson,	John.	Private
1230	Stanbra,	Thomas.	Private
	(1230 Stanbra, Thomas.)		
2319	Stanfield,	Charles.	Private
2627	Stannard,	George E.	Private
2637	Stannard*,	George.	Private
2294	Stanyard*,	Thomas.	Private
	(2296 Stanyard, Thomas.)		
2189	Steel*,	Thomas.	Private
	(2189 Steele, Thomas.)		
2990	Stevenson,	James.	Private
2088	Stewart,	Charles.	Private
2157	Stewart,	Thomas.	Private
2175	Stiles*,	William.	Private
2627	Stoney,	John.	Private
2562	Strange*,	James.	Private
2334	Studdart*,	Michael.	Private
2819	Sturgeon,	William.	Private
2177	Sullivan*,	Arthur.	Private
2704	Sullivan,	John.	Private
2736	Sullivan,	John.	Private
2601	Sullivan,	Patrick.	Private
1584	Swan*,	John.	Private

	(1582 Swan, John.)		
	Tweedie,	James.	Lieutenant
	Taylor,	John Robert.	Surgeon
2106	Tiley,	James.	Colour Sergeant
1730	Tabrar,	William.	Corporal
2273	Taylor*,	Charles.	Corporal
940	Taylor*,	William.	Drummer
2839	Tailor,	John.	Private
2044	Talbot,	James.	Private
2811	Tanner,	William.	Private
2254	Tate*,	Thomas.	Private
1598	Tate,	William.	Private
1673	Taylor*,	George.	Private
3032	Taylor*,	Henry.	Private
1965	Taylor*,	James.	Private
3019	Taylor*,	James.	Private
	(3010 Taylor, James.)		
2156	Thomas*,	Richard.	Private
	(2145 Thomas, Richard.)		
3031	Thompson*,	Ambrose.	Private
757	Thompson*,	William.	Private
1549	Thorndycroft*,	John.	Private
2732	Tickle,	William.	Private
2003	Toole*,	Patrick.	Private
2638	Tower*,	Robert.	Private
2889	Tracey*,	Joseph.	Private
2453	Tranton,	Robert.	Private
2541	Travel,	George.	Private
2539	Treanor,	Patrick.	Private
2342	Troy,	Thomas.	Private
2163	Tudor,	Richard.	Private
3088	Tully,	Thomas.	Private
768	Turnbull,	David.	Private
1342	Turnbull,	Walter.	Private
1792	Turner*,	Henry.	Private
1747	Turner*,	Richard,	Private
2660	Turner*,	Thomas.	Private
2866	Turner,	Thomas.	Private
2092	Tylor,	John.	Private
	(2092 Tyler, John.)		
1771	Tyrell,	John.	Private
2958	**Vincent**,	John.	Corporal
2538	Vickery,	Edward.	Private
3034	Vincent,	William B.	Private
	Welsh,	Astell Thomas.	Captain
	Whitehead,	William.	Lieutenant
	Wilkinson*,	John.	Lieutenant
	Wolseley*,	Garnet Joseph.	Ensign
2774	Woodford,	Arthur.	Orderly Room Clerk
2618	Watts,	George.	Colour Sergeant
2034	White,	John.	Colour Sergeant
1243	Watts*,	William.	Sergeant
2314	Weir*,	Alexander.	Sergeant
	(2316 Weir, Alexander.)		
2291	Woodland*,	John.	Sergeant
2261	Whitworth,	Thomas.	Corporal
1741	Williams,	Robert.	Corporal
1937	Wilson,	George.	Corporal
1780	Woods*,	Anthony.	Corporal
	(1780 Wood, Anthony.)		
2872	Woodley,	George.	Drummer
2679	Wright,	Henry.	Drummer
1573	Wade*,	John.	Private
2945	Wade,	Patrick.	Private
2814	Walker,	William.	Private
2565	Wall,	John.	Private
1310	Walley,	James.	Private
2671	Walsh,	James.	Private
2515	Walsh*,	John.	Private
2993	Walsh,	John.	Private
2367	Walsh,	Michael.	Private
2494	Walsh,	Michael.	Private
2975	Walsh,	Miles.	Private
2368	Walsh,	Robert.	Private

1712	Walton*,	Thomas.	Private		3086	Willerton*,	Henry.	Private
1315	Warburton*,	William.	Private		1693	Williams*,	George.	Private
3039	Ward,	George.	Private		2060	Williams,	John.	Private
2724	Waterhouse*,	Isaac.	Private		2191	Williams,	John.	Private
2533	Waters*,	Charles.	Private		2765	Williams,	Richard.	Private
2982	Waters,	William.	Private		2241	Williamson,	William.	Private
	Waterson,	John.	Private		2898	Willis,	William.	Private
2101	Webb,	James.	Private		1648	Wise,	George.	Private
1938	Webb,	William.	Private		1646	Wise,	Joseph.	Private
2873	Wedgewood*, Peter. (Alias McGinn, Peter) Private				2986	Wolfe,	Michael.	Private
2702	Weight*,	Benjamin.	Private		1199	Wolfenden,	Thomas.	Private
2197	Weldon*,	Henry.	Private		2673	Woodman,	George.	Private
2759	Welsh*,	Thomas.	Private		1589	Woods,	James.	Private
1612	West*,	John.	Private		2061	Woods*,	Thomas.	Private
2913	Whalin*,	Thomas.	Private			(2062 Wood, Thomas.)		
	(2913 Whalan, Thomas.)				2394	Woods,	William.	Private
3073	Whealan,	Michael.	Private		2770	Woods,	William.	Private
2611	Whealan,	William.	Private		3066	Woods,	William.	Private
2529	Wheeler*,	Stanislaus.	Private		1547	Woodward*,	Samuel.	Private
	(2529 Wheeler, Stanislaus Frederick.)				2773	Wright*,	George.	Private
2183	White*,	Charles.	Private		1563	Wright,	James.	Private
2575	White,	Thomas.	Private		1842	Wright,	John.	Private
2308	Whitehead,	Henry.	Private		1099	Wright,	Patrick.	Private
780	Whitfield*,	John.	Private		2068	Wright*,	Richard.	Private
2070	Whybrow*,	William.	Private		3105	Wrigley,	John.	Private
2690	Wiggins,	John.	Private		1234	**Yorstin***,	James.	Corporal
3392	Wigood*,	Robert.	Private			(1219 Yorstin, James.)		
2726	Wiles*,	William.	Private		1556	Young,	John.	Private

CASUALTIES, PEGU CAMPAIGN

The following list of 384 men has been taken from the Medal Roll dated January 9th 1855, the Monument in Lichfield Cathedral and its medal records. The majority of the soldiers died from cholera, dysentery and other diseases, whilst on active service with the Regiment. The place of death is identified wherever possible. Some men died in India not Burma and some even died back home in England. In the campaign, one colour sergeant and 9 privates were killed in action. One man was accidentally killed, one was drowned, and some 30 soldiers were discharged invalid or otherwise. At the time of writing, no records are available of wounded, however it is known that Lieutenant Nunn was slightly wounded when Rangoon was captured, and Ensigns Wolseley and Wilkinson were both wounded and mentioned in despatches for taking entrenchments not far from Kyon Tani on March 19th 1853. Ensign Garnet Joseph Wolseley was later to reach the rank of Field Marshal and become an outstanding soldier of the Victorian era.

The list also contains the names of 8 soldiers who died whilst serving with the Regiment in Burma but did not receive the Indian General Service Medal with the clasp 'Pegu'. These men can be identified by a (*), before their surname.

NB. (1). Some spellings and Army Numbers are slightly different between the Medal List and the Regiment's Nominal Roll. Those differences identified have been included, the Medal List version taking precedence, the Nominal Roll in brackets.

NB. (2). Ensign Wilkinson is shown as a Lieutenant on the Medal List

Killed in Action

2510	Baker,	John.	Private	Died of Wounds	13th Jan.	1853
2776	Bull,	Josiah.	Private	Murdered	10th Oct.	1852
1292	Dow,	Joseph.	Private		14th April	1852
3058	Fenlon,	George.	Private		15th March.	1853
1698	Hinton,	Israel.	Private	Died of Wounds & Infection	24th June	1852
2501	Lear,	William.	Private	Died of Wounds	21st May	1852
	(2508 Lear, William.)					
2929	Lonergan,	John.	Private		19th March.	1853
	(**NB.** Monument Lichfield Cathedral - Lonagan, John.- Nominal Roll Lonugan, John)					
2849	Lyons,	John.	Private	Date and place not known		
2724	Waterhouse,	Isaac.	Private		9th Oct.	1852
2314	Weir,	Alexander.	Sergeant		14th April	1852 Rangoon
	(2316 Weir, Alexander.)					

Wounded

	Nunn,	James Loftus Winniett.	Lieutenant	April 1852 (Storming Rangoon)
	Wilkinson,	John.	Lieutenant	19th March.	1853
	Wolseley,	Garnet Joseph.	Ensign	19th March.	1853

Died of Disease, Invalided or Accidently Killed

2480	Abrahams,	John.	Private	Died	10th June	1854
3110	Acton,	Thomas.	Private	Died	16th April	1854
1591	Ainsworth,	William.	Private	Died	29th Dec.	1852

3118	Allen,	Stephen.	Private	Died	16th Sept.	1853
1599	Arlett,	William.	Private	Died	31st Jan.	1854
2278	Armer,	Samuel.	Sergeant	Died	10th May	1853
2154	Arnold,	Joseph.	Private	Discharged	30th Dec.	1854
2997	Atkinson,	William.	Private	Died	30th Nov.	1852
2547	Baker,	Alfred.	Private	Died	12th April	1852
	(2549 Baker, Alfred.)					
2051	Balderson,	James.	Private	Died	1st Dec.	1853
2696	Banning,	John.	Private	Died	15th May	1852
1902	Banstead,	James.	Private	Discharged, Date and place not known		
	(1902 Benstead, James.)					
1530	Barnes,	Josiah.	Drummer	Died	1st July	1852 Rangoon
1305	Bathgate,	Robert.	Private	Died	3rd Nov.	1852
2728	Bayley,	John.	Private	Died	9th March	1853
1778	Beaumont,	Joseph.	Private	Died	12th July	1852 Rangoon
2150	Beck,	John.	Private	Died	26th Dec.	1853
973	Berry,	James.	Private	Discharged at Calcutta	1854 - Deceased	
3038	Bierne,	John.	Private	Killed	23rd March	1853
2199	Bird,	William.	Private	Died	23rd June	1853
2962	Blackall,	Alexander John.	Corporal	Died	22nd March	1854
	(2962 Blackhall, Alexander John.)					
2889	Blake,	Frederick.	Private	Died	20th Oct.	1853
	(2289 Blake, Frederick.)					
1346	Blake,	Thomas.	Colour Sergeant	Died	14th May	1853
	(1346 Bleack, Thomas.)					
3060	Bolkin,	John.	Private	Died	20th April	1853
2443	Booth,	John.	Private	Died	2nd April	1853
3008	Booton,	George.	Private	Died	21st Dec.	1852
	Bowler,	Henry George John.	Lieutenant	Died,	Date and place not known	
2804	Bradshaw,	George.	Sergeant	Died	Date and place not known	
1037	Brannagan,	Christopher.	Private	Died	14th Nov.	1852
	(1137 Brannagan, Chrisopher.)					
2656	Brennan,	Patrick.	Private	Died	10th June	1854
3022	Briggs,	Benjamin.	Private	Died	29th Sept.	1852
	(3026 Briggs, Benjamin.)					
2414	Bright,	John.	Private	Died	13th Oct.	1853
2960	Brock,	John Clear.	Private	Died	16th Oct.	1852
	(2960 Brook, John Clear.)					
2236	Brooks,	John.	Private	Died	9th Dec.	1852
2442	Brophy,	Patrick.	Private	Died	30th Dec.	1852
2187	Broughton,	George.	Private	Died	8th Dec.	1852
	(2178 Broughton, George.)					
1548	Brown,	William.	Private	Died	21st Nov.	1852
2853	Brown,	William.	Private	Died	28th June	1853
1610	Burchett,	Allan.	Private	Died	23rd June	1853
1776	Burgess,	John.	Private	Died	2nd May	1853
3082	Burgess,	William.	Private	Died	22nd July	1853
2093	Burrell,	Stephen.	Private	Died	18th May	1853
2762	Butterworth,	James.	Corporal	Died	1st April	1852
1804	Bye,	John.	Private	Died	22nd April	1852
	(1801 Bye, John.)					
3077	Byrne,	Mark.	Private	Died	5th July	1862
2020	Cavanagh,	William.	Private	Died	13th June	1853
2051	Cawley,	Patrick.	Private	Died	1st Dec.	1853
1781	Chippington,	George.	Private	Died,	Date and place not known	
1983	Churchman,	James.	Private	Died	26th March	1853 Prome
2408	Clarke,	Abraham.	Corporal	Discharged	31st Aug.	1854
2116	Clayson,	Thomas.	Private	Died	21st Sept.	1853
2453	Clinnon,	John.	Private	Died	16th March	1853
	(2455 Clinnan, John.)					
2185	Clydesdale,	John.	Private	Died	22nd March	1853 Prome
1909	Coadwell,	James.	Private	Died	31st July	1852
1841	Commisky,	Michael.	Private	Died	14th Jan.	1853 Prome
2332	Conlan,	Michael.	Private	Died	8th June	1853
	(2332 Conlon, Michael.)					
1688	Connell,	James.	Private	Died	28th Nov.	1853
1223	Connell,	John.	Private	Died	5th July	1853
2979	Connors,	Michael.	Private	Died	20th July	1852
2635	Connors,	Thomas.	Private	Died	9th May	1854
2812	Conway,	George.	Private	Died	15th July	1853
1907	Cook,	George.	Private	Died	9th April	1852
852	Cook,	Henry.	Private	Discharged	25th Aug.	1853 - Deceased
2227	Crawley,	John.	Private	Died,	Date and place not known	
	(2227 Crowley, John.)					

1586	Cromar,	William.	Private	Died		30th Sept.	1852
1054	Crook,	William.	Sergeant	Died		30th March	1853
2887	Crowe,	John.	Private	Died		28th Oct.	1854
	(2887 Crow, John.)						
2647	Curtis,	James.	Private	Died		6th April	1853
2351	Cutts,	Thomas James.	Private	Died		25th Nov.	1853
2862	Daley,	John.	Private	Died		10th July	1853
	(2862 Daly, James.)						
1652	Dare,	George.	Private	Died		6th May	1854
	*Daubeny (KH), Henry.		Lieutenant-General Died,			Date and place not known	
2858	Davis,	Samuel.	Private	Died		1st July	1853
	(2854 Davis, Samuel.)						
3112	Davis,	Thomas.	Private	Deserted July 1856	Deceased, Date and place not known		
3116	Davis,	William.	Private	Died		2nd May	1853
1888	Day,	John Stephen.	Pay Master Sergeant	Died		19th Oct.	1852
3099	Dean,	James.	Private	Died		13th July	1853
1070	Dean,	Matthew Martin.	Private	Died		11th July	1852
3087	Delany,	Cornelius.	Private	Died		19th March	1853
	(3078 Delany, Cornilius.)						
2706	Denby,	Jarvis.	Sergeant	Died		20th June	1853
2754	Dennison,	William.	Private	Died,		Date and place not known	
2622	Dewest,	James.	Private	Died		11th April	1853
	(2621 Dewest, James.)						
3098	Dickenson,	Joseph.	Private	Died		5th Oct.	1853
2926	Donoghue,	Michael.	Private	Died		27th Nov.	1852
2002	Donohoe,	Alexander.	Private	Discharged		11th Aug.	1853
2312	Donovan,	Daniel.	Private	Died		23rd May	1853
2877	Dordon,	Michael.	Private	Died		20th Dec.	1854
	(2877 Dordow, Michael.)						
2241	Dowling,	Richard.	Private	Died		20th Dec.	1854
3117	Down,	Samuel.	Private	Died		18th March	1853
	(3119 Down, Samuel.)						
3099	Doyle,	John.	Private	Died		19th July	1853
	(3079 Doyle, John.)						
2320	Drewitt,	Jacob.	Private	Died		3rd Jan.	1853
	(2320 Drewett, Jacob.)						
3074	Drury,	John.	Private	Died		23rd March	1853
2215	Duigan,	John.	Corporal	Died		2nd Feb.	1854
	*Dunn,	William Calvert.	Leiutenant	Died,		Date and place not known	
2521	Dwyer,	Michael.	Private	Discharged Invalid		26th Oct.	1854
1741	Dycks,	William.	Private	Died		14th Oct.	1853
	(1741 Dicks, William.)						
1715	Dyson,	Richard.	Private	Died,		Date and place not known	
2462	Eagle,	Francis.	Private	Died		21st Aug.	1853
	(2463 Eagar, Francis.)						
2951	Edwards,	Arthur.	Corporal	Died		14th Nov.	1852
	(2957 Edwards, Arthur.)						
2749	Edwards,	Henry.	Private	Died		11th Feb.	1853
3115	Emmett,	Robert.	Private	Died		28th June	1853
2911	Evans,	John.	Private	Died,		Date and place not known	
2040	Eyre,	Stephen.	Private	Died		17th April	1852
2378	Fannon,	William.	Private	Discharged		30th Dec.	1854
3068	Fawcett,	Mathew.	Private	Died		20th May	1853
	(3084 Fawcett, Matthew.)						
1702	Fielding,	Henry.	Private	Died		10th April	1852 Rangoon
2955	Finnigan,	Patrick.	Private	Died		12th Aug.	1853
1343	Fisher,	James.	Sergeant	Died		20th April	1853
2821	Fitzgerald,	John.	Private	Died		20th Oct.	1852 Rangoon
2418	Fitzpatrick,	James.	Private	Died		4th Feb.	1853
3070	Flannigan,	John.	Private	Died		2nd Oct.	1853
	(3070 Flannagan, John.)						
2237	Fletcher,	Francis.	Private	Died		13th May	1853
2275	Foden,	Jeffrey.	Private	Died		6th Jan.	1853
1010	Foot,	James.	Private	Died		13th Sept.	1853
2440	Foot,	James.	Private	Died		18th Dec.	1853
1721	Foot,	William.	Private	Drowned		7th April 1853 River Salween, Moulmein	
	(1721 Foote, William.)						
2999	Fox,	Michael.	Private	Died		2nd May	1853
2799	Fox,	Robert.	Private	Died		28th Sept.	1852
891	Fox,	Thomas.	Private	Discharged		25th Jan.	1854
1109	Frame,	George.	Private	Discharged Invalid		26th Oct.	1853
	*Freeman,	William Deane.	Lieutenant	Died,		Date and place not known	
1390	French,	Francis Thomas.	Private	Died		17th Dec.	1852 Prome

1623	Friend,	Thomas.	Colour Sergeant	Died	30th March	1853
2879	Fulcher,	Alfred.	Private	Died,	Date and place not known	
2361	Fulham,	James.	Private	Died,	Date and place not known	
1027	Galvin,	James.	Private	Discharged	13th Aug.	1853
2941	Galvin,	James.	Private	Died	4th Aug.	1853
1764	Gardner,	John.	Private	Discharged	30th April	1857
1811	Gardner,	William.	Corporal	Died	24th July	1853
1271	Garrick,	James.	Corporal	Died	27th Dec.	1852 Prome
1628	Geary,	William.	Private	Died	12th May	1853
	(1628 Gary, William.)					
1869	Geddes,	John.	Private	Died	20th Aug.	1860 Saugor
	(1869 Geddies, John.)					
1948	Giles,	Richard.	Private	Died	12th Oct.	1852 Prome
2554	Gilham,	Edward.	Private	Died	9th Dec.	1852
2884	Gill,	Henry.	Private	Died	31st March	1853 Prome
2571	Gittings,	Richard.	Private	Died	30th April	1853
3029	Goldsmith,	David.	Private	Died	27th Dec.	1852
2016	Gore,	Thomas.	Private	Died	14th May	1853
	Grant,	J.	Asst. Surgeon	Died,	Date and place not known	
1726	Green,	Thomas.	Private	Died	8th Nov.	1852
2164	Greenway,	James.	Private	Died	27th Aug.	1853
1735	Gregson,	Henry.	Private	Died	13th April	1853
	(1735 Gregson, Thomas George.)					
2354	Gresham,	George.	Private	Died	28th May	1853
	(2364 Gresham, George.)					
2210	Grimes,	Thomas.	Private	Died	19th Nov.	1853
	(2210 Grime, Thomas.)					
2786	Guise,	Charles.	Sergeant	Died	18th Jan.	1853
	(2756 Guise, Charles.)					
1919	Hale,	William.	Private	Died	8th April	1853
1947	Hall,	George.	Private	Died	17th March	1853
1950	Hamilton,	Joseph.	Private	Died	7th Sept.	1853
1152	Hancock,	Edward.	Private	Died	11th Dec.	1852
2937	Hand,	James.	Corporal	Died	20th Sept.	1853
2488	Hardbattle,	James.	Corporal	Died	26th Sept.	1852
2755	Harrison,	Thomas.	Private	Died	9th Jan.	1854
3040	Harrison,	William.	Private	Died	4th May	1853
3051	Hayes,	Robert.	Private	Died	30th April	1853
2789	Haylings,	John.	Private	Died	6th Feb.	1854
2649	Heagarty,	Thomas.	Private	Died	4th April	1853
2285	Healy,	Michael.	Private	Died	10th April	1853
2927	Heckett,	Patrick.	Private	Died	22nd Jan.	1852
2673	Hemmings,	Thomas.	Private	Died	11th Dec.	1853
2503	Henry,	Robert.	Private	Died	18th Oct.	1853
1930	Hercott,	George.	Private	Died	22nd Oct.	1853
	(1913 Hercott, George.)					
1025	Hewitt,	George.	Private	Discharged,	Date and place not known	
1787	Hick,	Thomas.	Private	Died	7th Dec.	1852 Prome
1788	Higgins,	Henry.	Private	Discharged	17th Aug	1854
1814	Hill,	David.	Private	Died	22nd April	1852
3014	Hodgskins,	Benjamin.	Private	Died	17th Oct.	1852 Prome
2841	Hogan,	Alexander.	Private	Died	14th Dec.	1852 Prome
2620	Holingshead,	George.	Private	Died	17th April	1852 Rangoon
1889	Holmes,	Henry.	Private	Died	16th April	1852
	(1889 Homes, Henry.)					
2381	Horan,	James.	Private	Died	28th Oct.	1853
1875	Huggins,	James.	Sergeant	Died	7th Oct.	1853
2558	Hulme,	James.	Private	Discharged,	Date and place not known	
3113	Humston,	Mark.	Private	Died	30th Jan.	1854
	Hunt,	Thomas William.	Lieutenant	Died,	Date and place not known	
	Hunt,	Thomas Bloomfield.	Pay Master	Died,	Date and place not known	
2973	Hutton,	Thomas.	Private	Died	27th Dec.	1852
1140	Imeson,	William.	Private	Died	15th April	1852
	(1040 Imeson, William.)					
1307	Impitt,	William.	Drummer	Died	21st Sept.	1852
	(1307 Impett, William.)					
2771	Ison,	Henry.	Private	Died	16th Sept.	1853
1930	Jay,	Henry.	Private	Died	13th Nov.	1852
	(1934 Jay, Henry.)					
1517	Johnstone,	Edward.	Private	Died	24th Dec.	1852
	(1517 Johnson, Edward.)					
972	Johnstone,	Frederick.	Sergeant	Died	13th April	1853
	(972 Johnston, Frederick.)					
2659	Johnstone,	Robert.	Private	Discharged	28th July	1853
	(2659 Johnson, Robert.)					

1582	Jones,	James.	Private	Discharged	10th Nov.	1853
	(1562 Jones,	James.)				
1973	Jones,	James.	Private	Died	24th March	1853 Prome
2575	Jones,	John.	Private	Died	14th Dec.	1852
2142	Jones,	Thomas.	Private	Died	4th April	1853
	(2152 Jones, Thomas.)					
2938	Jordan,	Patrick.	Private	Died	7th July	1852
1886	Jude,	Page.	Private	Discharged	9th Jan.	1854
2012	Kelly,	Charles.	Private	Died	16th Oct.	1852
3003	Kelly,	John.	Private	Died	29th March	1853
3091	Kelly,	William.	Private	Died	5th May	1853
2891	Kemp,	George.	Private	Died	27th Jan.	1852 Prome
1617	King,	David.	Sergeant	Died	20th July	1852 Rangoon
	*Kirkland,	Matthew.	Leiutenant	Died,	Date and place not known	
3061	Kyrne,	Patrick.	Private	Died	27th April	1853
	(3061 Kyne, Patrick.)					
2628	Lacey,	John.	Private	Died	28th July	1853
1796	Lacey,	William.	Private	Died	18th July	1852
2170	Lafargue,	Peter.	Private	Died	22nd Jan.	1854
1237	Lambourne,	John.	Corporal	Died	8th July	1852 Rangoon
	(1237 Lamborn, John.)					
2987	Lawler,	Christopher.	Private	Died	18th July	1853
	(2987 Lawlor, Christopher.)					
2396	Lawler,	John.	Private	Died	30th Dec.	1853
2410	Lawson.	James.	Private	Died	15th April	1852
1885	Leadbeater,	James.	Private	Died	3rd Oct.	1853
2470	Ledward,	Thomas.	Private	Died	24th July	1853
	(2470 Ledwards, Thomas.)					
1603	Lee,	Ralph.	Private	Died	30th Nov.	1853
2806	Leech,	Alfred.	Corporal	Died	21st April	1852 Rangoon
	*Lewis,	Charles.	Lieutenant Colonel	Died,	Date and place not known	
1509	Lilley,	Thomas.	Private	Died	1st Feb.	1853 Rangoon
	Lockhart,	Robert Alexander.	Major	Died,	Date and place not known	
3114	Loncester,	Peter.	Private	Died	29th June	1853
	(3114 Longcester, Peter.)					
1035	Long,	Robert.	Private	Died	31st March	1853
2553	Longmore,	John.	Private	Died	25th March	1853
1588	Lovegrove,	Levi.	Private	Died	21st Nov.	1853
	*Lucas,	Henry Carr.	Asst. Surgeon	Died,	Date and place not known	
2849	Lyons,	John.	Private	Died,	Date and place not known	
2640	McCann,	John.	Private	Died,	Date and place not known	
2984	McDermott,	John.	Private	Died	13th Feb.	1853
2809	McGregor,	Archibald.	Private	Died	4th May	1853
2363	McGuckin,	Thomas.	Private	Died	10th Jan.	1853
	(2362 McGuckin, Thomas.)					
2842	McGuire,	Edward.	Private	Died	18th Sept.	1853
2073	McKenny,	Thomas.	Private	Died	1st Nov.	1852
	(2073 McKinney, Thomas.)					
1134	McLaren,	James.	Private	Died,	Date and place not known	
2014	McMahon,	John.	Private	Died	11th Feb.	1853
	(2014 MacMahon, John.)					
2963	McMahon,	Michael.	Private	Died	24th June	1853
2354	McMahon,	Samuel.	Private	Died	24th Nov.	1852 Prome
3018	McNamara,	John.	Private	Died	2nd Sept.	1853
1380	Madden,	John.	Private	Died	5th Feb.	1853 Rangoon
2731	Mahoney,	Daniel.	Private	Died	14th Aug.	1853
3071	Malcolm,	John.	Private	Died	13th March	1853
	(3071 Malcolm, James.)					
2860	Maley,	Philip.	Private	Died	21st April	1852
3027	Mann,	John.	Private	Died	6th March	1853
2436	Mason,	John.	Private	Died	13th July	1853
2193	Mason,	William.	Private	Discharged	17th Sept.	1853
1791	Mathews,	James.	Private	Died	24th Nov.	1853
1755	May,	Charles.	Private	Discharged	31st Aug.	1854
2593	Meale,	James.	Private	Died	13th March	1853
	(2593 Male, James.)					
3057	Medicroft,	John.	Private	Died	4th Aug.	1853
2785	Meeson,	Edward.	Private	Died	23rd Feb.	1853
3109	Milner,	John.	Private	Died	4th May	1853
2404	Mingey,	William.	Private	Died	11th Dec.	1852
	(2405 Mingey, William.)					
	*Montgomerie	Rob. Hamilton.	Lieutenant	Died	May	1852
3007	Montgomery,	Archibald.	Private	Died on board 'Phlegethon'	17th Oct.	1852
2879	Mooney,	John.	Private	Died,	Date and place not known	

2968	Mooney,	John.	Private	Died	25th April	1853
3000	Moore,	Isaac.	Private	Died	20th April	1853
2609	Moore,	Michael.	Private	Died	11th Feb.	1853
3011	Moran,	Patrick.	Private	Died	28th Nov.	1852
2709	Morgan,	Michael.	Private	Died	20th Aug.	1852
2288	Morley,	William.	Private	Died	31st Aug.	1852 Martaban
1951	Morris,	George.	Private	Died	23rd June	1853
2557	Morris,	John.	Private	Died	15th Dec.	1852
	(2257 Morris, John.)					
1050	Morris,	William.	Private	Died	18th June	1852
	(1500 Morris, William.)					
2069	Murphy,	Jeremiah.	Private	Died	30th April	1853 Prome
3013	Murray,	John.	Private	Died	24th Jan.	1853
3027	Murray,	John.	Private	Died,	Date and place not known	
1833	Murray,	Robert.	Private	Died	4th Nov.	1852
1992	Myers,	John.	Private	Died	22nd Sept.	1853
1706	Nash,	James.	Corporal	Died	17th Oct.	1852 Prome
2930	Neagle,	John.	Private	Died	26th Feb.	1853
2434	Neil,	Stephen.	Private	Died	21st April	1853
2225	Newlan,	William.	Sergeant	Died	18th March	1853
2474	Newman,	Thomas.	Private	Died	5th April	1853
	(2474 Newmans, Thomas.)					
1061	Nixon,	James.	Private	Died	3rd March	1853
2006	Nocton,	Lawrence.	Private	Died,	Date and place not known	
	Nunn,	James Loftus Winniett.	Lieutenant	Wounded	April 1852 (Storming Rangoon)	
2710	Nuttall,	Henry.	Private	Died	1st July	1853
2159	Oldfield,	Simeon.	Private	Died	30th March	1853 Prome
867	O'Rielly,	Philip.	Private	Discharged	28th Nov.	1854
1511	Padgett,	Luke.	Private	Died	22nd Dec.	1852 Prome
2892	Page,	James.	Private	Died	21st April	1853
2745	Palmer,	William.	Private	Died	8th Aug.	1852
1901	Parcel,	Richard.	Corporal	Died	15th Dec.	1852 Prome
2824	Park,	George.	Corporal	Died	24th Oct.	1852 Prome
833	Parker,	John.	Private	Died	18th May	1852
2885	Parker,	William.	Private	Died	2nd July	1853
1520	Peake,	George.	Private	Died	23rd April	1853
2223	Phillips,	James.	Private	Discharged Invalid	28th Oct.	1854
2722	Pitchford,	Mark.	Private	Died	13th April	1853
	*Quill,	Thomas Predergast	Lieutenant	Died,	Date and place not known	
1091	Quinn,	Edward.	Private	Died	22nd May	1853
2666	Quinn,	Thomas.	Corporal	Died	25th Dec.	1852
2335	Quirke,	James.	Private	Died	29th Oct.	1853
2754	Randall,	Richard.	Private	Died	29th July	1853
1382	Ratcliffe,	James.	Private	Died	25th April	1853
2146	Ratcliffe,	Robert.	Private	Died	9th June	185
2630	Reader,	Henry.	Private	Died	3rd July	1853
	(2636 Reader, Hery.)					
1790	Reid,	John.	Private	Died	31st Oct.	1852
	(1790 Reed, John)					
3015	Rielley,	John.	Private	Died	15th Aug.	1853
	(3015 Reiley, John.)					
2353	Rielley,	Luke.	Private	Died	18th March	1853
	(2353 Riley, Luke.)					
1567	Roberts,	Joseph.	Sergeant Major	Discharged	30th Dec.	1854
2188	Roberts,	Thomas.	Private	Died	14th July	1853
3100	Robinson,	George.	Private	Died	13th March	1853
1666	Robinson,	James.	Private	Discharged	31st Aug.	1854
3096	Rogers,	William.	Private	Discharged	30th Sept.	1854
2944	Ryan,	James.	Private	Died	22nd June	1852
	(2946 Ryan, James.)					
3030	Ryan,	Mathew.	Private	Died	7th Jan.	1853
2356	Ryan,	Patrick.	Private	Died	14th Dec.	1852 Prome
2001	Salter,	John.	Private	Died	11th Oct.	1853
2907	Sammon,	Thomas.	Private	Died	28th Feb.	1853
1388	Sanderson,	George.	Private	Died	4th June	1853
	Sayers,	Richard Talbot.	Major	Died,	Date and place not known	
3032	Scott,	John.	Private	Discharged,	Date and place not known	
2576	Shoreland,	James.	Private	Died	1st July	1852
	(2576 Shorlain, James.)					
1274	Silvey,	Edward.	Private	Died	25th Jan.	1853
2786	Silvey,	George.	Private	Died	24th June	1853
	(2783 Silvey, George.)					
1232	Smeaton,	Charles.	Private	Died	31st Dec.	1853
2000	Smith,	Edward.	Private	Died	17th Aug.	1853

3049	Smith,	James.	Private	Died,	Date and place not known	
2205	Smith,	John.	Private	Died	17th Jan.	1854
2668	Smith,	John.	Private	Died	28th March	1853 Prome
2717	Smith,	Richard.	Private	Died	21st April	1853
2758	Smith,	Thomas.	Private	Died	18th March	1853
2844	Smith,	Thomas.	Private	Died	11th April	1853
3085	Smith,	Thomas.	Private	Died	17th July	1853
2942	St. John,	Patrick.	Private	Died,	Date and place not known	
2637	Stannard,	George.	Private	Died,	Date and place not known	
2294	Stanyard,	Thomas.	Private	Died	31st Jan.	1853
	(2296 Stanyard, Thomas.)					
2969	Starr,	Archibald.	Corporal	Died	9th Dec.	1852
2189	Steel,	Thomas.	Private	Died	7th Aug.	1852
	(2189 Steele, Thomas.)					
2175	Stiles,	William.	Private	Discharged	30th Sept.	1854
2177	Sullivan,	Arthur.	Private	Discharged,	Date and place not known	
2562	Strange,	James.	Private	Discharged	25th Aug 1853 Deceased Date and place not known	
2334	Studdart,	Michael.	Private	Died	8th April	1854
1584	Swan,	John.	Private	Died	11th July	1853
	(1582 Swan, John.)					
2254	Tate,	Thomas.	Private	Died	9th May	1853
2273	Taylor,	Charles.	Corporal	Died	24th July	1853
940	Taylor,	William.	Drummer	Died	19th June	1853
1673	Taylor,	George.	Private	Died	29th May	1853
3032	Taylor,	Henry.	Private	Died	23rd April	1853
1965	Taylor,	James.	Private	Died	11th April	1852
3019	Taylor,	James.	Private	Died	12th Jan.	1853
	(3010 Taylor, James.)					
2156	Thomas,	Richard.	Private	Died	18th April	1852
	(2145 Thomas, Richard.)					
3031	Thompson,	Ambrose.	Private	Died,	Date and place not known	
757	Thompson,	William.	Private	Discharged	26th Oct.	1854
1549	Thorndycroft,	John.	Private	Invalided - Died	9th March	1853
2003	Toole,	Patrick.	Private	Died	1st July	1853
2638	Tower,	Robert.	Private	Died	30th March	1853 Prome
2889	Tracey,	Joseph.	Private	Deserted	24th Aug.1853-Deceased Date and place not known	
1792	Turner,	Henry.	Private	Died	25th July	1853
1747	Turner,	Richard,	Private	Died	2nd Aug.	1853
2660	Turner,	Thomas.	Private	Died	3rd Aug.	1852 Amherst
1573	Wade,	John.	Private	Died	5th June.	1852
2515	Walsh,	John.	Private	Died	3rd Jan.	1853
1712	Walton,	Thomas.	Private	Died	25th April	1854
1315	Warburton,	William.	Private	Died	11th April	1853
2533	Waters,	Charles.	Private	Died	3rd Aug.	1853
1243	Watts,	William.	Sergeant	Died	7th Oct.	1852
2873	Wedgewood,	Peter(alias Peter McGinn),Private		Died	11th Oct.	1853
2702	Weight,	Benjamin.	Private	Died	7th May	1853
2197	Weldon,	Henry.	Private	Died	10th Sept.	1852 Rangoon
2759	Welsh,	Thomas.	Private	Died	8th May	1852 Rangoon
1612	West,	John.	Private	Died	2nd May	1853
2913	Whalin,	Thomas.	Private	Died	23rd Jan.	1853
	(2913 Whalan, Thomas.)					
2529	Wheeler,	Stanislaus.	Private	Died	29th Jan.	1852
	(2529 Wheeler, Stanislaus Frederick.)					
2183	White,	Charles.	Private	Died	16th Dec.	1852
780	Whitfield,	John.	Private	Died,	Date and place not known	
2070	Whybrow,	William.	Private	Died	11th Sept.	1853
3392	Wigood,	Robert.	Private	Discharged	31st Aug.	1854
2726	Wiles,	William.	Private	Died	10th Sept.	1853
	Wilkinson,	John.	Lieutenant	Wounded	19th March	1853 Kyon Tani
3086	Willerton,	Henry.	Private	Died	14th March	1853
1693	Williams,	George.	Private	Died	3rd Jan.	1854
2291	Woodland,	John.	Sergeant	Died	30th Jan.	1853
1780	Woods,	Anthony.	Corporal	Died	13th Oct.	1852
	(1780 Wood, Anthony.)					
2061	Woods,	Thomas.	Private	Died	12th March	1853
	(2062 Wood, Thomas.)					
1547	Woodward,	Samuel.	Private	Died	7th Jan.	1853 Rangoon
	Wolseley,	Garnet Joseph.	Ensign	Wounded	19th March	1853 Kyon Tani
2773	Wright,	George.	Private	Died	9th May	1852
2068	Wright,	Richard.	Private	Died	12th Sept.	1853
1234	Yorstin,	James.	Corporal	Died	24th Aug.	1854
	(1219 Yorstin, James.)					

INDIAN MUTINY MEDAL 1857-1858

The Indian General Service Medal was sanctioned under the General Order No.363 dated August 18th 1858 and General Order No.733 dated 1859, with the medal being issued to soldiers engaged against the mutineers. An additional General Order, No.771 dated 1868 was raised, allowing the medal to be awarded to all those persons who had borne arms or who had been under fire.

The medal was of silver and 36mm in diameter. The designers were for the obverse side, W.Wyon. RA, and the reverse L.C.Wyon. A ribbon 32mm wide, white with two 6mm red stripes, was attached by a cusped swivel suspender. On the obverse is the diademed head of Queen Victoria with the legend 'VICTORIA REGINA'. On the reverse, is a helmeted figure of Britannia, holding a wreath in her outstretched right hand with a Union shield over her left arm. A lion is standing behind her with the words, 'INDIA', above. The exergue on the reverse contains the dates '1857-1858'. The recipient's name and regiment, or ship is indented in Roman capitals. A total of five, 'bars', were issued:

Delhi	May 30th 1857 - September 14th 1857
Defence of Lucknow	June 29th 1857 - November 22nd 1857
Relief of Lucknow	November 1857
Lucknow	November 1857 - March 1858
Central India	January 1858 - June 1858

MEDAL LIST

INDIAN MUTINY MEDAL 1857 - 1858 Including Clasp 'Central India'

The following list is of 808 soldiers who served with the 80th Regiment of Foot (Staffordshire Volunteers) as officers, surgeons, non commissioned officers and men, and who were awarded the Indian Mutiny Medal. A total of 162 were awarded the clasp 'Central India' for being part of the force under the command of Major-General Sir Hugh Rose at the capture of Kalpi.

N.B. Some spellings and Army Numbers are slightly different between the Medal List and the Regiment's Nominal Roll. Those differences identified have been included, with the Medal List version taking presedence, the Nominal Roll format in brackets. Where an * is after the surname, it refer to the Casualty List.

No.	Surname	Forename	Rank	Clasp
2144	**Allen**,	John.	Sergeant	
4202	Allen,	John.	Drummer	
3464	Addison,	John.	Private	
4024	Airey*,	Thomas.	Private	
3172	Allen,	Edward.	Private	
3384	Allen*,	George.	Private	'Central India'
3705	Allen,	William.	Private	
4160	Anderson*,	John.	Private	'Central India'
4242	Anderson,	William.	Private	
3927	Andrews,	Edward.	Private	
3919	Andrews,	John.	Private	'Central India'
3232	Andrews,	Joseph.	Private	'Central India'
3251	Andrews,	Thomas.	Private	
4013	Anthony,	Benjamin.	Private	
4016	Anthony,	William.	Private	
4074	Archer,	James.	Private	
3859	Archer,	Job.	Private	
4049	Archer,	John.	Private	
3855	Askew,	John.	Private	
	Browne Hon.,	John Montague.	Captain	'Central India'
	Batchelor,	Horatio Pettus.	Lieutenant	
	Borrowes*,	Erasmus.	Adjutant	
	Browne,	Wellington.	Pay Master	
3574	Broadmeadow,	William.	Hospital Sergeant	
3169	Burke*,	John.	Drum Major	
1606	Bayley,	Charles.	Sergeant	'Central India
3721	Bennett,	William.	Sergean	
3161	Brown,	Patrick.	Sergeant	'Central India'
2345	Burke,	James.	Sergeant	
3131	Butler,	James.	Sergeant	
2943	Butterworth,	Joseph.	Corporal	
4245	Beadle,	Edward.	Drummer	'Central India'
3155	Bagnall,	Thomas.	Private	'Central India'
3708	Bailey*,	William.	Private	'Central India'
3213	Bailiss,	Thomas.	Private	
3868	Bakehouse,	Benjamin.	Private	
4057	Banham,	Edward.	Private	
3395	Bannister*,	James.	Private	'Central India'
3193	Barnes*,	Thomas. (Alias Thomas Lowe) Private		
3367	Barr,	William.	Private	
3823	Barrett,	Michael.	Private	
4165	Barry,	John.	Private	
3864	Bayliss*,	Joseph.	Private	
3484	Beale,	John.	Private	
3857	Beard,	George.	Private	
3760	Beckett,	John.	Private	'Central India'
3677	Bell,	Duncan.	Private	'Central India'
2624	Bell,	John.	Private	'Central India'
3666	Bells,	Dugald.	Private	
3943	Bennett,	George.	Private	
3700	Bennett,	James.	Private	'Central India
3295	Bennett,	William.	Private	
3592	Benson,	James.	Private	
3421	Bentley*,	Joseph.	Private	
3222	Berry,	William E.	Private	
2978	Birchall,	John.	Private	
4003	Bird,	James.	Private	
3479	Bishop,	William.	Private	'Central India'
3500	Blackwell*,	Samuel.	Private	'Central India'
3883	Blake,	Francis.	Private	
2476	Blake,	William.	Private	
3379	Blakely,	James.	Private	
3441	Bobbins,	John.	Private	
1878	Bobbins,	William.	Private	
3140	Bond,	Samuel.	Private	
2761	Bond,	William.	Private	'Central India'
2086	Borham,	Thomas.	Private	
3843	Borrowes,	Osmond.	Private	
2802	Bowler,	George.	Private	
2803	Bowler,	Robert.	Private	
4028	Brackley,	James.	Private	
3508	Bradley,	Edward.	Private	
4145	Bradley,	Henry.	Private	
3829	Bradshaw,	James.	Private	
3735	Brennan,	Edward.	Private	'Central India'
3162	Bresnahan,	Timothy.	Private	
3397	Brett,	Thomas.	Private	

No.	Surname	Forename	Rank	Honour
3485	Britton*,	Robert.	Private	
3739	Brooks,	George.	Private	
3994	Brooks,	Joseph.	Private	
1917	Brown,	David.	Private	
3158	Brown,	John.	Private	
4104	Brown,	John.	Private	
4227	Brown,	John.	Private	
3371	Brown,	Joshua.	Private	'Central India'
2599	Brown,	Robert.	Private	
3726	Brown,	William.	Private	
3862	Browne,	William.	Private	'Central India'
3754	Bruce,	Joseph.	Private	
4219	Bugg*,	Robert.	Private	
4020	Burgess,	John.	Private	
3385	Burke,	John.	Private	
3571	Burnes,	Joseph.	Private	
3291	Burrell,	Charles.	Private	
2010	Bush,	Charles.	Private	
2800	Bush,	George.	Private	
3871	Buxton,	George.	Private	'Central India'
3142	Byrne,	Charles.	Private	
3387	Byrne*,	John.	Private	
3077	Byrne,	Mark.	Private	
2522	Byson,	James.	Private	
	Christie*,	Samuel Tolfroy.	Colonel	
	Crauford,	Frederick Brown Numa.	Lieutenant	
	Christie,	William Beaver B.	Lieutenant	'Central India'
	Cosens,	George Weir.	Ensign	
2911	Collins,	William.	Paymaster Sergeant	
3848	Crawley,	John.	Orderly Room Clerk	
3130	Clements,	Joseph.	Colour Sergeant	
3012	Carson,	John.	Sergeant	'Central India'
2820	Chamberlain,	James.	Sergeant	
3135	Clarke*,	Thomas.	Sergeant	
3188	Caddick,	Richard.	Corporal	
2555	Clarke,	Patrick.	Corporal	
3625	Connolly,	Malcolm.	Corporal	
3151	Corikah,	William.	Corporal	
4010	Coulbourne,	Joseph.	Corporal	'Central India'
1880	Creek,	Thomas.	Corporal	
2780	Connolly*,	Michael.	Drummer	
2740	Cuddy,	Martin.	Drummer	
3178	Callaghan,	Daniel.	Private	
2936	Callaghan,	Peter.	Private	
4151	Callanan,	John.	Private	
4095	Cameron,	Robert.	Private	'Central India'
2274	Cannon,	James.	Private	
2991	Carbray,	Patrick.	Private	
3440	Carlton,	Peter.	Private	
3667	Carmichael,	Michael.	Private	
3595	Carr,	Patrick.	Private	'Central India'
1844	Carr,	Samuel.	Private	
2923	Carroll,	John.	Private	
3398	Carroll,	Malachi.	Private	
3956	Carswell,	Lachlan.	Private	
3610	Carthy,	Thomas.	Private	'Central India'
4200	Cashen,	Anthony.	Private	
3889	Cave,	Jabez.	Private	
4083	Chadd,	Samuel.	Private	'Central India'
4134	Chamberlain,	Edwin.	Private	'Central India'
3604	Chamberlain*,	William.	Private	
4022	Cherry,	George.	Private	
3402	Chester,	William.	Private	
3893	Church,	William.	Private	
4229	Clapper,	Henry.	Private	
4061	Clarke,	James.	Private	'Central India'
3694	Clarke,	Thomas.	Private	
3802	Cleary,	James.	Private	
3284	Clegg,	Lawrence.	Private	
4018	Clements,	Charles.	Private	
4040	Clements,	Henry.	Private	
4032	Clements,	Wals.	Private	
4	Clements,	William.	Private	
3139	Clemson,	George.	Private	
4163	Cockaday,	Charles.	Private	
2147	Coghlan,	John.	Private	
2586	Collins,	James.	Private	
1637	Collins,	James.	Private	
2857	Collins,	James.	Private	
3198	Collins,	James.	Private	
2902	Collins,	John.	Private	
3244	Collins,	John.	Private	
4177	Comber,	George.	Private	
2561	Commack,	James.	Private	
1995	Connolly,	John.	Private	
3752	Connolly*,	William Henry.	Private	
3067	Connors,	Patrick.	Private	
2653	Conroy,	John.	Private	'Central India'
3306	Conroy,	John.	Private	'Central India'
4092	Cook,	David.	Private	'Central India'
3866	Cook,	Edward.	Private	'Central India'
4126	Cook*,	Richard.	Private	'Central India'
2556	Cooke,	John.	Private	
3686	Cooke,	Thomas.	Private	
3406	Cooper,	William.	Private	
4189	Cope,	William.	Private	
4030	Corby,	George.	Private	
3434	Corrigan,	Hugh.	Private	
3202	Corthorn,	Henry.	Private	
3869	Couldrick,	James.	Private	'Central India'
3345	Cowley,	Robert Alexander.	Private	
3587	Coyle*,	James.	Private	
3443	Crawley,	Thomas.	Private	
2579	Creig,	John.	Private	
3454	Crenage*,	John.	Private	
3881	Crick*,	Henry John.	Private	
3909	Critchell,	Henry.	Private	
3407	Critchley,	William.	Private	
3725	Crossley,	Francis.	Private	'Central India'
3722	Crowther,	Henry.	Private	
4119	Crump.	Benjamin.	Private	'Central India'
4116	Crump,	Charles.	Private	'Central India'
3639	Cruikshank,	Alexander.	Private	
3271	Cullins,	Michael.	Private	
3528	Cummings*,	Alexander.	Private	
	(3582 Cummings, Alexander)			
3409	Cummins,	John.	Private	
4203	Cummins*,	William.	Private	
3707	Cunningham,	Robert.	Private '	'Central India'
3744	Curme,	James.	Private	'Central India'
3529	Curran,	John.	Private	
3145	Curtis,	George.	Private	'Central India'
2623	Cussen,	John.	Private	
4004	Custance,	Henry.	Private	
	Dudgeon,	James.	Lieutenant	
2719	Deegan,	James.	Sergeant	
3396	Dale,	William.	Corporal	
2850	Derry,	James.	Corporal	
4160	Donn,	Henry.	Corporal	
1891	Dempsey,	John.	Drummer	
3808	Dalby*,	Alfred.	Private	'Central India'
3999	Dalby,	William.	Private	
3388	Danahar,	John.	Private	
4039	Darnell,	Benjamin.	Private	
1993	Darrant,	John.	Private	
3562	Davis,	Thomas.	Private	
3931	Dawkins,	Richard.	Private	
4102	Dawson,	Robert.	Private	
1946	Day,	William.	Private	
3612	Dean,	James.	Private	
	(3612 Deane, James.)			
3390	Dean,	Samuel.	Private	'Central India'
3410	Dempsey,	James.	Private	
3626	Dempsey,	John.	Private	
3664	Dempsey,	Thomas.	Private	
2705	Depledge,	William.	Private	
3422	Dick,	John.	Private	
4098	Dickey,	John.	Private	
1996	Dickinson,	James.	Private	
4017	Dilley,	Phillip.	Private	

3776	Donnolly*,	Patrick.	Private
3510	Double*,	Henry.	Private
3325	Douglas,	John.	Private
3039	Downey,	John.	Private
3770	Drake*,	James.	Private
3237	Duffey,	John.	Private
3724	Duffey,	Thomas.	Private
3550	Duggan,	Thomas.	Private
3874	Duncan*,	Joseph.	Private
3494	Dunn*,	William.	Private
	(3494 Dunne, William.)		
3789	Durham,	James.	Private
4140	Dyson,	William.	Private
4233	**Easton***,	Daniel.	Sergeant
4075	Elborne,	William.	Corporal
3699	Ely,	Henry.	Corporal
1931	Eagle,	John.	Private
4005	Earl,	William.	Private	'Central India'
3491	Eattock,	William.	Private	'Central India'
3657	Edie,	William.	Private
3895	Edwards,	Henry.	Private
2457	Edwards,	Joseph.	Private
3298	Edwards,	William.	Private
4141	Edwards,	William.	Private
3248	Ellard,	Charles.	Private
3278	Ellard,	Edward.	Private	'Central India'
3894	Emm,	Henry.	Private
3781	Evans,	James.	Private	'Central India'
	Fraser,	Donald.	Lieutenant
	Frank,	Philip.	Assistant Surgeon
3133	Flemming,	William.	Sergeant
3238	Ferguson,	William.	Corporal
2980	Fogarty,	Edmund.	Corporal
4169	Fone,	Alfred.	Corporal
4065	Fox,	Frederick.	Corporal
3274	Foster,	Thomas.	Drummer
3540	Fannon*,	James.	Private
3922	Feltham,	William.	Private
3255	Ferns,	David.	Private
3216	Field,	George.	Private
4000	Finn,	James.	Private
3641	Fisher,	George.	Private	'Central India'
3868	Fitch,	Charles.	Private
3031	Flannagan,	Edward.	Private
3877	Fletcher*,	Enoch.	Private
3530	Fletcher*,	Thomas.	Private
3233	Flitcroft,	William.	Private
4154	Flood,	William.	Private
3654	Flynn,	William.	Private	'Central India'
3828	Foden,	Joseph.	Private	'Central India'
2502	Foley,	Timothy.	Private
3511	Folkard,	Daniel.	Private	'Central India'
3535	Ford*,	Charles.	Private
	(3531 Forde, Charles.)		
3272	Foster,	Francis.	Private
3980	Foster,	George.	Private
3423	Foster,	William.	Private	'Central India'
3830	Foucher,	Samuel.	Private
4021	Fowler,	David.	Private
1403	French,	Charles.	Private
3880	Fuller,	Daniel.	Private
3324	Fullerton,	Crawford.	Private
	Goddard,	Frederick FitzClarence. Lieutenant
	Leveson-Gower, Hugh Broke B.Lieutenant
3143	Gudgeon,	Richard.	Colour Sergeant
2084	Goodenough,	James.	Sergeant
1869	Geddes,	John.	Corporal
3938	Glazebrook,	William.	Corporal
3642	Graham,	Owen.	Corporal
2412	Gunn,	Henry.	Corporal
2075	Gaffney,	John.	Private
3709	Gallagher,	Bernard.	Private	'Central India'
3815	Gallagher,	Thomas.	Private	'Central India'
4223	Gardner,	James.	Private
1870	Garner,	Begley.	Private

3957	Geddis,	Henry.	Private
3598	Gee,	Herbert.	Private	'Central India'
4027	George*,	Jessie.	Private
2023	Gettings,	James.	Private
4077	Gill,	John.	Private	'Central India'
2947	Gill,	Patrick.	Private	'Central india'
2904	Gilligan,	Bernard.	Private
3908	Gilliland,	William.	Private
3068	Gleeson,	James.	Private
3339	Glen,	Thomas.	Private
3960	Goodall*,	James.	Private
2158	Gordon,	John.	Private
3461	Gould*,	John.	Private
3341	Goulding,	Benjamin.	Private
3662	Graham,	John.	Private
3523	Graham,	William.	Private	'Central India'
2411	Gready,	John.	Private
4239	Green*,	James.	Private	'Central India'
4041	Green,	Thomas.	Private	'Central India'
4096	Greenfield,	John.	Private	'Central India'
3693	Greig*,	James.	Private
3297	Grieve,	Robert.	Private
3167	Grogan,	William.	Private
4071	Groom*,	George.	Private	'Central India'
	Hutchison,	George Samuel. Colonel
	Hardinge,	Edward.	Captain
	Holditch,	Edward Alan. Captain
	Hume,	Bliss John.	Captain
	Huskisson,	Samuel George.Ensign
3184	Harrison,	Samuel.	Sergeant Major
2200	Harrison,	Thomas.	Colour Sergeant
2102	Hornan,	Richard.	Colour Sergeant
1536	Hirst,	Robert.	Sergeant
3543	Hulme,	Thomas.	Sergeant
2851	Humphries,	Frederick.	Sergeant
3166	Hurley,	William.	Sergeant	'Central India'
3913	Hall,	Frederick.	Corporal
3933	Hallett,	George.	Corporal
1867	Harrison,	James.	Corporal
3792	Harrison,	William.	Corporal
3507	Horn,	William.	Corporal
3432	Horton*,	George.	Corporal
3022	Hennessey,	Nicholas.	Drummer
3486	Haddon,	Samuel.	Private
3319	Hallowell,	Joseph.	Private
2283	Hamilton,	Richard.	Private
4035	Hammond,	Thomas.	Private
3558	Hampton*,	Frederick.	Private
3080	Hanlon,	Edward.	Private
3910	Hanson,	Charles.	Private
3698	Hanson,	George.	Private
3983	Hardinge,	George.	Private
4011	Hardinge*,	James.	Private	'Central India'
3449	Hardman*,	John.	Private
3024	Hargroves,	John.	Private
3746	Harris,	James.	Private
4045	Hart,	George.	Private
3821	Hart,	Thomas.	Private
3243	Hart,	Timothy.	Private
1725	Hartington,	George.	Private
3391	Harvey,	Elijah.	Private
4161	Haseman,	Henry.	Private
4097	Haveran,	Robert.	Private
3374	Hawley,	John.	Private
4087	Hayburn,	James.	Private
4093	Hayburn,	William.	Private
3787	Haycock*,	William.	Private
3399	Healey,	Daniel.	Private
4088	Healey,	John.	Private
3963	Heater,	Charles.	Private
1722	Heathcock,	Thomas.	Private
3228	Heavy,	John.	Private
3322	Harry,	Henry.	Private
1867	Herbert,	Edward.	Private
3411	Haywood,	Richard.	Private

No.	Surname	Forename	Rank	Honour
4129	Hick,	George.	Private	
3207	Hickey*,	James.	Private	
3381	Hill,	James.	Private	
3589	Hill,	James.	Private	
4181	Hill,	John.	Private	
3050	Hindle,	John.	Private	
4197	Hinson,	John.	Private	
4178	Hinty,	Thomas.	Private	
3230	Hoare,	Alfred.	Private	'Central India'
3959	Hoare*,	William.	Private	
3150	Holden,	Benjamin.	Private	
2778	Holland,	George.	Private	
4110	Holman*,	John.	Private	
2912	Holmes,	Thomas.	Private	
4072	Hood,	William.	Private	
3546	Hope,	James.	Private	
3163	Hopkins,	John.	Private	
3504	Hopkins,	John.	Private	
3769	Hopkins,	John.	Private	
3097	Hopkins,	Joseph.	Private	
3972	Hopkins*,	Philip.	Private	
3041	Horan*,	Owen.	Private	
3737	Houlson,	John.	Private	
3102	Howe,	Thomas.	Private	
3520	Huggan,	Duncan.	Private	'Central India'
3562	Hughes,	Richard.	Private	
4008	Hulks,	George.	Private	
3328	Hunt,	James.	Private	
4021	Hunter,	William.	Private	
4215	Hutchings*,	Thomas.	Private	
	Irwin,	William Nelson.	Surgeon	
3683	Ingram,	Hugh.	Sergeant	
3456	Irvine*,	William.	Corporal	
	(3456 Irwin, William.)			
2626	Irwin,	Jeremiah.	Private	
2921	Ivers,	John.	Private	
3923	**Jackson**,	George.	Corporal	
3183	James,	George.	Corporal	'Central India'
3126	Jones,	Edward.	Drummer	
3583	Jackson*,	Thomas.	Private	'Central India'
3853	James,	Andrew.	Private	
3	Jefferson,	John.	Private	
4107	Jefferson,	Ralph.	Private	
4118	Jenkins,	Thomas.	Private	
4001	Jessop,	John.	Private	
3366	Johnston,	Cornelius.	Private	
3623	Johnston,	Thomas.	Private	
4094	Johnston,	Thomas.	Private	
3982	Johnston,	William.	Private	
3920	Jolliffe,	William.	Private	
4062	Jones,	Charles.	Private	
4113	Jones,	Charles.	Private	'Central India'
3268	Jones*,	Edward.	Private	
3424	Jones,	George.	Private	
4228	Jones,	James.	Private	
3621	Jones*,	John.	Private	
3181	Jones,	Joseph.	Private	'Central India'
3729	Jones,	Joshua.	Private	
2753	Jones,	Thomas.	Private	
2792	Jones,	Thomas.	Private	
4132	Jones,	Thomas.	Private	
3403	Jones*,	William.	Private	
3477	Jones,	William.	Private	
3807	Jones,	William.	Private	
2100	**Kitching**,	Robert.	Colour Sergeant	'Central India'
4089	Kane,	Christopher.	Private	
3575	Kelly,	Charles.	Private	
3204	Kelly,	Henry.	Private	
1745	Kelly,	John.	Private	
2388	Kenny,	James.	Private	'Central India'
3961	Kenyon*,	John.	Private	'Central India'
3227	Kerr*,	Edward.	Private	
3838	Kramer,	James.	Private	
3190	Kyle,	Hugh.	Private	
	Lane,	Benjamin.	Assistant Surgeon	
3138	Lovett,	Joseph.	Sergeant	
4222	Langstone,	Joyce.	Corporal	
3663	Lownsdale,	William.	Corporal	'Central India'
3696	Lackey,	Charles,	Private	
3740	Lantaff,	Thomas.	Private	
3872	Laurence*,	Charles.	Private	'Central India'
3594	Lavery,	John.	Private	'Central India'
3229	Lawson,	Ellis.	Private	
3506	Lawson,	John.	Private	
3257	Learmouth,	James.	Private	
2939	Ledow*,	Mathew.	Private	
3404	Lee,	Michael.	Private	'Central India'
3790	Leigh,	James.	Private	'Central India'
3876	Lewis,	James.	Private	
4188	Liggins*,	George.	Private	
4081	Light,	Joseph.	Private	'Central India'
3217	Lindsdell,	Robert.	Private	
3619	Little,	Samuel.	Private	'Central India'
3428	Lloyd,	Isaac.	Private	
3906	Lockyer,	Charles.	Private	'Central India'
3865	Long,	Robert.	Private	
4041	Loughlin,	James.	Private	
3415	Loughlin,	Thomas.	Private	
4234	Lovegrove,	Henry.	Private	
3577	Lovell,	Robert.	Private	
3944	Lucas,	James.	Private	
4153	Lucas,	Thomas.	Private	
	Miller,	Frederick.	Captain	
	Maxwell,	Robert James.	Lieutenant	
	Mortimer,	William Picton.	Lieutenant	'Central India'
	Miller (M.D.),	Colin.	Assistant Surgeon	
	Maloney,	William.	Quarter Master	
3152	Morin,	James.	Colour Sergeant	
3165	Marshall,	Thomas.	Sergeant	
3638	McAllen*,	Charles.	Sergeant	
	(3638 MacAllan, Charles.)			
1446	Monneypenny,	John.	Sergeant	
2617	Morris,	William.	Sergeant	
2106	Moss,	Edgar.	Sergeant	
2695	Mullins,	James.	Sergeant	
1839	Murphy,	John.	Sergeant	
3918	McCreight,	James.	Corporal	
3223	Millen,	John.	Corporal	
3668	Milloy,	Archibald.	Corporal	
3335	Mitchell,	Edward.	Corporal	
3745	Moates*,	William.	Corporal	'Central India'
	(3745 Moats, William.)			
3125	McCann,	John.	Drummer	'Central India'
3177	McDonald,	Richard.	Drummer	
	(3177 McDonnell, Richard.)			
3468	McBride,	Patrick.	Private	'Central India'
2243	McCabe,	Joseph.	Private	
3673	McCaller*,	Henry.	Private '	'Central India'
3628	McCallum,	Alexander.	Private	'Central India'
3997	McCarty,	Daniel.	Private	
2680	McCashen,	Edward.	Private	
4099	McCauly,	Bernard.	Private	
3778	McCleary,	John.	Private	
3688	McConnell,*	William.	Private	
3294	McCracken,	Samuel.	Private	
3320	McCullough,	John.	Private	
3473	McDonald,	Thomas.	Private	
3056	McElra,	James.	Private	
3969	McElween,	Mathew.	Private	'Central India'
3605	McGeough,	Patrick.	Private	'Central India'
3809	McGiveron,	Hugh.	Private	
4146	McGulton,	Frederick.	Private	
3690	McIlveen,	John.	Private	
3451	McKaon*,	Francis.	Private	'Central India'
3774	McKee,	Robert.	Private	
3337	McKechnie,	William.	Private	
4257	McKenna,	John.	Private	
3025	McKernon,	William.	Private	
4179	McLachlan,	Mathew.	Private	'Central India'
3296	McLachlan,	William.	Private	

3643	McLean,	James.	Private
3632	McLean,	James.	Private
3495	McLeod,	Donald.	Private
3603	McMaster,	Thomas.	Private	'Central India'
3426	McMurter,	Henry.	Private
3633	McNeillage,	John.	Private
4198	McPeak*,	James.	Private
3675	McPherson,	Peter.	Private
3899	Maggie,	Frederick.	Private	'Central India'
	(3899 Maggi, Frederick)		
3452	Mahaffy,	Samuel.	Private	'Central India'
3734	Mahoney,	Stephen.	Private	'Central India'
3064	Mannagon,	Michael.	Private
3211	Mansfield,	George.	Private
4047	Mansfield*,	George.	Private
2855	Mansfield,	William.	Private
3563	Marmion,	Henry.	Private	'Central India'
2600	Marrick,	Thomas.	Private
1709	Marsh,	John.	Private
3175	Marsh,	Robert.	Private
2775	Marshall*,	James.	Private
4053	Mathews*,	John.	Private
4048	Meade*,	James.	Private
3121	Meadows,	George.	Private
1949	Meadows,	James.	Private
3317	Megrillan,	Arthur.	Private	'Central India'
3892	Meldrum,	Alexander.	Private	'Central India'
2871	Membry,	Thomas.	Private
3973	Mills*,	John.	Private
3890	Miffin,	John.	Private	'Central India'
3634	Milloy*,	Archibald.	Private
3763	Minnis,	John.	Private	'Central India'
	(3753 Minnis, John.)		
2784	Mitchell,	Edward.	Private
3081	Mitchell,	Michael.	Private
3420	Mitchell,	Patrick.	Private
3253	Mongon*,	Thomas.	Private
2822	Moran,	Edward.	Private
3573	Moran,	John.	Private
3160	Moriarty,	Daniel.	Private
3513	Morley*,	George.	Private
4125	Morris,	Robert.	Private
3635	Morrison,	John.	Private
3516	Mullinger,	James.	Private
3358	Mulligan,	James.	Private
3728	Murphy,	Henry.	Private
3331	Murphy,	James.	Private
3561	Murphy,	Michael.	Private
3260	Murphy,	Patrick.	Private	'Central India'
3332	Murphy,	Patrick.	Private
	Nunn,	James Loftus Winniett. Captain	
3417	Norman,	George.	Sergeant	'Central India'
3841	Neat,	James.	Corporal
3028	Naughton,	John.	Private
3005	Nelson,	Matthew.	Private
3748	Newman,	Joseph.	Private	'Central India'
3287	Newman,	William.	Private
2111	Nicholls*,	Alfred.	Private
1750	Nicholls,	James.	Private
3517	Nicholls,	Thomas.	Private
3904	Nightingale*,	John.	Private	'Central India'
3318	Nulty,	Michael.	Private
3431	Orr*,	George.	Sergeant
1952	O'Hara,	Daniel.	Private
3775	O'Niel,	John.	Private
4060	O'Niel*,	Peter.	Private
3934	Oddy,	William.	Private
3692	Ogden,	John.	Private
28	Owen,	Robert.	Private
2087	**Purchase,**	Nicholas.	Quartermaster Sergeant
1568	Porter,	James.	Sergeant
3689	Perry*,	William.	Corporal
1	Power,	Patrick.	Corporal
4115	Paice,	Thomas.	Drummer
1704	Pendry,	Edmund.	Drummer
3622	Pendry,	James.	Drummer	'Central India'
3387	Palmer,	William.	Private	'Central India'
1526	Parrett,	Frederick.	Private
4183	Partridge,	Joseph.	Private
3120	Parry,	John.	Private	'Central India'
3429	Payne,	Samuel	Private
4123	Pearcy,	William.	Private	'Central India'
2797	Peel,	John.	Private
4206	Perrin,	John.	Private
3316	Perry,	Charles.	Private
4208	Perry,	Charles.	Private
2212	Peto,	Edward.	Private
3072	Phillips,	Matthew.	Private
4124	Phillips*,	William.	Private	'Central India'
3493	Pickford,	Peter.	Private
2318	Pike,	James.	Private
3482	Pitt*,	William.	Private	'Central India'
3330	Platt,	Edwin.	Private
4236	Platt,	Thomas.	Private
4149	Platt,	William.	Private
3035	Polworth,	William.	Private
2920	Power,	Thomas.	Private
3949	Povell,	Thomas.	Private	'Central India'
4127	Preece*,	James.	Private
3346	Preece,	Thomas.	Private
3854	Press*,	Richard.	Private	'Central India'
	(3854 Press, William.)		
4191	Preston*,	William.	Private
4111	Price*,	William.	Private
3697	Pritchard,	William.	Private
2782	Probert,	James.	Private
3964	Proctor,	James.	Private	'Central India'
3442	Purdy,	John.	Private
3189	**Rooker,**	Thomas.	Armourer Sergeant
3559	Ralph,	Henry.	Corporal
1809	Richards,	Charles.	Drummer
3915	Randle,	John.	Private
3514	Ralph*,	George.	Private	'Central india'
3629	Rawlinson,	Charles.	Private
3250	Reeve,	Charles.	Private	'Central India'
3187	Reid,	John.	Private
3970	Reid,	John.	Private
4082	Reynolds,	Denham.	Private
3076	Reynolds,	Thomas.	Private
3361	Richardson,	John.	Private
3020	Risworth,	John.	Private
4173	Robson,	John.	Private
3676	Roddy*,	Hugh.	Private	'Central India'
3602	Roe,	William.	Private	'Central India'
3661	Rodgers,	William.	Private	'Central india'
3832	Rolfe,	Henry.	Private	'Central India'
3301	Rollings,	George.	Private
3426	Rooney,	Peter.	Private
2863	Ross,	David.	Private
3766	Ross,	Joseph.	Private
3834	Rowland*,	Thomas.	Private
3492	Royle,	Joseph P.	Private
3985	Ryan,	Michael.	Private	'Central India'
2928	Ryan*,	Patrick.	Private
	St. Ledger,	Henry Hungerford. Lieutenant 'Central India'	
	Sullivan,	George.	Lieutenant	'Central India'
	Savage,	Edward.	Instructor of Musketry
	Smith,	Hamilton Charles. Captain	'Central India'
3647	Skee,	John.	Sergeant
3536	Smith,	George.	Sergeant
3712	Smith,	James.	Sergeant
2401	Smyth,	William.	Sergeant
3533	Smallwood,	John.	Corporal	'Central India'
3711	Salter*,	Richard.	Private
2513	Saunders*,	William.	Private
3474	Scott,	William.	Private
3370	Scullard,	Michael.	Private
4128	Seabourn,	Thomas.	Private

3412	Sefton,	Thomas.	Private		2958	**Vincent***,	John.	Corporal
3186	Settle,	Henry.	Private		3548	Vaughan,	Thomas.	Private
4014	Shambrook,	William.	Private	'Central India'	2538	Vickroy,	Edward.	Private
3819	Sharman,	John.	Private	'Central India'		**Whitehead**,	William.	Lieutenant	'Central India'
4026	Sharp,	Charles.	Private		2618	Watts,	George.	Colour Sergeant
3504	Sharp,	Henry.	Private	'Central India'	3073	Whealan,	Michael.	Colour Sergeant
3655	Shaw,	William John.	Private		3156	Worral,	Francis.	Colour Sergeant 'Central India'
1884	Sherratt,	Robert.	Private			(3156 Worril, Francis.)		
2137	Shields,	David.	Private		1776	Williams,	Robert.	Sergeant
3122	Shore,	Charles.	Private		2975	Walsh,	Miles.	Corporal	'Central India'
3124	Shore,	Edward.	Private		2261	Whitworth,	Thomas.	Corporal
2908	Sida,	John.	Private	'Central India'	3761	Wild,	John.	Corporal
3393	Simcox,	Elijah.	Private		3342	Walker,	Charles.	Private
2763	Simon,	Charles.	Private		4059	Walker,	James.	Private
4007	Simpson,	Charles.	Private	'Central India'	3299	Walker,	John.	Private
1785	Sims,	Daniel.	Private		4076	Walker,	Josiah.	Private	'Central India'
3682	Sinclair*,	Peter.	Private		4109	Walker,	Samuel.	Private
3975	Singleton,	John.	Private		2814	Walker,	William.	Private
4035	Skipp,	Charles.	Private		2565	Wall,	John.	Private
4217	Slaughter,	John.	Private	'Central India'	3321	Wallace,	James.	Private
4114	Smith,	Charles.	Private		2368	Walsh,	Robert.	Private
3684	Smith,	Dugald.	Private	'Central India'	3950	Walsh,	Thomas.	Private	'Central India'
3955	Smith,	George.	Private		4034	Warboy,	Isaac.	Private
3277	Smith*,	James.	Private		4078	Warner,	William.	Private '	'Central India'
3665	Smith,	John.	Private		3212	Waters,	Thomas.	Private
326?	Smith,	John.	Private	'Central India'	4019	Watson,	Isaac.	Private	'Central India'
3644	Smith,	John.	Private		3515	Webb,	Samuel.	Private
3806	Smith,	Thomas.	Private	'Central India'	1938	Webb,	William.	Private
3844	Smith,	Thomas.	Private		3231	Webb,	William.	Private
3656	Smith*,	William.	Private		4006	Weedon,	John.	Private
3905	Smith,	William.	Private		3265	Wellman,	James.	Private
2195	Spicer,	George.	Private	'Central India'	3503	Wells,	George.	Private
3249	Spicer,	Thomas.	Private	'Central India'	3502	Wells,	James.	Private
3695	Squires,	William.	Private		3852	Wharboy,	Henry.	Private
2319	Stanfield,	Charles.	Private		4023	Wharton,	Edward.	Private
3645	Stevenson,	James.	Private		4221	Wheatley,	Joseph.	Private
4137	Stevenson,	Walter.	Private	'Central India'	3418	White,	Daniel.	Private	'Central India'
3951	Stiles,	William.	Private		3269	White,	James.	Private
3280	Stimpson,	William.	Private		2573	White*,	Thomas.	Private
3768	Stodhart*,	Samuel.	Private	'Central India'	3310	Whitlow,	Thomas.	Private
3576	Stokes,	James.	Private		3340	Whitty,	Peter.	Private
4182	Stokes,	Joseph.	Private		4244	Whitworth*,	William.	Private
3580	Stokes,	Thomas.	Private		4033	Wiggs*,	George.	Private '	'Central India'
3759	Stone,	Edwin.	Private	'Central India'	3795	Wilde,	William.	Private	'Central India'
3955	Stroud,	George.	Private		3856	Wilkins,	Charles.	Private	'Central India'
2334	Stuart,	Frederick.	Private		3555	Wilkinson,	Robert.	Private
3861	Suter,	James.	Private		4192	Willdig,	William.	Private
3185	Sutter,	David.	Private		3611	Williams,	Charles.	Private
4159	Swan,	William H.	Private		4199	Williams,	Francis.	Private	'Central india'
3732	Sweeney*,	James.	Private	'Central India'	3747	Williams,	Henry.	Private
	Trevor,	William Gordon.	Lieutenant		3947	Willis,	George.	Private
2452	Travel,	George.	Sergeant		3134	Wilson*,	John.	Private
3651	Tarrant,	Edward.	Corporal		3240	Wilson,	John.	Private
1598	Tate,	William.	Private	'Central India'	3620	Wilson,	John.	Private
2839	Taylor,	John.	Private		3618	Wilson,	Robert.	Private
	(2839 Tailor, John.)				3501	Wilson,	William.	Private	'Central India'
4241	Taylor,	Samuel.	Private		4015	Wiltshire,	George.	Private
3182	Tennant,	John.	Private		4112	Wiltshire,	John.	Private
3852	Tetlow,	John.	Private		1648	Wise,	George.	Private
3236	Thompson,	George.	Private		2394	Woods*,	William.	Private
3788	Thompson,	John.	Private		3879	Woods,	William.	Private
3954	Thompson,	William.	Private		3528	Worsley*,	James.	Private
4205	Thompson,	William.	Private		3907	Wortley,	Charles.	Private	'Central India'
3519	Tincey,	John.	Private	'Central India'	4002	Wren,	John.	Private
3347	Tinsley,	Richard.	Private		3833	Wright.	James.	Private
3476	Tovey,	Josiah.	Private	'Central India'	1842	Wright,	John.	Private
4232	Townley,	Henry.	Private	'Central India'	92	Wright*,	John.	Private
4084	Tracey,	James.	Private	'Central India'	2282	Wright,	Josiah.	Private
3307	Trantum,	William.	Private	'Central India'		**Young**,	George Samuel.	Captain
4117	Treherne*,	Zecheriah.	Private		3338	Young,	Andrew.	Private
4168	Trollop*,	Joseph.	Private		1566	Young,	John.	Private
3088	Tulley,	Thomas.	Private		4051	Young,	Thomas.	Private	'Central India'
3153	Turner*,	Benjamin.	Private					
3552	Turner,	James.	Private					

CASUALTIES INDIAN MUTINY
Including 'CENTRAL INDIA' CAMPAIGN

A total of 160 casualties are listed for the period of the Indian mutiny, 43 men are not included in the preceding medal list and those men can be identified by a (*) prior to their surname. Three men were killed in action and four were wounded, one man was burnt to death and two were drowned. For the remaining soldiers who died, the cause of death is not known; three men had been sent home, with one place of death recorded as Chatham. The worst period was May 1858 when 42 deaths were recorded, followed by 20 deaths in both June and September 1858.

It should be noted that many more members of the 80th Regiment of Foot succumbed to the climatic conditions and disease whilst the Regiment served in India after the actual conflict, and those men are not included.

3110	*Acton,	Thomas.	Private	Died at Allahabad	16th May	1858
4024	Airey,	Thomas.	Private	Died (Place not known)	8th May	1858
3384	Allen,	George.	Private	Died at Allahabad	12th April	1858
4160	Anderson,	John.	Private	Died (Place not known)	15th May	1858
3708	Bailey,	William.	Private	Died at Cawnpore	1st July	1858
3395	Bannister,	James.	Private	Died at Cawnpore	13th June	1858
3193	Barnes,	Thomas.(Alias Thomas Lowe)	Private	Died at Cawnpore	7th Sept.	1858
3823	Barrett,	Michael.	Private	Died at Hillianpore	11th June	1858
3864	Bayliss,	Joseph.	Private	Died (Place not Known)	19th May	1858
3421	Bentley,	Joseph.	Private	Died at Lucknow	12th Dec.	1858
3500	Blackwell,	Samuel.	Private	Died at Cawnpore	9th July	1858
	Borrowes,	Erasmus.	Adjutant	Wounded Simree	9th Nov.	1858
3485	Britton,	Robert.	Private	Died at Allahabad	18th April	1858
4219	Bugg,	Robert.	Private	Died (Place not Known)	21st May	1858
3169	Burke,	John.	Drum Major	Died at Cawnpore	14th June	1858
3387	Byrne,	John.	Private	Died (Place not Known)	8th Aug.	1858
	*Caddy,	Enoch.	Private	Died (Place not Known)	5th Oct.	1858
3607	*Carpenter,	Henry.	Private	Died (Place not Known)	29th Aug.	1858
3604	Chamberlain,	William.	Private	Died (Place not Known)	26th May	1858
	Christie,	Samuel Tolfrey.	Colonel	Wounded (Place not known)	(Date not known)	
	*Clancy,	John.	Private	Died at Calcutta	14th Aug.	1858
	*Clarke,	John.	Private	Died (Place not Known)	15th Aug.	1858
3135	Clarke,	Thomas.	Sergeant	Died at Futteghur	21st May	1858
3783	*Clegg,	Charles.	Private	Died at Dumdum	18th Sept.	1858
	*Colligan,	Cornelius.	Private	Died at Chatham	25th Dec.	1858
	*Concah,	William.	Private	Died (Place not Known)	25th May	1858
	*Conley,	William.	Private	Died (Place not Known)	5th Nov.	1858
3752	Connelly,	William Henry.	Private	Died at Allahabad	27th May	1858
2780	Connolly,	Michael.	Drummer	Died at Cawnpore	5th Dec.	1858
4126	Cook,	Richard.	Private	Died at Cawnpore	23rd June	1858
	*Cortells,	John.	Private	Died (Place not Known)	6th Dec.	1858
3587	Coyle,	James.	Private	Died (Place not known)	21st May	1858
3454	Crenage,	John.	Private	Died at Cawnpore	25th May	1858
3881	Crick,	Henry John.	Private	Died at Cawnpore	8th Sept.	1858
3528	Cummings,	Alexander.	Private	Died (Place not Known)	12th June	1858
	(3582 Cummings, Alexander.)					
4203	Cummins,	William.	Private	Died at Cawnpore	24th Aug.	1858
3808	Dalby,	Alfred.	Private	Died at Cawnpore	19th Sept.	1858
3612	Dean,	James.	Private	Died at Allahabad	24th May	1858
	(3612 Deane, James)					
3776	Donnolly,	Patrick.	Private	Died at Kidderpore	11th Dec.	1858
3510	Double,	Henry.	Private	Died at Futteghur	13th July	1858
3770	Drake,	James.	Private	Died at Cawnpore	16th Sept.	1858
3874	Duncan,	Joseph.	Private	Died at Cawnpore	24th May	1858
3494	Dunn,	William.	Private	Died at Futteghur	25th May	1858
	(3494 Dunne, William.)					
	*Durrell,	Charles.	Private	Died at Futteghur	24th May	1858
4233	Easton,	Daniel.	Sergeant	Died at Cawnpore	15th May	1858
	*Fairlewin,	James.	Private	Died (Place not Known)	5th Aug.	1858
3540	Fannon,	James.	Private	Died at Futteghur	5th May	1858
	*Farrell,	Patrick.	Private	Died (Place not Known)	31st Aug.	1858
	*Fisher,	William.	Private	Died (Place not Known)	15th Aug.	1858
3460	*Fissman,	Cormick.	Private	Died at Cawnpore	26th April	1858
3877	Fletcher,	Enoch.	Private	Died at Allahabad	8th April	1858
3530	Fletcher,	Thomas.	Private	Died at Cawnpore	20th Sept.	1858
3535	Ford,	Charles.	Private	Died at Cawnpore	10th Oct.	1858
	(3537 Forde, Charles.)					
4027	George,	Jessie.	Private	Died at Cawnpore	6th Oct.	1858
3815	*Golhaugher,	Thomas.	Private	Died (Place not Known)	18th Aug.	1858
3960	Goodall,	James.	Private	Drowned in Ganges	25th April	1858

3461	Gould,	John.	Private	Died at Allahabad	2nd May	1858
4239	Green,	James.	Private	Died at Cawnpore	4th Dec.	1858
3693	Greig,	James.	Private	Died at Allahabad	27th April	1858
4071	Groom,	George.	Private	Died at Allahabad	29th July	1858
	*Gurry,	John.	Private	Died (Place not Known)	29th Aug.	1858
3558	Hampton,	Frederick.	Private	Died at Cawnpore	13th May	1858
4011	Hardinge,	James.	Private	Died (Place not known)	9th Sept.	1858
3449	Hardman,	John.	Private	Died at Cawnpore	26th Sept.	1858
3787	Haycock,	William.	Private	Died at Baunbaunge	7th Nov.	1858
	*Harran,	Robens.	Private	Died at Futteghur	14th May	1858
3207	Hickey,	James.	Private	Wounded (Place unknown)	5th Mar.	1858
3959	Hoare,	William.	Private	Died at Calcutta	25th July	1858
4110	Holman,	John.	Private	Died (Place not known)	12th May	1858
3972	Hopkins,	Philip.	Private	Died (Place not known)	27th April	1858
3041	Horan,	Owen.	Private	Died at Cawnpore	6th July	1858
3432	Horton,	George.	Corporal	Wounded (Place not known) (Date not known)		
4215	Hutchings,	Thomas.	Private	Died at Cawnpore	7th May	1858
3206	*Hutchinson,	Frances.	Private	Died (Place not Known)	29th July	1858
3456	Irvine,	William.	Corporal	Died at Cawnpore	29th Dec.	1858
	(3456 Irwin, William.)					
3583	Jackson,	Thomas.	Private	Died (Place not known)	21st May	1858
3268	Jones,	Edward.	Drummer	Died at Allahabad	9th Dec.	1858
3621	Jones,	John.	Private	Died at Buscan	13th Sept.	1858
3403	Jones,	William.	Private	Died at Hellianpore	11th June	1858
3816	*Kay,	James.	Private	Died at Allahabad	8th Oct.	1858
4248	*Kelly,	Richard.	Private	Died (Place not Known)	31st Aug.	1858
3961	Kenyon,	John.	Private	Died (Place not known)	22nd May	1858
3227	Kerr,	Edward.	Private	Died at Cawnpore	12th June	1858
	*King,	John.	Private	Died (Place not Known)	13th Aug.	1858
3518	*Kinsey,	James.	Private	Died at Futteghur	14th May	1858
3839	*Knight,	Charles.	Private	Died at Cawnpore	21st Nov.	1858
3872	Laurence,	Charles.	Private	Died at Cawnpore	24th May	1858
2939	Ledlow,	Matthew.	Private	Drowned at Cawnpore	10th July	1858
4188	Liggins,	George.	Private	Died at Allahabad	22nd April	1858
3111	*Longstont,	Thomas.	Private	Died at Cawnpore	14th June	1858
4044	*Lovegrove,	Henry.	Private	Died (Place not Known)	13th April	1858
3673	McCaller,	Henry.	Private	Died at Cawnpore	15th Dec.	1858
3688	McConnell,	William.	Private	Died (Place not known)	14th June	1858
3177	McDonald,	Richard.	Drummer	Died at Cawnpore	28th Aug.	1858
	(3177 McDonnell, Richard.)					
3451	McKaon,	Francis.	Private	Died at Cawnpore	23rd May	1858
	*McOliver,	James.	Private	Died at Kidderpore	14th Sept.	1858
4198	McPeak,	James.	Private	Died at Allahabad	28th April	1858
3638	McAllen,	Charles.	Sergeant	Died at Hulliampore	11th June	1858
	(3638 MacAllan, Charles.)					
3899	Maggie,	Frederick.	Private	Died (Place not known)	12th June	1858
	(3899 Maggi, Frederick.)					
4047	Mansfield,	George.	Private	Killed in Action Dundea Khera	24th Nov.	1858
2775	Marshall,	James.	Private	Died at Cawnpore	14th June	1858
4053	Mathews,	John.	Private	Died at Futteghur	12th May	1858
4048	Meade,	James.	Private	Died (Place not known)	6th May	1858
4230	*Miller,	William.	Private	Died (Place not Known)	14th Aug.	1858
3634	Milloy,	Archibald.	Private	Died at Allahabad	16th May	1858
3973	Mills,	John.	Private	Died (Place not known)	29th April	1858
3763	Minnis,	John.	Private	Died (Place not known)	6th May	1858
	(3753 Minnis, John.)					
3745	Moates,	William.	Corporal	Died (Place not Known)	21st May	1858
	(3745 Moats, William.)					
3253	Mongon,	Thomas.	Private	Died at Cawnpore	12th May	1858
3513	Morley,	George.	Private	Died (Place not known)	13th May	1858
	*Morris,	James.	Private	Died (Place not Known)	5th Aug.	1858
2111	Nicholls,	Alfred.	Private	Killed in Action Simree	9th Nov.	1858
3904	Nightingale,	John.	Private	Died (Place not known)	21st May	1858
4060	O'Niel,	Peter.	Private	Died at Cawnpore	7th Dec.	1858
3431	Orr,	George.	Sergeant.	Died at Allahabad	24th April	1858
	*Perkins,	Robert.	Private	Died at Futteghur	27th April	1858
3689	Perry,	William.	Corporal	Died at Cawnpore	4th April	1858
4124	Phillips,	William.	Private	Died at Cawnpore	18th Sept.	1858
3482	Pitt,	William.	Private	Died (Place not known)	22nd May	1858
4127	Preece,	James.	Private	Died (Place not known)	26th June	1858
3854	Press,	Richard.	Private	Died at Cawnpore	9th Sept.	1858
	(3854 Press, William.)					
4191	Preston,	William.	Private	Died at Cawnpore	30th Sept.	1858
4111	Price,	William.	Private	Died (Place not Known)	9th Sept.	1858

3514	Ralph,	George.	Private	Died at Cawnpore	22nd June	1858
	*Roche,	John.	Private	Sent Home }	20th April	1858
				Died }	20th Aug.	1858
3676	Roddy,	Hugh.	Private	Died at Cawnpore	23rd Sept.	1858
3834	Rowland,	Thomas.	Private	Died at Cawnpore	22nd June	1858
2928	Ryan,	Patrick.	Private	Died at Cawnpore	9th July	1858
3711	Salter,	Richard.	Private	Died at Cawnpore	17th Sept.	1858
2513	Saunders,	William.	Private	Died at Futteghur	12th Mar.	1858
	*Shore,	John.	Private	Died at Cawnpore	17th Oct.	1858
3682	Sinclair,	Peter.	Private	Died at Cawnpore	21st Sept.	1858
3536	*Smith,	George.	Sergeant	Died at Cawnpore	25th May	1858
3277	Smith,	James.	Private	Died at Futteghur	13th May	1858
3656	Smith,	William.	Private	Killed in Action Dundea Khera	24th Nov.	1858
3768	Stodhart,	Samuel.	Private	Died (Place not known)	14th May	1858
3732	Sweeney,	James.	Private	Died at Allahabad	27th Nov.	1858
	*Taylor,	Fergus.	Private	Died at Calcutta	9th Oct.	1858
2839	Taylor,	John.	Private	Burnt to Death	23rd May	1858
	(2839 Tailor, John.)					
	*Thompson,	Robert.	Private	Died (Place not Known)	5th June	1858
	*Tranter,	Thomas.	Private	Died (Place not Known)	30th July	1858
	*Travis,	Thomas.	Private	Died (Place not Known)	8th Aug.	1858
2539	*Treanor,	Patrick.	Private	Sent Home }	20th April	1858
				Died }	6th May	1858
4117	Treherne,	Zecheriah.	Private	Died at Allahabad	11th July	1858
4168	Trollop,	Joseph.	Private	Died at Allahabad	18th April	1858
3153	Turner,	Benjamin.	Private	Died at Cawnpore	15th May	1858
1771	*Tyrell,	John.	Private	Died at Dinapore	15th Sept.	1858
2958	Vincent,	John.	Corporal	Died at Cawnpore	18th June	1858
4043	*Warboy,	Isaac.	Private	Died at Allahabad	13th April	1858
3882	*Warby,	Henry.	Private	Died (Place not Known)	23rd May	1858
2573	White,	Thomas.	Private	Died at Cawnpore	19th July	1858
4244	Whitworth,	William.	Private	Died at Cawnpore	17th Dec.	1858
4033	Wiggs,	George.	Private	Died (Place not Known)	6th June	1858
	*Williamson,	Samuel.	Private	Died (Place not Known)	27th Aug.	1858
3134	Wilson,	John.	Private	Died at Cawnpore	21st May	1858
	*Wise,	Joseph.	Private	Died at Calcutta	20th June	1858
2394	Woods,	William.	Private	Died at Cawnpore	21st Sept.	1858
3156	Worral,	Francis.	Colour Sergeant	Wounded at Kalpi	23rd May	1857
	(3156 Worril, Francis.)			Died at Hiddespore	16th Nov.	1858
3528	Worsley,	James.	Private	Died at Cawnpore	14th June	1858
92	Wright,	John.	Private	Died at Cawnpore	4th July	1858

SOUTH AFRICA MEDAL
26th SEPTEMBER 1877 - 2nd DECEMBER 1879

The first Royal Warrant for the issue of the South Africa Medal was applied for in January 1880. At this time the War Office decided that two 'bars' would be issued, 'Caffraria 1877-9' and 'Zululand 1879'. This was to recognise the operations that had taken place against the various tribes, Gcalekas, Caikas, Griquas and the Zulus. A third bar was decided on in April for operations against the Basuto Chief, Sekukuni in 1879. A fourth 'bar', was envisaged, to recognise further fighting against the Basutos and the Moirosi tribes. Because of the possibilities of additional 'bars', the War Office re-examined the issue, and to minimise the number of medals and 'bars', finally issued General Order No.103. However, a further order was required to cover the campaign in 1878 against Chief Sekukuni, General Order No.134, issued October 1880. The General Orders 103 and 134 are as follows:

G.O. 103 - Medals

I.   The Queen in consideration of the arduous duties performed, and the successful conclusion of the operations referred to in the next paragraph, has been graciously pleased to command that a medal be granted to Her Majesty's imperial Forces and to such of Her Majesty's Colonial Forces, European or Native, as were regularly organised and disciplined as combatants, whether raised by the Colonial Government or by the General Officer Commanding.

II.   The medal will be granted to the Forces employed against-

a.   The Gcalekas, Gaikas, and other Kaffir Tribes from the 26th September 1877 to the 28th June 1878 inclusive.

b.   Against Pokwane, from the 21st to the 28th January 1878 inclusive.

c.   Against the Griquas, from the 24th April to the 12th November 1878 inclusive.

d.   Against the Zulus, from the 11th January to the 1st September 1879 inclusive.

e.   Against Sekukuni, from the 11th November to the 2nd December 1879, and including the troops stationed at Fort Burghers, Fort Albert Edward, Seven Mile Post, Fort Oliphants, Fort Weeber, and in Sekukuni's Valley.

f.   Against Moirosi's stronghold.

III.   Her Majesty has also been pleased to approve of a clasp being attached to the said medal, on which will be indicated the year or years in which the recipients of the medal were engaged in the late war, thus -

		Year on Clasp
For operations against the	Gcalekas, &c.	1877-8
	Pokwane and the Griquas	1878
" "	in the Zulu and Sekukuni campaigns respectively or both	1879
" "	as specified in Paragraph II., in 1878-8-9	1878-8-9
" "	as specified in paragraph II., in 1878-9	1878-9

the principle being that the year or years on the clasp confirm all the operations in which the recipient may have been engaged in such year or years.

IV.   Those troops employed in Natal from the 11th January 1879 to the 1st September 1879, but who never crossed the border into Zululand, will be granted the medal without clasp.

V.   The medal will be granted by Her Majesty to commemorate the successful termination of previous wars in South Africa; and those officers, non-commissioned officers and men who are already in prossession of this medal, will if they have been engaged in the operations referred to in paragraph II., receive the clasp with the year or years inscribed thereon in accordance with paragraph III.

VI.   Staff Officers and Special Service Officers will forward their applications through the General Officers under whom they served.

VII.   Officers who served as Heads of Departments will furnish returns of Staff Officers and others who served under their command.

VIII.   Commanding Officers of Royal Artillery and Royal Engineers, and Officers Commanding Regiments of Cavalry and Infantry (Regular Forces), will forward nominal rolls of Officers, non-commissioned officers, and men to the Adjutant-General of the Forces. The names of men who, except for desertion or misconduct, would have been recommended for the medal, are also to be included in the rolls, and in the column of remarks the reasons which have rendered them ineligible are to be stated. All rolls will be made out on foolscap, ruled cross-wise, with a margin of an inch on each side of the fold, so as to admit of ready reference when the sheets are bound. The names will be entered alphabetically, in order of rank.

IX.   All applications on behalf of Imperial Forces are to be prepared in duplicate, in conformity with the form given in Appendix (see p.121), and forwarded to the Adjutant-General of the Forces, Horse Guards, War Office, Pall Mall, London.

G.O. 134 - Medals

I.   The provisions of G.O. 103 of 1880 will apply to the Forces engaged against Sekukuni in 1878.

II.   In the applications for medals on behalf of such forces, a column will be inserted in the rolls, showing that they were employed in the operation referred to.

The medal was silver, 36mm in diameter. The designers of the medal were for the obverse side, W.Wyon RA, and the reverse side, L.C.Wyon. Ribbon 32mm wide, watery orange-yellow with two, 5mm and two, 1mm dark blue stripes. The ribbon attached by means of an ornamented scroll swivelling suspender, slightly wider than the previous South Africa medal issued in 1853. On the obverse side is the diademed head of Queen Victoria with the legend, 'VICTORIA REGINA'. On the reverse side is a lion, representing Africa, in a crouching position as though in the act of submission. Behind the lion is a Protea bush. In the exergue on the reverse is a Zulu shield and four (crossed), assegais. The naming was engraved in capital letters. A total of seven, 'bars', was issued: 1877; 1877-8; 1877-8-9; 1877-9; 1878; 1878-9 and 1879. Approximately 36,600 medals were struck and about 5600 were issued with no Bar'.

MEDAL LIST
SOUTH AFRICA MEDAL 26th SEPTEMBER 1877 - 2nd DECEMBER 1879

This list contains the names of officers, non-commissioned officers and men who served with the 80th Regiment of Foot (Staffordshire Volunteers) and were awarded the South Africa Medal, a total of 1211 medals. Of these 750 were awarded under General Order No.103, and 171 under General Order No.134. Included are 290 names identified by D.R.Forsyth, shown by the insertion (F) after the name. A total of 120 medals were awarded with no 'clasp'.

The spellings of the soldiers' names have been taken directly from the medal lists, however, where the soldier's army number or name vary from the Regiments Nominal Rolls, both are shown, the medal list taking precedence with the Nominal Roll in brackets. The list shows the rank held by the soldier, with, in brackets, the rank held at the time of earning the award.

NB. Where an * is indicated after the surname , refer to Casualty List.

No.	Surname	Forename	Rank	Clasp
	Anderson,	Wilfred Turner.	Captain	
4202	Allen,	John.	Sergeant Major	
894	Allen,	Charles.	Sergeant	
1968	Attride,	George. (Alias George Eve)	Sergeant	
93	Arthurs,	William.	Corporal	
1822	Allen,	Amos.	Corporal (Private)	
1188	Appleby(F),	James.	Drummer	
304	Abbott,	John.	Private	
1505	Adair,	Henry.	Private	
1856	Adams(F),	George.	Private	No clasp
704	Adams*,	Robert.	Private	
546	Adey*,	Jonah.	Private	
976	Adey,	Walter.	Private	
1916	Aher(F),	James.	Private	No clasp
1206	Ainsworth,	Henry.	Private	
1850	Allen,	Frederick.	Private	
1968	Allen(F),	John.	Private	No clasp
1444	Allen,	Victor.	Private	
1283	Allison,	John.	Private	
1236	Allport(F),	Cornelius.	Private	
1017	Allsop,	Joseph.	Private	
	(1017 Allsop, George.)			
231	Anderson,	Frederick.	Private	
573	Andrews,	William.	Private	
1916	Annals,	Alfred.	Private	
1817	Ansell(F),	Joseph.	Private	No clasp
19/585	Anthony*,	John.	Private	
1521	Appleton,	Thomas.	Private	
1058	Archer,	Harry.	Private	
857	Archer(F),	Richard.	Private	
922	Archer(F),	Thomas.	Private	
1970	Archer(F),	William.	Private	No clasp
1437	Arkell,	James.	Private	
441	Armstrong,	John.	Private	
7	Armstrong,	Thomas W.	Private	
1055	Armstrong,	William.	Private	
108	Arthurs,	Michael.	Private	
2033	Atkins,	Charles.	Private	
1452	Atkinson,	James.	Private	
1874	Atkinson(F),	Seymour.	Private	No clasp
1918	Attwater(F),	John.	Private	No clasp
1907	Austin,	Edward.	Private	
	Bradshaw(F),	James Lewis.	Brevet Major	
	Bird,	H. J.	School Master	
919	Booth v.c.,	Anthony Clarke.	Colour Sergeant	
1103	Baxter,	James.	Sergeant (Corporal)	
1054	Beal,	Wallace.	Sergeant (Corporal)	
36	Beverley,	James.	Sergeant	
98	Butler,	John.	Sergeant	
200	Bailey,	John J.	Lance Sergeant (Private)	
1387	Brown*,	Thomas.	Lance Sergeant	
19/636	Beecroft*,	Alfred.	Corporal (Private)	
762	Brew,	George.	Corporal	
2038	Barnwell,	William.	Drummer	
759	Backett,	John.	Private	
1065	Bagnall,	John.	Private	
779	Bagnall,	Thomas.	Private	
1998	Bailey,	Frederick.	Private	
1199	Bailey(F),	Jno. Davies.	Private	
1788	Bailey,	Robert.	Private	
1223	Bailey,	Thomas.	Private	
577	Baker,	John.	Private	
397	Baker(F),	Philip.	Private	
560	Baker,	William.	Private	
22	Bale,	Robert.	Private	
1870	Ball(F),	John.	Private	No clasp
2056	Balshaw,	Albert Edward.	Private	
19/202	Banks*,	Arthur.	Private	
1049	Banks,	Thomas.	Private	
1086	Banks(F),	William.	Private	
943	Banner*,	John.	Private	
1883	Bannon(F),	Patrick.	Private	No clasp
1448	Barber,	Alexander.	Private	
1382	Barcklie,	Matthew.	Private	
1908	Bargery(F),	Henry.	Private	No clasp
1935	Barker(F),	William.	Private	No clasp
1514	Barnes,	James.	Private	
531	Barnett,	Richard.	Private	
1928	Barr,	Thomas.	Private	
2053	Barrett,	Denis.	Private	
1591	Barron,	Anthony.	Private	
1872	Barsby,	Thomas.	Private	
1634	Barter(F),	Robert.	Private	
1859	Bartley(F),	Myles W.	Private	No clasp
1520	Baskoth(F),	Thomas.	Private	
1038	Bateman,	William.	Private	
1259	Baverstock(F),	George.	Private	
1145	Bayless(F),	John.	Private	
865	Baxter,	Samuel.	Private	
349	Baxter,	William.	Private	
1358	Baxter,	William.	Private	
1535	Beamer,	John.	Private	
1110	Beatson,	Matthew.	Private	
1028	Beaumont,	Alfred.	Private	
276	Bebbington,	William.	Private	
1164	Bedwith,	Alfred.	Private	
736	Bell,	James.	Private	
1070	Bellerson,	Thomas.	Private	
680	Bennett,	William.	Private	
105	Bentley,	John.	Private	
275	Bentley,	John.	Private	
975	Benton,	Samuel.	Private	
513	Betts,	Henry.	Private	
1687	Bickerton,	Joseph.	Private	
1081	Biddle(F),	James.	Private	
280	Biernes,	Thomas.	Private	
1076	Billingham,	Thomas.	Private	

(1076 Billingham, James.)

No.	Surname	Forename	Rank	Clasp
1251	Bills(F),	Thomas.	Private	
1174	Birch(F),	Joseph.	Private	
29	Birch,	William.	Private	
109	Bird,	Francis.	Private	
1854	Blackham(F), William.		Private	No clasp
412	Blakeway,	John.	Private	
719	Boden,	John.	Private	
16	Bond*,	William.	Private	
1015	Bond,	William.	Private	
1897	Booker,	Alfred.	Private	
1155	Booth,	Enoch.	Private	
766	Booth,	Frederick.	Private	
265	Bourn,	William.	Private	
1138	Bow,	Spencer.	Private	
519	Bowen,	Thomas.	Private	
1277	Bowker,	Robert.	Private	
534	Bown,	Ebinezer	Private	
349	Boyd(F),	Thomas.	Private	
489	Boyle,	Martin.	Private	
2102	Boyle,	Thomas.	Private	
1564	Bradshaw,	William.	Private	
1919	Brady(F),	Robert.	Private	No clasp
567	Bramill,	William.	Private	
1877	Braze,	Thomas.	Private	
273	Brereton,	Thomas.	Private	
722	Brew,	George.	Private	
415	Bridgewood. William.		Private	
633	Brindley(F), Alfred.		Private	
647	Brindley(F), William.		Private	
1358	Brisbane,	William.	Private	
1556	Britton(F),	Edward.	Private	
1664	Broadhurst,	Amos.	Private	
19/745	Broughton*, George.		Private	
1914	Brown(F),	George.	Private	No clasp
48	Brown*,	James.	Private	
122	Brown,	John.	Private	
542	Brown,	John.	Private	
576	Brown,	Samuel.	Private	
1553	Brown,	William.	Private	
19/488	Brownson*, Henry.		Private	
659	Buckler,	Thomas.	Private	
1134	Bullock(F),	George.	Private	
907	Bullock(F),	William.	Private	
1172	Bunday,	David.	Private	
1728	Bunday,	Henry.	Private	
2044	Burden,	Joseph.	Private	
2054	Burgess,	William.	Private	
169	Burgwin*,	Thomas.	Private	
2055	Burke,	Daniel.	Private	
1856	Burnett,	John.	Private	
79	Burns(F),	H.	Private	
323	Burns(F),	Harry.	Private	
736	Burns,	Hugh.	Private	
1078	Burnes(F),	William.	Private	
2071	Burrett,	William.	Private	
1922	Bursnell(F),	James.	Private	No clasp
1609	Burtenshaw*, Henry.		Private	
99	Burton,	Alfred.	Private	
1737	Burton,	Joseph.	Private	
1984	Burton,	Thomas.	Private	
1936	Bush(F),	John.	Private	
278	Butler*,	Frederick.	Private	
574	Butler,	John.	Private	
603	Byrne,	Christopher.	Private (Sergeant)	
	Cole(F),	Charles Christopher.	Captain	

No.	Surname	Forename	Rank	Clasp
	Creagh,	Chas Augustus Fitzgerald	Brevet Major	
	Cameron,	Saumarez William.	Lieutenant	
	Chamberlain, Tankerville James.		Lieutenant	
995	Cameron,	Harry.	Sergeant	
1044	Carter,	Samuel.	Sergeant	
222	Cleaver(F),	William.	Sergeant	
3244	Collins,	John.	Sergeant	
1063	Cox,	George William.	Sergeant (Corporal)	
1389	Carter(F),	Henry.	Lance Sergeant	
966	Cooper,	Albert.	Lance Sergeant (Private)	
545	Constable,	Thomas.	Corporal (Private)	
1241	Corraskry,	James.	Corporal	
301	Collier,	Alfred.	Drummer	
1769	Cunningham, Thomas.		Drummer	
1139	Cairns(F),	Edward.	Private	
1222	Callaghan(F), Michael.		Private	
159	Callaghan,	Patrick.	Private	
1129	Cameron,	Frederick.	Private	
1938	Camp(F),	Daniel.	Private	No clasp
406	Carberry,	Richard.	Private	
1340	Carey,	Francis.	Private (Corporal)	
112	Carpenter,	John.	Private	
2100	Carr,	Joseph.	Private	
1578	Carroll,	James.	Private	
18	Carroll,	John.	Private	
986	Carter,	Charles.	Private	
387	*Carter(F),	John.	Private	
1140	Cartwright(F), Samuel.		Private	
818	Cash(F),	William.	Private	
1913	Cassidy(F),	William.	Private	No clasp
387	*Cater(F),	John.	Private	
1290	Chadwick*,	John.	Private	
1656	Chadwick,	Henry.	Private	
1974	Champion(F),	John P.	Private	No clasp
287	Chare*,	Calib Edwin.	Private	
1914	Chase,	Robert.	Private	
1944	Cherrie,	William.	Private	
1043	Cheshire,	John.	Private	
1377	Chesterton*,	John.	Private	
1906	Childerstone(F), Stephen.		Private	No clasp
2171	Childs,	Edward.	Private	
1797	Christie*,	James.	Private	
	(1797 Christy, James.)			
1967	Cinamond(F),	Thomas E.	Private	No clasp
1884	Clarke,	Alfred George.	Private	
507	Clarke,	John.	Private	
1052	Clarke(F),	John.	Private	
1911	Clarke(F),	John.	Private	No clasp
2026	Clarke,	Owen.	Private (Sergeant)	
983	Clarke,	Thomas.	Private	
1497	Clarke,	Thomas.	Private	
1014	Clarke,	Thomas.	Private	
94	Clarke,	William.	Private	
1934	Clarke(F),	William.	Private	No clasp
1827	Clay,	Isaac.	Private	
1982	Clayton,	George.	Private	
1658	Clayton,	Herbert.	Private	
487	Cleaton,	William.	Private	
2	Cleaver,	John.	Private	
551	Cluit,	John.	Private	
413	Clulec,	Thomas.	Private	
2044	Colbridge(F),	William.	Private	No clasp
755	Colclough,	George.	Private	
1550	Cole(F),	Charles Edwin.	Private	
298	Cole,	Frederick.	Private	
561	Cole,	William.	Private	

No.	Surname	Forename	Rank	Clasp
1969	Coleman(F),	John.	Private	No clasp
485	Coleman,	Thomas.	Private	
1478	Collier,	William.	Private	
1324	Collinson,	Robert.	Private	
1989	Colyer,	William.	Private	
1098	Concaly(F),	John.	Private	
314	Conlon,	John.	Private	
739	Connell,	James.	Private	
690	Connell,	John.	Private	
1221	Connolly(F),	William.	Private	
988	Convey,	John.	Private	
1232	Cook*(F),	Thomas.	Private	
1935	Cooke,	Albert.	Private	
1371	Cooke,	Charles.	Private	
82	Cooke,	George.	Private	
1913	Cooke,	George.	Private	
	(1913 Cook, George.)			
2072	Cooper,	Edwin.	Private	
1245	Cooper(F),	Jas. Frederick.	Private	
696	Cope,	Samuel.	Private	
736	Cope(F),	Thomas.	Private	
1051	Corbett,	David.	Private	
1871	Corbett(F),	Thomas.	Private	No clasp
753	Corns,	John.	Private	
1169	Corry*(F),	John.	Private	
1029	Costello(F),	S.	Private	
502	Cowdrell,	Richard.	Private	
601	Cox,	Joseph.	Private	
1966	Cox(F),	William.	Private	No clasp
1874	Coy,	William.	Private	
123	Coyne,	John.	Private	
499	Crawford,	William.	Private	
1905	Creagh(F),	William.	Private	No clasp
194	Crudington(F),	Richard.	Private	
1198	Cruise(F),	Samuel.	Private	
1111	Cruite,	George.	Private	
1524	Cullen,	Peter.	Private	
232	Cullen,	Michael.	Private	
1650	Culley,	Frederick.	Private	
1889	Cullum(F),	John.	Private	No clasp
631	Curtin,	John.	Private	
	Daubeney,	Edward Kaye.	Lieutenant (2nd Lieutenant)	
909	Davis,	John.	Quartermaster Sergeant (Sergeant)	
1048	Day,	Hugh H.	Colour Sergeant (Sergeant)	
2101	Davis,	Charles G.	Sergeant	
947	Davis,	Peter.	Sergeant	
488	Dickey,	William.	Sergeant	
1804	Duncan,	John.	Sergeant	
900	Duggan*,	Myles.	Lance Sergeant	
594	Donovan,	William.	Drummer	
465	Dabbs,	Robert.	Private	
1272	Dagger,	Henry.	Private	
78	Dailey(F),	John.	Private	No clasp
1158	Dakin(F),	George.	Private	
410	Dale(F),	Henry.	Private	
1364	Daniels,	George.	Private	
1728	Daniels(F),	Samuel.	Private	
209	Daniels,	William.	Private	
1213	Darby(F),	William.	Private	
614	Davis,	John.	Private	
846	Davis(F),	Samuel.	Private	No clasp
1312	Davis,	William.	Private	
19/1042	Day*,	Alfred.	Private	
1930	Day,	William.	Private	
1119	Deacon,	William.	Private	
1115	Delany,	Michael.	Private	
1633	Delany,	Michael J.	Private	
1464	Dempsey,	Andrew.	Private	
1361	Dermott,	James.	Private	
256	Dobson,	Edward.	Private	
19/953	Dodd*,	John.	Private	
1971	Doe,	Joseph.	Private	
1076	Dollin,	Robert.	Private (Sergeant)	
1271	Donnelly(F),	Patrick.	Private	
1879	Donohoe(F),	Michael.	Private	No clasp
101	Donovan,	Thomas.	Private	
1071	Done,	Benjamin.	Private	
1901	Double(F),	Charles.	Private	No clasp
1330	Doyle,	Augustine.	Private	
	(1330 Doyle, Augustin.)			
243	Drinkwater,	Enoch.	Private	
2005	Dudley,	Alfred.	Private	
274	Dudley,	Joseph.	Private	
1616	Duffy*,	Michael.	Private	
1231	Dudley(F),	Thomas.	Private	
1219	Dudwell(F),	John.	Private	
2079	Dumbleton,	Benjamin.	Private	
507	Dunn,	Charles.	Private	
260	Dutton*,	John Henry.	Private	
1202	Dutton*(F),	Noah.	Private	
1900	Dyball*,	William.	Private	
8	Dyer,	George.	Private	
895	**Else,**	Willam.	Colour Sergeant (Sergeant)	
1383	Ermion.	George.	Sergeant	
794	Eady,	John.	Private	
1876	Eaton(F),	William.	Private	No clasp
1973	Ede(F),	Thomas.	Private	No clasp
718	Edwards,	Edward.	Private	
379	Edwards,	Eli.	Private	
1554	Edwards(F),	Emanuel.	Private	
1094	Edwards(F),	Michael.	Private	
1624	Edwards,	Robert.	Private	
1035	Edwards,	William.	Private	
1141	Edwards,	William.	Private	
750	Egerton(F),	Samuel.	Private	
421	Eley,	Frederick.	Private	
376	Ellis,	George.	Private	
1543	Ellis,	George.	Private	
1162	Ellis,	Henry.	Private	
84	Ellison,	Robert.	Private	
143	England,	William.	Private	
1003	Evens,	Even.	Private	
	(1003 Evans, Even.)			
214	Evens,	George.	Private	
	(214 Evans, George.)			
713	Evens,	Henry.	Private	
	(713 Evans, Henry)			
1074	Evens,	John.	Private	
	(1074 Evans, John.)			
570	Everitt,	William.	Private	
	(570 Everett, William.)			
2109	**Frayling,**	William Walter.	Band Master	
1362	Foulks,	John.	Colour Sergeant (Sergeant)	
459	Fredericks*,	Henry.	Colour Sergeant	
1917	Ferguson,	Donald.	Drummer	
1026	Fallon,	John.	Private	
1045	Fallon,	Josiah.	Private (Corporal)	
1830	Farmer,	William.	Private	

No.	Surname	Forename	Rank	Note
1028	Farnell*,	William.	Private	
2019	Farrell,	Patrick.	Private	
1643	Faulkner,	William.	Private	
467	Fawcett,	Thomas.	Private	
1884	Feltwell(F),	John.	Private	No clasp
2052	Ferris(F),	James.	Private	
1114	Field,	Edward.	Private	
222	Findley*,	William.	Private	
520	Finn,	James.	Private	
1860	Finnegan,	Patrick.	Private	
230	Fisher,	John.	Private	
1228	Fisher,	John.	Private	
1947	Fisher,	Thomas.	Private	
1857	Fitton(F),	James.	Private	No clasp
1286	Fitzmorris,	Thomas.	Private	
604	Fitzpatrick,	Patrick T.	Private	
1512	Fletcher(F),	Albert.	Private	
233	Fletcher,	James.	Private	
1695	Flewitt,	James.	Private	
701	Flint,	John.	Private	
1892	Floyd*,	Joseph.	Private	
19/176	Flyfield*,	William.	Private	
785	Flynn,	Robert.	Private	
490	Foden,	Joseph.	Private	
613	Follows,	George.	Private	
812	Ford,	James.	Private	
1342	Ford(F),	Patrick.	Private	
340	Ford,	Thomas.	Private	
303	Foreman,	Henry.	Private	
1886	Foster(F),	Benjamin.	Private	No clasp
1820	Foster,	Robert.	Private	
754	Foster(F),	Thomas.	Private	
778	Foster,	William.	Private	
1597	Foulk,	John.	Private	
1030	Fox,	John.	Private	
1465	Fox*,	William.	Private	
2080	Francis,	James.	Private	
1552	Frayne(F),	Joseph.	Private	
1918	Fricker,	Joseph.	Private	
677	Frighney,	Robert.	Private	
151	Fryer,	William.	Private	
1449	Fulton,	William.	Private	
2089	Furness,	Albert.	Private	
679	Furness,	Richard.	Private	
1925	Furniaux*,	John.	Private	
	Griffin,	Thomas Edward.	Lieutenant & Adjutant	
1279	Grant,	John.	Sergeant (Corporal)	
1439	Garner,	George.	Corporal	
1915	Green,	Henry.	Corporal	
3642	Graham*,	Ewen.	Lance Corporal	
1196	Gallagher(F),	James.	Private	
1544	Gallagher(F),	Patrick.	Private	
2015	Gardiner,	Charles.	Private	
1024	Garford(F),	Edward.	Private	No clasp
1813	Garvey*(F),	Thomas.	Private	No clasp
925	Gibbons(F),	Joseph.	Private	
469	Giblin,	Owen.	Private	
173	Gibson,	John.	Private	
700	Gillham,	James.	Private	
1335	Gilligan,	William.	Private	
19/500	Gittins*,	Edwin.	Private	
1261	Glinnon(F),	Thomas.	Private	No clasp
	(1261 Glennon, Thomas.)			
1390	Goddard,	William.	Private	
1901	Godden,	Thomas.	Private	
699	Godwin,	William.	Private	
1184	Goulden(F),	Patrick.	Private	
936	Granger(F),	Thomas.	Private	
1182	Grant,	John.	Private	
854	Grantley,	Thomas.	Private (Paymaster Sergeant)	
603	Gratton,	John.	Private	
743	Greatback,	James.	Private	
1131	Greatrix(F),	Benjamin.	Private	
1697	Green*,	Joseph.	Private	
1800	Gretton,	William.	Private	
239	Grey,	William.	Private	
	(239 Gray, William.)			
1851	Griffin(F),	George W.	Private	No clasp
1463	Griffiths,	Edward.	Private	
1550	Griffiths,	Henry.	Private	
1538	Griffiths(F),	Jas. Thornton.	Private	
639	Griffiths(F),	Thomas.	Private	
835	Griffiths(F),	William.	Private	
836	Gubbins,	Nicholas.	Private	
1044	Guest,	Joseph.	Private	
1239	Guest(F),	Thomas.	Private	
1671	Guilfoy,	James.	Private	
1999	Gutterege,	Arthur.	Private	
	(1999 Gutteridge, Arthur.)			
1031	Gutteredge,	George.	Private	
	(1031 Gutalage, George.)			
1034	Guy,	Peter.	Private	
368	Guy,	William.	Private	
	Howard,	Walter.	Major (Captain)	
	Harward,	Henry Hollingworth.	Lieutenant	
	Hast,	Arthur Wellesley.	Lieutenant	
	Horsburgh,	Archibald Borthwick.	Lieutenant	
	Huskisson(F),	Samuel George.	Captain & Brevet Major No clasp	
1802	Hopkins,	Harry.	Colour Sergeant (Corporal)	
1646	Harcourt,	Frederick.	Sergeant (Corporal)	
889	Horton,	Thomas.	Sergeant (Corporal)	
288	Hamner,	George.	Lance Sergeant (Corporal)	
1176	Hacker,	William.	Private	
820	Hackley(F),	James.	Private	
1502	Hackman,	Samuel.	Private	
19/536	Hadley*,	George.	Private	
1518	Hadley(F),	William.	Private	
538	Hale,	Charles.	Private	
539	Hale,	William.	Private	
580	Halford,	John.	Private	
1937	Hall(F),	James.	Private	No clasp
1777	Hall*,	John.	Private	
957	Hall,	William.	Private	
1812	Halligan,	James.	Private	
1539	Halligan(F),	Thomas.	Private	
1859	Hamerton,	Thomas.	Private	
1853	Hamilton(F),	James.	Private	No clasp
1513	Hammonds,	Francis.	Private	
1891	Hammonds(F),	William.	Private	
3	Hancox,	Samuel.	Private (Sergeant)	
281	Handcox,	Joseph.	Private	
492	Hands,	William.	Private	
937	Hanes(F),	E.	Private	
1558	Hankinson,	Richard.	Private	
702	Hannon,	Johm.	Private	
	(702 Hannen, John.)			
1368	Hanson,	William.	Private	
512	Harbattle,	George.	Private	

1880	Harbridge(F),	George.	Private	No clasp	543	Howard,	Henry.	Private
1325	Hardy,	William.	Private		1721	Howard,	Owen.	Private
121	Harper,	Josiah.	Private		2067	Howes,	John.	Private
643	Harris,	Henry.	Private		1933	Hoyle(F),	Joseph.	Private	No clasp
1824	Hart,	George.	Private		495	Hughes,	Benjamin.	Private
1253	Hart(F),	John.	Private		525	Hughes(F),	George.	Private
2008	Hart*,	Julian.	Private		552	Hughes,	James.	Private
135	Hartrick,	William.	Private		1499	Hughes*,	John.	Private
1816	Harvey,	John.	Private		1589	Hughes,	Joseph.	Private
1231	Harvey,	William.	Private		1814	Hughes(F),	Richard.	Private	No clasp
1562	Haslem,	Richard.	Private		1060	Hughes(F),	Thomas.	Private
1073	Hatton,	Frederick.	Private		1132	Hughes(F),	William.	Private
1864	Haven(F),	John.	Private	No clasp	1898	Hunt,	Frederick.	Private
134	Hawkes,	Charles.	Private		925	Hunt,	John.	Private
19/999	Hawkes*,	Eli.	Private		1900	Hunt(F),	William.	Private	No clasp
1129	Hawkesworth(F),	George.	Private	No clasp	1072	Hurd,	Walter.	Private
147	Hawkins,	William.	Private		945	Hussell,	William.	Private
1951	Hayden,	George.	Private		535	Husselbee,	John.	Private
1975	Hayelton,	William.	Private		229	Hutchinson,	Thomas.	Private
1966	Hayes,	Dennis.	Private		1887	Hyem(F),	Henry.	Private
	(1966 Hayes, Dennies.)				902	**Ingham***,	John.	Private
1818	Hayes(F),	Edward.	Private	No clasp	1838	Irvine,	William Thomas.	Private
19/227	Haynes*,	George.	Private			**Johnson**,	Henry James.	Captain (Lieutenant)
	(19/227 Haines, George.)				366	Jones,	Nicholas,	Sergeant Instructor Musketry
1268	Haynes(F),	John.	Private					
921	Haywood(F),	Charles.	Private		442	Jervis(F),	James.	Sergeant
1267	Haywood(F),	Henry.	Private		1271	Johnson*,	William.	Sergeant
235	Haywood,	Joseph.	Private		1783	Joyce,	William.	Lance Sergeant (Private)
	(235 Hayward, Joseph.)				2107	Jennings,	Edgar.	Corporal
761	Haywood,	Mark.	Private		19/544	Johnson*,	Ernest.	Corporal
19/783	Healey*,	Thomas.	Private		1965	Jackman(F),	Eli.	Private	No clasp
871	Heath(F),	Robert.	Private		1509	Jackson(F),	Benjamin.	Private
599	Heath,	William.	Private		566	Jackson,	Joseph.	Private
1576	Heavey,	Bartholomuew.	Private		272	Jackson,	Thomas.	Private
1906	Herman,	George.	Private		742	Jackson,	Thomas.	Private
167	Herryman,	Ephraim.	Private		1919	Jacobs*,	Henry.	Private
1868	Hickey(F),	Joseph.	Private	No clasp	823	James(F),	Joseph.	Private
19/1021	Hill*,	Henry.	Private		1083	Jefferson,	William.	Private
1848	Hill(F),	Joseph.	Private		285	Jenkins,	Henry Charles.	Private
256	Hill,	Thomas.	Private			(285 Jenkin, Henry Charles.)		
721	Hill,	Thomas.	Private		1059	Jenkins(F),	Richard.	Private
1068	Hill,	Thomas.	Private		241	Jennings,	George.	Private
207	Hince,	Thomas.	Private		223	Jennings(F),	Thomas.	Private
737	Hing,	Thomas.	Private		1005	Jobbourn,	Henry.	Private
2047	Hippenstall(F),	John.	Private	No clasp		(1005 Jobburn, Henry.)		
604	Hixon,	Henry.	Private		776	Johnson,	Harry.	Private
	(604 Hickson, Henry.)				653	Johnson,	Hubert.	Private
881	Hockley,	Philip.	Private		1723	Johnson,	John.	Private
709	Hodges*,	Thomas.	Private		1679	Johnson,	Joseph.	Private
740	Hogan,	Martin.	Private		891	Johnson(F),	William.	Private
498	Holden,	Samuel.	Private		2058	Johnson,	William.	Private
1032	Holman,	Charles.	Private		226	Jones,	Charles.	Private
1433	Holman*,	Edwin.	Private		1819	Jones(F),	Daniel.	Private	No clasp
97	Holmes,	Archibald.	Private		240	Jones,	Henry.	Private
29	Holmes,	James.	Private		155	Jones,	James.	Private
894	Hope(F),	James.	Private		997	Jones,	Joel.	Private
820	Hopkins,	George.	Private		437	Jones(F),	John.	Private
1994	Hopkins,	John T.	Private		1619	Jones,	John.	Private
2094	Hopkins,	William Francis.	Private		1961	Jones(F),	Samuel.	Private	No clasp
979	Hopley,	William.	Private		1214	Jones(F),	Thomas.	Private
2083	Hopson,	John.	Private		1260	Jones(F),	Thomas.	Private
890	Horn,	William.	Private (Corporal)		1391	Jones,	William.	Private
1522	Hough,	John.	Private		1488	Jones,	William John.	Private
129	Hoult,	Edward.	Private		1814	Jones,	William.	Private
1720	Howard,	Charles.	Private		1964	Jones,	William Jas.	Private
1945	Howard,	Frank.	Private		1976	Joyce(F),	Eli.	Private	No clasp

No.	Surname	Forename	Rank	
1251	Joyce.	Martin.	Private	
589	Judd,	Thomas.	Private	
668	**Kelly**,	Patrick.	Sergeant	
1567	King,	John.	Sergeant (Corporal)	
1711	Kelly,	Thomas.	Corporal	
1344	Kilsill,	Henry.	Corporal	
461	Kynaston,	John.	Corporal	
418	Keats,	Joseph.	Private	
1907	Keen(F),	John.	Private	No clasp
115	Keenan,	William.	Private	
2045	Kelly(F),	John.	Private	No clasp
682	Kelly,	Peter.	Private	
1477	Kelly,	Thomas.	Private	
578	Kesterton,	William.	Private	
1357	Kettle,	John.	Private	
526	Kilbride,	John.	Private	
914	King(F),	Charles.	Private	
456	King,	James.	Private	
1217	King(F),	Peter.	Private	
1632	Kitchen,	Joseph.	Private	
182	Knowles(F),	Henry.	Private	
	Lindop,	Alfred Henry.	Lieutenant (2nd Lieutenant)	
	Lyons,	Frederick William.	Lieutenant (2nd Lieutenant)	
1321	Lynch,	Thomas.	Colour Sergeant (Sergeant)	
2065	Laurence*,	Robert.	Sergeant	
374	Lockett,	Joseph.	Lance Sergeant (Private)	
185	Lowbridge,	David.	Lance Sergeant (Private)	
1833	Lewis,	William.	Corporal	
2066	Little,	William.	Corporal	
999	Lovegrove,	Richard.	Corporal (Private)	
595	Lawrence,	Charles.	Drummer	
1647	Leather*,	John.	Drummer	
110	Lewis,	John.	Drummer	
1376	Lacy,	John.	Private	
1865	Lafferty*,	John.	Private	
393	Lawley,	Henry.	Private	
357	Lawrence,	William.	Private	
1885	Lawson(F),	John.	Private	No clasp
1902	Lawton,	Henry.	Private	
1795	Leigh,	Ralph.	Private	
632	Leek,	John.	Private	
19/996	Leese*,	Ralph.	Private	
1029	Lewis,	Henry.	Private	
1506	Lewis,	Peter.	Private	
1958	Lineham(F),	Jeremiah.	Private	No clasp
267	Linksey,	Patrick.	Private	
1625	Linkston,	Robert.	Private	
1834	Linnett,	John.	Private	
27	Lloyd,	William.	Private	
	(27 Loyd, William.)			
1990	Loage,	James.	Private	
917	Locker(F),	George Thomas.	Private	
19/1931	Lodge*,	Henry. (Alias Henry Cook)	Private	
1903	Loney(F),	Thomas.	Private	No clasp
583	Longstaff,	George.	Private	
1863	Loomes(F),	Reuban Thomas.	Private	
1657	Lord,	William.	Private	
	(1657 Lord, William H.)			
1230	Lowder(F),	John.	Private	
271	Lowe,	Samuel.	Private	
1653	Lowrie,	James.	Private	
1532	Luck(F),	John.	Private	No clasp
773	Lunn,	John.	Private	
1213	Lunt*,	William.	Private	
1645	Lynch,	William.	Private	
1771	Lyons,	Thomas.	Private	
	Marshall,	Francis MacLeon Hastings,	Lieutenant (2nd Lieutenant)	
	Moriarty*,	David Barry.	Captain	
	Moore,	William.	Lieutenant	
1012	McGuiness,	Christopher.	Orderly Room Clerk	
918	Machin,	Frederick.	Colour Sergeant	
416	Markwell,	Thomas.	Sergeant	
1761	McDonald,	Nicholas.	Sergeant	
124	McMullen,	John.	Sergeant (Corporal)	
1487	Major,	Robert.	Corporal	
2000	Martin,	Charles.	Corporal	
714	Maynard,	William J.	Corporal	
1525	McCready,	Robert.	Corporal	
19/733	McCoy*,	John.	Corporal	
1303	McDonald,	John.	Corporal	
1618	McMullen(F),	Henry.	Corporal	
1867	Mellon(F),	James.	Corporal	No clasp
1866	Moon(F),	Richard.	Corporal	No clasp
1372	Moore,	George.	Corporal	
1319	Moore,	Henry.	Corporal (Drummer)	
1534	Murch,	Samuel.	Corporal (Private)	
596	Maker(F),	James.	Drummer	
1767	McQuillan,	John.	Drummer	
1336	Moran,	William.	Drummer	
2108	McAuliff,	Edmond.	Private	
300	McCaffrey,	Hugh.	Private	
2007	McCall,	Martin.	Private	
2017	McCann,	Patrick.	Private	
62	McCleary,	Dennis.	Private	
	(62 McClarey, Dennis.)			
1253	McClennon(F),	Jno.	Private	No clasp
1314	McCormack,	Michael.	Private	
1120	McCue(F),	John.	Private	
1349	McCullough,	James.	Private	
765	McDermott(F),	John.	Private	
559	McDonald*,	William.	Private	
1858	McGillan,	Thomas.	Private	
1975	McGlocklin(F),	James.	Private	
1799	McGookin.	John.	Private	
1972	McGrath(F),	Dennis.	Private	No clasp
1875	McGrath(F),	William.	Private	No clasp
1719	McGurk,	Peter.	Private	
2282	McKee,	Edward.	Private	
1546	McKee,	James.	Private	
1775	McKenny,	William.	Private	
309	McKenzie,	John.	Private	
1960	McLoughlin(F),	John.	Private	No clasp
1159	McMahon,	Robert.	Private	
1177	McNichols(F),	Nicholas.	Private	
77	McNeil,	Michael.	Private	
19/1378	McSherry*,	Bernard.	Private	
	(19/1378 McSherry, Edward.)			
305	Mace(F),	John.	Private	
1012	Machin,	Joseph.	Private	
1981	Macklin(F),	James.	Private	
	(1981 Macklan, James.)			
2092	Maden,	George.	Private	
1426	Makepeace,	John.	Private	
1568	Malloy,	John.	Private	
879	Manning(F),	John.	Private	
1351	Manning,	Stephen.	Private	
963	Mannison(F),	Michael.	Private	
181	Manson*(F),	Alexander.	Private	

No.	Surname	Forename	Rank	Clasp
1927	Mantell,	Henry.	Private	
1161	Marlow,	James.	Private	
1890	Marsdin,	Mark.	Private	
	(1890 Marsden, Mark.)			
2046	Marshall(F),	Henry.	Private	No clasp
2103	Marson,	William.	Private	
206	Martin,	Frederick.	Private	
1909	Martin,	Thomas.	Private	
1397	Martin(F),	William.	Private	
588	Mason,	Edward.	Private	
1522	Mason(F),	John.	Private	
1712	Massey,	Thomas.	Private	
732	Masterson,	Peter.	Private	
1933	Matthews,	Alfred.	Private	
170	Matthews,	Charles.	Private	
1846	May,	John.	Private	
1801	Mayfield(F),	Frank.	Private	No clasp
1580	Meachin*,	Alfred.	Private	
1010	Mead,	Isaac.	Private	
1983	Mead,	Thomas.	Private	
19/590	Meadows*,	Henry.	Private	
1025	Meekin,	Edward.	Private	
1492	Meers,	Edward.	Private	
432	Melsop,	John.	Private	
1683	Mercer,	George.	Private	
344	Merrill(F),	Thomas.	Private	
678	Merryman,	John.	Private	
83	Middleton,	Edward.	Private	
	(83 Middleton, Edwin.)			
2063	Middow*,	Arthur.	Private	
1910	Midgley(F),	James.	Private	No clasp
49	Millar,	John.	Private	
851	Millership(F),	William.	Private	
586	Millington,	Thomas.	Private	
1109	Mills(F),	Henry.	Private	
1976	Mitchell*,	George.	Private	
268	Moffatt,	John.	Private	
1057	Moffatt,	John.	Private	
1083	Moffatt(F),	Thomas.	Private	
2106	Monaghan,	Patrick.	Private	
1033	Monckton,	Edward.	Private	
554	Moore,	George.	Private	
2048	Moore*,	Robert.	Private	
924	Moran(F),	James.	Private	
310	Moran,	Martin.	Private	
1032	Moran*.	William.	Private	
1397	Moreton,	William.	Private	
787	Morgan,	Bernard.	Private	
1084	Morley(F),	Michael.	Private	
2049	Morris(F),	George.	Private	No clasp
180	Morris,	John.	Private	
476	Morris,	John.	Private	
	(476 Morriss, John.)			
504	Morris,	Joseph.	Private	
1821	Morris,	Joseph.	Private	
681	Morris,	Michael.	Private	
964	Morris*,	Thomaas.	Private	
161	Morris,	William.	Private	
768	Morris,	William.	Private	
1920	Morris(F),	William.	Private	No clasp
315	Mountford,	William.	Private	
1904	Muddell,	Charles.	Private	
1678	Mulgrew,	James.	Private	
2043	Mulligan(F),	John.	Private	No clasp
1579	Mullholland,	Joseph.	Private	
1964	Murphy(F),	Peter.	Private	No clasp
127	Mullins,	Thomas.	Private	
1501	Murphy,	William.	Private	
1226	Musson(F),	William.	Private	
201	**Norton**,	William.	Colour Sergeant	
1555	Newman(F),	J.	Corporal	No clasp
1962	Nash(F),	George.	Private	No clasp
157	Navan,	John.	Private	
1493	Nayler,	George.	Private	
984	Neale,	Joseph.	Private	
758	Newey,	William.	Private	
	(758 Newey, John.)			
958	Newman(F),	Alfred.	Private	
1963	Newman(F),	Edward.	Private	No clasp
1868	Newton,	Henry.	Private	
468	Nicklin,	Thomas.	Private	
1508	Nicholl(F),	George.	Private	
555	Nichols,	Benjamin.	Private	
1926	Night*,	Henry.	Private	
263	Nixon,	Joseph.	Private	
2023	Nolan,	John.	Private	
1339	Nolan,	Patrick.	Private	
548	Nolan,	Phillip.	Private	
1681	Nolan,	Thomas.	Private	
772	Noonan,	Thomas.	Private	
1062	Norton*,	John.	Private	
1566	Nunnerley,	John.	Private	
692	**O'Day**,	Owen.	Drum Major	
1249	O'Neill*,	Thomas.	Colour Sergeant (Sergeant)	
119	Oakley,	Thomas.	Private	
1117	O'Brien,	Richard.	Private	
478	O'Gera,	William.	Private	
1812	O'Gilvie(F),	James.	Private	No clasp
1456	O'Neill,	John.	Private	
1736	Ovens,	Williams.	Private	
166	Owen,	Edward.	Private	
1162	Owen,	George.	Private	
1840	Owen,	James.	Private	
165	Owen,	William.	Private	
2087	Owens(F),	Henry.	Private	No clasp
1240	Owens*(F),	Richard.	Private	
1858	Owens(F),	Thomas.	Private	No clasp
	Prior,	John Edward Hale.	Major (Captain)	
	Potts,	Lipton Comming.	Captain (Lieutenant)	
	Pendrey,	James.	Quartermaster	
784	Pendergast,	Henry.	Sergeant (Corporal)	
1257	Penketh,	James.	Sergeant (Corporal)	
98	Perkins,	Benjamin.	Sergeant	
1401	Pritchard(F),	Samuel.	Corporal	No clasp
582	Page,	Albert.	Private	
1147	Parker(F),	Thomas.	Private	
1027	Parks,	Charles.	Private	
1256	Parks,	Henry.	Private	
1885	Parrott,	George.	Private	
172	Parry,	Henry.	Private	
1903	Parson(F),	John W.	Private	No clasp
719	Parsons(F),	Richard.	Private	No clasp
1160	Patey,	John.	Private	
527	Payne,	Edward.	Private	
971	Payne,	Thomas.	Private	
698	Pearse.	Charles.	Private	
805	Pemberton,	Henry.	Private	
399	Pepper,	John.	Private	
685	Perkins,	Albert.	Private	
662	Perkins,	John.	Private	
116	Perkins,	Joseph.	Private	

No.	Surname	Forename	Rank	Clasp
92	Peters,	Frank.	Private	
246	Phillips,	Alfred.	Private	
477	Phillips,	Thomas.	Private	
612	Phillips,	Thomas.	Private	
220	Phipps*,	William.	Private	
649	Picken,	George.	Private	
1225	Picken(F),	James.	Private	No clasp
286	Pitcher,	Joseph.	Private	
	(286 Pittcher,Joseph.)			
360	Plant,	Henry.	Private	
1604	Plant,	William.	Private	
1917	Plummer(F),	Peter.	Private	No clasp
1549	Poole,	John.	Private	
904	Potts(F),	John.	Private	No clasp
706	Powell,	Edward.	Private	
1234	Powers,	John.	Private	
1852	Powis(F),	Noah.	Private	No clasp
717	Powis,	Samuel.	Private	
186	Preece,	George.	Private	
1909	Preston(F),	John.	Private	No clasp
1265	Price(F),	John.	Private	
1816	Price(F),	John.	Private	No clasp
2031	Prince,	John.	Private	
757	Prince,	Joseph.	Private	
2085	Pritchard*,	Charles.	Private	
1053	Proud,	Peter.	Private	
	(1053 Proud, Robert.)			
1163	Pummell*,	Arthur.	Private	
645	**Queeny**,	Owen.	Private	
2047	Quick,	James.	Private	
824	Quinn(F),	John.	Private	
	Roworth,	Charles Edward Whitaker.	Captain	
	Raitt,	Herbert Aveling.	Lieutenant (2nd Lieutenant)	
2098	Richardson,	William.	Colour Sergeant (Sergeant)	
829	Rafferty(F),	James.	Private	
1974	Ralphs*,	Frederick.	Private	
201	Ramsey,	George.	Private	
414	Randle,	Henry.	Private	
1094	Ratcliffe(F),	George.	Private	No clasp
1953	Raymond,	Charles.	Private	
533	Reed,	George Thomas.	Private	
869	Reilly(F),	Michael.	Private	
158	Renfrey,	Alfred.	Private	
1183	Reeves(F),	James.	Private	No clasp
1541	Reynolds(F),	John.	Private	
609	Rhoades,	Roland.	Private	
	(609 Rhodes, Roland.)			
1894	Rhoades,	Thomas.	Private	
	(1894 Rhoads, Thomas.)			
1093	Rice(F),	Andrew.	Private	
528	Richardson,	Charles.	Private	
2012	Richardson,	George.	Private	
1099	Richardson(F),	Robert.	Private	
1108	Rickman,	George.	Private	
933	Riley(F),	Albert.	Private	
995	Riley,	Martin.	Private	
1963	Ring,	Edward.	Private	
878	Roach(F),	Thomas.	Private	
578	Robbins,	William.	Private	
1960	Roberts,	Henry.	Private	
1959	Robertson(F),	Samuel.	Private	No clasp
19/259	Robinson*,	John.	Private	
1483	Robinson,	Robert.	Private	
1000	Robinson,	Samuel.	Private	
1047	Robson,	James.	Private	
1393	Rochell,	Henry.	Private	
1296	Rodgers(F),	John.	Private	
965	Rodgers,	Samuel.	Private	
1881	Roe(F),	John.	Private	No clasp
486	Rohen*,	Peter.	Private	
1540	Rollason(F),	Henry.	Private	
1811	Rose(F),	Richard W.	Private	No clasp
358	Rouse,	William.	Private	
744	Rowan,	Thomas.	Private	
1573	Rowe(F),	James.	Private	
975	Rowe,	John.	Private	
853	Rowley(F),	George.	Private	
663	Rowley,	Thomas.	Private	
1337	Rubie,	George.	Private	
1085	Rubie,	Robert.	Private	
2070	Ruffle*,	Henry.	Private	
711	Rush,	Frank.	Private	
2010	Russell,	James.	Private	
1923	Rutledge(F),	John.	Private	No clasp
1254	Ryan,	Daniel.	Private	
1912	Ryan,	Henry.	Private	
1263	Ryan(F),	John.	Private	
1971	Ryan(F),	John.	Private	No clasp
1423	Ryan*,	Joseph.	Private	
1878	Ryan(F),	Richard.	Private	No clasp
1007	Ryder,	Thomas.	Private	
	Saunders,	Allan.	Captain	
	Savage,	Henry Charles.	Lieutenant & Adjutant	
	Sherrard,	James Ormsby.	Captain (Lieutenant)	
3124	Shore,	Edward.	Colour Sergeant	
149	Smallwood,	Samuel.	Armourer Sergeant	
1863	Searl(F),	Henry.	Sergeant	No clasp
1503	Stevenson,	Joseph.	Sergeant	
1627	Sansam*,	George.	Lance Sergeant	
2062	Stephens,	Edward.	Corporal	
375	Salt,	George.	Private	
1889	Salter,	Charles.	Private	
1873	Sample(F),	Thomas.	Private	No clasp
972	Sanders,	John.	Private	
439	Sands,	William.	Private	
	(439 Sandes, William.)			
968	Sargeant,	Henry.	Private	
	(967 Sargeant, Henry.)			
1533	Satterley,	William.	Private	
972	Saunders(F),	John.	Private	Clasp '1878-9'
	(972 Sanders, John.)			
962	Saville,	Edward.	Private	
1019	Savage,	James.	Private	
670	Saxton,	Josiah.	Private	
	(670 Saxton, Joseph.)			
2074	Scott,	Edward.	Private	
1253	Seddons,	Thomas.	Private	
	(1253 Seddon,Thomas.)			
377	Sedgeley,	William Henry.	Private	
1888	Selby(F),	George.	Private	No clasp
262	Senior,	John.	Private	
650	Sergeant,	John W.	Private	
1904	Sewell(F),	John.	Private	No clasp
675	Seymour*,	William.	Private	
	(695 Seymour, William.)			
484	Shapcott,	Henry.	Private	
970	Shaw,	Frederick.	Private	
1535	Shaw(F),	Jonathan.	Private	
1534	Shaw(F),	Robert.	Private	
1165	Shaw,	Samuel.	Private	

1810	Shaw(F),	William.	Private	No clasp	2060	Summersby,	Henry.	Private	
323	Shea(F),	Cornelius.	Private	No clasp	1988	Sutton,	James.	Private	
2035	Shellock,	James.	Private			**Tucker** (C.B.)	Charles.	Lt. Colonel (Major)	
19/615	Sherridan*,	Michael.	Private			Tyler,	Charles John Roper.	Major	
514	Shirley,	Henry William.	Private		2003	Thompson,	John.	Orderly Room Clerk	
508	Sigley,	John.	Private					(Quartermaster Sergeant)	
1770	Silcock*,	Joseph.	Private		1163	Tolley,	William.	Sergeant	
324	Simcock,	John.	Private		1011	Tidball,	Henry.	Corporal (Private)	
819	Simpson*,	Arthur.	Private		1757	Terry,	Alfred.	Drummer	
511	Simpson,	William.	Private		120	Tallice,	George.	Private	
607	Sinclair,	William.	Private		1245	Tansley*(F),	Jas. Frederick.	Private	
378	Sivorns,	William.	Private		630	Tarver,	Jonathan.	Private	
1864	Skellam,	Thomas.	Private		1244	Taylor(F),	Alfred.	Private	
	(1864 Skellam, Thomas Everard.)				1121	Taylor(F),	James.	Private	
610	Slack,	Edward.	Private		1207	Taylor(F),	James.	Private	
1557	Slater(F),	John.	Private		735	Taylor,	John.	Private	
608	Sleigh,	Walter.	Private		720	Taylor,	Joshua Thomas.	Private	
684	Smallman,	John.	Private		1330	Taylor,	Robert.	Private	
376	Smith,	Charles.	Private		1895	Taylor,	Thomas.	Private	
386	Smith,	Daniel.	Private		255	Taylor,	William.	Private	
1018	Smith,	Daniel.	Private		368	Taylor(F),	William.	Private	
893	Smith(F),	David.	Private		1536	Taylor,	William.	Private	
1048	Smith,	George.	Private		373	Teehan,	John.	Private	
1171	Smith(F),	George.	Private	No clasp	435	Terry,	Joseph.	Private	
479	Smith,	Henry.	Private		816	Tetlow,	Edward.	Private	
19/510	Smith*,	Henry.	Private		162	Thirley(F),	Thomas.	Private Clasp '1878-9'	
646	Smith,	Henry.	Private		1511	Thomas(F),	Daniel.	Private	
	(646 Smith, Henry George.)				1794	Thompson,	Alexander.	Private	
725	Smith,	Henry.	Private		2096	Thompson,	E.D.A.	Private	
424	Smith,	James.	Private		2081	Thompson*,	Henry.	Private	
144	Smith,	John.	Private		1957	Thompson,	Robert.	Private	
1050	Smith,	John.	Private		811	Thompson,	Thomas.	Private	
1350	Smith,	John.	Private		2002	Thompson,	William.	Private	
1523	Smith(F),	John.	Private			(2002 Thomson, William.)			
1948	Smith,	John.	Private		162	Thorley,	Thomas.	Private	
1063	Smith*,	Johnson.	Private		19/587	Tibbott*,	Joseph.	Private	
258	Smith,	Joseph.	Private		1061	Tilley,	George.	Private	
657	Smith*,	Joseph.	Private		1826	Toal,	James.	Private	
61	Smith,	Mark.	Private		649	Tomlin,	Thomas.	Private	
1240	Smith,	Michael.	Private		1291	Tomlinson*,	Richard.	Private	
664	Smith,	Thomas.	Private		1529	Tomlinson,	William.	Private	
705	Smith,	Thomas.	Private		329	Topp,	Charles.	Private	
1494	Smith,	William.	Private		1108	Toy(F),	James.	Private	
200	Snape,	James.	Private		63	Trott,	Charles.	Private (Sergeant)	
2029	Soan,	Benjamin.	Private		19/1705	Tucker*,	George.	Private	
1902	Southworth(F),	Benjamin.	Private	No clasp	19/104	Tucker*,	Thomas.	Private	
1805	Speers,	James.	Private		487	Tulley,	Charles.	Private	
729	Spence,	Robert.	Private		669	Tully*,	Patrick.	Private	
1077	Spencer,	Henry.	Private		1091	Tunstall(F),	Arthur.	Private	
746	Spink,	James.	Private		1887	Turner,	Charles.	Private	
2009	Stabbs(F),	John.	Private	No clasp	459	Turner,	Edward.	Private	
1526	Stacey,	Arthur.	Private		782	Turner,	William.	Private	
2016	Stanley,	Alfred.	Private		1322	Tyldesley,	Thomas.	Private	
1776	Sterling,	Henry.	Private		501	Tyler,	James.	Private	
1107	Stevenson,	George.	Private			**Ussher**,	Beverley William Reid.	Lieutenant (2nd	
1137	Stevenson,	Thomas.	Private					Lieutenant)	
473	Stokes,	David.	Private		188	Upperdine,	Joseph.	Private	
138	Stokes,	Frank.	Private		1872	Upsdale(F),	Henry.	Private	No clasp
1067	Stokes,	John.	Private		902	Upton*(F),	Henry.	Private	
1987	Storas,	William.	Private		540	**Vyse**,	Joseph.	Drummer	
225	Storer,	Walter.	Private		993	Vanston,	Francis.	Private	
229	Street,	Walter.	Private		1516	Vaughan(F),	Frank.	Private	
1792	Sturges,	Warren.	Private		1941	Vaughan,	Henry.	Private	
1396	Sugden,	Richard.	Private		1046	Vaughan,	John.	Private	
2042	Sullivan,	Michael.	Private		423	Varley*,	John.	Private	
1274	Summers(F),	Jonathan.	Private		370	Vernon*,	James.	Private	

1080	Vickery,	Samuel.	Private
	Williams(F), George Albanus.		2nd Lieutenant
336	Waters,	James.	Colour Sergeant
1965	Woods,	Alfred H.	Colour Sergeant
1665	Walker,	Harry.	Sergeant
1217	Ward,	Henry.	Sergeant
1630	Watts*,	James Henry.	Sergeant
1320	Weldon,	Peter.	Corporal (Drummer)
1911	Wakeling,	George.	Private
530	Walker(F),	Edward.	Private. No clasp
1546	Walker(F),	George.	Private
563	Walker,	Thomas.	Private
124	Walkley,	Thomas.	Private
549	Walsh,	Anthony.	Private
	(549 Welsh, Anthony.)		
219	Walsh,	John.	Private
803	Walsh,	John.	Private
1495	Walsh,	William.	Private
1851	Ward(F),	Issaac.	Private No clasp
1530	Ward(F),	John.	Private
1921	Ward(F),	John.	Private No clasp
62	Ward,	William.	Private
1144	Ware(F),	William.	Private
204	Warner,	Cornelius.	Private
1092	Washington(F), William.		Private
427	Wassall v.c.,	Samuel.	Private
1016	Wassall,	Charles.	Private
1924	Waxham,	Thomas.	Private
730	Weaver,	Benjamin.	Private
606	Weaver,	Job:	Private
1289	Weaver*,	John.	Private
19/716	Weaver*,	Joseph.	Private
605	Webster,	John.	Private
1009	Wedge,	Henry.	Private
987	Welch,	John B.	Private
1704	Wells,	Edward.	Private
1905	Wells,	James.	Private
1002	West,	Eli.	Private
1815	Westcoth(F),	James R.	Private No clasp
990	Western,	Charles.	Private
1269	Weston(F),	Patrick.	Private
294	Westwood,	James.	Private
228	Westwood,	Thomas.	Private
1506	Wheat(F),	Clement.	Private
1097	Wheeler,	Richard.	Private
752	While,	William.	Private
1069	Whitby,	Charles.	Private
2061	White,	George.	Private
624	White,	John.	Private
1536	White(F),	Joseph R.	Private
1095	White,	William.	Private
1041	Whitehouse,	David.	Private
9/60	Whitehouse*,	Joseph.	Private
769	Whitehouse,	Richard.	Private
	(769 Whitehead, Richard.)		
774	Whitehouse,	William.	Private
1250	Whittaker(F),	David.	Private
2091	Whittaker,	William.	Private
2097	Whyman,	Thomas.	Private
247	Wiley,	Charles.	Private
137	Wiley,	Thomas.	Private
1555	Wilkes(F),	William.	Private
24	Wilkins,	Henry.	Private

815	Wilkinson(F),	David.	Private
791	Wilkinson,	Samuel.	Private
1006	Wilkinson,	William.	Private
1549	Wilks(F),	John.	Private
450	Willings,	Enoch.	Private
1039	William,	William.	Private
	(1039 Williams, William.)		
991	Williams,	Charles.	Private
1876	Williams,	George.	Private
691	Williams,	Harry.	Private
1915	Williams(F),	John.	Private No clasp
997	Williams,	Shadrack.	Private
361	Williams,	Thomas.	Private
1809	Williams(F),	Thomas.	Private No clasp
	(1809 Williamson, Thomas.)		
573	Williams,	Thomas.	Private
617	Williams,	William.	Private
442	Williamson,	Frank.	Private
2013	Wilmott,	William.	Private
	(2013 Wilmot, William.)		
1896	Wilson,	Charles.	Private
627	Wilson,	Frederick.	Private
1175	Wilson,	Henry.	Private
1375	Wiltshire,	Benjamin.	Private
686	Winter,	John.	Private
1020	Winwood,	Joseph.	Private
295	Wood,	Charles.	Private
446	Wood,	David.	Private
515	Wood,	James.	Private
1486	Wooding,	Issaac.	Private
1535	Woodford,	Joseph.	Private
1605	Woodward*,	Herbert.	Private
977	Woodward,	James.	Private
724	Woodward,	Jason.	Private
980	Woodward,	John.	Private
1394	Woolcot,	Henry.	Private (Corporal)
	(1394 Woolcox, Henry.)		
1871	Woollams,	Frederick.	Private
1551	Worrolls(F)	, Henry.	Private
1912	Worth(F),	Richard.	Private No clasp
2078	Worty,	James.	Private
2048	Wrick(F),	William.	Private No clasp
	(2048 Wride, William.)		
598	Wright,	Frederick.	Private
564	Wright,	George.	Private
1882	Wright(F),	John.	Private No clasp
2051	Wright,	Joseph.	Private
1023	Wright,	William.	Private
566	Wroe,	John.	Private
1972	**Young**,	Henry.	Private
1888	Young,	Thomas.	Private
1013	Yoxall,	Frederick.	Private
*387	Carter,	John.	} This may me the same person
387	Cater,	John.	

Attached to the 80th Regiment of Foot

Commissariat & Transport

Whittington,	Joseph.	Waggon Conductor

Army Medical Department

Cobbin,	William Ingram.	Civil Surgeon

CASUALTIES SOUTH AFRICA SEKUKUNI CAMPAIGNS AND ZULU WAR

A total of 122 names are contained in the list of casualties for the 80th Regiment of Foot. 70 men were killed in actions during the campaigns, 7 men were killed at Isandhlwana, 61 at the Intombi River and two at the battle at Ulundi. It is reported that 5 men were wounded at the final battle at Ulundi. Civil Surgeon William Ingram Cobbin of the Army Medical Department and Joseph Whittington, a waggon conductor of the Commissariat and Transport Department, both attached to the 80th Regiment were also killed at the battle at the Intombi River on March 12th 1879. During the final conflict with Chief Sekukuni at the taking of Sekukuni Kraal on November 28th 1879, one member of the 80th was wounded.

The list also contains the names of 43 soldiers who died whilst serving with the Regiment in South Africa. Of these some fifteen soldiers were not awarded the South Africa Medal and these can be identified by a (*), before their surname.

704	Adams,	Robert.	Private	Died (Place not Known)	14th Feb.	1880
546	Adey,	Jonah.	Private	Killed in Action, Intombi River	12th Mar.	1879
19/585	Anthony,	John.	Private	Killed in Action, Intombi River	12th Mar.	1879
19/202	Banks,	Arthur.	Private	Killed in Action, Intombi River	12th Mar.	1879
943	Banner,	John.	Private	Killed in Action, Intombi River	12th Mar.	1879
19/636	Beecroft,	Alfred.	Corporal (Private)	Severly Wounded, Ulundi	4th July	1879
	*Belt,	John	Quarter Master	Died at Mooi River	5th Aug.	1878
16	Bond,	William.	Private	Died at Lydenburg	29th Dec.	1878
19/745	Broughton,	George.	Private	Killed in Action, Intombi River	12th Mar.	1879
48	Brown,	James.	Private	Killed in Action, Intombi River	12th Mar.	1879
1387	Brown,	Thomas.	Lce Sergeant	Severely Wounded, Kambula,	29th Mar.	1879
19/488	Brownson,	Henry.	Private	Killed in Action, Intombi River	12th Mar.	1879
1609	Burtenshaw,	Henry.	Private	Died in South Africa	30th Mar.	1880
509	*Burton,	Thomas.	Private	Died at Pietermaritzburg	28th June	1878
278	Butler,	Frederick.	Private	Died (Place not known)	18th July	1879
169	Burgwin,	Thomas.	Private	Died at Sea	10th May	1880
1290	Chadwick,	John.	Private	Killed in Action, Intombi River	12th Mar.	1879
287	Chare,	Calib Edwin.	Private	Slightly Wounded, Sekukuni's Kraal	28th Nov.	1879
1377	Chesterton,	John.	Private	Killed in Action, Isandhlwana	22nd Jan.	1879
1797	Christie,	James.	Private	Killed in Action, Intombi River	12th Mar.	1879
	(1797 Christy, James.)					
641	*Collins,	Hugh.	Private	Died at Durban	3rd April	1877
1232	Cook,	Thomas.	Private	Died in Transvaal	8th Oct.	1879
1169	Corry,	John.	Private	Died at Whistletroom	19th Sept.	1879
19/1042	Day,	Alfred.	Private	Killed in Action, Intombi River	12th Mar.	1879
19/953	Dodd,	John.	Private	Killed in Action, Intombi River	12th Mar.	1879
1616	Duffy,	Michael.	Private	Severely Wounded, Ulundi	4th July	1879
900	Duggan,	Myles.	Lce. Sergeant	Died at Mooi River	1st Oct.	1879
260	Dutton,	John Henry.	Private	Killed in Action, Intombi River	12th Mar.	1879
1202	Dutton,	Noah.	Private	Died at Sea	17th April	1880
1900	Dyball,	William.	Private	Died at Lydenburg	29th Jan.	1879
559	*Edwards,	James.	Private	Died Transvaal	12th Oct.	1878
1028	Farnell,	William.	Private	Killed in Action, Intombi River	12th Mar.	1879
222	Findley,	William.	Private	Killed in Action, Intombi River	12th Mar.	1879
1892	Floyd,	Joseph.	Private	Killed in Action, Ulundi	4th July	1879
19/176	Flyfield,	William.	Private	Killed in Action, Intombi River	12th Mar.	1879
1465	Fox,	William.	Private	Killed in Action, Intombi River	12th Mar.	1879
459	Fredericks,	Henry.	Colour Sergeant	Killed in Action, Intombi River	12th Mar.	1879
1925	Furniaux,	John.	Private	Killed in Action, Intombi River	12th Mar.	1879
1813	Garvey,	Thomas.	Private	Died at Pinetown	19th Dec.	1879
1274	*Gissio,	Harry.	Private	Died at Pretoria	28th Sept.	1878
19/500	Gittins,	Edwin.	Private	Killed in Action, Intombi River	12th Mar.	1879
3642	Graham,	Ewen.	Lce. Corporal	Died at Middleburg	4th Jan.	1879
1697	Green,	Joseph.	Private	Killed in Action, Intombi River	12th Mar.	1879
19/536	Hadley,	George.	Private	Killed in Action, Intombi River	12th Mar.	1879
150	*Hain,	William.	Private	Died at Pietermaritzburg	19th Feb.	1878
1777	Hall,	John.	Private	Died in South Africa	7th Mar.	1880
2008	Hart,	Julian.	Private	Killed in Action, Intombi River	12th Mar.	1879
19/999	Hawkes,	Eli.	Private	Killed in Action, Intombi River	12th Mar.	1879
19/227	Haynes,	George.	Private	Killed in Action, Intombi River	12th Mar.	1879
	(19/227 Haines, George.)					
19/783	Healey,	Thomas.	Private	Killed in Action, Intombi River	12th Mar.	1879
19/1021	Hill,	Henry.	Private	Killed in Action, Intombi River	12th Mar.	1879
709	Hodges,	Thomas.	Private	Killed in Action, Intombi River	12th Mar.	1879
1433	Holman,	Edwin.	Private	Killed in Action, Isandhlwana	22nd Jan.	1879
1499	Hughes,	John.	Private	Killed in Action, Intombi River	12th Mar.	1879
902	Ingham,	John.	Private	Killed in Action, Intombi River	12th Mar.	1879
1919	Jacobs,	Henry.	Private	Killed in Action, Intombi River	12th Mar.	1879
19/544	Johnson,	Ernest.	Corporal	Killed in Action, Intombi River	12th Mar.	1879

1271	Johnson,	William.	Sergeant	Killed in Action, Isandhlwana	22nd Jan.	1879
1865	Lafferty,	John.	Private	Killed in Action, Intombi River	12th Mar.	1879
2065	Lawrence,	Robert.	Sergeant	Died (Place not Known)	30th Oct.	1879
1647	Leather,	John.	Drummer	Killed in Action, Intombi River	12th Mar.	1879
19/996	Leese,	Ralph.	Private	Killed in Action, Intombi River	12th Mar.	1879
19/1931	Lodge,	Henry. (Alias Henry Cook.) Private		Killed in Action, Intombi River	12th Mar.	1879
1213	Lunt,	William.	Private	Dangerously Wounded, Ulundi	4th July	1879
19/733	McCoy,	John.	Corporal	Killed in Action, Intombi River	12th Mar.	1879
559	McDonald,	William.	Private	Killed in Action, Isandhlwana	22nd Jan.	1879
19/1378	McSherry,	Bernard.	Private	Killed in Action, Intombi River	12th Mar.	1879
	(19/1378 McSherry, Edward.)					
181	Manson,	Alexander.	Private	Died at Utrecht	10th Sept.	1879
1580	Meachin,	Alfred.	Private	Died at Pietermaritzburg	29th Dec.	1880
19/590	Meadows,	Henry.	Private	Killed in Action, Intombi River	12th Mar.	1879
2063	Middow,	Arthur.	Private	Killed in Action, Intombi River	12th Mar.	1879
1976	Mitchell,	George.	Private	Killed in Action, Intombi River	12th Mar.	1879
277	*Mollast,	John.	Private	Died (Place not Known)	1st Nov.	1877
2048	Moore,	Robert.	Private	Killed in Action, Intombi River	12th Mar.	1879
1032	Moran.	William.	Private	Killed in Action, Intombi River	12th Mar.	1879
	Moriarty,	David Barry	Captain	Killed in Action, Intombi River	12th Mar.	1879
964	Morris,	Thomas.	Private	Died (Place not Known)	19th Nov.	1879
181	*Moss,	John.	Private	Died (Place not Known)	23rd April	1879
1926	Night,	Henry.	Private	Killed in Action, Intombi River	12th Mar.	1879
1062	Norton,	John.	Private	Died at Whistlestroom	16th Sept.	1879
1249	O'Neill,	Thomas.	Colour Sergeant	Severely Wounded, Ulundi	4th July	1879
1240	Owens,	Richard.	Private	Died (Place not Known)	26th Oct.	1879
276	*Parr,	Joseph.	Private	Died (Place not Known)	13th May	1879
220	Phipps,	William.	Private	Killed in Action, Intombi River	12th Mar.	1879
2085	Pritchard,	Charles.	Private	Killed in Action, Intombi River	12th Mar.	1879
1163	Pummell,	Arthur.	Private	Killed in Action, Intombi River	12th Mar.	1879
1974	Ralphs,	Frederick.	Private	Killed in Action, Intombi River	12th Mar.	1879
19/259	Robinson,	John.	Private	Killed in Action, Intombi River	12th Mar.	1879
486	Rohen,	Peter.	Private	Died at Netley, England	29th Mar.	1880
	*Rowlands,	Henry.	Major	Died at Newcastle	17th Nov.	1877
2070	Ruffle,	Henry.	Private	Killed in Action, Intombi River	12th Mar.	1879
1423	Ryan,	Joseph.	Private	Died (Place not Known)	(Date not known)	
1627	Sansam,	George.	Lce. Sergeant	Killed in Action, Intombi River	12th Mar.	1879
675	Seymour,	William.	Private	Killed in Action, Isandhlwana	22nd Jan.	1879
	(695 Seymour, William.)					
19/615	Sherridan,	Michael.	Private	Killed in Action, Intombi River	12th Mar.	1879
1770	Silcock,	Joseph.	Private	Killed in Action, Intombi River	12th Mar.	1879
819	Simpson,	Arthur.	Private	Died (Place not Known)	21st July	1879
19/510	Smith,	Henry.	Private	Killed in Action, Intombi River	12th Mar.	1879
1063	Smith,	Johnson.	Private	Died at Fort Weeber, Transvaal	10th Dec.	1879
657	Smith,	Joseph.	Private	Died (Place not Known)	14th Oct.	1879
1245	Tansley,	Jas. Frederick.	Private	Died (Place not Known)	13th May	1880
2104	*Tatum,	Charles.	Sergeant	Died at Pretoria	5th Mar.	1879
1536	*Taylor,	William.	Private	Died at Newcastle	18th Aug.	1878
2081	Thompson,	Henry.	Private	Killed in Action, Isandhlwana	22nd Jan.	1879
19/587	Tibbott,	Joseph.	Private	Killed in Action, Intombi River	12th Mar.	1879
1291	Tomlinson,	Richard.	Private	Killed in Action, Intombi River	12th Mar.	1879
19/1705	Tucker,	George.	Private	Killed in Action, Intombi River	12th Mar.	1879
19/104	Tucker,	Thomas.	Private	Killed in Action, Intombi River	12th Mar.	1879
	*Twenlow,	George Hamilton.	Lt. Colonel	Died at King William's Town	8th Nov.	1877
669	Tully,	Patrick.	Private	Dangerously Wounded, Ulundi	4th July	1879
902	Upton,	Henry.	Private	Died (Place not Known)	22nd Nov.	1879
423	Varley,	John.	Private	Died at Pietermaritzburg	22nd July	1880
370	Vernon,	James.	Private	Killed in Action, Intombi River	12th Mar.	1879
1630	Watts,	James Henry.	Sergeant	Killed in Action, Ulundi	4th July	1879
270	*Weatherer,	James.	Private	Died at Newcastle	25th Feb.	1878
1289	Weaver,	John.	Private	Died (Place not Known)	26th Mar.	1880
19/716	Weaver,	Joseph.	Private	Killed in Action, Intombi River	12th Mar.	1879
9/60	Whitehouse,	Joseph.	Private	Killed in Action, Isandhlwana	22nd Jan.	1879
2076	*Wiltshire,	Samuel.	Private	Died at King William's Town	26th May	1877
1605	Woodward,	Herbert.	Private	Killed in Action, Intombi River	12th Mar.	1879

Attached to the 80th Regiment of Foot

Commissariat & Transport

	Whittington,	Joseph.	Waggon Conductor	Killed in Action, Intombi River	12th Mar.	1879

Army Medical Departmen

	Cobbin,	William Ingram.	Civil Surgeon	Killed in Action, Intombi River	12th Mar.	1879

THE VICTORIA CROSS

The highest award that this country can bestow on a person employed by the Military or indirectly as a civilian, man or woman, for an act of bravery in time of war, is the Victoria Cross. The Victoria Cross medal is not made of valuable metal, it is made of simple bronze, the material being taken from captured guns in the Crimea. Recent research also shows that some medals may have been struck from the metal of guns manufactured in China. It is acknowledged throughout the world that the recipient has been identified as one of the 'Bravest of the Brave', and they will receive just acquiescence, be it a nod of the head or salute from the highest ranking officer, senior state official or ordinary person in the street.

The medal was named after Queen Victoria, and the award allegedly came from an idea of Prince Albert's. It came into being following numerous discussions with the Queen, Prince Albert, officers of the armed forces and Ministers of State, with the Royal Warrant for the Victoria Cross being signed on 29th January 1856. It was agreed to award it retrospectively back to the autumn of 1854 for actions during the Crimean War 1853-1856.

The original idea was that it would be awarded only to members of the Royal Navy and the British Army and only for some single act of valour or devotion to duty whilst serving their Country in the presence of the enemy. Her Majesty took great pains to point out that the award was not an Order such as the Most Honourable Order of the Garter and that it offered no knighthood or companionage. The medal was to be highly prized and eagerly sought after by both officers and men. Since the introduction of the Victoria Cross, a total of 1354 'crosses' have been awarded. Today, the value of the medal lies not in the materials of its manufacture, but in the stories, myths and legends of the person awarded, and how, when and where it was earned.

Where a body of men and/or women merit the award of the Victoria Cross, then the officers and non-commissioned officers and men select one person by ballot to receive it. As stated in the Royal Warrant, in awarding the Victoria Cross *'neither rank, nor long service, nor wounds, nor any other circumstances or condition whatsoever save the merit of conspicuous bravery'....* thereby placing.... *'all persons on a perfectly even footing in relation to eligibility for the decoration'.*

Various warrants for amendments over the years have been approved . In 1858 an amendment was introduced so that the Victoria Cross could be won by those who, *'may perform acts of conspicuous courage and bravery .... in circumstances of extreme danger such as the occurrence of a fire on board ship, or the foundering of a vessel at sea, or under any other circumstances in which......life or public property may be saved'.* In 1881 a further amendment was introduced - *'our will and pleasure is that the qualification shall be conspicuous bravery or devotion to the country in the presence of the enemy'.*

At first no provision was made for the medal to be awarded posthumously. In 1902 King Edward VII approved that following the death of a person who would have been so decorated if alive, it would now be acknowledged in death, with the next of kin or representative accepting the award on behalf of the dead recipient. Many have been awarded posthumously since that time.

On the 21st October 1911 King George V signed the warrant to allow native officers and men of the Indian Army the award. Then on the 22nd May 1920 a major review of the award was undertaken and further amendments were sanctioned so that the award could be extended to include the Royal Air Force and *'Air Forces of the Dominions, Colonies, Dependencies or Protectorates of the Commonwealth'* and *'matrons, sisters, nurses and staff of the Nursing Services and other Services pertaining to hospitals and nursing and civilians of either sex regularly or temporary under the orders, direction or supervision........of the Military Authorities'.* The warrant again emphasised that the Victoria Cross, *'shall only be awarded for most conspicuous bravery or some daring pre-eminent act of valour or self sacrifice or extreme devotion to duty in the presence of the enemy'.* During the review of the award in 1920, the original colour of blue ribbon for the Navy and crimson for the Army was changed so that the standard colour for the ribbon was crimson. Since 1918 all Victoria Crosses have had a crimson ribbon.

The earliest recorded incident that merited the award was on the 21st June 1854 in the Baltic when Charles Davis Lucas, a mate on board Her Majesty's Ship 'Hecla' raced forward and picked up a 'live' shell which had landed on the deck of the ship and with its fuse hissing threw it over board, thus saving the ship and many lives. The last Victoria Cross was awarded posthumously to Sergeant Ian John McKay of the 3rd Battalion Parachute Regiment for his action on 11th/12th June 1982 during the Battle of the Falkland Islands.

On six occasions the Victoria Cross has gone to people whose actions where not carried out in the presence of the enemy. Four privates and an assistant surgeon, all of the 24th Regiment of Foot, were awarded the medal for saving lives at sea in a storm in the Andaman Islands in 1867. The sixth was awarded to a private of the Rifle Brigade who at Danville railway station in Quebec, Canada in 1866 put out a fire that had started in a railway car that contained 2000lbs of ammunition.

The medal has only been awarded to four civilians, the first three during the Indian Mutiny 1857-58, two to members of the Bengal Civil Service and a member of the Indian Civil Service. The fourth civilian was a member of the Bengal Ecclesiastical Department of the Indian Army, who earned his award during the Afghanistan War 1878-1880. Only three men (no woman has yet been awarded the medal) have been awarded the Victoria Cross twice, these being Lieutenant Arthur Martin-Leake VC, RAMC., Captain Noel Godfrey Chavasse VC, MC, MA, RAMC and Captain Charles Hazlitt Upham VC, New Zealand Military Forces.

Originally when the Victoria Cross was awarded for those below commissioned rank and in the navy below warrant officer rank, a pension of £10 per annum for life went with it, and a further £5.00 for any subsequent 'Bar'. In certain situations the pension was increased dependent on circumstances. Throughout the years the 'pension' has been reviewed and increased periodically. Should a recipient of the Victoria Cross be found guilty of treason, felony, cowardice or any infamous crime, the medal and pension can be confiscated and the name of the recipient be removed from the register of the award. Unfortunately, on occasions when this happened, eight medals were withdrawn and the names struck off the register between 1863-1908. However, this practice ceased after the First World War following comments made by the King George V, and all 8 names were reinstated on the medal list, although in theory the medal and pension can still be confiscated.

One medal was presented to the United States of America on the 28th October 1920, awarded to their Unknown Warrior who is buried in the Arlington National Cemetery, Washington D.C.

The Victoria Cross is a most coveted award and although highly prized cannot be 'bought' or 'wangled' and is devoid of all distinctions of rank. The design of the medal is that of a cross/pattée (maltese cross), 34mm across the raised edges. In the centre of the obverse side of the medal is a lion passant guardant standing upon the Royal Crest. Below the crown on a semi-circular scroll there are the words 'FOR VALOUR'. On the reverse side in the centre panel is recorded the date(s) for which the decoration was awarded. The cross is suspended by means of a bar that is ornamented with laurel, and this bar incorporates a seriffed 'V' by which is suspended a single link. On the reverse of the laurel decorated bar is inscribed the name, rank, regiment or squadron of the recipient. The ribbon is 40mm in width, for the navy VCs originally blue and for the army crimson. Royal Warrant amendments in 1920 specified henceforth a crimson ribbon irrespective of the branch of service.

For those who receive the award a miniature cross is worn on the ribbon alone in undress uniform. To those who are awarded a second medal a further miniature cross is added to distinguish that a 'bar' has been awarded.

RECIPIENTS OF THE VICTORIA CROSS
80th REGIMENT OF FOOT (STAFFORDSHIRE VOLUNTEERS)

SAMUEL WASSALL (No. 427 Private) 1856 - 1927
Wassall, Samuel. Born: Moor Lane, Kingswinford, Staffordshire, Enlisted Dudley 28th November 1874
Age: 18 years. Height 5ft 4ins. Complexion fair, Eyes grey, Hair light brown, Trade Dyer.
Citation for the Victoria Cross
Private Samuel Wassall 80th Regiment of Foot, *"For his gallant conduct in having, at the imminent risk of his own life, saved that of Private Westwood, of the same Regiment. On the 22nd January 1879, when the camp at Isandhlwana was taken by the enemy, Private Wassall retreated towards the Buffalo River, in which he saw a comrade struggling, and apparently drowning. He rode to the bank, dismounted, leaving his horse on the Zulu side, rescued the man from the stream, and again mounted his horse, dragging Private Westwood across the river under a heavy shower of bullets."*
Award Published in the London Gazette dated 17th June 1879
Place/date of deed Isandhlwana, Zululand, South Africa, 22nd January 1879
Presented at Utrecht 11/09/79 by Sir Garnet Wolseley

ANTHONY CLARKE BOOTH (No. 919 Colour Sergeant) 1846 - 1899
Booth, Anthony Clarke Colour Sergeant Born: Carrington, Basford, Nottinghamshire,
Enlisted Sheffield 28th October 1864. Age: 18 years 6 months. Height: 5ft 6ins. Complexion fresh. Eyes grey, Hair brown, Trade Tailor
Citation for the Victoria Cross
Colour Sergeant Anthony Clarke Booth 80th Regiment of Foot, *"For his gallant conduct on the 12th March 1879, during the Zulu attack on the Intombi River, in having when considerably outnumbered by the enemy, rallied a few men on the south bank of the river, and covered the retreat of fifty soldiers and others for a distance of three miles. The Officer Commanding 80th Regiment reports that, had it not been for the coolness displayed by this Non-Commissioned Officer, not one man would have escaped."*
Date in the London Gazette 24th February 1880
Place/date of deed: Intombi River, Zululand, South Africa, 12th March 1879
Presented at Windsor Castle 26th June 1880 By HM Queen Victoria

THE REGIMENT

The history of the 80th Regiment of Foot (Staffordshire Volunteers) is a grand and fine record. Throughout their existence they set a good example and were well respected, and happily that some of their traditions and honours are still remembered to this day.

Throughout the eighty-eight years the Regiment existed, they served sovereign and country well. The seven battle honours awarded to the 80th were but a few events in the history of the Regiment. Over many years, the vast array of characters that swelled the ranks came from many walks of life, from the privileged upper classes purchasing their rank, to those who through hunger, cold and unemployment joined the army to obtain regular food and clothing. Some joined in the hope of seeking wealth and fortune, others simply sought adventure.

The dull life in barracks when serving at 'home', with its routines and duties, could become monotonous, but this was soon forgotten when campaigning abroad and out in the 'open'. Adventure and hardships were experienced, and the dangers and horrors of war. The soldiers of the 80th Regiment of Foot who served and took part in the campaigns which resulted in seven Battle Honours, were awarded a total of three thousand, eight hundred and seventy-eight medals. Two men were awarded the Victoria Cross, this country's premier award for gallantry.

Following their service in the army, men reaching the maximum age limit or time expired date, would be retired from the army. In later years they were first placed on the Army Reserve list for a period of time and then finally retired. For some life was not so kind; through injury or wounds, sickness or simply being worn out by the exertions and demands of army life, some men were forced to retire. The majority retired having served loyally, but records show that a very small minority were dismissed from the army with ignominy.

The rigors of army life and service abroad, exposed to the elements and the diseases associated with a foreign clime, brought an early death to many a soldier. Likewise, many a life was lost through accident such as drowning and fire. At least one man, it is recorded, was murdered. From the casualty lists shown here, one can clearly see that there was more loss of life due to sickness than being killed in action or dying of wounds received in battle. Many never returned to these shores, remaining forever in a foreign land, their names perhaps inscribed on some plaque or monument in a church, market place or village green.

In this book all those who served and were awarded medals associated with the seven battle honours have been included and it is hoped that it will be a fitting tribute to those who took part in events which form part of our history and which helped shape the world as we know it today.

Officers shako badge
c. 1816 - 1822

Shako Helmet Plate
Other Ranks 1878 -1881

The Regimental Tree

The South Staffordshire Regiment

The North Staffordshire Regiment

1705
Lillingston's Regiment
(During this period known
by name of Colonel at the time)

1751
38th Regiment of Foot

1756
2/11th Regiment of Foot

1758
64th Regiment of Foot

1782
38th Regiment of Foot
(First Staffordshire)

1782
64th Regiment of Foot
(Second Staffordshire)

1793
80th Regiment
of Foot
(Staffordshire Volunteers)

1824
98th Regiment
of Foot

1876
98th (or Prince
of Wales's)
Regiment of Foot

1881
The South Staffordshire
Regiment

1st Battalion   2nd Battalion

1881
The Prince of Wales's (North
Staffordshire) Regiment

1st Battalion   2nd Battalion

1920
The North Staffordshire Regiment
(The Prince of Wales's)

1948
1st Battalion

1948
1st Battalion

1959
The Staffordshire Regiment
(The Prince of Wales's)

BIBLIOGRAPHY

PUBLISHED BOOKS

Bancroft, JW	THE VICTORIA CROSS ROLL OF HONOUR	Aim High Productions, London 1989
Bancroft, JW	THE ZULU WAR VCs	J.W.Bancroft, Manchester 1992
Barthorp, M	THE ZULU WAR A PICTORIAL HISTORY	Blandford 1980 Reprint 1981 P/back 1984 & 1985
Bennett, IHW	EYEWITNESS IN ZULULAND	Greenhill Books, London 1989
Clammer, D.	THE ZULU WAR	Pan Books, London 1973
Cook, HCB	THE BATTLE HONOURS OF THE BRITISH & INDIAN ARMIES 1662-1982	Leo Cooper, London 1987
Cook, HCB	THE SIKH WARS 1845-1846 & 1848-1849	Leo Cooper, London 1975
Droogleever, RWF	THE ROAD TO ISANDHLWANA Colonel Anthony Durford IN NATAL AND ZULULAND	Greenhill Books, London 1992
Dupuy E, Dupuy TN	THE COLLINS ENCYCLOPEDIA OF MILITARY HISTORY	
Emery, F	THE RED SOLDIER THE ZULU WAR 1879	Hodder & Stoughton 1997; Jonathan Ball J/burg 1983
Edgerton, RB	LIKE LIONS THEY FOUGHT THE LAST ZULU WAR	Weidenfeld and Nicholson, London 1988
Farmer, JS	THE REGIMENTAL RECORDS OF THE BRITISH ARMY 1660 - 1901	Grant Richards 1901 Crecy (Cathedral Publicishing.) Bristol 1984
Featherstone, D	VICTORIAN COLONIAL WARFARE - AFRICA	Cassell, London 1992
Featherstone, D	VICTORIAN COLONIAL WARFARE - INDIA	Cassell, London 1992 & 1993
Forsyth DR	SOUTH AFRICAN WAR MEDAL 1877-8-9. THE MEDAL ROLL	D.R. Forsyth.
Furneaux, R.	THE ZULU WAR ISANDHLWANA & RORKE'S DRIFT	Weidenfeld and Nicholson, London 1963
George, B, Ryan, N	WORTH SAVING - The Story of the Staffordshire Regiment's Fight for Survival.	Smith Settle, Otley. 1996
Gough, C, VC, Innes, A, Sir	THE SIKHS AND THE SIKH WARS	A.D. Inness & Co. London 1897 Inness, A.
Hallows, IS	REGIMENTS AND CORPS OF THE BRITISH ARMY	Arms & Armour, London, 1991, Cassell London 1994
Haythornthwaite,PJ	THE COLONIAL WARS SOURCE BOOK	Arms & Armour, London
Hope, R	THE ZULU WAR AND THE 80th REGIMENT OF FOOT	Churnet Valley Books, Leek 1997
Jocelyn, Arthur	AWARDS OF HONOUR	Adam & Charles Black, London 1956
Jones, JP	HISTORY OF THE SOUTH STAFFORDSHIRE REGIMENT 1705-1923	Whitehead, Wolverhampton 1923
Joslin, EC, Litherland, AR, Simkin, BT	BRITISH BATTLES & MEDALS	Spink & Son, London 1988
Lock, R	BLOOD ON THE PAINTED MOUNTAIN	Greenhill Books, London 1995
Knight, I	ZULU ISANDLWANA & RORKE'S DRIFT 22-23 JANUARY 1879	Windrow & Greene, London 1992
Knight, I, Castle, I	THE ZULU WAR THEN AND NOW	After the Battle, London 1993
Laband, J	FIGHT US IN THE OPEN	Shuter & Shooter, South Africa 1985, 1987
Laband, J	THE BATTLE OF ULUNDI	Shuter & Shooter, South Africa 1988
Laband, JPC & Thompson, PS	FIELD GUIDE TO THE WAR IN ZULULAND AND THE DEFENCE OF NATAL 1879	University of Natal, South Africa 1987
Laurie, WBF	THE SECOND BURMESE WAR	Smith & Taylor, London 1853
Mackay, J &Mussell, J	THE MEDAL YEAR BOOK - 1998	Token Publishing Honiton, Devon 1997
Morris, DR	THE WASHING OF SPEARS	Abacus, London 1966
Norris-Newman, CL	IN ZULULAND WITH THE BRITISH THROUGHOUT THE WAR 1879	Greenhill Books, London 1988
Percival, J	FOR VALOUR, THE VICTORIA CROSS COURAGE IN ACTION	Thomas Methven, London 1985
Roe, FG	THE BRONZE CROSS	P.R. Gawthorn, London 1945
Smyth, J Sir	THE VICTORIA CROSS 1856-1964	Frederick Muller, London, 1965
Snodgrass, Major	NARRATIVE OF THE BURMESE WAR	London 1853
Tavender IT	CASUALTY ROLL FOR THE ZULU AND BASUTO WARS SOUTH AFRICA 1877-79	Howard, Suffolk 1985
Vale, WL	HISTORY OF THE STAFFORDSHIRE REGIMENT	Golden Polden Ltd, Aldershot 1969
War Office Intelligence	NARRATIVE OF THE FIELD OPERATIONS CONNECTED WITH THE ZULU WAR OF 1879	London, 1881 Reprint Greenhill Books, London 1989
Young, J	THEY FELL LIKE STONES BATTLES & CASUALTIES OF THE ZULU WAR 1879	Greenhill, London 1991
This England Books	THE REGISTER OF THE VICTORIA CROSS	This England Books, Cheltenham 1981

PUBLICATIONS
THERE WILL BE AN AWFUL ROW AT HOME ABOUT THIS Zulu Study Group, Victorian Study Group 1987 The Zulu War
Introduction by Morris, D.R. Edited by Knight, I.J.

BLACK COUNTRY V.Cs. Harris, B The Black Country Society 1985

NEWSPAPERS AND JOURNALS
THE STAFFORD KNOT (THE JOURNAL OF THE STAFFORDSHIRE REGIMENT) Issue No. 40 April 1979
THE STAFFORD KNOT (THE JOURNAL OF THE STAFFORDSHIRE REGIMENT) Issue No. 41 October 1979
LONDON GAZETTE   TAMWORTH HERALD   ILLUSTRATED LONDON NEWS   NATAL MERCURY

OFFICIAL SOURCES (Crown Copyright)Public Record Office
WO 16 Series Regimental and Corps Pay Lists   WO 100/47   Medal Lists (South African Campaign)
WO 1/7 Colours   WO 27/98 Colours

MEDAL LISTS (Crown Copyright)

Military General Service Medal	Kingsley-Foster	Military General Service Roll
Sutlej Campaign Medal	India Office Records	
India General Service Medal	India Office Records	
Indian Mutiny Medal	India Office Records	
South Africa Medal	WO 100/47 Medal Lists (South African Campaign)	
	D R Forsyth SOUTH AFRICAN WAR MEDAL 1877-8-9	

UNPUBLISHED WORKS
Savage Lt. Col. A HISTORY OF THE SOUTH STAFFORDSHIRE REGIMENT (38th & 80th)
Original copies: Royal United Services Institute, Regimental Museum, Whittington Barracks.

Appendix A
OFFICERS OF THE REGIMENT

For the majority of the 80th Regiment's life, the officers who served in the Regiment purchased their commissions. They were drawn from the privileged upper class of society, the sons of nobility and gentry and the professional middle classes. It was a custom to purchase a commission for newly born offspring. However, there were provisions for the ordinary 'private soldier' to advance into the officer classes, to be promoted and even reach high rank. But generally higher rank depended not on ability, intellect or bravery, but on the purse. Officers could even exchange their commissions to serve with other Regiments in order to serve in a particular part of the world and to participate in a particular campaign, for the chance to be noticed in battle and perhaps achieve fame and fortune.

In the early 1800s, the Duke of York Reforms prevented officers advancing too quickly. No subaltern could be promoted until he had served at least 2 years, and no rank of major could be commissioned without serving a minimum of 6 years. In the 1870s Viscount Edward Cardwell, the Secretary of State for War 1868-1874, implemented further reforms to the British Army. The system of purchasing commissions was ended and officers or prospective officers had to be educated in the art, technology, tactics and theory of warfare. Institutions like the Royal Military Academy, Sandhurst and 'the shop' at Woolwich became military centres of world renown.

1794

Rank	Name	Regiment	Army
Leiut. Colonel Commandant	Henry, Lord Paget	12 Sept 1793	
Majors Lt. Col.	Forbes Champagné	12 Sept 1793	
	Josiah Champagné	13 Sept 1793	
Captains	William Sneyd	12 Sept 1793	20 Aug 1782
	Jeremiah French	13 Sept 1793	19 June 1783
	William Harness	14 Sept 1793	24 Jan 1791
	William Forster	15 Sept 1793	
	John Ford	16 Sept 1793	
	William, Lord Craven	18 Sept 1793	
Captain Lieut. and Captain	Stephen Fauchey	17 Sept 1793	
Lieutenants	Mark William Carr	12 Sept 1793	3 Feb 1778
	Francis Castello	13 Sept 1793	16 June 1782
	James Rooke	14 Sept 1793	
	Archibald Campbell	15 Sept 1793	
Ensigns	George Reynolds	12 Sept 1793	
	Charles Reynolds	13 Sept 1793	
	Thomas Edwards	14 Sept 1793	
	Thomas Howard	15 Sept 1793	
	Robert Bullock	16 Sept 1793	
	William Haston	17 Sept 1793	
	Thomas Archer	18 Sept 1793	
Chaplain	Edward Remington	12 Sept 1793	
Adjutant	Stephen Fauchey	12 Sept 1793	
Quarter-Master	John Mason	12 Sept 1793	

Agent, Messrs. Cox and Greenwood, Craig's Court

1795

Rank	Name	Regiment	Army
Leiut. Colonel Commandant	Henry, Lord Paget	12 Sept 1793	
Lieut. Colonel	Forbes Champagné	18 Dec 1793	
	Josiah Champagné	19 Dec 1793	
Major	William Armstrong	18 Dec 1793	
	William Harness	19 Dec 1793	
Captains	William Forster	15 Sept 1793	
	John Ford	16 Sept 1793	
	Stephen Fauchey	17 Sept 1793	
	James Rooke	6 Mar 1794	
	John White	7 Mar 1794	
	John White	13 Sept	
	William Howe Delancey	1 Oct	25 Mar 1794
Captain Lieut. and Captain	Mark William Carr	5 Mar 1794	
Lieutenants	Francis Castello	13 Sept 1793	16 June 1782
	Robert Smith	14 Jan 1794	
	John Edwards	5 Mar 1794	
	George Reynolds	6 Mar	
	Charles Reynolds	31 Mar	
	Thomas Howard	1 Apr	
	John Dalrymple	20 Apr	
	John Banks Cox	13 June	
	Robert Bullock	16 July	
Ensigns	Thomas Archer	18 Sept 1793	
	Thomas Bal. St George	22 Feb 1794	
	Harry Cary	14 Mar	
	Brownl Vil. Layard	30 May	
	Solomon Welch	17 Sept	
	John Harvey	18 Sept	
Chaplain	Edward Remington	12 Sept 1793	
Adjutant	Solomon Welch	6 June 1794	
Quarter-Master	John Mason	12 Sept 1793	

Agent, Messrs. Cox and Greenwood, Craig's Court

1796

Rank	Name	Regiment	Army
Leiut. Colonel Commandant	John St Ledger	16 June 1795	M.Gen. 26 Feb 1795
Lieut. Colonel	Josiah Champagné	19 Dec 1793	
	William Ramsey	16 June 1795	
Major	William Harness	19 Dec 1793	
	John Ford	1 July 1795	
Captains	William Forster	15 Sept 1793	
	Stephen Fauchey	17 Sept 1793	
	James Rooke	6 Mar 1794	
	John White	7 Mar 1794	
	John White	13 Sept	
	William Howe Delancey	1 Oct	25 Mar 1794
	John Banks Cox	15 July 1795	
	William Johnstone	11 Aug	Major 1 Mar 1794
	Hon. Stirling St Clair	11 Aug	6 June 1794
	Thomas Baldwin St George		
Captain Lieut. and Captain	Mark William Carr	5 Mar 1794	

Rank	Name	Regiment	Army
Lieutenants	Robert Smith	14 Jan 1794	
	John Edwards	5 Mar 1794	
	Thomas Howard	1 Apr	
	John Dalrymple	2 Apr	
	Robert Bullock	16 July	
	Henry Cary	15 July 1795	
	Solomon Walsh	15 July1795	
	John Harvey	15 July 1795	
	Willam Bolton	1 Sept	
	Dennis Kingdon	2 Sept	
	John Bradshaw	3 Sept	22 Aug 1794
	William Moore	4 Sept	22 Aug 1794
	Charles Malony	6 Sept	4 Oct 1794
	John Bradish	7 Sept	3 Nov 1794
	Robert Boyce	8 Sept 1795	26 Nov 1794
	William Moore	9 Sept 1795	26 Nov 1794
	Joseph Halliday	10 Sept 1795	29 Nov 1794
	Peter Kearnes	11 Sept 1795	8 July 1795
	John Mahoney	12 Sept 1795	31 May 1794
	William Jones	13 Sept 1795	15 Aug 1795
	Mich. Henry Dundas	14 Sept 1795	
	Judge Tho. D'Arcey	26 Sept 1795	
	George Edwards	18 Nov	24 Aug 1795
	Samuel Pocock		
Ensigns	John Fearon	20 May 1795	
	Whitmore Blashfield	15 July	
	Robert Ashe	15 Aug	
	Cha. Smith McCarthy	19 Aug	
	Robert Mowbray	24 Aug	
	Robert Mather	1 Sept	22 July 1794
	Walter Nangle	3 Sept	3 Sept 1794
	David Chalmers	4 Nov	
Chaplain	Edward Remington	12 Sept 1793	
Adjutant	Solomon Welch	6 June 1794	
Quarter-Master	John Mason	12 Sept 1793	

Agent, Messrs. Cox and Greenwood, Craig's Court

1797

Rank	Name	Regiment	Army
Leiut. Colonel Commandant	John St Ledger	16 June 1795	M.Gen. 26 Feb1795
Lieut. Colonel	Josiah Champagné	19 Dec1793	
	William Ramsey	16 June1795	1 Mar 1794
Majors	William Harness	19 Dec1793	Lt.Col. 3 May 1796
	John Ford	1July 1795	
Captains	William Forster	15 Sept 1793	
	Stephen Fauchey	17 Sept 1793	
	Mark William Carr	5 Mar 1794	
	James Rooke	6 Mar 1794	
	John White	7 Mar 1794	
	John White	13 Sept	
	John Banks Cox	15 July 1795	
	Thomas Baldwin St. George	26 Jan 1796	
	John Ashley Sturt	19 Aug 1794	
Captain Lieut. and Captain	Robert Smith	19 Mar 1796	
Lieutenants	John Edwards	5 Mar 1794	
	Thomas Howard	1 Apr	
	John Dalrymple	2 Apr	
	Henry Cary	15 July 1795	
	Solomon Walsh	15 July 1795	
	John Harvey	15 July 1795	
	Willam Bolton	1 Sept	
	Dennis Kingdon	2 Sept	
	Charles Molony	6 Sept	4 Oct 1794
	John Bradish	7 Sept	3 Nov 1794
	Robert Boyce	8 Sept	26 Nov 1794
	Joseph Halliday	10 Sept	29 Nov 1794
	Peter Kearnes	11 Sept 1795	8 July 1795
	William Jones	13 Sept 1795	5 Aug 1795
	Mich. Henry Dundas	14 Sept 1795	
	Judge Tho. D'Arcey	26 Sept 1795	
	Samuel Pocock	20 Jan 1796	
	Robert Mowbray	2 Feb	
	Joseph Curtis	27 Feb	5 Sept 1795
	Robert Ashe	19 Mar	
	John Grosser	5 Apr	
	Allen Campbell	12 Apr	
	James Cookson	10 May	
	George De Laney	17 May	
	Barnard De Laney	6 July	
Ensigns	John Fearon	20 May 1795	
	Whitmore Blashfield	15 July	
	Cha. Smith McCarthy	19 Aug	
	Robert Mather	1 Sept	22 July 1794
	David Chalmers	4 Nov	
	John St George	12 Mar 1796	
	--- Thompson	19 Mar 1796	
	Barrington Bradshaw	25 Apr	
	John Lewis	29 July	
Chaplain	Edward Remington	12 Sept 1793	
Adjutant	Solomon Welch	6 June 1794	
Quarter-Master	John Mason	12 Sept 1793	

Agent, Messrs. Cox and Greenwood, Craig's Court

1798

Rank	Name	Regiment	Army
Leiut. Colonel Commandant	John St.Ledger	16 June 1795	M.Gen. 26 Feb 1795
Lieut. Colonel	Josiah Champagné	19 Dec 1793	Col. 26 Jan 1797
	William Ramsey	16 June 1795	1 Mar 1794
Majors	William Harness	19 Dec 1793	Lt.Col. 3 May 1796
	John Ford	1July 1795	

Captains	William Forster	15 Sept 1793	
	Stephen Fauchey	17 Sept 1793	
	Mark William Carr	5 Mar 1794	
	John White	7 Mar 1794	
	John White	13 Sept	
	John Banks Cox	15 July 1795	
	Thomas Baldwin St George	26 Jan 1796	
	John Ashley Sturt	20 Oct	19 Aug 1794
Captain Lieut. and Captain	Robert Smith	19 Mar 1796	
Lieutenants	John Edwards	5 Mar 1794	
	Thomas Howard	1 Apr	
	John Dalrymple	2 Apr	
	Henry Cary	15 July 1795	
	Solomon Walsh	15 July 1795	
	John Harvey	15 July 1795	
	Willam Bolton	1 Sept	
	Dennis Kingdon	2 Sept	
	Charles Molony	6 Sept	4 Oct 1794
	John Bradish	7 Sept	3 Nov 1794
	Robert Boyce	8 Sept	26 Nov 1794
	Joseph Halliday	10 Sept	29 Nov 1794
	Peter Kearnes	11 Sept	8 July 1795
	William Jones	13 Sept	15 Aug 1795
	Mich. Henry Dundas	14 Sept 1795	
	Judge Tho. D'Arcey	26 Sept 1795	
	Samuel Pocock	20 Jan 1796	
	Robert Mowbray	2 Feb	
	Robert Ashe	19 Mar	
	John Grosser	5 Apr	
	Allen Campbell	12 Apr	
	James Cookson	10 May	
	Barnard De Laney	6 July	
	John St Ledger Halford	25 Oct	30 Sept 1794
	Whitmore Blashfield	17 Nov	
Ensigns	John Fearon	20 May 1795	
	Cha. Smith McCarthy	19 Aug	
	Robert Mather	1 Sept	22 July 1795
	David Chalmers	4 Nov	
	John St George	12 Mar 1796	
	Thompson	19 Mar 1796	
	Barrington Bradshaw	25 Apr	
	John Lewis	29 July	
Adjutant	Solomon Welch	6 June 1794	
Quarter-Master	John Mason	12 Sept 1793	

Agent, Messrs. Cox and Greenwood, Craig's Court

1799

Rank	Name	Regiment	Army
Leiut. Colonel Commandant	John St Ledger	16 June 1795	M.Gen. 26 Feb 1795
Lieut. Colonel	Josiah Champagné	19 Dec 1793	Col. 26 Jan 1797
	William Ramsey	16 June 1795	1 Mar 1798
Major	William Harness	19 Dec 1793	Lt.Col. .3 May 1796
	John Ford	1 July 1795	
Captains	Stephen Fauchey	17 Sept 1793	
	Mark William Carr	5 Mar 1794	
	John White	7 Mar 1794	
	John Banks Cox	15 July 1795	
	Thomas Baldwin St. George	26 Jan 1796	
	Robert Smith	20 Mar 1796	
	John Ashley Sturt	20 Oct	19 Aug 1794
	Hugh McPherson	17 May 1798	8 July 1795
Captain Lieut. and Captain	John Edwards	28 Apr 1797	
Lieutenants	Thomas Howard	1 Apr 1794	
	John Dalrymple	2 Apr 1794	
	Henry Cary	15 July 1795	
	Solomon Walsh	15 July 1795	
	John Harvey	15 July 1795	
	Willam Bolton	1 Sept	
	Dennis Kingdon	2 Sept	
	Charles Molony	6 Sept	4 Oct 1794
	John Bradish	7 Sept	3 Nov 1794
	Robert Boyce	8 Sept	26 Nov 1794
	Joseph Halliday	10 Sept	29 Nov 1794
	Peter Kearnes	11 Sept	8 July 1795
	Mich. Henry Dundas	14 Sept	
	Judge Tho. D'Arcey	26 Sept	
	Samuel Pocock	20 Jan 1796	
	Robert Mowbray	2 Feb	
	Robert Ashe	19 Mar	
	Allen Campbell	12 Apr	
	James Cookson	10 May	
	Barnard De Laney	6 July	
	John St Ledger Hansard	25 Oct	30 Sept 1794
	Whitmore Blashfield	17 Nov	
	Samuel Allen Wheeler	1 July 1797	
	John St George	24 May 1798	
Ensigns	John Fearon	20 May 1795	
	Thompson	19 Mar 1796	
	John Lewis	29 July	
	Fra. Howard Willington	3 Jan 1797	
	Arth. Cuthbert Campbell	2 May	
	Charles Rowan	15 May	
	Thomas Douglas	17 May	
	James Morisset	1 Feb 1798	
	Robert Dashwood	20 June	
Adjutant	Solomon Welch	6 June 1794	
Quarter-Master	John Mason	12 Sept 1793	

Agent, Messrs. Cox and Greenwood, Craig's Court

1800

Rank	Name	Regiment	Army
Leiut. Colonel Commandant	John St Ledger	16 June 1795	M.Gen. 26 Feb 1795
Lieut. Colonel	Josiah Champagné	19 Dec 1793	Col. 26 Jan 1797
	William Ramsey	16 June 1795	Col. 1 Jan 1798
Majors	William Harness	19 Dec 1793	Lt.Col. .3 May 1796
	John Ford	1 July 1795	
Captains	Mark William Carr	5 Mar 1794	
	John White	7 Mar 1794	
	John Banks Cox	15 July 1795	
	Thomas Baldwin St George	26 Jan 1796	
	Robert Smith	20 Mar 1796	
	John Ashley Sturt	20 Oct	19 Aug 1794
	John Mac Rae	4 Oct 1797	2 Sept 1795
	Hugh McPherson	17 May 1798	8 July 1795
Captain Lieut. and Captain	John Edwards	28 Apr 1797	
Lieutenants	John Dalrymple	2 Apr 1794	
	Henry Cary	15 July 1795	
	Solomon Walsh	15 July 1795	
	John Harvey	15 July 1795	
	Willam Bolton	1 Sept	
	Dennis Kingdon	2 Sept	
	Charles Molony	6 Sept	4 Oct 1794
	John Bradish	7 Sept	3 Nov 1794
	Robert Boyce	8 Sept	26 Nov 1794
	Joseph Halliday	10 Sept	29 Nov 1794
	Peter Kearnes	11 Sept	8 July 1795
	Mich. Henry Dundas	14 Sept	
	Judge Tho. D'Arcey	26 Sept	
	Samuel Pocock	20 Jan 1796	
	Robert Mowbray	2 Feb 1796	
	Robert Ashe	19 Mar	
	James Cookson	10 May	
	John St Ledger Hansard	25 Oct	30 Sept 1794
	Samuel Allen Wheeler	1 July 1797	
	Barrington Bradshaw	1 Oct	2 May 1797
	John St George	24 May 1798	
	Thomas Douglas	15 June	
	Charles Hardy	3 July 1799	2 Dec 1795
Ensigns	John Fearon	20 May 1795	
	John Lewis	29 July 1796	
	Arth. Cuthbert Campbell	2 May 1797	
	Lionel Hooke	24 Nov	20 Dec 1796
	Thomas Ker	14 Dec	
	James Morisset	1 Feb 1798	
	Robert Dashwood	20 June	
Adjutant	Solomon Welch	6 June 1794	
Quarter-Master	John Mason	12 Sept 1793	
Asst Surgeon	William Brown	25 Dec 1796	
	------ Dick	15 May 1798	

Agent, Messrs. Cox and Greenwood, Craig's Court

1801

Rank	Name	Regiment	Army
Colonel	Gerard Lake	14 Feb 1800	Lt.Gen. 26 Jan 1797
Lieut. Colonel	Josiah Champagné	19 Dec 1793	Col. 26 Jan 1797
	William Ramsey	16 June 1795	Col. 1 Jan 1798
Majors	William Harness	19 Dec 1793	Lt.Col. .3 May 1796
	John Ford	1 July 1795	
Captains	Mark William Carr	5 Mar 1794	
	John White	7 Mar 1794	
	John Banks Cox	15 July 1795	
	Thomas Baldwin St George	26 Jan 1796	
	Robert Smith	20 Mar 1796	
	John Ashley Sturt	20 Oct	19 Aug 1794
	John Mac Rae	4 Oct 1797	2 Sept 1795
	Robert Mowbray	3 Aug 1799	
Captain Lieut. and Captain	John Edwards	28 Apr 1797	
Lieutenants	John Dalrymple	2 Apr 1794	
	Solomon Walsh	15 July 1795	
	John Harvey	15 July 1795	
	William Bolton	1 Sept	
	Dennis Kingdon	2 Sept	
	John Bradish	7 Sept	3 Nov 1794
	Robert Boyce	8 Sept	26 Nov 1794
	Joseph Halliday	10 Sept	29 Nov 1794
	Peter Kearnes	11 Sept	8 July 1795
	Mich. Henry Dundas	14 Sept	
	Judge Tho. D'Arcey	26 Sept	
	James Cookson	10 May 1796	
	John St Ledger Hansard	25 Oct	30 Sept 1794
	John St George	28 Apr 1797	
	Samuel Allen Wheeler	1 July 1797	
	Barrington Bradshaw	1 Oct	2 May 1797
	Thomas Douglas	15 June 1798	
	John Lewis	26 Apr 1799	
	Thomas Kerr	15 May	8 Feb 1792
	Lionel Hooke	21 Aug	
	Charles Hardy	3 July	2 Dec 1795
Ensigns	James Walsh	10 May 1797	
	Thomas Ker	14 Dec	
	James Morisset	1 Feb 1798	
	Robert Dashwood	20 June	
	Matthew R. Freeman	8 Mar 1799	
	George Colquhoun Bt.	5 Oct	
Adjutant	Solomon Welch	6 June 1794	
Quarter-Master	John Mason	12 Sept 1793	
Asst Surgeon	William Brown	25 Dec 1796	
	------ Dick	15 May 1798	

1802

Rank	Name	Regiment	Army
Colonel	Gerard Lake	14 Feb 1800	Lt.Gen. 26 Jan 1797
Lieut. Colonel	John Mortresor	25 Apr 1801	22 June 1795
	William Harness	26 Apr 1801	3 May 1796
Major	John Ford	1 July 1795	Lt. Col. 1 Jan 1801
Captains	Mark William Carr	5 Mar 1794	
	John White	7 Mar 1794	
	John Banks Cox	15 July 1795	
	Thomas Baldwin St. George	26 Jan 1796	
	Robert Smith	20 Mar 1796	
	John Ashley Sturt	20 Oct	19 Aug 1794
	John Mac Rae	4 Oct 1797	2 Sept 1795
	Robert Mowbray	3 Aug 1799	
Captain Lieut. and Captain	John Edwards	28 Apr 1797	
Lieutenants	John Dalrymple	2 Apr 1794	
	Solomon Walsh	15 July 1795	
	John Harvey	15 July 1795	
	Willam Bolton	1 Sept	
	Dennis Kingdon	2 Sept	
	John Bradish	7 Sept	3 Nov 1794
	RobertBoyce	8 Sept	26 Nov 1794
	Joseph Halliday	10 Sept	29 Nov 1794
	Mich. Henry Dundas	14 Sept	
	Judge Tho. D'Arcey	26 Sept	
	James Cookson	10 May 1796	
	John St.Ledger Hansard	25 Oct	30 Sept 1794
	John St George	28 Apr 1797	
	Samuel Allen Wheeler	1 July	
	Barrington Bradshaw	1 Oct 1797	2 May 1797
	Thomas Douglas	15 June 1798	
	John Lewis	26 Apr 1799	
	Thomas William Kerr	15 May	8 Feb 1792
	Charles Hardy	3 July	2 Dec 1795
	Lionel Hooke	21 Aug	
	James Morisset	9 May 1800	
	Robert Dashwood	10 May 1800	
Ensigns	James Walsh	10 May 1797	
	Matthew R. Freeman	8 Mar 1799	
	Henry Jones Groves	9 Sept 1800	
	Philip Rowson Stepney	9 Nov	
	------ Harness	10 Nov	
	Andrew Kelly	14 May 1801	25 May 1796
Adjutant	Solomon Welch	6 June 1794	
Quarter-Master	John Mason	12 Sept 1793	
Asst Surgeon }	William Brown	25 Dec 1796	
	----- Dick	15 May 1798	

Agent, Messrs. Cox, Greenwood and Cox, Craig's Court

1803

Rank	Name	Regiment	Army
Colonel	Gerard Lake	14 Feb 1800	Gen. 29 Apr 1802
Lieut. Colonel	John Mortresor	25 Apr 1801	Col. 29 Apr 1802
	William Harness	26 Apr 1801	3 May 1796
Majors	John Ford	1 July 1795	Lt. Col. 1 Jan 1801
	Benjamin Forbes	17 June1802	Lt. Col. 1 Jan 1800
Captains	Mark William Carr	5 Mar 1794	
	John White	7 Mar 1794	
	John Banks Cox	15 July 1795	
	Thomas Baldwin St George	26 Jan 1796	
	Robert Smith	20 Mar 1796	
	John Ashley Sturt	20 Oct	19 Aug 1794
	John Mac Rae	4 Oct 1797	2 Sept 1795
	Robert Mowbray	3 Aug1799	
Captain Lieut. and Captain	John Edwards	28 Apr 1797	
Lieutenants	John Dalrymple	2 Apr 1794	
	Solomon Welch	15 July 1795	Adjutant
	John Harvey	15 July 1795	
	Willam Bolton	1 Sept	
	Dennis Kingdon	2 Sept	
	John Bradish	7 Sept	3 Nov 1794
	Robert Boyce	8 Sept	26 Nov 1794
	Joseph Halliday	10 Sept	29 Nov 1794
	Mich. Henry Dundas	14 Sept	
	Judge Tho. D'Arcey	26 Sept	
	James Cookson	10 May 1796	
	John St Ledger Hansard	25 Oct	30 Sept 1794
	John St George	28 Apr 1797	
	Samuel Allen Wheeler	1 July	
	Barrington Bradshaw	1 Oct 1797	2 May 1797
	Thomas Douglas	15 June 1798	
	John Lewis	26 Apr 1799	
	Thomas William Kerr	15 May	8 Feb 1792
	Charles Hardy	3 July	2 Dec 1795
	Lionel Hooke	21 Aug	
	James Morisset	9 Nov 1800	
	Robert Dashwood	10 Nov 1800	
	Matthew Robert Freeman	24 Jan 1801	
Ensigns	James Walsh	10 May 1797	
	Henry Jones Groves	9 Sept 1800	
	Philip Rowson Stepney	9 Nov	
	------ Harness	10 Nov	
	Andrew Adamson	1 Apr 1801	
	Andrew Kelly	14 May	25 May 1796
	Clement John Cozens	8 Jan 1802	
Adjutant	Solomon Welch	6 June 1794	Lieut. 15 July 1795
Quarter-Master	John Mason	12 Sept 1793	
Asst Surgeon }	William Brown	25 Dec 1796	
	------ Dick	15 May 1798	

1804

Rank	Name	Regiment	Army
Colonel	Gerard Lake	14 Feb 1800	Gen. 29 Apr 1802
Lieut. Colonel	John Mortresor	25 Apr 1801	Col. 29 Apr 1802
	William Harness	26 Apr 1801	3 May 1796
Majors	John Ford	1 July 1795	Lt. Col. 1 Jan 1801
	Benjamin Forbes	17 June 1802	Lt. Col. 1 Jan 1800
Captains	John White	7 Mar 1794	Major 25 Sept 1803
	Thomas Baldwin St George	26 Jan 1796	
	Robert Smith	20 Mar 1796	
	John Ashley Sturt	20 Oct	19 Aug 1794
	John Edwards	28 Apr 1797	
	John Mac Rae	4 Oct	2 Sept 1795
	Robert Mowbray	3 Aug 1799	
	Joseph Cookson	17 Mar 1803	9 Mar 1803
	John Dalrymple	25 June	
	John St George	10 Sept	
Lieutenants	Solomon Welch	15 July	1795 Adjutant
	John Harvey	15 July 1795	
	Willam Bolton	1 Sept	
	Dennis Kingdon	2 Sept	
	Robert Boyce	8 Sept	26 Nov 1794
	Judge Tho. D'Arcey	26 Sept	
	Samuel Allen Wheeler	1 July 1797	
	Barrington Bradshaw	1 Oct	2 May 1797
	John Lewis	26 Apr 1799	
	Charles Hardy	3 July	2 Dec 1795
	Lionel Hooke	21 Aug	
	James Morisset	9 Nov 1800	
	Robert Dashwood	10 Nov 1800	
	Matthew Robert Freeman	24 Jan 1801	
	Henry Jones Groves	1Jan 1802	
	Andrew Adamson	20 Oct	
	Andrew Kelly	21 Oct	
	Edward Lenn	16 June 1803	23 Mar 1800
	Geo. Robert Lascelles	3 Dec	17 Oct 1799
	James Walsh		
Ensigns	Philip Rowson Stepney	9 Nov 1800	
	------ Harness	10 Nov	
	Clement John Cozens	8 Jan 1802	
	James Henry Bloomfield	1 June	
	J. Lawford Watson	20 Oct	
	Charles Forrest	21 Oct	
Paymaster	Tho. John Gataker	31 Mar 1803	
Adjutant	Solomon Welch	6 June 1794	Lieut. 15 July 1795
Quarter-Master	John Middleton	27 Jan 1803	
Asst Surgeon }	William Brown	25 Dec 1796	
	--------- Dick	15 May 1798	

Agent, Messrs. Greenwood and Cox, Craig's Court

1805

Rank	Name	Regiment	Army
Colonel	Gerard Lord Lake	14 Feb 1800	Gen. 29 Apr 1802
Lieut. Colonel	John Mortresor	25 Apr 1801	Col. 29 Apr 1802
	William Wallace	14 Nov 1804	1 Jan 1798
Major	Benjamin Forbes	17 June 1802	Lt. Col. 1 Jan 1800
	John White	25 Sept 1803	
Captains	Robert Smith	20 Mar 1796	
	John Ashley Sturt	20 Oct	19 Aug 1794
	John Edwards	28 Apr 1797	
	John Mac Rae	4 Oct 1797	2 Sept 1795
	Robert Mowbray	3 Aug 1799	
	Joseph Cookson	17 Mar 1803	9 Mar 1803
	John Dalrymple	25 June	
	John St George	10 Sept	
	J. Murray	14 Sept 1804	9 July 1803
Lieutenants	Solomon Welch	15 July 1795	Adjutant
	John Harvey	15 July 1795	
	Willam Bolton	1 Sept	
	Dennis Kingdon	2 Sept	
	Robert Boyce	8 Sept	26 Nov 1794
	Judge Tho. D'Arcey	26 Sept 1795	
	Samuel Allen Wheeler	1 July 1797	
	John Lewis	26 Apr 1799	
	Charles Hardy	3 July	2 Dec 1795
	Lionel Hooke	21 Aug	
	James Morisset	9 Nov 1800	
	Robert Dashwood	10 Nov 1800	
	Matthew Robert Freeman	24 Jan 1801	
	Henry Jones Groves	1 Jan 1802	
	Andrew Adamson	20 Oct	
	Andrew Kelly	21 Oct	
	Geo. Robert Lascelles	3 Dec 1803	17 Oct 1799
	Stepney Rawson Stepney	26 May 1804	
	James H. Walsh	27 Sept	
	Clement John Cozens	18 Oct	
Ensigns	------ Harness	10 Nov 1800	
	J. Lawford Watson	20 Oct 1802	
	Charles Forrest	21 Oct	
	------ Grove	1 Apr 1803	
	------ Mosse	1 Aug	
	Charles Campbell	27 Sept	
	William Musgrave	15 Jan 1804	
	Henry Stoddart	16 Aug	
Paymaster	Thomas John Gataker	31 Mar 1803	
Adjutant	Solomon Welch	6 June 1794	Lieut. 15 July 1795
Quarter-Master	John Middleton	27 Jan 1803	
Asst Surgeon }	William Brown	25 Dec 1796	
	------ Dick	15 May 1798	

Agent, Messrs. Greenwood and Cox, Craig's Court

1806

Rank	Name	Regiment	Army
Colonel	Gerard Lord Lake	14 Feb 1800	Gen. 29 Apr 1802
Lieut. Colonel	William Wallace	14 Nov 1804	1 Jan 1798
	Benjamin Forbes	4 Apr 1805	1 Jan 1800
Major	John White	26 May 1803	
Captains	Robert Smith	20 Mar 1796	
	John Ashley Sturt	20 Oct	Major 1 Jan 1805
	John Edwards	28 Apr 1797	
	Robert Mowbray	3 Aug 1799	
	Joseph Cookson	17 Mar 1803	9 Mar 1803
	John Dalrymple	25 June	
	John St George	10 Sept	
	Solomon Welch	2 Jan 1804	
	John Harvey	8 Jan 1804	
	J. Murray	14 Apr	9 July 1803
Lieutenants	William Bolton	1 Sept 1795	
	Dennis Kingdon	2 Sept	
	Robert Boyce	8 Sept 1795	26 Nov 1794
	Judge Tho. D'Arcey	26 Sept 1795	
	Samuel Allen Wheeler	1 July 1797	
	Charles Hardy	3 July 1799	2 Dec 1795
	James Morisset	9 Nov 1800	
	Robert Dashwood	10 Nov 1800	
	Matthew Robert Freeman	24 Jan 1801	
	Henry Jones Groves	1 Jan 1802	
	Andrew Adamson	20 Oct	
	Andrew Kelly	21 Oct	
	Stepney Rawson Stepney	26 May 1803	
	James H. Walsh	27 Sept	
	Clement John Cozens	18 Oct	
	Geo. Robert Lascelles	3 Dec 1803	17 Oct 1799
	P. W. Harness	2 Jan 1804	
	William Henry Macarmick	17 Feb	30 Oct 1801
	Thomas Mosse	29 Feb	
Ensigns	J. Lawford Watson	20 Oct 1802	
	Charles Forrest	21 Oct 1802	
	------ Grove	1 Apr 1803	
	William Musgrave	15 Jan 1804	
	Paul Secluno	16 Jan 1804	
	Colin Thompson	13 Apr	
	James F. Hadden	2 May	
	Henry Stoddart	16 Aug	
Paymaster	Thomas John Gataker	31 Mar 1803	
Quarter-Master	John Middleton	27 Jan 1803	
Asst Surgeon }	William Brown	25 Dec 1796	
	------ Dick	15 May 1798	

Agent, Messrs. Cox and Greenwood, Craig's Court

1807

Rank	Name	Regiment	Army
Colonel	Gerard Lord Lake	14 Feb 1800	Gen. 29 Apr 1802
Lieut. Colonel	William Wallace	14 Nov 1804	1 Jan 1798
	Benjamin Forbes	4 Apr 1805	1 Jan 1800
Majors	John White	26 May 1803	
	Robert Smyth	4 Apr 1805	
Captains	John Ashley Sturt	20 Oct 1796	Major 1 Jan 1805
	John Edwards	28 Apr 1797	
	Joseph Cookson	17 Mar 1803	9 Mar 1803
	John Dalrymple	25 June	
	John St George	10 Sept	
	Solomon Walsh	2 Jan 1804	
	John Harvey	8 Jan 1804	
	J.Murray	14 Apr	9 July 1803
	William Bolton	4 Apr 1805	
	Robert Dashwood	30 Oct 1806	
Lieutenants	Dennis Kingdon	2 Sept 1795	Adjutant
	Robert Boyce	8 Sept 1795	26 Nov 1794
	Judge Tho. D'Arcey	26 Sept 1795	
	Samuel Allen Wheeler	1 July 1797	
	James Morisset	9 Nov 1800	
	Matthew Robert Freeman	24 Jan 1801	
	Henry Jones Groves	1 Jan 1802	
	Andrew Adamson	20 Oct	
	Andrew Kelly	21 Oct	
	Stepney Rawson Stepney	26 May 1803	
	James H. Walsh	27 Sept	
	Clement John Cozens	18 Oct	
	Geo. Robert Lascelles	3 Dec 1803	17 Oct 1799
	P. W. Harness	2 Jan 1804	
	William Henry Macarmick	17 Feb	30 Oct 1801
	Thomas Mosse	29 Feb	
	William Musgrave	15 Sept	
	Paul Secluno	16 Sept	
	F. Grove	17 Sept	
	J. Lawford Watson	4 Apr 1805	
Ensigns	Charles Forrest	21 Oct 1802	
	James F. Hadden	2 May 1804	
	Henry Stoddart	16 Aug	
	Charles Dick	15 Sept	
	James Kirby	4 Apr 1805	
	Abel Craven	6 Mar 1806	
	Thomas Bailie	31 July	
Paymaster	Thomas John Gataker	31 Mar 1803	
Adjutant	Dennis Kingdon	12 Sept 1804	Lieut. 2 Sept 1795
Quarter-Master	John Middleton	27 Jan 1803	
Asst Surgeon }	William Brown	25 Dec 1796	
	------- Dick	15 May 1798	

Agent, Messrs. Greenwood and Cox, Craig's Court

1808

Rank	Name	Regiment	Army
Colonel	Gerard Viscount Lake	14 Feb 1800	Gen. 29 Apr 1802
Lieut. Colonel	William Wallace	14 Nov 1804	1 Jan 1798
	Benjamin Forbes	4 Apr 1805	1 Jan 1800
Majors	John White	26 May 1803	
	Robert Smyth	4 Apr 1805	
Captains	John Ashley Sturt	20 Oct 1796	Major 1 Jan 1805
	John Edwards	28 Apr 1797	
	Joseph Cookson	17 Mar 1803	9 Mar 1803
	John Dalrymple	25 June	
	John St George	10 Sept	
	Solomon Walsh	2 Jan 1804	
	John Harvey	8 Jan 1804	
	Dennis Kingdon	15 Apr	
	Robert Dashwood	30 Oct 1806	
	Eyre Evans Kenny	22 Jan 1807	24 Dec 1804
	Henry James Phelps	12 Nov	
Lieutenants	Robert Boyce	8 Sept 1795	26 Nov 1794
	Judge Tho. D'Arcey	26 Sept 1795	
	Samuel Allen Wheeler	1 July 1797	
	James Morisset	9 Nov 1800	
	Matthew Robert Freeman	24 Jan 1801	
	Henry Jones Groves	1 Jan 1802	
	AndrewAdamson	20 Oct	
	AndrewKelly	21 Oct	
	Stepney Rawson Stepney	26 May 1803	
	James H. Walsh	27 Sept	
	Geo. Robert Lascelles	3 Dec 1803	17 Oct 1799
	P. W. Harness	2 Jan 1804	
	Thomas Mosse	29 Feb	
	William Musgrave	15 Sept	
	Paul Secluno	16 Sept	
	F. Grove	17 Sept	
	J. Lawford Watson	4 Apr 1805	
	Henry Stoddart	2 Nov	
	W. K. Burton	2 Jan 1807	1 June 1806
	Thomas Bailie	29 Jan 1807	
	Richard John Castell	1 Feb	
Ensigns	Charles Forrest	21 Oct 1802	
	Charles Dick	15 Sept 1804	
	Abel Craven	6 Mar 1806	
	John P. McGregor	1 July	
	J. Dale	21 Aug	25 Apr 1805
	Joseph Coles	22 Aug 1806	
	Charles Curtis	28 May 1807	
	Thomas Langley Colt	25 Aug	
Paymaster	Thomas John Gataker	31 Mar 1803	
Quarter-Master	John Middleton	27 Jan 1803	
Asst Surgeon	William Brown	25 Dec 1796	
	--------- Dick	15 May 1798	

Agent, Messrs. Greenwood, Cox and Co. Craig's Court

1809

Rank	Name	Regiment	Army
Colonel	Hon. Edward Paget	23 Feb 1808	M. Gen. 1 Jan 180
Lieut. Colonel	William Wallace	14 Nov 1804	Col. 25 Apr 1808
	Benjamin Forbes	4 Apr 1805	1 Jan 1800
Majors	John White	26 May 1803	
	John Ashley Sturt	12 May 1808	1 Jan 1805
Captains	John Edwards	28 Apr 1797	
	Joseph Cookson	17 Mar 1803	9 Mar 1803
	John Dalrymple	25 June	
	JohnSt George	10 Sept	
	Solomon Walsh	2 Jan 1804	
	Dennis Kingdon	15 Apr	
	Robert Dashwood	30 Oct 1806	
	Eyre Evans Kenny	22 Jan 1807	24 Dec 1804
	Henry James Phelps	12 Nov	27 June 1805
	Judge Thomas D'Arcey	11 May 1808	
	Samuel Allen Wheeler	12 May 1808	
Lieutenants	Matthew Robert Freeman	24 Jan 1801	
	Henry Jones Groves	1 Jan 1802	
	Andrew Adamson	20 Oct	
	Andrew Kelly	21 Oct	
	Stepney Rawson Stepney	26 May 1803	
	James H. Walsh	27 Sept	
	Geo. Robert Lascelles	3 Dec 1803	17 Oct 1799
	P. W. Harness	2 Jan 1804	
	Thomas Mosse	29 Feb	Adjutant
	William Musgrave	15 Sept	
	Paul Secluno	16 Sep	
	F. Grove	17 Sept	
	Henry Stoddart	2 Nov 1805	
	Thomas Bailie	29 Jan 1807	
	Charles Dick	1 Feb	
	Richard John Castell	1 Feb	
	John Bowler	1 July	
	Alexander Lumsden	22 Sept	14 May 1805
	Acheson French	17 Dec	
	Narborough Baker	10 Mar 1808	
	William Trant	7 July	25 May 1808
	P.F. Edward Cadenski	14 July	30 Apr 1807
	Joseph Ellis	1 Dec	22 Sept 1808
Ensigns	Charles Forrest	21 Oct 1802	
	Joseph Coles	22 Aug 1806	
	Charles Curtis	28 May 1807	
	George Barrs	25 Apr	
	Francis Browne	27 July	

	Name	Regiment	Army
	Thomas Langley Colt	25 Aug	
	Peter Maclaine	28 Jan 1808	
	Henry Nott	22 Sept	
	Charles Anderson	12 Jan 1809	
Adjutant	Thomas Mosse	29 Aug 1806	Lieut. 29 Feb 1804
Quarter-Master	John Middleton	27 Jan 1803	
Surgeon	William Browne	25 Jan 1808	
Asst Surgeon	--------- Dick	15 May 1798	
Agent, Mr. Watson, No. 37 Argyll Street.			

1810

Rank	Name	Regiment	Army
Colonel	Hon. Edward Paget	23 Feb 1808	M. Gen. 1 Jan 1805
Lieut. Colonel	William Wallace	14 Nov 1804	Col. 25 Apr 1808
	Benjamin Forbes	14 Apr 1805	1 Jan 1800
Majors	John White	26 May 1803	
	John Ashley Sturt	12 May 1808	1 Jan 1805
Captains	John Edwards	28 Apr 1797	Major 25 Oct 1809
	Joseph Cookson	17 Mar 1803	9 Mar 1803
	John Dalrymple	25 June	
	John St George	10 Sept	
	Solomon Walsh	2 Jan 1804	
	Dennis Kingdon	15 Apr	
	Robert Dashwood	30 Oct 1806	
	Eyre Evans Kenny	22 Jan 1807	24 Dec 1804
	Henry James Phelps	12 Nov	27 June 1805
	Judge Thomas D'Arcey	11 May 1808	
	Samuel Allen Wheeler	12 May 1808	
Lieutenants	Matthew Robert Freeman	24 Jan 1801	
	Henry Jones Groves	1 Jan 1802	
	Andrew Adamson	20 Oct	
	Andrew Kelly	21 Oct	
	Stepney Rawson Stepney	26 May 1803	
	James H.Walsh	27 Sept	
	P. W. Harness	2 Jan 1804	
	Thomas Mosse	29 Feb	Adjutant
	William Musgrave	15 Sept	
	Paul Secluno	16 Sept	
	F. Grove	17 Sept	
	Henry Stoddart	2 Nov 1805	
	Thomas Bailie	29 Jan 1807	
	Charles Dick	1 Feb	
	Richard John Castell	1 Feb	
	John Bowler	1 Jul	
	Alexander Lumsden	22 Sept	14 May 1805
	Acheson French	17 Dec	
	Narborough Baker	10 Mar 1808	
	Henry Benson	1 June	10 No 1804
	William Trant	7 July	25 May 1808
	P.F. Edward Cadenski	14 July	30 Apr 1807
	Joseph Ellis	1 Dec	22 Sept 1808
Ensigns	Charles Forrest	21 Oct 1802	
	Joseph Coles	22 Aug 1806	
	George Barrs	25 Apr 1807	
	Charles Curtis	28 May	
	Francis Browne	27 July	
	Thomas Langley Colt	25 Aug	
	Peter Maclaine	28 Jan 1808	
	Henry Nott	22 Sept	
	Charles Anderson	12 Jan 1809	
Adjutant	Thomas Mosse	29 Aug 1806	Lieut. 29 Feb 1804
Quarter-Master	John Middleton	27 Jan 1803	
Surgeon	William Browne	25 Jan 1808	
Asst Surgeon	--------- Dick	15 May 1798	
Agent, Mr. Watson, No. 37 Argyll Street.			

1811

Rank	Name	Regiment	Army
Colonel	Hon. Edward Paget	23 Feb 1808	M. Gen. 1 Jan 1805
Lieut. Colonel	Benjamin Forbes	14 Apr 1805	1 Jan 1800
	John White	14 Dec 1809	
Majors	John Ashley Sturt	28 Aug 1806	1 Jan 1805
	John Edwards	14 Dec 1809	25 Oct 1809
Captains	Joseph Cookson	17 Mar 1803	9 Mar 1803
	John Dalrymple	25 June	
	John St. George	10 Sept	
	Solomon Walsh	2 Jan 1804	
	Dennis Kingdon	15 Apr 1804	
	Robert Dashwood	30 Oct 1806	
	Eyre Evans Kenny	22 Jan 1807	24 Dec 1804
	Henry James Phelps	12 Nov	27 June 1805
	Samuel Allen Wheeler	12 May 1808	
	Charles Knatchbull	5 Apr 1810	18 Aug 1808
	Henry Jones Groves	1 Nov	
Lieutenants	Andrew Adamson	20 Oct 1802	
	Andrew Kelly	21 Oct 1802	
	Stepney Rawson Stepney	26 May 1803	
	James H. Walsh	27 Sept	
	P. W. Harness	2 Jan 1804	
	Thomas Mosse	29 Feb	Adjutant
	William Musgrave	15 Sept	
	Paul Secluno	16 Sept	
	F. Grove	17 Sept	
	Henry Stoddart	2 Nov 1805	
	Thomas Bailie	29 Jan 1807	
	Charles Dick	1 Feb	
	Richard John Castell	1 Feb	
	John Bowler	1 July	
	Alexander Lumsden	22 Sept	14 May 1805
	S. S. Burns	1 Dec	

	Acheson French	17 Dec	
	Narborough Baker	10 Mar 1808	
	William Trant	7 July	25 May 1808
	P.F. Edward Cadenski	14 July	30 Apr 1807
	Joseph Ellis	1 Dec	22 Sept 1808
	Thomas Langley Colt	18 Jan 1809	
	Charles Curtis	25 June	
Ensigns	Henry Nott	22 Sept 1808	
	John Malony	25 Sept 1808	
	Charles Anderson	12 Jan 1809	
	Peter Mosse	20 May 1810	
	Thomas Darke	14 June	
	James Skelton	19 July	
	Benjamin Swain Ward	16 Aug	
	Michael Nugent	6 Dec	
Adjutant	Thomas Mosse	29 Aug 1806	Lieut. 29 Feb 1804
Quarter-Master	John Middleton	27 Jan 1803	6 Nov 1797
Surgeon	William Browne	25 Jan 1808	
Asst Surgeon }	---------- Dick	15 May 1798	
	Andrew Nicoll	21 Feb 1811	

Agent, Mr. Watson, No. 1 Poland Street.

1812

Rank	Name	Regiment	Army
Colonel	Hon. Edward Paget	23 Feb 1808	Lt. Gen. 4 June 181
Lieut. Colonel	Benjamin Forbes	14 Apr 1805	Col. 25 July 1811
	John White	14 Dec 1809	
Majors	John Ashley Sturt	28 Aug 1806	1 Jan 1805
	John Edwards	14 Dec 1809	25 Oct 1809
Captains	Joseph Cookson	17 Mar 1803	9 Mar 1803
	John Dalrymple	25 June	
	John St George	10 Sept	
	Solomon Walsh	2 Jan 1804	
	Dennis Kingdon	15 Apr	
	Robert Dashwood	30 Oct 1806	
	Eyre Evans Kenny	22 Jan 1807	24 Dec 1804
	Henry James Phelps	12 Nov	27 June 1805
	Samuel Allen Wheeler	12 May 1808	
	Charles Knatchbull	5 Apr 1810	18 Aug 1808
	Henry Jones Grove	1 Nov	
Lieutenants	Andrew Adamson	20 Oct 1802	
	Andrew Kelly	21 Oct 1802	
	Stepney Rawson Stepney	26 May 1803	
	James H.Walsh	27 Sept	
	P. W. Harness	2 Jan 1804	
	Thomas Mosse	29 Feb	Adjutant
	William Musgrave	15 Sept	
	F. Grove	17 Sept	
	Henry Stoddart	2 Nov 1805	
	Thomas Bailie	29 Jan 1807	
	Charles Dick	1 Feb	
	Richard John Castell	1 Feb	
	John Bowler	1 July	
	Alexander Lumsden	22 Sept	14 May 1805
	S. S. Burns	1 Dec	
	Acheson French	17 Dec	
	Narborough Baker	10 Mar 1808	
	William Trant	7 July	25 May 1808
	P.F. Edward Cadenski	14 July	30 Apr1807
	Joseph Ellis	1 Dec	22 Sept1808
	Thomas Langley Colt	18 Jan 1809	
	Francis Brown	1 Aug 1810	1 Apr 1810
	Henry Nott	1 Oct	
	William Penny	25 Oct	15 June 1808
	John Molony	25 Mar 1811	
Ensigns	Charles Anderson	12 Jan 1809	
	Peter Mosse	20 May 1810	
	Thomas Darke	14 June	
	Benjamin Swain Ward	16 Aug	
	Michael Nugent	6 Dec	
	------- Wilson	25 Mar 1811	
	James Inkson	11 Apr	
Adjutant	Thomas Mosse	29 Aug 1806	Lieut. 29 Feb 1804
Quarter-Master	John Middleton	27 Jan 1803	
Surgeon	William Browne	25 Jan 1808	
Asst Surgeon }	-------- Dick	15 May 1798	
	Andrew Nicoll	21 Feb 1811	

Agent, Mr. Watson, No. 1 Poland Street.

1813

Rank	Name	Regiment	Army
Colonel	Hon. Sir Edward Paget K.B.	23 Feb 1808	Lt. Gen. 4 June 1811
Lieut. Colonel	Benjamin Forbes	14 Apr 1805	Col. 25 July 1811
	John White	12 May 1809	
Majors	John Ashley Sturt	28 Aug 1806	Lt. Col. 1 Jan 1812
	John Edwards	12 May 1809	
Captains	Joseph Cookson	17 Mar 1803	9 Mar 1803
	John Dalrymple	25 June	
	Solomon Walsh	2 Jan 1804	
	Dennis Kingdon	15 Apr	
	Robert Dashwood	30 Oct 1806	
	Eyre Evans Kenny	22 Jan 1807	24 Dec 1804
	Henry James Phelps	12 Nov 1805	27 June 1805
	Samuel Allen Wheeler	12 May 1808	
	Charles Knatchbull	5 Apr 1810	18 Aug 1808
	Henry Jones Grove	1 Nov	
	P. W. Harness	28 May 1812	
Lieutenants	Andrew Kelly	21 Oct 1802	
	Stepney Rawson Stepney	26 May 1803	
	James H. Walsh	27 Sept	

Rank	Name	Regiment	Army
	Thomas Mosse	29 Feb	
	William Musgrave	15 Sept 1804	
	F. Grove	17 Sept	
	Henry Stoddart	2 Nov 1805	
	Thomas Bailie	29 Jan 1807	
	Charles Dick	1 Feb	
	Richard John Castell	1 Feb	
	John Bowler	1 July	
	S. S. Burns	1 Dec 1807	Adjutant
	Acheson French	17 Dec	
	Narborough Baker	10 Mar 1808	
	William Trant	7 July	25 May 1808
	P. F. Edward Cadenski	14 July	30 Apr 1807
	Joseph Ellis	1 Dec	22 Sept 1808
	Thomas Langley Colt	18 Jan 1809	
	Francis Brown	1 Aug 1810	1 Apr 1810
	Henry Nott	1 Oct	
	William Penny	25 Oct	15 June 1808
	John Molony	25 Mar 1811	
	Charles Anderson	27 Aug 1811	
	Thomas Darke	11 June 1812	
Ensigns	Peter Mosse	20 May 1810	
	Michael Nugent	6 Dec	
	------ Wilson	25 Mar 1811	
	James Inkson	11 Apr	
	Thomas Barlow	12 Dec	
	Rich. Robertus Halahan	23 July 1812	
	Joseph Stokes	29 Oct	
Adjutant	S. S. Burns	1 Sept 1811	Lieut. 1 Dec 1807
Quarter-Master	John Middleton	27 Jan 1803	
Surgeon	William Browne	25 Jan 1808	
Asst Surgeon	J. Dick	15 May 1798	
	Andrew Nicoll	21 Feb 1811	

Agent, Mr. Watson, No. 1 Poland Street.

1814

Rank	Name	Regiment	Army
Colonel	Hon. Sir Edward Paget K.B.	23 Feb 1808	Lt. Gen. 4 June 1811
Lieut. Colonel	Benjamin Forbes	14 Apr 1805	Col. 25 July 1811
	John White	12 May 1809	
	John Ashley Sturt	4 June 1813	
Majors	John Edwards	12 May 1809	
	Joseph Cookson	4 June 1813	
Captains	John Dalrymple	25 June 1803	
	Dennis Kingdon	15 Apr 1804	
	Robert Dashwood	30 Oct 1806	
	Eyre Evans Kenny	22 Jan 1807	24 Dec 1804
	Henry James Phelps	12 Nov 1805	27 June 1805
	Charles Knatchbull	5 Apr 1810	18 Aug 1808
	Henry Jones Grove	1 Nov	
	P. W. Harness	28 May 1812	
	William Thorne	30 June	30 Aug 1810
	Andrew Kelly	4 June 1813	
Lieutenants	Stepney Rawson Stepney	26 May 1803	
	James H. Walsh	27 Sept	
	William Musgrave	15 Sept 1804	
	F. Grove	17 Sept 1804	
	Henry Stoddart	2 Nov 1805	
	Thomas Bailie	29 Jan 1807	
	Charles Dick	1 Feb	
	Richard John Castell	1 Feb	
	John Bowler	1 July	
	S. S. Burns	1 Dec 1807	Adjutant
	Acheson French	17 Dec 1807	
	Narborough Baker	10 Mar 1808	
	William Trant	7 July	25 May 1808
	Joseph Ellis	1 Dec	22 Sept 1808
	Thomas Langley Colt	18 Jan 1809	
	Francis Brown	1 Aug 1810	1 Apr 1810
	Henry Nott	1 Oct	
	William Penny	25 Oct	15 June 1808
	John Molony	25 Mar 1811	
	Charles Anderson	27 Aug 1811	
	Peter Mosse	3 May 1812	
	Thomas Darke	11 June 1812	
	------ Wilson	5 Aug 1813	
	John Donavan Verner	12 Aug 1813	27 Nov 1812
Ensigns	James Inkson	11 Apr 1811	
	Thomas Barlow	12 Dec	
	------ Archer	3 May 1812	
	Clement Wolseley	4 June	
	Rich. Robertus Halahan	23 July 1812	
	Joseph Southwell Stokes	29 Oct	
	William Burke	10 Dec	
	Robert Greaves	8 Apr 1813	
	William Harvey	5 Aug	
Paymaster	James Cruckshanks	16 Sept 1813	
Adjutant	S. S. Burns	1 Sept 1811	Lieut. 1 Dec 1807
Quarter-Master	John Middleton	27 Jan 1803	
Surgeon	William Browne	25 Jan 1808	
Asst Surgeon	Andrew Nicoll	21 Feb 1811	

Agent, Mr. Watson, No. 1 Poland Street.

1815

Rank	Name	Regiment	Army
Colonel	Hon. Sir Edward Paget K.B	23 Feb 1808	Lt. Gen. 4 June 1811
Lieut. Colonel	John White	12 May 1809	
	John Ashley Sturt	4 June 1813	1 Jan 1812
Majors	John Edwards	12 May 1809	Lt. Col. 4 June 1814
	Joseph Cookson	4 June 1813	

Rank	Name	Regiment	Army
Captains	John Dalrymple	25 June 1803	Major 4 June 1814
	Dennis Kingdon	15 Apr 1804	Major 4 June 1814
	Robert Dashwood	30 Oct 1806	
	Eyre Evans Kenny	22 Jan 1807	24 Dec 1804
	Henry James Phelps	12 Nov 1805	27 June 1805
	Henry Jones Grove	1 Nov 1810	
	P. W. Harness	28 May 1812	
	William Thorne	30 June	30 Aug 1810
	James Maclean	25 Oct	18 Oct 1810
	Andrew Kelly	4 June 1813	
	Stepney Rawson Stepney	30 Mar 1814	
Lieutenants	James H. Walsh	27 Sept 1803	
	William Musgrave	15 Sept 1804	
	F. Grove	17 Sept 1804	
	Henry Stoddart	2 Nov 1805	
	Thomas Bailie	29 Jan 1807	
	Charles Dick	1 Feb	
	Richard John Castell	1 Feb	
	John Bowler	1 July	
	S. S. Burns	1 Dec 1807	Adjutant
	Acheson French	17 Dec 1807	
	Narborough Baker	10 Mar 1808	
	William Trant	7 July	25 May 1808
	Joseph Ellis	1 Dec	22 Sept 1808
	Thomas Langley Colt	18 Jan 1809	
	Francis Brown	1 Aug 1810	1 Apr 1810
	Henry Nott	1 Oct	
	William Penny	25 Oct	15 June 1808
	John Molony	25 Mar 1811	
	Charles Anderson	27 Aug 1811	
	Peter Mosse	3 May 1812	
	Thomas Darke	11 June 1812	
	------ Wilson	5 Aug 1813	
	John Donavan Verner	12 Aug 1813	27 Nov 1812
	James Inkson	30 Dec	
	------ Archer	30 Mar 1814	
Ensigns	Clement Wolseley	4 June 1812	
	Rich. Robertus Halahan	23 July 1812	
	Joseph Southwell Stokes	29 Oct	
	William Burke	10 Dec	
	Robert C. Greaves	8 Apr 1813	
	William Harvey	5 Aug	
	William Clarke	30 Dec	
	John McQueen	30 Mar 1814	
	James McQueen	31 Mar 1814	
	George Vernon	5 May	
Paymaster	James Cruckshanks	16 Sept 1813	
Adjutant	S. S. Burns	1 Sept 1811	Lieut. 1 Dec 1807
Quarter-Master	John Middleton	27 Jan 1803	
Surgeon	William Browne	25 Jan 1808	
Asst Surgeon }	Andrew Nicoll	21 Feb 1811	
	Louis Sheppard	17 Mar 1814	

Agent, Mr. Watson, No. 1 Poland Street.

1816

Rank	Name	Regiment	Army
Colonel	Hon. Sir Edward Paget K.B.	23 Feb 1808	Lt. Gen. 4 June 1811
Lieut. Colonel	John White	12 May 1809	
	John Ashley Sturt	4 June 1813	1 Jan 1812
Majors	John Edwards	12 May 1809	Lt. Col. 4 June 1814
	Joseph Cookson	4 Jun 1813	
Captains	John Dalrymple	25 June 1803	Major 4 June 1814
	Dennis Kingdon	15 Apr 1804	Major 4 June 1814
	Robert Dashwood	30 Oct 1806	
	Eyre Evans Kenny	22 Jan 1807	Major 4 June 1814
	Henry James Phelps	12 Nov 1805	27 June 1805
	Henry Jones Grove	12 Nov 1809	
	P. W. Harness	28 May 1812	
	William Thorne	30 June	30 Aug 1810
	James Maclean	25 Oct	18 Oct 1810
	Andrew Kelly	4 June 1813	
	William Henry Taynton	1 June 1815	Major 4 June 1813
Lieutenants	James H. Walsh	27 Sept 1803	
	William Musgrave	15 Sept 1804	
	F. Grove	17 Sept 1804	
	Henry Stoddart	2 Nov 1805	
	Charles Dick	1 Feb 1807	
	Richard John Castell	1 Feb 1807	
	John Bowler	1 July	
	S. S. Burns	1 Dec 1807	Adjutant
	Acheson French	17 Dec 1807	
	Narborough Baker	10 Mar 1808	
	William Trant	7 July	25 May 1808
	Joseph Ellis	1 Dec	22 Sept 1808
	Thomas Langley Colt	18 Jan 1809	
	Francis Brown	1 Aug 1810	1 Apr 1810
	Henry Nott	1 Oct	
	William Penny	25 Oct	15 June 1808
	John Molony	25 Mar 1811	
	Charles Anderson	27 Aug 1811	
	Peter Mosse	3 May 1812	
	Thomas Darke	11 June 1812	
	------ Wilson	5 Aug 1813	
	John Donavan Verner	12 Aug 1813	27 Nov 1812
	James Inkson	30 Dec	
	------ Archer	30 Mar 1814	
	William Illius	19 Jan 1815	29 June 1813
Ensigns	Clement Wolseley	4 June 1812	
	Rich. Robertus Halahan	23 July 1812	

Rank	Name	Regiment	Army
	Joseph Southwell Stokes	29 Oct	
	William Burke	10 Dec	
	William Harvey	5 Aug	
	William Clarke	30 Dec	
	John McQueen	30 Mar 1814	
	James McQueen	31 Mar 1814	
	George Vernon	5 May	
Paymaster	James Cruckshanks	16 Sept 1813	
Adjutant	S. S. Burns	1 Sept 1811	Lieut. 1 Dec 1807
Quarter-Master	John Middleton	27 Jan 1803	
Surgeon	William Browne	25 Jan 1808	
Asst Surgeon }	Andrew Nicoll	21 Feb 1811	
	Louis Sheppard	17 Mar 1814	

Agent, Mr. Watson, No. 1 Poland Street.

1817

Rank	Name	Regiment	Army
Colonel	Sir Alex.Campbell, Bt.	26 Dec 1815	Lt. Gen. 4 June 1814
Lieut. Colonel	John Ashley Sturt	4 June 1813	1 Jan 1812
	John Edwards	16 Oct 1815	4 June 1814
Majors	Joseph Cookson	4 June 1813	
	John Dalrymple	16 Oct 1815	4 June 1814
Captains	Dennis Kingdon	15 Apr 1804	Major 4 June 1814
	Robert Dashwood	30 Oct 1806	
	Eyre Evans Kenny	22 Jan 1807	Major 4 June 1814
	Henry James Phelps	12 Nov 1805	27 June 1805
	Henry Jones Grove	12 May 1809	
	William Thome	30 June 1812	30 Aug 1810
	James Maclean	25 Oct	18 Oct 1810
	Andrew Kelly	4 Jun 1813	
	James H.Walsh	1 July 1815	
	Frederick Grove	16 Oct	
	James Winniett Nunn	7 Dec 1815	13 Dec 1810
Lieutenants	Henry Stoddart	2 Nov 1805	
	Charles Dick	1 Feb 1807	
	Richard John Castell	1 Feb 1807	
	John Bowler	1 July	
	S. S. Burns	1 Dec 1807	Adjutant
	Acheson French	17 Dec 1807	
	Narborough Baker	10 Mar 1808	
	William Trant	7 July	25 May 1808
	Joseph Ellis	1 Dec	22 Sept 1808
	Francis Brown	1 Aug 1810	1 Apr 1810
	Henry Nott	1 Oct	
	William Penny	25 Oct	15 June 1808
	John Molony	25 Mar 1811	
	Charles Anderson	27 Aug 1811	
	Peter Mosse	3 May 1812	
	Thomas Darke	11 June 1812	
	------ Wilson	5 Aug 1813	
	James Inkson	30 Dec 1814	
	------ Archer	30 Mar 1814	
	Clement Wolseley	1 Nov	
	William Illius	18 Jan 1815	29 June 1813
	Rich. Robertus Halahan	25 Aug	
	Joseph Southwell Stokes	26 Aug	
	William Burke	27 Aug	
	William Harvey	16 Oct	
Ensigns	William Clarke	30 Dec 1813	
	John McQueen	30 Mar 1814	
	James McQueen	31 Mar 1814	
	George Vernon	5 May	
	A. J. Caldwell	22 May	
	Charle Rumley	25 Aug	
	John Bowness	26 Aug	
	Henry Augustus Jackson	27 Aug	
	John Buchanan	15 Feb 1816	
	John Howe	21 Nov	
Paymaster	James Cruckshanks	16 Sept 1813	
Adjutant	S. S. Burns	1 Sept 1811	Lieut. 1 Dec 1807
Quarter-Master	John Middleton	27 Jan 1803	
Surgeon	William Brown	25 Jan 1808	
Asst Surgeon }	Andrew Nicoll	21 Feb 1811	
	Louis Sheppard	17 Mar 1814	

Agent, Mr. Macdonald, Pall Mall Court, Pall Mall.

1818

Rank	Name	Regiment	Army
Colonel	Sir Alex. Campbell, Bt. K.C.B.	26 Dec 1815	Lt. Gen. 4 June 1814
Lieut. Colonel	Joseph Cookson	7 Feb 1817	
	Walter Symes	11 Dec	27 Aug 1811
Majors	John Dalrymple	16 Oct 1815	4 June 1814
	Dennis Kingdon	7 Feb 1817	4 June 1814
Captains	Robert Dashwood	30 Oct 1806	
	Eyre Evans Kenny	22 Jan 1807	Major 4 June 1814
	Henry James Phelps	12 Nov 1805	27 June 1805
	Henry Jones Grove	12 May 1809	
	James Maclean	25 Oct 1812	18 Oct 1810
	James H.Walsh	1 July 1815	
	James Winniett Nunn	7 Dec 1815	13 Dec 1810
	W. C. Harpur	1 July 1817	1 Sept 1813
	Charles Dick	14 Aug	
	Richard John Castell	27 Nov	
Lieutenants	John Bowler	1 July 1807	
	S. S. Burns	1 Dec 1807	Adjutant
	Acheson French	17 Dec 1807	
	Narborough Baker	10 Mar 1808	
	Joseph Ellis	1 Dec	22 Sept 1808
	Francis Brown	1 Aug 1810	1 Apr 1810
	Henry Nott	1 Oct	

Rank	Name	Regiment	Army
	William Penny	25 Oct	15 June 1808
	John Molony	25 Mar 1811	
	Charles Anderson	27 Aug 1811	
	Thomas Darke	11 June 1812	
	James Inkson	30 Dec 1813	
	John McQueen	27 Nov 1817	
Ensigns	James McQueen	31 Mar 1814	
	George Vernon	5 May	
	A. J. Caldwell	22 May	
	John Bowness	26 Aug 1815	
	Henry Augustus Jackson	27 Aug 1815	
	John Buchanan	15 Feb 1816	
	------ Hayes	1 Mar 1817	
	Frederick Liardet	11 Sept	25 May 1815
	Ernest Stewart Toole	27 Nov	
Paymaster	James Cruckshanks	16 Sept 1813	
Adjutant	S. S. Burns	1 Sept 1811	Lieut. 1 Dec 1807
Quarter-Master	------ Smyth	14 Aug 1817	
Surgeon	William Browne	25 Jan 1808	
Asst Surgeon }	Andrew Nicoll	21 Feb 1811	
	Louis Sheppard	17 Mar 1814	

Agent, Messrs. A. Campbell and Co. No. 18, Suffolk Street, Charing Cross.

1819

Rank	Name	Regiment	Army
Colonel	Sir Alex. Campbell, Bt. K.C.B.	26 Dec 1815	Lt. Gen. 4 June 1814
Lieut. Colonel	Joseph Cookson	7 Feb 1817	
Majors	Dennis Kingdon	7 Feb 1817	4 June 1814
	Morris William Bailey	25 Dec	Lt. Col. 4 June 1814
Captains	Robert Dashwood	30 Oct 1806	
	Eyre Evans Kenny	22 Jan 1807	Major 4 June 1814
	Henry James Phelps	12 Nov 1805	27 June 1805
	Henry Jones Grove	12 May 1809	
	James Maclean	25 Oct 1812	18 Oct 1810
	James H.Walsh	1 July 1815	
	James Winniett Nunn	7 Dec 1815	13 Dec 1810
	W. C. Harpur	1 July 1817	1 Sept 1813
	Charles Dick	14 Aug	
	Richard John Castell	27 Nov	
Lieutenants	Acheson French	2 Feb 1807	
	John Bowler	1 July	
	S. S. Burns	1 Dec 1807	Adjutant
	Narborough Baker	10 Mar 1808	
	Joseph Ellis	1 Dec	22 Sept 1808
	William Penny	25 Oct 1810	15 June 1808
	John Molony	25 Mar 1811	
	John Charles Anderson	27 Aug 1811	
	Thomas Darke	11 June 1812	
	James Inkson	30 Dec 1814	
	Andrew Williams	2 Apr 818	2 Oct 1814
	Clement Wolseley	8 July	1 Nov 1814
	William J. Maginnis	9 July	4 Aug 1813
Ensigns	James McQueen	31 Mar 1814	
	A. J. Caldwell	22 May	
	John Bowness	26 Aug 1815	
	Henry Augustus Jackson	27 Aug 1815	
	John Buchanan	15 Feb 1816	
	Thomas Hayes	1 Mar 1817	
	Frederick Liardet	11 Sept 1815	25 May 1815
	Ernest Stuart Toole	27 Nov	
Paymaster	MichaelJones	2 July 1818	21 Apr 1798
Adjutant	S. S. Burns	1 Sept 1811	Lieut. 1 Dec 1807
Quarter-Master	------ Smyth	14 Aug 1817	
Surgeon	John Lightbody	7 May 1818	15 Oct 1812
Asst Surgeon	John Regan	5 Mar 1818	1 Sept 1814

1820

Rank	Name	Regiment	Army
Colonel	Sir Alex. Campbell, Bt. K.C.B.	26 Dec	1815 Lt. Gen.4 June 181
Lieut. Colonel	Joseph Cookson	7 Feb 1817	
Majors	George Dean Pitt	19 Aug 1819	13 Jan 1814
	James Maclean	18 Nov	
Captains	Eyre Evans Kenny	22 Jan 1807	Major 4 June 1814
	Henry James Phelps	12 Nov 1805	Major 12 Aug 1819
	Henry Jones Grove	12 May 1809	
	James H. Walsh	1 July 1815	
	James Winniett Nunn	7 Dec 1815	13 Dec 1810
	W. C. Harpur	1 July 1817	1 Sept 1813
	Charles Dick	14 Aug	
	Richard John Castell	27 Nov	
	S. S. Burns	11 Feb 1819	
	Narborough Baker	18 Nov 1819	
Lieutenants	Acheson French	2 Feb 1807	
	John Bowler	1 July	
	Joseph Ellis	1 Dec 1808	22 Sept 1808
	William Penny	25 Oct 1810	15 June 1808 Adjut.
	John Molony	25 Mar 1811	
	John Charles Anderson	27 Aug 1811	
	Thomas Darke	11 June 1812	
	James Inkson	30 Dec 1813	
	Andrew Williams	2 Apr 1818	2 Oct 1814
	Clement Wolseley	8 July	1 Nov 1814
	William J. Maginnis	9 July	4 Aug 1813
	James McQueen	11 Feb 1819	
	A. James Caldwell	18 Nov	
Ensigns	John Bowness	26 Aug 1815	
	Henry Augustus Jackson	27 Aug 1815	
	John Buchanan	15 Feb 1816	
	Frederick Liardet	11 Sept 1817	25 May 1815
	Ernest Stuart Toole	27 Nov	

Rank	Name	Regiment	Army
	Ronald Macdonald	11 Feb 1819	
	Westropp Peard Watkins	11 Nov	18 Feb 1813
	Charles Crickitt	18 Nov	
Paymaster	William Leslie	4 Nov 1819	Lieut. 24 Sept 1812
Adjutant	William Penny	11 Feb 1819	Lieut. 15 June 1808
Quarter-Master	Thomas Smyth	14 Aug1817	
Surgeon	John Lightbody	7 May 1818 1	5 Oct 1812
Asst Surgeon	John Regan	5 Mar 1818	1 Sept 1814

1821

Rank	Name	Regiment	Army
Colonel	Sir Alex.Campbell, Bt. K.C.B.	26 Dec 1815	Lt. Gen. 4 June 1814
Lieut. Colonel	Joseph Cookson	7 Feb 1817	
Majors	George Dean Pitt	19 Aug 1819	13 Jan 1814
	James Maclean	18 Nov	
Captains	Eyre Evans Kenny	22 Jan 1807	Major 4 June 1814
	Henry James Phelps	12 Nov 1805	Major 12 Aug 1819
	Henry Jones Grove	12 May 1809	
	James H. Walsh	1 July 1815	
	James Winniett Nunn	7 Dec 1815	13 Dec 1810
	W. C. Harpur	1 Jul 1817	1 Sept 1813
	Richard John Castell	27 Nov	
	S. S. Burns	11 Feb 1819	
	Narborough Baker	18 Nov 1819	
	Charles Addison	16 Mar 1820	Major 12 Aug 1819
Lieutenants	Acheson French	2 Feb 1807	
	John Bowler	1 July	
	Joseph Ellis	1 Dec 1808	22 Sept 1808
	William Penny	25 Oct 1810	15 June 1808 Adjut.
	John Molony	25 Mar 1811	
	John Charles Anderson	27 Aug 1811	
	James Inkson	30 Dec 1813	
	Andrew Williams	2 Apr 1818	2 Oct 1814
	William J. Maginnis	9 July	4 Aug 1813
	George Stoat Jeffery	17 Aug 1820	5 Aug 1815
	Samuel Paul Baghott	9 Nov	27 July 1820
	John Twigg	7 Dec	24 Aug 1813
	Arthur Grueber	8 Dec	16 Dec 1813
Ensigns	John Bowness	26 Aug 1815	
	Henry Augustus Jackson	27 Aug 1815	
	John Buchanan	15 Feb 1816	
	Frederick Liardet	11 Sept 1817	25 May 1815
	Ernest Stuart Toole	27 Nov	
	Ronald Macdonald	11 Feb 1819	
	Westropp Peard Watkins	11 Nov	18 Feb 1813
	Charles Crickitt	18 Nov	
Paymaster	William Leslie	4 Nov 1819	Lieut. 24 Sept 1812
Adjutant	William Penny	11 Feb 1819	Lieut. 15 June 1808
Quarter-Master	Hugh McDougall	21 Dec 1820	Lieut. 12 Aug 1813
Surgeon	John Lightbody	7 May 1818	15 Oct 1812
Asst Surgeon	John Regan	5 Mar 1818	1 Sept 1814

Agent, Messrs. A. Campbell and Co. Regent Street, St James's.

1822

Rank	Name	Regiment	Army
Colonel	Sir Alex Campbell, Bt. K.C.B.	26 Dec 1815	Lt. Gen. 4 June 1814
Lieut. Colonel	Joseph Cookson	7 Feb 1817	
Majors	George Dean Pitt	19 Aug 1819	13 Jan 1814
	James Maclean	18 Nov	
Captains	Eyre Evans Kenny	22 Jan 1807	Major 4 June 1814
	Henry James Phelps	12 Nov 1805	Major 12 Aug 1819
	Henry Jones Grove	12 May 1809	
	James H.Walsh	1 July 1815	
	James Winniett Nunn	7 Dec 1815	13 Dec 1810
	W. C. Harpur	1 July 1817	1 Sept 1813
	Richard John Castell	27 Nov	
	Narborough Baker	18 Nov 1819	
	Charles Addison	16 Mar 1820	Major 12 Aug 1819
Lieutenants	Acheson French	2 Feb 1807	
	John Bowler	1 July	
	Joseph Ellis	1 Dec 1808	22 Sept 1808
	William Penny	25 Oct 1810	15 June 1808 Adjut.
	John Molony	25 Mar 1811	
	John Charles Anderson	27 Aug 1811	
	James Inkson	30 Dec 1813	
	Andrew Williams	2 Apr 1818	2 Oct 1814
	William J. Maginnis	9 July	4 Aug 1813
	George Stoat Jeffery	17 Aug 1820	5 Aug 1815
	John Twigg	7 Dec	24 Aug 1813
	Arthur Grueber	8 Dec	16 Dec 1813
Ensigns	John Bowness	26 Aug 1815	
	Henry Augustus Jackson	27 Aug 1815	
	John Buchanan	15 Feb 1816	
	Frederick Liardet	11 Sept 1817	25 May 1815
	Ernest Stuart Toole	27 Nov	
	Ronald Macdonald	11 Feb 1819	
	Westropp Peard Watkins	11 Nov	18 Feb 1813
Paymaster	William Leslie	4 Nov 1819	Lieut. 24 Sept 1812
Adjutant	William Penny	11 Feb 1819	Lieut. 15 June 1808
Surgeon	John Lightbody	7 May 1818	15 Oct 1812
Asst Surgeon	John Regan	5 Mar 1818	1 Sept 1814

Agent, Messrs. Campbell and Co. Regent Street, St James's.

1823

Rank	Name	Regiment	Army
Colonel	Sir Alex. Campbell, Bt. K.C.B.	26 Dec 1815	Lt. Gen. 4 June 1814
Lieut. Colonel	George Dean Pitt	8 Apr 1822	
Majors	James Maclean	18 Nov 1819	
	Wm. C. Harpur	18 Apr 1822	
Captains	Eyre Evans Kenny	22 Jan 1807	Major 4 June 1814
	Henry James Phelps	12 Nov 1805	Major 12 Aug 1819

	Henry Jones Grove	12 May 1809	
	James H, Walsh	1 July 1815	
	James Winniett Nunn	7 Dec 1815	13 Dec 1810
	Narborough Baker	18 Nov 1819	
	Charles Addison	16 Mar 1820	Major 12 Aug 1819
Lieutenants	Acheson French	2 Feb 1807	
	John Bowler	1 July	
	Joseph Ellis	1 Dec 1808	22 Sept 1808
	William Penny	25 Oct 1810	15 June 1808 Adjut.
	John Molony	25 Mar 1811	
	John Charles Anderson	27 Aug 1811	
	James Inkson	30 Dec 1813	
	Andrew Williams	2 Apr 1818	2 Oct 1814
	William J. Maginnis	9 July	4 Aug 1813
	George Stoat Jeffery	17 Aug 1820	5 Aug 1815
	John Twigg	7 Dec	24 Aug 1813
	Arthur Grueber	8 Dec	16 Dec 1813
Ensigns	John Bowness	26 Aug 1815	
	Henry Augustus Jackson	27 Aug 1815	
	John Buchanan	15 Feb 1816	
	Frederick Liardet	11 Sept 1817	25 May 1815
	Ernest Stuart Toole	27 Nov 1817	
	Ronald Macdonald	11 Feb 1819	
	John Thomas	25 Aug 1814	
Paymaster	William Leslie	4 Nov 1819	Lieut. 24 Sept 1812
Adjutant	William Penny	11 Feb 1819	Lieut. 15 June 1808
Quarter-Master	W. Campbell	31 Jan 1822	
Surgeon	John Lightbody	7 May 1818	15 Oct 1812
Asst Surgeon	John Regan	5 Mar 1818	1 Sept 1814

Agent, Messrs. Campbell and Co. Regent Street, St James's.

1824

Rank	Name	Regiment	Army
Colonel	Sir Alex. Campbell, Bt. K.C.B.	26 Dec 1815	Lt. Gen. 4 June 1814
Lieut. Colonel	George Dean Pitt	8 Apr 1822	
Majors	James Maclean	18 Nov 1819	
	Wm. C. Harpur	18 Apr 1822	
Captains	Eyre Evans Kenny	22 Jan 1807	Major 4 June 1814
	Henry James Phelps	12 Nov 1805	Major 12 Aug 1819
	Henry Jones Grove	12 May 1809	
	James Winniett Nunn	7 Dec 1815	13 Dec 1810
	Narborough Baker	18 Nov 1819	
	Charles Addison	16 Mar 1820	Major 12 Aug 1819
	Thomas Bunbury	25 Oct 1814	
	James Arthur Butler	31 July 1823	18 Apr 1816
Lieutenants	Acheson French	2 Feb 1807	
	John Bowler	1 July	
	Joseph Ellis	1 Dec 1808	22 Sept 1808
	William Penny	25 Oct 1810	15 June 1808 Adjut.
	John Molony	25 Mar 1811	
	John Charles Anderson	27 Aug 1811	
	James Inkson	30 Dec 1813	
	Andrew Williams	2 Apr 1818	2 Oct 1814
	William J. Maginnis	9 July	4 Aug 1813
	George Stoat Jeffery	17 Aug 1820	5 Aug 1815
	John Twigg	7 Dec	24 Aug 1813
	Arthur Grueber	8 Dec	16 Dec 1813
Ensigns	John Bowness	26 Aug 1815	
	Henry Augustus Jackson	27 Aug 1815	
	John Buchanan	15 Feb 1816	
	Frederick Liardet	11 Sept 1817	25 May 1815
	Ernest Stuart Toole	27 Nov 1817	
	Ronald Macdonald	11 Feb 1819	
	John Thomas	25 Aug 1814	
Paymaster	William Leslie	4 Nov 1819	Lieut. 24 Sept 1812
Adjutant	William Penny	11 Feb 1819	Lieut. 15 June 1808
Quarter-Master	W. Campbell	31 Jan 1822	
Surgeon	John Lightbody	7 May 1818	15 Oct 1812
Asst Surgeon	John Regan	5 Mar 1818	1 Sept 1814

Agent, Messrs. Campbell and Co. Regent Street, St James's.

1825

Rank	Name	Regiment	Army
Colonel	Sir Alex. Campbell, Bt. K.C.B.	26 Dec 1815	Lt. Gen. 4 June 1814
Lieut. Colonel	George Dean Pitt	18 Apr 1822	
Majors	James Maclean	18 Nov 1819	
	William C. Harpur	18 Apr 1822	
Captains	Eyre Evans Kenny	22 Jan 1807	Major 4 June 1814
	Henry James Phelps	12 Nov 1805	Major 12 Aug 1819
	Henry Jones Grove	12 May 1809	
	James Winniett Nunn	7 Dec 1815	13 Dec 1810
	Narborough Baker	18 Nov 1819	
	Charles Addison	16 Mar 1820	Major 12 Aug 1819
	Thomas Bunbury	10 Oct 1822	25 Oct 1814
	James Arthur Butler	31 July 1823	18 Apr 1816
Lieutenants	Acheson French	2 Feb 1807	
	John Bowler	1 July	
	Joseph Ellis	1 Dec 1808	22 Sept 1808
	William Penny	25 Oct 1810	15 June 1808 Adjut.
	John Molony	25 Nov 1811	
	John Charles Anderson	27 Aug 1811	
	James Inkson	30 Dec 1813	
	Andrew Williams	2 Apr 1818	2 Oct 1814
	William J. Maginnis	9 July	4 Aug 1813
	George Stoat Jeffery	17 Aug 1820	5 Aug 1815
	John Twigg	7 Dec	24 Aug 1813
	Arthur Grueber	8 Dec	16 Dec 1813
Ensigns	John Bowness	26 Aug 1815	
	Henry Augustus Jackson	27 Aug 1815	
	John Buchanan	15 Feb 1816	

Rank	Name	Regiment	Army
	Frederick Liardet	11 Sept 1817	25 May 1815
	Ronald Macdonald	11 Feb 1819	
	John Thomas	30 May 1822	
Paymaster	William Leslie	4 Nov 1819	Lieut. 24 Sept 1812
Adjutant	William Penny	11 Feb 1819	Lieut. 15 June 1808
Quarter-Master	William Campbell	31 Jan 1822	
Surgeon	John Lightbody	7 May 1818	15 Oct 1812
Asst Surgeon	John Regan	5 Mar 1818	1 Sept 1814

Agent, Messrs. Campbell and Co. Regent Street, St James's.

1826

Rank	Name	Regiment	Army
Colonel	Sir Rufane Shawe Donkin, KCB, GCH	20 Apr 1825	Lt. Gen. 19 July 1821
Lieut. Colonel	George Dean Pitt	18 Apr 1822	
Majors	James Maclean	18 Nov 1819	
	William C. Harpur	18 Apr 1822	
Captains	Eyre Evans Kenny	22 Jan 1807	Major 4 June 1814
	Henry Jones Grove	12 May 1809	
	James Winniett Nunn	7 Dec 1815	13 Dec 1810
	Narborough Baker	18 Nov 1819	
	Thomas Bunbury	10 Oct 1822	25 Oct 1814
	Acheson French	7 Apr 1825	
	John Bowler	8 Apr 1825	
	John Routledge Majendie	4 Aug	30 June 1825
	Joseph Ellis	29 Sept	
	Tho. W. O. McNiven	19 Nov	29 Oct 1825
Lieutenants	William Penny	25 Oct 1810	15 June 1808 Adjut.
	John Charles Anderson	27 Aug 1811	
	James Inkson	30 Dec 1813	
	William J. Maginnis	9 July 1818	4 Aug 1813
	George Stoat Jeffery	17 Aug 1820	5 Aug 1815
	James Leche	17 Mar 1825	10 Mar 1814
	John Bowness	7 Apr	
	Henry Augustus Jackson	8 Apr	
	George Hind Edwards	9 Apr	16 Aug 1810
	Ronald Macdonald	20 Aug	25 Jan 1825
	John Thomas	15 Sept	
	Edward Every	22 Dec	27 Aug 1825
	Willoughby Moore	19 Jan 1826	17 July 1823
Ensigns	John West	25 Jan 1825	
	Francis Norris Toole	7 Apr	2nd Lt. 11 Nov 1824
	William Harvie Christie	8 Apr	
	George Black	9 Apr	
	Charles Augustus Brooke	10 Apr	
	James Lacy	11 Apr	
	Francis Hay Graham	15 Oct	
Paymaster	William Leslie	4 Nov 1819	Lieut. 24 Sept 1812
Adjutant	William Penny	11 Feb 1819	Lieut. 15 June 1808
Quarter-Master	William Campbell	31 Jan 1822	
Surgeon	John Lightbody	7 May 1818	15 Oct 1812
Asst Surgeon }	John Regan	5 Mar 1818	1 Sept 1814
}	Robert Johnson, M. D.	29 Dec 1825	

Agent, Messrs. Greenwood, Cox and Hammersley.

1827

Rank	Name	Regiment	Army
Colonel	Sir Rufane Shawe Donkin, KCB, GCH	20 Apr 1825	Lt. Gen. 19 July 1821
Lieut. Colonel	George Deane Pitt	18 Ap 1822	
Majors	James Maclean	18 Nov 1819	
	William C. Harpur	18 Apr 1822	
Captains	Henry Jones Grove	12 May 1809	
	James Winniett Nunn	7 Dec 1815	13 Dec 1810
	Narborough Baker	18 Nov 1819	
	Thomas Bunbury	10 Oct 1822	25 Oct 1814
	Acheson French	7 Apr 1825	
	John Bowler	8 Apr 1825	
	John Routledge Majendie	4 Aug	30 June 1825
	Joseph Ellis	29 Sept	
	Tho. William Ogilvy McNiven	19 Nov	29 Oct 1825
	George Falconar	31 Aug 1826	22 Apr 1825
Lieutenants	William Penny	25 Oct 1810	15 June 1808 Adjut.
	John Charles Anderson	27 Aug 1811	
	James Inkson	30 Dec 1813	
	William J. Maginnis	9 July 1818	4 Aug 1813
	George Stoat Jeffery	17 Aug 1820	5 Aug 1815
	John Bowness	7 Apr 1825	
	Henry Augustus Jackson	8 Apr 1825	
	George Hind Edwards	9 Apr 1825	16 Aug 1810
	Ronald Macdonald	20 Aug 1825	25 Jan 1825
	John Thomas	15 Sept	
	Edward Every	22 Dec	27 Aug 1825
	John West	16 Mar 1826	
	Francis Norris Toole	17 Aug	
Ensigns	William Harvie Christie	8 Apr 1825	
	George Black	9 Apr 1825	
	Charles Augustus Brooke	10 Apr 1825	
	James Lacy	11 Apr 1825	
	Francis Hay Graham	15 Oct	
	Rinaldo Scheberras	16 Mar 1826	
	Franci Blake Knox	19 Oct	
Paymaster	William Leslie	4 Nov 1819	Lieut. 24 Sept 1812
Adjutant	William Penny	11 Feb 1819	Lieut. 15 June 1808
Quarter-Master	William Campbell	31 Jan 1822	
Surgeon	John Lightbody	7 May 1818	15 Oct 1812
Asst Surgeon }	John Regan	5 Mar 1818	1 Sept 1814
	Robert Johnson, M. D.	29 Dec 1825	

Agent, Messrs. Greenwood, Cox and Hammersley.

1828

Rank	Name	Regiment	Army
Colonel	Sir Rufane Shawe Donkin, KCB, GCH	20 Apr 1825	Lt. Gen. 19 July 1821
Majors	William C. Harpur	18 Apr 1822	
	Charles St. John Fancourt	16 Aug 1827	28 June 1827
Captains	Henry Grove	12 May 1809	
	James Winniett Nunn	7 Dec 1815	13 Dec 1810
	Narborough Baker	18 Nov 1819	
	Thomas Bunbury	10 Oct 1822	25 Oct 1814
	Acheson French	7 Apr 1825	
	John Bowler	8 Apr 1825	
	John Routledge Majendie	4 Aug	30 June 1825
	Tho. William Ogilvy McNiven	19 Nov	29 Oct 1825
	George Falconar	31 Aug 1826	22 Apr 1825
	Hon. Cadwallader Davis Blaney	7 June 1827	8 Apr 1826
Lieutenants	John Charles Anderson	27 Aug 1811	
	James Inkson	30 Dec 1813	
	William J. Maginnis	9 July 1818	4 Aug 1813
	John Bowness	7 Apr 1825	
	Henry Augustus Jackson	8 Apr 1825	
	Ronald Macdonald	20 Aug 1825	25 Jan 1825
	John Thomas	15 Sept	
	Edward Every	22 Dec	27 Aug 1825
	John West	16 Mar 1826	
	Francis Norris Toole	17 Aug	
	William Harvie Christie	13 Mar 1827	6 Mar 1827
	Francis Hay Graham	12 Apr	
	Rob. John Napier Kellette	19 June	22 Apr 1826
	George Black	12 July 1827	Adjutant
Ensigns	Rinaldo Scheberras	16 Mar 1826	
	Samuel Lettsom	6 Mar 1827	
	Rich. Thomson Hopkins	12 Apr 1827	
	Richard Talbot Sayers	19 Apr 1827	
	William Thomas Colman	28 June	7 Sept 1815
	George Denshire	28 June	8 Apr 1826
	Henry West	22 Nov	
Paymaster	William Leslie	4 Nov 1819	Lieut. 24 Sept 1812
Adjutant	George Black	19 June 1827	Lieut. 12 July 1827
Quarter-Master	William Campbell	31 Jan 1822	
Surgeon	John Lightbody	7 May 1818	15 Oct 1812
Asst Surgeon }	JohnRegan	5 Mar 1818	1 Sept 1814
	Robert Johnson, M. D.	29 Dec 1825	

Agent, Messrs. Greenwood, Cox and Hammersley.

1829

Rank	Name	Regiment	Army
Colonel	Sir Rufane Shawe Donkin, KCB, GCH	20 Apr 1825	Lt. Gen. 19 July 1821
Lieut. Colonel	George Deane Pitt	18 Apr 1822	
Majors	William C. Harpur	18 Apr 1822	
	Henry Grove	24 July 1828	
Captains	James Winniett Nunn	7 Dec 1815	13 Dec 1810
	Narborough Baker	18 Nov 1819	
	Thomas Bunbury	10 Oct 1822	25 Oct 1814
	Acheson French	7 Apr 1825	
	John Bowler	8 Apr 1825	
	Tho. William Ogilvy McNiven	19 Nov	29 Oct 1825
	George Falconar	31 Aug 1826	22 Apr 1826
	Hon. Cadwallader Davis Blaney	7 June 1827	8 Apr 1826
	Lord Wm. Francis Monatagu	15 May 1828	8 Apr 1826
	John Charles Anderson	24 Jul 1828	
Lieutenants	James Inkson	30 Dec 1813	
	William J. Maginnis	9 July 1818	4 Aug 1813
	John Bowness	7 Apr 1825	
	Henry Augustus Jackson	8 Apr 1825	
	Ronald Macdonald	20 Aug 1825	5 Jan 1825
	John Thomas	15 Sept	
	Edward Every	22 Dec	27 Aug 1825
	John West	16 Mar 1826	
	Francis Norris Toole	17 Aug	
	William Harvie Christie	13 Mar 1827	6 Mar 1827
	Rob. John Napier Kellette	19 June	22 Apr 1826
	George Black	12 July 1827	Adjutant
	Bingley Broadhead	21 Nov 1828	20 Sept 1826
Ensigns	Rinaldo Scheberras	16 Mar 1826	
	Samuel Lettsom	6 Mar 1827	
	Rich. Thomson Hopkins	12 Apr 1827	
	Richard Talbot Sayers	19 Apr 1827	
	William Thomas Colman	28 June	7 Sept 1815
	George Denshire	28 June	8 Apr 1826
	Henry West	22 Nov	
	Gilbert W. Robinson	31 July 1828	
Paymaster	William Leslie	4 Nov 1819	Lieut. 24 Sept 1812
Adjutant	George Black	19 June 1827	Lieut. 12 July 1827
Quarter-Master	William Campbell	31 Jan 1822	
Surgeon	John Lightbody	7 May 1818	15 Oct 1812
Asst Surgeon }	John Regan	5 Mar 1818	1 Sept 1814
	Robert Johnson, M. D.	29 Dec 1825	

Agent, Messrs. Greenwood, Cox and Hammersley.

1830

Rank	Name	Regiment	Army
Colonel	Sir Rufane Shawe Donkin, KCB, GCH	20 Apr 1825	Lt. Gen. 19 July 1821
Lieut. Colonel	George Deane Pitt	18 Apr 1822	
Majors	William C. Harpur	18 Apr 1822	
	Henry Grove	24 July 1828	
Captains	James Winniett Nunn	7 Dec 1815	13 Dec 1810
	Narborough Baker	18 Nov 1819	
	Thomas Bunbury	10 Oct 1822	25 Oct 1814
	Acheson French	7 Apr 1825	
	John Bowler	8 Apr 1825	

Rank	Name	Regiment	Army
	Tho. William Ogilvy McNiven	19 Nov	29 Oct 1825
	George Falconar	31 Aug 1826	22 Apr 1825
	Hon. Cadwallader Davis Blaney	7 June 1827	8 Apr 1826
	Lord Wm. Francis Monatagu	15 May 1828	8 Apr 1826
	John Charles Anderson	24 July 1828	
Lieutenants	James Inkson	30 Dec 1813	
	William J. Maginnis	9 July 1818	4 Aug 1813
	John Bowness	7 Apr 1825	
	Henry Augustus Jackson	8 Apr 1825	
	Ronald Macdonald	20 Aug 1825	25 Jan 1825
	John Thomas	15 Sept	
	Edward Every	22 Dec	27 Aug 1825
	John West	16 Mar 1826	
	Francis Norris Toole	17 Aug	
	William Harvie Christie	13 Mar 1827	6 Mar 1827
	George Black	12 July 1827	Adjutant
	Bingley Broadhead	21 Nov 1828	20 Sept 1826
	Samuel Lettsom	2 Apr 1829	
Ensigns	Rinaldo Scheberras	16 Mar 1826	
	Rich. Thomson Hopkins	12 Apr 1827	
	Richard Talbot Sayers	19 Apr 1827	
	William Thomas Colman	28 June	7 Sept 1815
	George Denshire	28 June	8 Apr 1826
	Henry West	22 Nov	
	Gilbert W. Robinson	31 July 1828	
	John Smith	2 Apr 1829	
Paymaster	William Leslie	4 Nov 1819	Lieut. 24 Sept 1812
Adjutant	George Black	19 June 1827	Lieut. 12 July 1827
Quarter-Master	William Campbell	31 Jan 1822	
Surgeon	John Lightbody	7 May 1818	15 Oct 1812
Asst Surgeon	John Regan	5 Mar 1818	1 Sept 1814
	Robert Johnson, M. D.	29 Dec 1825	

Agent, Messrs. Greenwood, Cox and Hammersley.

1831

Rank	Name	Regiment	Army
Colonel	Sir Rufane Shawe Donkin, KCB, GCH	20 Apr 1825	Lt. Gen. 19 July 1821
Lieut. Colonel	George Deane Pitt	18 Apr 1822	
Majors	William C. Harpur	18 Apr 1822	
	Henry Grove	24 July 1828	
Captains	James Winniett Nunn	7 Dec 1815	13 Dec 1810
	Narborough Baker	18 Nov 1819	
	Thomas Bunbury	10 Oct 1822	25 Oct 1814
	John Bowler	8 Apr 1825	
	Tho. William Ogilvy McNiven	19 Nov	29 Oct 1825
	George Falconar	31 Aug 1826	22 Apr 1825
	John Charles Anderson	24 July 1828	
	John Bowness	11 June 1830	
	John Haggerstone	16 July	7 July 1825
	William Henry Page	8 Nov	Major 22 July 1830
Lieutenants	James Inkson	30 Dec 1813	
	Henry Augustus Jackson	8 Apr 1825	
	Ronald Macdonald	20 Aug 1825	25 Jan 1825
	John Thomas	15 Sept	
	Edward Every	22 Dec	27 Aug 1825
	John West	16 Mar 1826	
	William J. Maginnis	17 Mar 1826	4 Aug 1813
	William Harvie Christie	13 Mar 1827	6 Mar 1827
	George Black	12 July 1827	Adjutant
	Bingley Broadhead	21 Nov 1828	20 Sept 1826
	Samuel Lettsom	2 Apr 1829	
	Rich. Thomson Hopkins	11 June 1830	
	Francis Crowther	28 Sept	16 Nov 1815
Ensigns	Rinaldo Scheberras	16 Mar 1826	
	Richard Talbot Sayers	19 Apr 1827	
	George Denshire	28 June	8 Apr 1826
	Henry West	22 Nov	
	Gilbert W. Robinson	31 July 1828	
	John Smith	2 Apr 1829	
	John Scully	11 June 1830	
	Charles Robert Raitt	13 June 1830	
Paymaster	William Leslie	4 Nov 1819	Lieut. 24 Sept 1812
Adjutant	George Black	19 June 1827	Lieut. 12 July 1827
Quarter-Master	William Campbell	31 Jan 1822	
Surgeon	John Lightbody	7 May 1818	15 Oct 1812
Asst Surgeon	RobertJohnson, M.D.	29 Dec 1825	
	William Wallace, M.D.	26 Nov 1830	8 Mar 1827

Agent, Messrs. Greenwood, Cox and Co.

1832

Rank	Name	Regiment	Army
Colonel	Sir Rufane Shawe Donkin, KCB, GCH	20 Apr 1825	Lt. Gen. 19 July 1821
Lieut. Colonel	George Deane Pitt	18 Apr 1822	
Majors	William C. Harpur	18 Apr 1822	
	Henry Grove	24 July 1828	
Captains	James Winniett Nunn	7 Dec 1815	13 Dec 1810
	Narborough Baker	18 Nov 1819	
	Thomas Bunbury	10 Oct 1822	25 Oct 1814
	John Bowler	8 Apr 1825	
	Tho. William Ogilvy McNiven	19 Nov	29 Oct 1825
	GeorgeFalconar	31 Aug 1826	22 Apr 1825
	John Charles Anderson	24 July 1828	
	John Bowness	11 June 1830	
	John Haggerstone	16 July	17 July 1825
	William Henry Page	9 Nov	Major 22 July 1830
Lieutenants	James Inkson	30 Dec 1813	
	Henry Augustus Jackson	8 Apr 1825	
	Ronald Macdonald	20 Aug 1825	25 Jan 1825
	John Thomas	15 Sept	
	Edward Every	22 Dec	27 Aug 1825

Rank	Name	Regiment	Army
	John West	16 Mar 1826	
	William J. Maginnis	17 Mar.1826	4 Aug 1813
	William Harvie Christie	13 Mar.1827	6 Mar 1827
	George Black	12 July.1827	Adjutant
	Bingley Broadhead	21 Nov.1828	20 Sept 1826
	Samuel Lettsom	2 Apr.1829	
	Rich. Thomson Hopkins	11 June.1830	
	Francis Crowther	28 Sept	16 Nov 1815
Ensigns	Rinaldo Scheberras	16 Mar 1826	
	Richard Talbot Sayers	19 Apr 1827	
	George Denshire	28 June	8 Apr 1826
	Henry West	22 Nov	
	Gilbert W. Robinson	31 July 1828	
	John Smith	2 Apr 1829	
	John Scully	11 June 1830	
	Charles Robert Raitt	13 June 1830	
Paymaster	William Leslie	4 Nov 1819	Lieut. 24 Sept 1812
Adjutant	George Black	19 June 1827	Lieut. 12 July 1827
Quarter-Master	William Campbell	31 Jan 1822	
Surgeon	John Lightbody	7 May 1818	15 Oct 1812
Asst Surgeon	Joseph Ewing	6 Sept 1831	7 Sept 1809

Agent, Messrs. Greenwood, Cox and Co.

1833

Rank	Name	Regiment	Army
Colonel	Sir Rufane Shawe Donkin, KCB, GCH	20 Apr 1825	Lt. Gen. 19 July 1821
Lieut. Colonel	George Deane Pitt	18 Apr 1822	
Majors	Henry Grove	24 July 1828	
	Narborough Baker	25 May 1832	
Captains	James Winniett Nunn	7 Dec 1815	Major 22 July 1830
	Thomas Bunbury	10 Oct 1822	25 Oct 1814
	John Bowler	8 Apr 1825	
	Tho. William Ogilvy McNiven	19 Nov	29 Oct 1825
	George Falconar	31 Aug 1826	22 Apr 1825
	John Bowness	11 June 1830	
	John Haggerstone	16 July	17 July 1825
	William Henry Page	9 Nov	Major 22 July 1830
	Edward Every	25 May 1832	
	John West	22 June 1832	
Lieutenants	James Inkson	30 Dec 1813	
	Henry Augustus Jackson	8 Apr 1825	
	Ronald Macdonald	20 Aug 1825	25 Jan 1825
	John Thomas	15 Sept	
	William J. Maginnis	17 Mar 1826	4 Aug 1813
	William Harvie Christie	13 Mar 1827	6 Mar 1827
	George Black	12 July 1827	Adjutant
	Samuel Lettsom	2 Apr 1829	
	Rich. Thomson Hopkins	11 June 1830	
	Francis Crowther	28 Sept	16 Nov 1815
	Robert Edw. Fullerton	18 May 1832	20 Jan 1832
	Richard Talbot Sayers	25 May 1832	
	George Denshire	22 June	
Ensigns	Rinaldo Scheberras	16 Mar 1826	
	John Smith	2 Apr 1829	
	John Scully	11 June 1830	
	Charles Robert Raitt	13 June 1830	
	John Lightbody	25 May 1832	
	Horatio Rob. Maydwell Gulston	26 May 1832	
	Charles Richard Ilderton	22 June	
	William Godfrey Jervis	21 Dec	16 Nov 1832
Adjutant	George Black	19 June 1827	Lieut. 12 July 1827
Quarter-Master	William Campbell	31 Jan 1822	
Surgeon	John Lightbody	7 May 1818	15 Oct 1812
Asst Surgeon	Joseph Ewing	6 Sept 1831	7 Sept 1809

Agent, Messrs. Greenwood, Cox and Co.

1834

Rank	Name	Regiment	Army
Colonel	Sir Rufane Shawe Donkin, KCB, GCH	20 Apr 1825	Lt. Gen. 19 July 1821
Lieut. Colonel	George Deane Pitt	18 Apr 1822	
Majors	Henry Grove	24 July 1828	
	Narborough Baker	25 May 1832	
Captains	James Winniett Nunn	7 Dec 1815	Major 22 July 1830
	Thomas Bunbury	10 Oct 1822	25 Oct 1814
	John Bowler	8 Apr 1825	
	George Falconar	31 Aug 1826	22 Apr 1825
	John Bowness	11 June 1830	
	William Henry Page	9 Nov	Major 22 July 1830
	Edward Every	25 May 1832	
	John West	22 June 1832	
	William Harvie Christie	24 May 1833	
	Samuel Lettsom	4 Oct 1833	
Lieutenants	Henry Augustus Jackson	8 Apr 1825	
	Ronald Macdonald	20 Aug 1825	25 Jan 1825
	William J. Maginnis	17 Mar 1826	4 Aug 1813
	George Black	12 July 1827	Adjutant
	Rich. Thomson Hopkins	11 June 1830	
	Robert Edw. Fullerton	18 May 1832	20 Jan 1832
	Richard Talbot Sayers	25 May 1832	
	George Denshire	22 June	
	Rinaldo Scheberras	16 Apr 1833	
	John Smith	24 May	
	John Scully	26 July	
	Charles Robert Raitt	4 Oct 1833	
	James Deavers Morris	8 Nov	25 June 1818
Ensigns	John Lightbody	25 May 1832	
	Horatio Rob. Maydwell Gulston	26 May 1832	
	Charles Richard Ilderton	22 June	
	Walter Farquhar Christie	19 Apr 1833	
	Mascie Domville Taylor	10 May	

Rank	Name	Regiment	Army
	Wilmot Henry Bradford	24 May	
	George Denis Pack	26 July 1833	
	William Hawkins	4 Oct	
Paymaster	John Grant	1 June 1833	24 Mar 1829 Lt. 24 July 1811
Adjutant	George Black	19 June 1827	Lieut. 12 July 1827
Quarter-Master	William Campbell	31 Jan 1822	
Surgeon	John Lightbody	May 1818	15 Oct 1812
Asst Surgeon	Joseph Ewing	6 Sept 1831	7 Sept 1809
Agent, Messrs. Greenwood, Cox and Co.			

1835

Rank	Name	Regiment	Army
Colonel	Sir Rufane Shawe Donkin, KCB, GCH	20 Apr 1825	Lt. Gen. 19 July 1821
Lieut. Colonel	George Deane Pitt	18 Apr 1822	
Majors	Narborough Baker	25 May 1832	
	Thomas Bunbury	21 Nov 1834	
Captains	James Winniett Nunn	7 Dec 1815	Major 22 July 1830
	John Bowler	8 Apr 1825	
	George Falconar	31 Aug 1826	22 Apr 1825
	John Bowness	11 June 1830	
	William Henry Page	9 Nov	Major 22 July 1830
	Edward Every	25 May 1832	
	John West	22 June 1832	
	William Harvie Christie	24 May 1833	
	Samuel Lettsom	4 Oct 1833	
	Rich. Thomson Hopkins	21 Nov 1834	
Lieutenants	Henry Augustus Jackson	8 Apr 1825	
	Ronald Macdonald	20 Aug 1825	25 Jan 1825
	George Black	12 July 1827	Adjutant
	Robert Edw. Fullerton	18 May 1832	20 Jan 1832
	Richard Talbot Sayers	25 May 1832	
	George Denshire	22 June	
	Rinaldo Scheberras	16 Apr 1833	
	John Smith	24 May	
	John Scully	26 July	
	Charles Robert Raitt	4 Oct 1833	
	James Deavers Morris	8 Nov	25 June 1818
	John Lightbody	9 May 1834	
	Horatio Rob. Maydwell Gulston	21 Nov	
Ensigns	Charles Richard Ilderton	22 June 1832	
	Walter Farquhar Christie	19 Apr 1833	
	Mascie Domville Taylor	10 May	
	Wilmot Henry Bradford	24 May	
	George Denis Pack	26 July 1833	
	William Hawkins	4 Oct	
	Hon. Wm. Ant. Skeffington Foster	9 May 1834	
	Henry Cowell Boys	21 Nov	
Paymaster	John Grant	1 June 1833	24 Mar 1829 Lt. 24 July 1811
Adjutant	George Black	19 June 1827	Lieut. 12 July 1827
Quarter-Master	William Campbell	31 Jan 1822	
Surgeon	John Lightbody	7 May 1818	15 Oct 1812
Asst Surgeon	Joseph Ewing	6 Sept 1831	7 Sept 1809
Agent, Messrs. Cox and Co.			

1836

Rank	Name	Regiment	Army
Colonel	Sir Rufane Shawe Donkin, KCB, GCH	20 Apr 1825	Lt. Gen. 19 July 1821
Lieut. Colonel	George Deane Pitt	18 Apr 1822	
Majors	Narborough Baker	25 May 1832	
	Thomas Bunbury	21 Nov 1834	
Captains	James Winniett Nunn	7 Dec 1815	Major 22 July 1830
	John Bowler	8 Apr 1825	
	John Bowness	11 June 1830	
	John West	22 June 1832	
	William Harvie Christie	24 May 1833	
	Samuel Lettsom	4 Oct 1833	
	Robert Edw. Fullerton	30 Jan 1835	
	Patrick Plunkett	31 July 1835	19 Dec 1834
	George Denshire	4 Sept	
	Nathaniel Kane	20 Nov	13 Nov 1832
Lieutenants	Henry Augustus Jackson	8 Apr 1825	
	Ronald Macdonald	20 Aug 1825	25 Jan 1825
	George Black	12 July 1827	Adjutant
	Richard Talbot Sayers	25 May 1832	
	Rinaldo Scheberras	16 Apr 1833	
	John Smith	24 May	
	John Scully	26 July	
	Charles Robert Raitt	4 Oct 1833	
	James Deavers Morris	8 Nov	25 June 1818
	John Lightbody	9 May 1834	
	Horatio Rob. Maydwell Gulston	21 Nov	
	Charles Richard Ilderton	30 Jan 1835	
	Walter Farquhar Christie	4 Sept 1835	
Ensigns	Mascie Domville Taylor	10 May 1833	
	Wilmot Henry Bradford	24 May	
	George Denis Pack	26 July 1833	
	William Hawkins	4 Oct	
	Hon. Wm. Ant. Skeffington Foster	9 May 1834	
	William Hougham Tyssen	30 Jan 1835	
	Hon. Theodore Torkington	14 Aug 1835	
	James Edward Amiraux	25 Sept	
Paymaster	John Grant	1 June 1833	24 Mar 1829 Lt. 24 July 1811
Adjutant	George Black	19 June 1827	Lieut. 12 July 1827
Quarter-Master	William Campbell	31 Jan 1822	
Surgeon	Joseph Ewing	6 Sept 1831	7 Sept 1809
Asst Surgeon	John Reid	4 Dec 1835	6 Oct 1814
Agent, Messrs. Cox and Co			

1837

Rank	Name	Regiment	Army
Colonel	Sir Rufane Shawe Donkin, KCB, GCH	20 Apr 1825	Lt. Gen. 19 July 1821
Lieut. Colonel	George Dean Pitt, KH.	18 Apr 1822	Col. 10 Jan 1837
Majors	Narborough Baker	25 May 1832	
	Thomas Bunbury	21 Nov 1834	
Captains	James Winniett Nunn	7 Dec 1815	Major 22 July 1830
	John Bowler	8 Apr 1825	
	John West	22 June 1832	
	William Harvie Christie	24 May 1833	
	Samuel Lettsom	4 Oct 1833	
	Patrick Plunkett	31 July 1835	19 Dec 1834
	Nathaniel Kane	20 Nov	13 Nov 1832
	Richard Tasker Furlong	22 Apr 1836	19 Dec 1834
	John Smith	26 Aug	
	Henry Hutton Jacob	23 Sept	Major 10 Jan 1837
Lieutenants	Ronald Macdonald	20 Aug 1825	25 Jan 1825
	George Black	12 July 1827	Adjutant
	Richard Talbot Sayers	25 May 1832	
	Rinaldo Scheberras	16 Apr 1833	
	John Scully	26 July	
	Charles Robert Raitt	4 Oct 1833	
	James Deavers Morris	8 Nov	25 June 1818
	John Lightbody	9 May 1834	
	Horatio Rob. Maydwell Gulston	21 Nov	
	Walter Farquhar Christie	4 Sept 1835	
	George Brunswick Smyth	6 May 1836	4 Mar 1836
	Joseph North	5 Aug	11 June 1830
	Robert Alex. Lockhart	16 Sept	5 Oct 1832
Ensigns	George Denis Pack	26 July 1833	
	William Hawkins	4 Oct	
	Hon. Wm. Ant. Skeffington Foster	9 May 1834	
	William Hougham Tyssen	30 Jan 1835	
	Hon. Theodore Torkington	14 Aug 1835	
	Samuel Tolfrey Christie	22 Jan 1836	
	Samuel Wellington Corbet Singleton	29 Jan 1836	
	Charles Henry Mortimer Kelson	26 Aug	
Paymaster	John Grant	1 June 1833	24 Mar 1829 Lt. 24 July 1811
Adjutant	George Black	19 June 1827	Lieut. 12 July 1827
Quarter-Master	William Campbell	31 Jan 1822	
Surgeon	Robert Turnbull	28 June 1836	
Asst Surgeon }	John Reid	4 Dec 1835	6 Oct 1814
	Patrick Gammie	17 June 1836	

Agent, Messrs. Cox and Co.

1838

Rank	Name	Regiment	Army
Colonel	Sir John Taylor, KC.B15	Mar 1837	Lt. Gen. 10 Jan 1837
Lieut. Colonel	Narborough Baker	24 Mar 1837	
Majors	Thomas Bunbury	21 Nov 1834	
	John Bowler	24 Mar 1837	
Captains	James Winniett Nunn	7 Dec 1815	Major 22 July 1830
	John West	22 June 1832	
	William Harvie Christie	24 May 1833	
	Samuel Lettsom	4 Oct 1833	
	Patrick Plunkett	31 July 1835	19 Dec 1834
	Nathaniel Kane	20 Nov	13 Nov 1832
	Richard Tasker Furlong	22 Apr 1836	19 Dec 1834
	Henry Hutton Jacob	23 Sept	Major 10 Jan 1837
	John Scully	24 Mar 1837	
	William Kemp	31 Mar 1837	Major 10 Jan 1837
Lieutenants	Ronald Macdonald	20 Aug 1825	25 Jan 1825
	George Black	12 July 1827	Adjutant
	Richard Talbot Sayers	25 May 1832	
	Rinaldo Scheberras	16 Apr 1833	
	Charles Robert Raitt	4 Oct 1833	
	James Deavers Morris	8 Nov	25 June 1818
	John Lightbody	9 May 1834	Adjutant
	Horatio Rob. Maydwell Gulston	21 Nov	
	Walter Farquhar Christie	4 Sept 1835	
	George Brunswick Smyth	6 May 1836	4 Mar 1836
	Joseph North	5 Aug	11 June 1830
	Robert Alex. Lockhart	16 Sept	5 Oct 1832
	William Hawkins	21 Apr 1837	
Ensigns	George Denis Pack	26 July 1833	
	Hon. Wm. Ant. Skeffington Foster	9 May 1834	
	William Hougham Tyssen	30 Jan 1835	
	Hon. Theodore Torkington	14 Aug 1835	
	Samuel Tolfrey Christie	22 Jan 1836	
	Samuel Wellington Corbet Singleton	29 Jan 1836	
	Charles Henry Mortimer Kelson	26 Aug	
	Abel Dottin Wm. Best	21 Apr 1837	
Paymaster	Thomas Bloomfield Hunt	1 Aug 1837	Lieut. 25 Oct 1833
Adjutant	John Lightbody	24 Mar 1837	Leiut. 9 May 1837
Quarter-Master	Frederick Hayes	10 Feb 1837	
Surgeon	Robert Turnbull	28 June 1836	
Asst Surgeon }	John Reid	4 Dec 1835	6 Oct 1814
	Patrick Gammie	17 June 1836	

Agent, Mr. Lawrie, Charles Street, St. James's.

1839

Rank	Name	Regiment	Army
Colonel	Sir John Taylor, KC.B	15 Mar 1837	Lt. Gen. 10 Jan 1837
Lieut. Colonel	Narborough Baker	24 Mar 1837	
Majors	Thomas Bunbury	21 Nov 1834	
	William Harvie Christie	9 Nov 1838	
Captains	James Winniett Nunn	7 Dec 1815	Major 22 July 1830
	Samuel Lettsom	4 Oct 1833	
	Richard Tasker Furlong	22 Apr 1836	19 Dec 1834
	Henry Hutton Jacob	23 Sept	Major 10 Jan 1837

Rank	Name	Regiment	Army
	William Kemp	31 Mar 1837	Major 10 Jan 1837
	Charles Robert Raitt	22 June 1838	
	Horatio Robert Maydwell Gulston	23 June 1838	
	George Brunswick Smyth	26 June 1838	
	Robert Alex. Lockhart	13 July 1838	
	Charles Steuart	9 Nov	
Lieutenants	Ronald Macdonald	20 Aug 1825	25 Jan 1825
	George Black	12 July 1827	Adjutant
	Richard Talbot Sayers	25 May 1832	
	Rinaldo Scheberras	16 Apr 1833	
	James Deavers Morris	8 Nov	25 June 1818
	John Lightbody	9 May 1834	Adjutant
	Owen Gorman	1 June 1838	27 Feb 1836
	Hon. Wm. Ant. Skeffington Foster	22 June	
	William Hougham Tyssen	23 June	
	Walter Farquhar Christie	4 Sept 1835	
	Hon. Theodore Torkington	26 June	
	Samuel Tolfrey Christie	13 July	
	Simon Fraser	28 Aug	17 July 1811
	George Denis Pack	19 Oct	
Ensigns	Abel Dottin Wm. Best	21 Apr 1837	
	Lambert Lyons Montgomery	22 June 1838	
	William Cookson	23 June 1838	
	Alexander William Riley	26 June 1838	
	Anthony Ormsby	13 July	
	Charles Henry Leslie	20 July	
	Hen. Andrew Hollinsworth	1 Nov	8 July 1837
	William Henry Hopper	2 Nov	29 Dec
Paymaster	Thomas Bloomfield Hunt	1 Aug 1837	Lieut. 25 Oct 1833
Adjutant	John Lightbody	24 Mar 1837	Lieut. 9 May 1837
Quarter-Master	Frederick Hayes	10 Feb 1837	
Surgeon	Robert Turnbull	28 June 1836	
Asst Surgeon }	John Reid	4 Dec 1835	6 Oct 1814
	Patrick Gammie	17 June 1836	

Agent, Mr. Lawrie, Charles Street, St. James's.

1840

Rank	Name	Regiment	Army
Colonel	Sir John Taylor, KC.B15	Mar 1837	Lt. Gen. 10 Jan 1837
Lieut. Colonel	Narborough Baker	24 Mar 1837	
Majors	Thomas Bunbury	21 Nov 1834	
	Samuel Lettsom	17 Jan 1840	
Captains	James Winniett Nunn	7 Dec 1815	Major 22 July 1830
	Richard Tasker Furlong	22 Apr 1836	19 Dec 1834
	William Kemp	31 Mar 1837	Major 10 Jan 1837
	Charles Robert Raitt	22 June 1838	
	Horatio Robert Maydwell Gulston	23 June 1838	
	George Brunswick Smyth	26 June 1838	
	Robert Alex. Lockhart	13 July 1838	
	Charles Steuart	9 Nov 1838	
	Hon. Wm. Ant. Skeffington Foster	17 Jan 1840	
Lieutenants	Ronald Macdonald	20 Aug 1825	25 Jan 1825
	George Black	12 July 1827	Adjutant
	Richard Talbot Sayers	25 May 1832	
	Rinaldo Scheberras	16 Apr 1833	
	James Deavers Morris	8 Nov	25 June 1818
	John Lightbody	9 May 1834	Adjutant
	Owen Gorman	1 June 1838	27 Feb 1836
	William Hougham Tyssen	23 June 1838	
	Hon. Theodore Torkington	26 June 1838	
	Samuel Tolfrey Christie	13 July 1838	
	Simon Fraser	28 Aug	17 July 1811
	Abel Dottin Wm. Best	4 Oct 1839	
	Lambert Lyons Montgomery	17 Jan 1840	
Ensigns	William Cookson	23 June 1838	
	Alexander William Riley	26 June 1838	
	Anthony Ormsby	13 July 1838	
	Charles Henry Leslie	20 July 1838	
	Hen. Andrew Hollinsworth	1 Nov	8 July 1837
	William Henry Hopper	2 Nov	29 Dec 1837
	John Charles Hay	4 Oct 1839	
	Hercules Atkin Welman	17 Jan 1840	
Paymaster	Thomas Bloomfield Hunt	1 Aug 1837	Lieut. 25 Oct 1833
Adjutant	John Lightbody	24 Mar 1837	Lieut. 9 May 1837
Quarter-Master	Frederick Hayes	10 Feb 1837	
Surgeon	Robert Turnbull	28 June 1836	
Asst Surgeon }	Patrick Gammie	17 June 1836	
	Arthur Colquhoun Macnish	5 July 1839	

Agent, Mr. Lawrie, Charles Street, St. James's.

1841

Rank	Name	Regiment	Army
Colonel	Sir John Taylor, KC.B	15 Mar 1837	Lt. Gen. 10 Jan 1837
Lieut. Colonel	Narborough Baker	24 Mar 1837	
Majors	Thomas Bunbury	21 Nov 1834	
	Samuel Lettsom	17 Jan 1840	
Captains	James Winniett Nunn	7 Dec 1815	Major 22 July 1830
	Charles Robert Raitt	22 June 1838	
	Horatio Robert Maydwell Gulston	23 June 1838	
	Robert Alex. Lockhart	13 July 1838	
	Charles Steuart	9 Nov 1838	
	Hon. Wm. Ant. Skeffington Foster	17 Jan 1840	
	Francis Marsh	14 Feb 1840	
	William Hougham Tyssen	27 Mar 1840	
	Philip Grove Beers	29 May 1840	
Lieutenants	Ronald Macdonald	20 Aug 1825	25 Jan 1825
	George Black	12 July 1827	
	Richard Talbot Sayers	25 May 1832	
	Rinaldo Scheberras	16 Apr 1833	
	James Deavers Morris	8 Nov	25 June 1818

Rank	Name	Regiment	Army
	John Lightbody	9 May 1834	Adjutant
	Owen Gorman	1 June 1838	27 Feb 1836
	Hon. Theodore Torkington	26 June 1838	
	Samuel Tolfrey Christie	13 July 1838	
	Simon Fraser	28 Aug	17 July 1811
	Abel Dottin Wm. Best	4 Oct 1839	
	Lambert Lyons Montgomery	17 Jan 1840	
	William Cookson	27 Mar 1840	
Ensigns	Alexander William Riley	26 June 1838	
	Anthony Ormsby	13 July 1838	
	Charles Henry Leslie	20 July 1838	
	Hen. Andrew Hollinsworth	1 Nov	8 July 1837
	William Henry Hopper	2 Nov	29 Dec 1837
	Hercules Atkin Welman	17 Jan 1840	
	Rob. Boyle Warren	27 Mar 1840	
	Mathew Deane Freeman	6 Nov 1840	
Paymaster	Thomas Bloomfield Hunt	1 Aug 1837	Lieut. 25 Oct 1833
Adjutant	John Lightbody	24 Mar 1837	Lieut. 9 May 1837
Quarter-Master	Frederick Hayes	10 Feb 1837	
Surgeon	Robert Turnbull	28 June 1836	
Asst Surgeon }	Patrick Gammie	17 June 1836	
	Arthur Colquhoun Macnish	5 July 1839	

1842

Rank	Name	Regiment	Army
Colonel	Sir John Taylor, KC.B	15 Mar 1837	Lt. Gen. 10 Jan 1837
Lieut. Colonel	Narborough Baker	24 Mar 1837	
Majors	Thomas Bunbury	21 Nov 1834	
	Charles Robert Raitt	29 Oct 1841	
Captains	James Winniett Nunn	7 Dec 1815	Major 22 July 1830
	Robert Alex. Lockhart	13 July 1838	
	Hon. Wm. Ant. Skeffington Foster	17 Jan 1840	
	Francis Marsh	14 Feb 1840	4 Jan 1833
	William Hougham Tyssen	27 Mar 1840	
	Philip Grove Beers	29 May 1840	
	Ronald Macdonald	26 Jan 1841	
	Charles Lewis	18 May 1841	22 Mar 1832
	Abel Dottin Wm. Best	2 July 1841	
	Robert Geroge Hughes	3 Dec 1841	
Lieutenants	Richard Talbot Sayers	25 May 1832	
	Rinaldo Scheberras	16 Apr 1833	
	James Deavers Morris	8 Nov	25 June 1818
	John Lightbody	9 May 1834	Adjutant
	Owen Gorman	1 June 1838	27 Feb 1836
	Hon. Theodore Torkington	26 June 1838	
	Samuel Tolfrey Christie	13 July 1838	
	Simon Fraser	28 Aug	17 July 1811
	Lambert Lyons Montgomery	17 Jan 1840	
	William Cookson	27 Mar 1840	
	Alexander William Riley	19 Feb 1841	
	Anthony Ormsby	2 July 1841	
	Charles Henry Leslie	16 July 1841	
Ensigns	Hen. Andrew Hollinsworth	1 Nov	8 July 1837
	Hercules Atkin Welman	17 Jan 1840	
	Rob. Boyle Warren	27 Mar 1840	
	Mathew Deane Freeman	6 Nov 1840	
	Geo. Cha. Glossop Bythesea	19 Feb 1841	
	Astell Thomas Welsh	21 May 1841	
	Edward Alan Holdich	2 July 1841	
	George Samuel Young	16 July 1841	
Paymaster	Thomas Bloomfield Hunt	1 Aug 1837	Lieut. 25 Oct 1833
Adjutant	John Lightbody	24 Mar 1837	Lieut. 9 May 1837
Quarter-Master	Frederick Hayes	10 Feb 1837	
Surgeon	Robert Turnbull	28 June 1836	
Asst Surgeon }	Patrick Gammie	17 June 1836	
	Arthur Colquhoun Macnish	5 July 1839	

Agent, Mr. John Lawrie.

1843

Rank	Name	Regiment	Army
Colonel	Sir John Taylor, KC.B	15 Mar 1837	Lt. Gen. 10 Jan 1837
Lieut. Colonel	Narborough Baker	24 Mar 1837	
Majors	Thomas Bunbury	21 Nov 1834	
	Charles Robert Raitt	29 Oct 1841	
Captains	James Winniett Nunn	7 Dec 1815	Major 22 July 1830
	Robert Alex. Lockhart	13 July 1838	
	Francis Marsh	14 Feb 1840	4 Jan 1833
	William Hougham Tyssen	27 Mar 1840	
	Charles Lewis	18 May 1841	22 Mar 1832
	Abel Dottin Wm. Best	2 July 1841	
	Robert Geroge Hughes	3 Dec 1841	
	William Hay	29 Mar 1842	22 Apr 1836
Lieutenants	Richard Talbot Sayers	25 May 1832	
	Rinaldo Scheberras	16 Apr 1833	
	James Deavers Morris	8 Nov	25 June 1818
	John Lightbody	9 May 1834	Adjutant
	Owen Gorman	1 June 1838	27 Feb 1836
	Samuel Tolfrey Christie	13 July 1838	
	Simon Fraser	28 Aug	17 July 1811
	Lambert Lyons Montgomery	17 Jan 1840	
	William Cookson	27 Mar 1840	
	Alexander William Riley	19 Feb 1841	
	Anthony Ormsby	2 July 1841	
	Charles Henry Leslie	16 July 1841	
	Edw. Hamilton Ffinney	29 Mar 1842	13 June 1830
Ensigns	Hercules Atkin Welman	17 Jan 1840	
	Rob. Boyle Warren	27 Mar 1840	
	Mathew Deane Freeman	6 Nov 1840	
	Geo. Cha. Glossop Bythesea	19 Feb 1841	
	Astell Thomas Welsh	21 May 1841	

Rank	Name	Regiment	Army
	Edward Alan Holdich	2 July 1841	
	George Samuel Young	16 July 1841	
	William Hunter	20 May 1842	
Paymaster	Thomas Bloomfield Hunt	1 Aug 1837	Lieut. 25 Oct 1833
Adjutant	John Lightbody	24 Mar 1837	Lieut. 9 May 1837
Quarter-Master	Frederick Hayes	10 Feb 1837	
Surgeon	Alex. Sheriff Macdonell	2 Dec 1842	
Asst Surgeon }	Patrick Gammie	17 June 1836	
	Arthur Colquhoun Macnish	5 July 1839	
Agent, Mr. Lawrie			

1844

Rank	Name	Regiment	Army
Colonel	Sir Maurice Charles O'Connell KCH	15 Jan 1844	Lt. Gen. 23 Nov 1841
Lieut. Colonel	Narborough Baker	24 Mar 1837	
Majors	Thomas Bunbury	21 Nov 1834	
	Charles Robert Raitt	29 Oct 1841	
Captains	James Winniett Nunn	7 Dec 1815	Major 22 July 1830
	Robert Alex. Lockhart	13 July 1838	
	Francis Marsh	14 Feb 1840	4 Jan 1833
	Charles Lewis	18 May 1841	22 Mar 1833
	Abel Dottin Wm. Best	2 July 1841	
	Robert Geroge Hughes	3 Dec 1841	
	Richard Talbot Sayers	16 Mar 1843	
	Rinaldo Scheberras	17 Mar 1843	
	James Deavers Morris	18 Mar 1843	
	Lambert Lyons Montgomery	28 July 1843	
Lieutenants	John Lightbody	9 May 1834	Adjutant
	Owen Gorman	1 June 1838	27 Feb 1836
	Samuel Tolfrey Christie	13 July 1838	
	Simon Fraser	28 Aug	17 July 1811
	William Cookson	27 Mar 1840	
	Alexander William Riley	19 Feb 1841	
	Anthony Ormsby	2 July 1841	
	Charles Henry Leslie	16 July 1841	
	Edw. Hamilton Ffinney	29 Mar 1842	13 June 1830
	Hercules Atkin Welman	16 Mar 1843	
	Rob. Boyle Warren	17 Mar 1843	
	Mathew Deane Freeman	18 Mar 1843	
	Geo. Cha. Glossop Bythesea	28 July 1843	
Ensigns	Astell Thomas Welsh	21 May 1841	
	Edward Alan Holdich	2 July 1841	
	George Samuel Young	16 July 1841	
	William Hunter	20 May 1842	
	Wm. Fred. Adams Colman	15 June 1843	
	Henry Geo. John Bowler	16 June 1843	
	William Davis	5 Nov	
	W. Wm. Oliver St John	4 Aug 1843	
Paymaster	Thomas Bloomfield Hunt	1 Aug 1837	Lieut. 25 Oct 1833
Adjutant	John Lightbody	24 Mar 1837	Lieut. 9 May 1837
Quarter-Master	Frederick Hayes	10 Feb 1837	
Surgeon	Alexander Sheriff Macdonell	2 Dec 1842	
Asst Surgeon }	Patrick Gammie	17 June 1836	
	Arthur Colquhoun Macnish	5 July 1839	
Agent, John Lawrie Esq.			

1845

Rank	Name	Regiment	Army
Colonel	Sir Maurice Charles O'Connell KCH	15 Jan 1844	Lt. Gen. 23 Nov 1841
Lieut. Colonel	Narborough Baker	24 Mar 1837	
	Thomas Bunbury	26 Jul 1844	
Majors	Charles Robert Raitt	29 Oct 1841	
Captains	James Winniett Nunn	26 Jul 1844	
	Robert Alex. Lockhart	13 July 1838	
	Charles Lewis	18 May 1841	22 Mar 1832
	Abel Dottin Wm. Best	2 July 1841	
	Robert Geroge Hughes	3 Dec 1841	
	Richard Talbot Sayers	16 Mar 1843	
	Rinaldo Scheberras	17 Mar 1843	
	James Deavers Morris	18 Mar 1843	
	Lambert Lyons Montgomery	28 July 1843	
	John Lightbody	26 July 1844	
	William Cookson	13 Dec 1844	
Lieutenants	Owen Gorman	1 June 1838	27 Feb 1836
	Samuel Tolfrey Christie	13 July 1838	
	Simon Fraser	28 Aug	17 July 1811
	Alexander William Riley	19 Feb 1841	
	Anthony Ormsby	2 July 1841	
	Charles Henry Leslie	16 July 1841	
	Edw. Hamilton Ffinney	29 Mar 18421	3 June 1830
	Hercules Atkin Welman	16 Mar 1843	
	Robert Boyle Warren	17 Mar 1843	
	Matthew Deane Freeman	18 Mar 1843	
	Geo. Cha. Glossop Bythesea	28 July 1843	
	John Cumming	26 July 1844	
	Edward Hardinge	26 July 1844	
	Richard Crawley		
	Theodore Richard Hickson	26 July 1844	
	George Dean Pitt		
	Charles Duperier	26 July 1844	
	Astell Thomas Welsh	26 July 1844	
	Edward Alan Holdich	26 July 1844	
	George Samuel Young	26 July 1844	
	William Hunter	26 July 1844	
	W. Wm. Oliver St. John	13 Dec 1844	
Ensigns	Wm. Fred. Adams Colman	15 June 1843	
	Henry Geo. John Bowler	16 June 1843	
	William Davis		
	Benjamin Hallowell Boxer		
	Stewart Alex. Kershaw	26 July 1844	

	Geo. Carnaby Robertson	27 July 1844	
	James Lloyd Fraser	28 July 1844	
	Hen. Wm. John A. Brahan	13 Dec 1844	
Paymaster	Thomas Bloomfield Hunt	1 Aug 1837	Lieut. 25 Oct 1833 Adjutant
Quarter-Master	Frederick Hayes	10 Feb 1837	
Surgeon	Alexander Sheriff Macdonell	2 Dec 1842	
Asst Surgeon }	Patrick Gammie	17 June 1836	
	Arthur Colquhoun Macnish	5 July 1839	
	Miah William Murphy	22 July 1842	
Agent, Messrs. Cox and Co.			

1846

Rank	Name	Regiment	Army
Colonel	Sir Maurice Charles O'Connell KCH	15 Jan 1844	Lt. Gen. 23 Nov 1841
Lieut. Colonel	Narborough Baker	24 Mar 1837	
	Thomas Bunbury	26 Jul 1844	
Majors	James Winniett Nunn	26 July 1844	
	Robert Blucher Wood	17 May 1844	
Captains	Robert Alex. Lockhart	13 July 1838	
	Charles Lewis	18 May 1841	
	Abel Dottin Wm. Best	2 July 1841	
	Robert Geroge Hughes	3 Dec 1841	
	Richard Talbot Sayers	16 Mar 1843	
	Rinaldo Scheberras	17 Mar 1843	
	James Deavers Morris	18 Mar 1843	
	Lambert Lyons Montgomery	28 July 1843	
	William Cookson	13 Dec 1844	
Lieutenants	Owen Gorman	1 June 1838	27 Feb 1836
	Samuel Tolfrey Christie	13 July 1838	
	Simon Fraser	28 Aug	17 July 1811
	Alexander William Riley	19 Feb 1841	
	Anthony Ormsby	2 July 1841	
	Charles Henry Leslie	16 July 1841	
	Hercules Atkin Welman	16 Mar 1843	Adjutant
	Robert Boyle Warren	17 Mar 1843	
	Mathew Deane Freeman	18 Mar 1843	
	Geo. Cha. Glossop Bythesea	28 July 1843	
	John Cumming	26 July 1844	
	Edward Hardinge	26 July 1844	
	Richard Crawley		
	Theodore Rich. Hickson	26 July 1844	
	George Dean Pitt	26 July 1844	
	Charles Duperier	26 July 1844	
	Astell Thomas Welsh	26 July 1844	
	Edward Alan Holdich	26 July 1844	
	George Samuel Young	26 July 1844	
	William Hunter	26 July 1844	
	W. Wm. Oliver St. John	13 Dec 1844	
	Wm. Fred. Adams Colman	10 Mar 1845	
	Henry Geo. John Bowler	13 July 1845	
Ensigns	Benjamin Hallowell Boxer	21 May	
	Stewart Alex. Kershaw	26 July 1844	
	Geo. Carnaby Robertson	27 July 1844	
	James Lloyd Fraser	28 July 1844	
	George Bodle	23 May 1845	
	Paul Fred. de Quincey	2 May 1845	
	Walter Butler Charles S. Wandesforde	4 July 1845	
	Henry Leslie Grove	17 Oct 1845	
Paymaster	Thomas Bloomfield Hunt	1 Aug 1837	Lieut. 25 Oct 1833 Adjutant
	Hercules Atkin Welman	10 Mar 1845	
Quarter-Master	Frederick Hayes	10 Feb 1837	
Surgeon	Alexander Sheriff Macdonell	2 Dec 1842	
Asst Surgeon }	Patrick Gammie	17 June 1836	
	Arthur Colquhoun Macnish	5 July 1839	
	Miah William Murphy	22 July 1842	
Agent, Messrs. Cox and Co.			

1847

Rank	Name	Regiment	Army
Colonel	Sir Maurice Charles O'Connell KCH	15 Jan 1844	Lt. Gen. 23 Nov 1841
Lieut. Colonel	Thomas Bunbury	26 July 1844	
	Robert Blucher Wood, C.B.	30 Dec 1845	
Majors	James Winniett Nunn	26 July 1844	
	Robert Alex. Lockhart	30 Dec 1845	
Captains	Charles Lewis	18 May 1841	
	Robert Geroge Hughes	3 Dec 1841	
	Richard Talbot Sayers	16 Mar 1843	
	James Deavers Morris	18 Mar 1843	
	Lambert Lyons Montgomery	28 July 1843	
	William Cookson	13 Dec 1844	
	Samuel Tolfrey Christie	28 Aug 1845	
	Alexander William Riley	22 Dec 1845	
	Anthony Ormsby	25 Dec 1845	
	Charles Henry Leslie	14 Apr 1846	
Lieutenants	Hercules Atkin Welman	16 Mar 1843	Adjutant
	John Cumming	26 July 1844	8 May 1840
	Edward Hardinge	26 July 1844	31 Dec 1841
	Theodore Richard Hickson	26 July 1844	15 July 1843
	George Dean Pitt	26 July 1844	19 Jan 1844
	Charles Duperier	26 July 1844	
	Astell Thomas Welsh	26 July 1844	
	Edward Alan Holdich	26 July 1844	
	George Samuel Young	26 July 1844	
	William Hunter	26 July 1844	
	Wm. Fred. Adams Colman	10 Mar 1845	
	Henry Geo. John Bowler	13 July 1845	
	Benjamin Hallowell Boxer	28 Aug 1845	
	Hon. Arth. E. Hardinge	22 Dec 1845	
	Ed. Wm. Pincke Kingsley	23 Dec 1845	
	Hamilton Charles Smith	24 Dec 1845	

Rank	Name	Regiment	Army
	Walter Butler Charles S. Wandesforde	14 Apr 1846	
	William Calvert Dunn	12 June 1846	3 Apr 1846
	Paul Fred. de Quincey	31 July 1846	
	Robert Clifton Gordon	1 Aug 1846	
	William Deane Freeman	9 Oct	
	Hon. John Howe M. Browne	11 Dec 1846	
Ensigns	Edward Browne Hart	9 Dec 1845	
	Matthew Kirkland	22 Dec 1845	
	Attilio Scheberras	21 Apr 1846	
	Donald Maclean Fraser	8 May 1846	
	Robert Crawford	18 Sept 1846	
	Edward John Mathias	9 Oct	18 Sept 1846
	Thomas Airey	20 Oct	21 Apr 1846
	William Patterson	11 Dec 1846	
Paymaster	Thomas Bloomfield Hunt	1 Aug 1837	Lieut. 25 Oct 1833 Adjutant
	Hercules Atkin Welman	10 Mar 1845	
Quarter-Master	George Bodle	21 May 1847	
Surgeon	Alexander Sheriff Macdonell	2 Dec 1842	
Asst Surgeon	Patrick Gammie	17 June 1836	
	Miah William Murphy	22 July 1842	
	David Stuart Eskine Bain	23 Jan 1846	

Agent, Messrs. Cox and Co.

1848 - 1849

Rank	Name	Regiment	Army
Colonel	Sir Maurice Charles O'Connell KCH	15 Jan 1844	Lt. Gen. 23 Nov 1841
Lieut. Colonel	Thomas Bunbury	26 July 1844	
	Robert Blucher Wood, C.B.	30 Dec 1845	
Majors	Robert Alex. Lockhart	30 Dec 1845	
	Charles Lewis	3 Feb 1847	19 June 1846
Captains	Robert Geroge Hughes	3 Dec 1841	
	Richard Talbot Sayers	16 Mar 1843	
	James Deavers Morris	18 Mar 1843	
	Lambert Lyons Montgomery	28 July 1843	
	Samuel Tolfrey Christie	28 Aug 1845	
	Alexander William Riley	22 Dec 1845	
	Anthony Ormsby	25 Dec 1845	
	Charles Myers Creagh	21 Nov 1846	19 Dec 1845
	Robert Hawkes	13 Aug 1847	11 Oct 1844
	Henry Cricket Tyler	3 Sept	27 June 1845
Lieutenants	John Cumming	26 July 1844	8 May 1840
	Edward Hardinge	26 July 1844	31 Dec 1841
	Theodore Richard Hickson	26 July 1844	15 July 1843
	George Dean Pitt	26 July 1844	19 Jan 1844
	Charles Duperier	26 July 1844	
	Astell Thomas Welsh	26 July 1844	
	Edward Alan Holdich	26 July 1844	
	George Samuel Young	26 July 1844	
	Willia Hunter	26 July 1844	
	Wm. Fred. Adams Colman	10 Mar 1845	
	Henry Geo. John Bowler	13 July 1845	
	Benjamin Hallowell Boxer	28 Aug 1845	
	Hon. Arth. E. Hardinge	22 Dec 1845	
	Ed. Wm. Pincke Kingsley	23 Dec 1845	
	Hamilton Charles Smith	24 Dec 1845	
	Walter Butler Charles S. Wandesforde	14 Apr 1846	
	William Calvert Dunn	12 June 1846	3 Apr 1846
	Paul Fred. de Quincey	31 July 1846	
	William Deane Freeman	9 Oct	
	Robert Cassels Oliphant	30 Nov	
	Hon. John Howe M. Browne	11 Dec 1846	
	George Bodle	21 May 1847	21 Feb 1846 Adjut.
	Attilio Scheberras	21 Jan 1848	
Ensigns	Matthew Kirkland	22 Dec 1845	
	Donald Maclean Fraser	8 May 1846	
	Edward John Mathias	9 Oct	18 Sept 1846
	Thomas Airey	20 Oct	21 Apr 1846
	William Patterson	11 Dec 1846	
	Thomas William Hunt	21 May 1847	
	Jas. Loftus Winniett Nunn	29 Oct	
	Rob. Daniel David Lecky	21 Jan 1848	
Paymaster	Thomas Bloomfield Hunt	1 Aug 1837	Lieut. 25 Oct 1833
Adjutant	George Bodle	21 May 1847	Lieut. 21 Feb 1847
Quarter-Master	George Crawford	21 May 1847	Ens. 18 Sept 1846
Surgeon	Alexander Sheriff Macdonell	2 Dec 1842	
Asst Surgeon }	Miah William Murphy	1 Nov 1844	22 July 1842
	David Stuart Eskine Bain	23 Jan 1846	
	Henry Carr Lucas	2 Mar 1847	

Agent, Messrs. Cox and Co.

1850 - 1851

Rank	Name	Regiment	Army
Colonel	Henry Daubeney, KH	31 Jan 1850	Maj. Gen. 23 Nov 1841
Lieut. Colonel	Robert Blucher Wood, C.B.	30 Dec 1845	
	Charles Lewis	22 Feb 1850	
Majors	Robert Alex. Lockhart	30 Dec 1845	
	Robert Geroge Hughes	22 Feb 1850	
Captains	Richard Talbot Sayers	16 Mar 1843	
	Lambert Lyons Montgomery	28 July 1843	
	Samuel Tolfrey Christie	28 Aug 1845	
	Anthony Ormsby	25 Dec 1845	
	Robert Hawkes	13 Aug 1847	11 Oct 1844
	Edward Hardinge	22 Dec 1848	
	George Dean Pitt	4 May 1849	
	Chas. Fitzgerald Studdert	13 July	4 May 1849
	John Cumming	10 June	
	Edward Alan Holdich	22 Feb 1850	
Lieutenants	Theodore Richard Hickson	26 July 1844	15 July 1843
	Charles Duperier	26 July 1844	
	Astell Thomas Welsh	26 July 1844	

Rank	Name	Regiment	Army
	George Samuel Young	26 July 1844	
	William Hunter	26 July 1844	
	Wm. Fred. Adams Colman	10 Mar 1845	
	Henry Geo. John Bowler	13 July 1845	
	Benjamin Hallowell Boxer	28 Aug 1845	
	Hamilton Charles Smith	24 Dec 1845	
	William Calvert Dunn	12 June 1846	3 Apr 1846
	William Deane Freeman	9 Oct 1846	
	Robert Cassels Oliphant	30 Nov	
	Hon. John Howe M. Browne	11 Dec 1846	
	George Bodle	21 May 1847	21 Feb 1846 Adjut.
	Bliss John Hume	30 June 1848	17 Mar 1848
	Matthew Kirkland	20 Oct	
	Frederick Miller	22 Dec	4 Apr 1846
	Charles Frederick Amiel	22 Dec 1848	25 Sept
	James John Dudgeon	22 Dec 1848	
	George Newton Fendall	4 May 1849	
	Donald Maclean Fraser	10 June 1849	
	Jas. Loftus Winniett Nunn	22 Feb 1850	
	Samuel Head	8 Mar	20 Nov 1848
Ensigns	William Patterson	11 Dec 1846	
	Thomas William Hunt	21 May 1847	
	Rob. Daniel David Lecky	21 Jan 1848	
	George Sullivan	9 Jan 1849	
	John Wilkinson	9 Mar 1849	
	Thomas Prendergast Quill	10 Apr	
	William Whitehead	18 Sept	22 Aug 1849
Paymaster	Thomas Bloomfield Hunt	1 Aug 1837	Lieut. 25 Oct 1833
Adjutant	George Bodle	21 May 1847	Lieut. 21 Feb 1847
Quarter-Master	George Crawford	21 May 1847	Ens. 18 Sept 1846
Surgeon	John Robert Taylor	7 July 1848	14 June 1842
Asst Surgeon }	Miah William Murphy	1 Nov 1844	22 July 1842
	David Stuart Eskine Bain	23 Jan 1846	
	Henry Carr Lucas	2 Mar 1847	

Agent, Messrs. Cox and Co.

1852 - 1853

Rank	Name	Regiment	Army
Colonel	Henry Daubeney, KH	31 Jan 1850	Maj. Gen. 23 Nov 1841
Lieut. Colonel	Robert Blucher Wood, C.B.	30 Dec 1845	
	Charles Lewis	22 Feb 1850	
Majors	Robert Alex. Lockhart	30 Dec 1845	
	Robert Geroge Hughes	22 Feb 1850	
Captains	Richard Talbot Sayers	16 Mar 1843	
	Lambert Lyons Montgomery	28 July 1843	
	Samuel Tolfrey Christie	28 Aug 1845	
	Anthony Ormsby	25 Dec 1845	
	Robert Hawkes	13 Aug 1847	11 Oct 1844
	Edward Hardinge	22 Dec 1848	
	George Dean Pitt	4 May 1849	
	Chas. Fitzgerald Studdert	13 July	4 May 1849
	Edward Alan Holdich	22 Feb 1850	
Lieutenants	Charles Duperier	26 July 1844	
	Astell Thomas Welsh	26 July 1844	
	George Samuel Young	26 July 1844	
	William Gray	26 July 1844	
	Wm. Fred. Adams Colman	10 Mar 1845	
	Henry Geo. John Bowler	13 July 1845	
	Benjamin Hallowell Boxer	28 Aug 1845	
	Hamilton Charles Smith	24 Dec 1845	
	William Deane Freeman	9 Oct 1846	
	Hon. John Howe Montague Browne	11 Dec 1846	
	George Bodle	21 May 1847	21 Feb 1846 Adjut.
	Bliss John Hume	30 June 1848	17 Mar 1848
	Matthew Kirkland	20 Oct	
	Frederick Miller	22 Dec	4 Apr 1846
	Charles Frederick Amiel	22 Dec 1848	25 Sept 1846
	James John Dudgeon	22 Dec 1848	
	Donald Maclean Fraser	10 June 1849	
	Jas. Loftus Winniett Nunn	22 Feb 1850	
	Chas. Henry Theodore Bruce de Ruvignes	2 Apr	2 Nov 1849
	George Sullivan	31 Oct 1851	
	William Patterson	13 Oct 1851	2 Nov 1849
	Rob. Hamilton Montgomerie	13 Jan 1852	4 Apr 1851
Ensigns	Thomas William Hunt	21 May 1847	
	Rob. Daniel David Lecky	21 Jan 1848	
	John Wilkinson	9 Mar 1849	
	Thomas Prendergast Quill	10 Apr	
	William Whitehead	18 Sept	22 Aug 1849
	Fred. Earnest Appleyard	14 June 1850	
	Richard Swift	21 Nov 1851	
	James Tweedie	5 Mar	27 Feb 1852
Paymaster	Thomas Bloomfield Hunt	1 Aug 1837	Lieut. 25 Oct 1833
Adjutant	George Bodle	21 May 1847	Lieut. 21 Feb 1847
Quarter-Master	George Crawford	21 May 1847	Ens. 18 Sept 1846
Surgeon	John Robert Taylor	7 July 1848	14 June 1842
Asst Surgeon }	Miah William Murphy	1 Nov 1844	22 July 1842
	Henry Carr Lucas	2 Mar 1847	

Agent, Messrs. Cox and Co.

1854 - 1855

Rank	Name	Regiment	Army
Colonel	Lawrence Arguimbau, C.B	30 Apr 1853	Maj Gen. 9 Nov 1846
Lieut. Colonel	George Hutchison	2 Apr 1852	7 June 1850
Majors	Lambert Lyons Montgomery	17 Oct 1852	
	Samuel Tolfrey Christie	31 Oct 1852	
Captains	Anthony Ormsby	25 Dec 1845	
	Robert Hawkes	13 Aug 1847	11 Oct 1844
	Edward Hardinge	22 Dec 1848	
	George Dean Pitt	4 May 1849	

	Name	Regiment	Army
	Chas. Fitzgerald Studdert	13 July	4 May 1849
	Edward Alan Holdich C.B.	22 Feb 1850	Lt. Col. 28 May 1853
	Charles Duperier	7 May 1852	
	Benjamin Hallowell Boxer	12 Oct	
	Astell Thomas Welsh	17 Oct	
	George Samuel Young	31 Oct 1852	
	Hamilton Charles Smith	1 May 1853	
Lieutenants	Hon. John Howe Montague Browne	11 Dec 1846	
	Bliss John Hume	30 June 1848	17 Mar 1848
	Frederick Miller	22 Dec	4 Apr 1846
	Charles Frederick Amiel	22 Dec 1848	25 Sept 1846
	James John Dudgeon	22 Dec 1848	
	Donald Maclean Fraser	10 June 1849	
	Jas. Loftus Winniett Nunn	22 Feb 1850	
	Chas. Henry Theodore Bruce de Ruvignes	2 Apr	2 Nov 1849
	William Patterson	13 Oct 1851	2 Nov 1849
	George Sullivan	31 Oct 1851	
	William Whitehead	17 Aug 1852	
	Erasmus Borrowes	1 May 1853	Adjutant
	Thomas Clement Belmore St George	7 Jan 1854	10 Nov 1848
Ensigns	F. Brown Numa Craufurd	21 Sept 1852	21 Sept 1852
	Horatio Pettus Batchelor	23 Nov	
	William Picton Mortimer	24 Nov	
	Thomas Arundell	20 Jan 1854	
Paymaster	George Bodle	8 Apr 1853	Lieut. 21 Feb 1846
Adjutant	Erasmus Borrowes	8 Apr 1853	Ens. 13 Feb 1852
Quarter-Master	Wellington Browne	22 Apr 1853	
Surgeon	Wm. Nelson Irwin	3 Mar 1854	
Agent, Messrs. Cox and Co.			

1856 - 1857

Rank	Name	Regiment	Army
Colonel	Thomas William Robbins	12 Mar 1855	Maj Gen.20 June 1854
Lieut. Colonel	George Hutchison	2 Apr 1852	7 June 1850
Majors	Samuel Tolfrey Christie	31 Oct 1852	
	Anthony Ormsby	28 July 1854	
Captains	Robert Hawkes	13 Aug 1847	11 Oct 1844
	Edward Hardinge	22 Dec 1848	
	George Dean Pitt	4 May 1849	
	Chas. Fitzgerald Studdert	13 July	4 May 1849
	Edward Alan Holdich C.B.	22 Feb 1850	Lt. Col. 28 May 1853
	Astell Thomas Welsh	17 Oct	
	George Samuel Young	31 Oct 1852	
	Hamilton Charles Smith	1 May 1853	
	Hon. John Howe Montague Browne	6 June 1854	
	Bliss John Hume	4 Aug 1854	
	Herbert Morris	24 Nov	
	Frederick Miller	1 Dec 1854	
Lieutenants	Charles Frederick Amiel	22 Dec 1848	25 Sept 1846
	James John Dudgeon	22 Dec 1848	
	Donald Maclean Fraser	10 June 1849	
	James Loftus Winniett Nunn	22 Feb 1850	
	Chas. Henry Theodore Bruce de Ruvignes	2 Apr	2 Nov 1849
	William Patterson	13 Oct 1851	2 Nov 1849
	George Sullivan	31 Oct 1851	
	William Whitehead	17 Aug 1852	
	Erasmus Borrowes	1 May 1853	Adjutant
	Thomas Clement Belmore St. George	27 Jan 1854	10 Nov 1848
	F. Brown Numa Craufurd	6 June 1854	
	Horatio Pettus Batchelor	6 June 1854	
	William Picton Mortimer	11 Aug 1854	
	Henry Hungerford St. Ledger	1 Dec	
	Henry Geo. Pattisson	1 June 1855	
Ensigns	Robert James Maxwell	25 Aug 1854	
	William Gordon Trevor	31 Aug 1854	
	Hugh Broke B. Leveson Gower	1 Sept 1854	
	Frederick FitzClarence Goddard	2 Sept 1854	
	William Beaver B. Christie	13 Oct 1854	
	William Maclean	1 May 1855	
	Samuel George Huskisson	15 May 1855	
	Henry Grattan	15 June	
	Anthony Robert Keogh	27 July	5 July 1855
	George Weir Cosens	2 Oct	
Paymaster	Wellington Browne	1 July 1855	Q-Mr 22 Apr 1853
Adjutant	Erasmus Borrowes	8 Apr 1853	Lieut. 13 Feb 1852
Quarter-Master	William Maloney	23 Oct 1855	
Surgeon	Wm. Nelson Irwin	3 Mar 1854	
Asst Surgeon }	Benjamin Lane	23 July 1852	
	Alfred Hoyte	27 Mar 1855	
Agent, Messrs. Cox and Co.			

1857 - 1858

Rank	Name	Regiment	Army
Colonel	Thomas William Robbins	12 Mar 1855	Maj Gen. 20 June 1854
Lieut. Colonel	George Hutchison	2 Apr 1852	Col. 28 Nov 1854
Majors	Samuel Tolfrey Christie	31 Oct 1852	Lt. Col. 9 Dec 1853
	Anthony Ormsby	28 July 1854	
Captains	Robert Hawkes	13 Aug 1847	Major 16 Dec 1856
	Edward Hardinge	22 Dec 1848	
	George Dean Pitt	4 May 1849	
	Chas. Fitzgerald Studdert	13 July	4 May 1849
	Edward Alan Holdich C.B.	22 Feb 1850	Lt. Col. 28 May 1853
	George Samuel Young	31 Oct 1852	
	Hamilton Charles Smith	1 May 1853	
	Hon. John Howe Montague Browne	6 June 1854	
	Bliss John Hume	4 Aug 1854	
	Herbert Morris	24 Nov	24 June 1853
	Frederick Miller	1 Dec 1854	Major 6 June 1856
	Richard William Woods	22 July 1856	12 Apr 1856
Lieutenants	Charles Frederick Amiel	22 Dec 1848	25 Sept 1846

Rank	Name	Regiment	Army
	James John Dudgeon	22 Dec 1848	
	Donald Maclean Fraser	10 June 1849	
	James Loftus Winniett Nunn	22 Feb 1850	
	George Sullivan	31 Oct 1851	
	William Whitehead	17 Aug 1852	
	Erasmus Borrowes	1 May 1853	Adjutant 10 Nov 1848
	Thomas Clement Belmore St George	27 Jan 1854	
	F. Brown Numa Craufurd	6 June 1854	
	Horatio Pettus Batchelor	6 June 1854	
	William Picton Mortimer	11 Aug 1854	
	Henry Hungerford St. Ledger	1 Dec	
	Henry Geo. Pattisson	1 June 1855	
	Robert James Maxwell	1 Apr 1856	
	John Bennett	22 July	3 Aug 1855
Ensigns	William Gordon Trevor	31 Aug 1854	
	Hugh Broke B. Leveson Gower	1 Sept 1854	
	Frederick FitzClarence Goddard	2 Sept 1854	
	William Beaver B. Christie	13 Oct 1854	
	William Maclean	1 May 1855	
	Samuel George Huskisson	15 May 1855	
	Anthony Robert Keogh	27 July	5 July 1855
	George Weir Cosens	2 Oct	
	Robert Cuninghame Graham	1 Apr 1856	
	Dudley Beaumont	8 July 1856	
	Valentine O'Connor	17 Feb 1857	
Paymaster	Wellington Browne	1 July 1855	Q-Mr 22 Apr 1853
Adjutant	Erasmus Borrowes	8 Apr 1853	Lieut. 13 Feb 1852
Quarter-Master	William Maloney	23 Oct 1855	
Surgeon	Wm. Nelson Irwin	3 Mar 1854	
Asst Surgeon }	Benjamin Lane	23 July 1852	
	Colin Matheson Milne Miller, MD.	18 Apr 1856	7 Nov 1851

Agent, Messrs. Cox and Co.

1859 - 1860

Rank	Name	Regiment	Army
Colonel	Thomas William Robbins	12 Mar 1855	Maj. Gen. 20 June 1854
Lieut. Colonel	George Hutchison	2 Apr 1852	Col. 28 Nov 1854
	Samuel Tolfrey Christie	4 May 1859	
Majors	Anthony Ormsby	28 July 1854	
	Robert Hawkes	5 Mar 1858	
Captains	Edward Hardinge	22 Dec 1848	
	George Dean Pitt	4 May 1849	
	Chas. Fitzgerald Studdert	13 July	4 May 1849
	George Samuel Young	31 Oct 1852	
	Hamilton Charles Smith	1 May 1853	
	Hon. John Howe Montague Browne	6 June 1854	
	Bliss John Hume	4 Aug 1854	
	Herbert Morris	24 Nov	24 June 1853
	Frederick Miller	1 Dec 1854	Major 6 June 1856
	Richard William Woods	22 July 1856	12 Apr 1856
	James Loftus Winniett Nunn	27 Nov 1857	Inst. of Musketry
	Charles Frederick Amiel	5 Mar 1858	
	James John Dudgeon	30 Mar 1858	
Lieutenants	George Sullivan	31 Oct 1851	
	William Whitehead	17 Aug 1852	
	Erasmus Borrowes	1 May 1853	Adjutant
	Fred. Brown Numa Craufurd	6 June 854	
	Horatio Pettus Batchelor	6 June 1854	
	William Picton Mortimer	11 Aug 1854	
	Henry Hungerford St Ledger	1 Dec	
	Henry Geo. Pattisson	1 June 1855	
	Robert James Maxwell	1 Apr 1856	
	John Bennett	22 July	3 Aug 1855
	William Gordon Trevor	27 Nov 1857	
	Hugh Broke B. Leveson Gower	12 Feb 1858	
	Frederick FitzClarence Goddard	5 Mar 1858	
	William Beaver B. Christie	30 Mar 1858	
	William Maclean	30 Mar 1858	
Ensigns	Samuel George Huskisson	15 May 1855	
	George Weir Cosens	2 Oct	
	Robert Cuninghame C. Graham	1 Apr 1856	
	Dudley Beaumont	8 July 1856	
	Valentine O'Connor	17 Feb 1857	
	Henry James Brown	12 Feb 1858	
	Walter Howard	16 Mar 1858	
	Joseph Bramley Ridout	13 Apr 1858	
	Samuel Pollock Muirhead	26 Nov 1858	
	Thomas Bernard Mitchell	19 Feb 1858	
Paymaster	Wellington Browne	1 July 1855	Q-Mr 22 Apr 1853
Instructor of Musketry	James Loftus Winniett Nunn	23 Sept 1857	
Adjutant	Erasmus Borrowes	8 Apr 1853	Lieut. 13 Feb 1852
Quarter-Master	William Maloney	23 Oct 1855	
Surgeon	Wm. Nelson Irwin	3 Mar 1854	
Asst Surgeon }	Colin Matheson Milne Miller, MD	18 Apr 1856	7 Nov 1851
	Philip Frank, M.D.	14 Dec 1854	
	Issac Hoysted	10 Mar 1858	

Agent, Messrs. Cox and Co.

1861 - 1862

Rank	Name	Regiment	Army
Colonel	Thomas William Robbins	12 Mar 1855	Maj. Gen. 20 June 1854
Lieut. Colonel	Samuel Tolfrey Christie	4 May 1859	
	Robert Hawkes	4 May 1859	
Majors	Edward Hardinge	4 May 1859	
	Hamilton Charles Smith	18 Oct 1859	
Captains	George Dean Pitt	4 May 1849	
	George Samuel Young	31 Oct 1852	
	Bliss John Hume	4 Aug 1854	
	Frederick Miller	1 Dec 1854	Major 6 June 1856
	Richard William Woods	22 July 1856	12 Apr 1856

Rank	Name		
	James Loftus Winniett Nunn	27 Nov 1857	Inst. of Musketry
	Charles Frederick Amiel	6 Nov 1858	
	George Sullivan	4 May 1859	
	Robert James Maxwell	18 Oct 1859	
	Henry Rowland	26 Mar 1858	
	William Whitehead	6 June 1860	
	John Wilkinson	13 Dec 1859	
	Charles Tucker	6 Nov 1860	
Lieutenants	Fred. Brown Numa Craufurd	6 June 1854	Adjutant
	William Picton Mortimer	11 Aug 1854	
	William Gordon Trevor	27 Nov 1857	
	Hugh Broke B. Leveson Gower	12 Feb 1858	
	Frederick FitzClarence Goddard	5 Mar 1858	
	William Beaver B. Christie	30 Mar 1858	
	Samuel George Huskisson	1 Jan 1859	
	Alexander Ewing	20 July 1858	
	Charles B. Steward	23 July 1858	
	Dudley Beaumont	4 May 1859	
	Valentine O'Connor	26 Aug 1859	
	Walter Howard	26 Aug 1859	
	Joseph Bramley Ridout	18 Oct 1859	
	Samuel Harrison	25 May 1860	
	Henry James Brown	6 June 1860	
Ensigns	Samuel Pollock Muirhead	26 Nov 1858	
	Thomas Bernard Mitchell	19 Feb 1858	
	Charles George Norris	31 May 1859	
	John Hall Green	1 July 1860	
	Patrick Joseph Cowan	29 July 1859	
	Paul Swinburne	28 Oct 1859	
	William Kelly Westropp	6 Jan 1860	
	Edmond Richard Purcell	12 June 1860	
	John Christopher Robinson	3 July 1860	
	Thomas Theobald Willington	10 July 1860	
Paymaster	Wellington Browne	1 July 1855	Q-Mr 22 Apr 1853
Instructor of Musketry	James Loftus Winniett Nunn	23 Sept 1857	
Adjutant	Fred. Brown Numa Craufurd	21 May 1859	
Quarter-Master	Patrick Sheeran	10 May 1860	22 July 1855
Surgeon	John Alex. Wm. Thompson, M.D.	26 Feb 1856	
Asst Surgeon }	William Jackson	9 Nov 1857	
	James. Inkson, M.D.	19 Oct 1857	
	Richard Muir Gilhurst, M.D.	14 Dec 1858	
Agent, Messrs. Cox and Co.	Irish Agent Sir E. Borough, Bt. and Co.		

1863 - 1864

Rank	Name	Regiment	Army
Colonel	Thomas William Robbins	12 Mar 1855	Maj. Gen. 20 June 1854
Lieut. Colonel	Samuel Tolfrey Christie C.B.	4 May 1859	
	Robert Hawkes	4 May 1859	
Majors	Edward Hardinge	4 May 1859	
	Hamilton Charles Smith	18 Oct 1859	
Captains	George Dean Pitt	4 May 1849	
	Bliss John Hume	4 Aug 1854	
	Frederick Miller	1 Dec 1854	Major 6 June 1856
	James Loftus Winniett Nunn	27 Nov 1857	Inst. of Musketry
	Charles Frederick Amiel	5 Mar 1858	
	George Sullivan	4 May 1859	
	Robert James Maxwell	18 Oct 1859	
	Henry Rowland	26 Mar 1858	
	William Whitehead	6 June 1860	
	John Wilkinson	13 Dec 1859	
	Charles Tucker	6 Nov 1860	
	Charles John Roper Tyler	16 Sept 1860	
	Hugh Broke B. Leveson Gower	4 Mar 1862	
Lieutenants	Fred. Brown Numa Craufurd	6 June 1854	
	William Picton Mortimer	11 Aug 1854	
	William Gordon Trevor	27 Nov 1857	
	Frederick FitzClarence Goddard	5 Mar 1858	
	William Beaver B. Christie	30 Mar 1858	
	Samuel George Huskisson	1 Jan 1859	Adjutant
	Dudley Beaumont	4 May 1859	
	Valentine O'Connor	26 Aug 1859	
	Walter Howard	26 Aug 1859	
	Joseph Bramley Ridout	18 Oct 1859	Inst. of Musketry
	Samuel Harrison	25 May 1860	
	Henry James Brown	6 June 1860	
	Charles George Norris	22 Oct 1861	
	Charles Stuart Wms. Furlong	7 Apr 1862	
	Samuel Pollock Muirhead	1 Aug 1862	
	Paul Swinburne	21 Nov 1862	
Ensigns	Thomas Bernard Michell	19 Feb 1858	
	John Hall Green	1 July 1860	
	William Kelly Westropp	6 Jan 1860	
	Edmond Richard Purcell	12 June 1860	
	John Christopher Robinson	3 July 1860	
	Allan Saunders	23 Aug 1861	
	James McMillan	4 Mar 1862	
	Henry James Barr	10 June 1862	
	John White Tunbull	5 Sept 1862	
	Basil Henry S. Gower	7 Nov 1862	
Paymaster	Wellington Browne	1 July 1855	Q-Mr 22 Apr 1853
Instructor of Musketry	Joseph Bramley Ridout	28 Jan 1861	
Adjutant	Samuel George Huskisson	8 Feb 1862	
Quarter-Master	Patrick Sheeran	10 May 1860	22 July 1855
Surgeon	John Alex. Wm. Thompson, M.D.	26 Feb 1856	
Asst Surgeon }	James.Inkson, M.D.	19 Oct 1857	
	Thomas White, M.D.	19 Jan 1860	
	James B. Baker	28 May 1857	
Agent, Messrs. Cox and Co.	Irish Agent Sir E. Borough, Bt. and Co.		

1865 - 1866

Rank	Name	Regiment	Army
Colonel	James Robert Young	28 Oct 1864	
Lieut. Colonel	Samuel Tolfrey Christie C.B.	4 May 1859	
	Robert Hawkes	4 May 1859	
Majors	Edward Hardinge	4 May 1859	
	Hamilton Charles Smith	18 Oct 1859	
Captains	Bliss John Hume	4 Aug 1854	
	Frederick Miller	1 Dec 1854	Major 6 June 1856
	James Loftus Winniett Nunn	27 Nov 1857	
	Charles Frederick Amiel	5 Mar 1858	
	George Sullivan	4 May 1859	
	Robert James Maxwell	18 Oct 1859	
	Henry Rowland	26 Mar 1858	
	William Whitehead	6 June 1860	
	John Wilkinson	13 Dec 1859	
	Charles Tucker	6 Nov 1860	
	Charles John Roper Tyler	16 Sept 1860	
	Alfred Rob. Ord	22 Apr 1862	
Lieutenants	Fred. Brown Numa Craufurd	6 June 1854	
	William Picton Mortimer	11 Aug 1854	
	William Gordon Trevor	27 Nov 1857	
	Frederick Fitz Clarence Goddard	5 Mar 1858	
	William Beaver B. Christie	30 Mar 1858	
	Samuel George Huskisson	1 Jan 1859	Adjutant
	Dudley Beaumont	4 May 1859	
	Valentine O'Connor	26 Aug 1859	
	Walter Howard	26 Aug 1859	
	Joseph Bramley Ridout	18 Oct 1859	Inst. of Musketry
	Samuel Harrison	25 May 1860	
	Henry James Brown	6 June 1860	
	Charles George Norris	22 Oct 1861	
	Charles Stuart Wms. Furlong	7 Apr 1862	
	Paul Swinburne	21 Nov 1862	
	William Kelly Westropp	14 June 1864	
Ensigns	Thomas Bernard Michell	19 Feb 1858	
	John Hall Green	1 July 1860	
	Edmond Richard Purcell	12 June 1860	
	John Christopher Robinson	3 July 1860	
	Allan Saunders	23 Aug 1861	
	James McMillan	4 Mar 1862	
	Henry James Barr	10 June 1862	
	Basil Henry S. Gower	7 Nov 1862	
	Joseph Renny Macy	14 June 1864	
	Art. Hippisley Smith	5 July 1864	
Paymaster	Wellington Browne	1 July 1855	Q-Mr 22 Apr 1853
Instructor of Musketry	Joseph Bramley Ridout	28 Jan 1861	
Adjutant	Samuel George Huskisson	8 Feb 1862	
Quarter-Master	Patrick Sheeran	10 May 1860	22 July 1855
Surgeon	John Alex. Wm. Thompson, MD	26 Feb 1856	
Asst Surgeon }	James Inkson, M.D.	19 Oct 1857	
	Rich. W. Hare, M.B.	1 Oct 1862	

Agent, Messrs. Alex. F. Ridgeway and Sons.　　　Irish Agent Messrs Cane and Sons.

1867 - 1868

Rank	Name	Regiment	Army
Colonel	James Robert Young	28 Oct 1864	
Lieut. Colonel	Robert Prescott Harrison	9 Nov 1866	
Majors	Hamilton Charles Smith	18 Oct 1859	
	William George Maresson	16 Oct 1866	
Captains	James Loftus Winniett Nunn	27 Nov 1857	
	Charles Frederick Amiel	5 Mar 1858	
	George Sullivan	4 May 1859	
	Robert James Maxwell	18 Oct 1859	
	Henry Rowland	26 Mar 1858	
	William Whitehead	6 June 1860	
	John Wilkinson	13 Dec 1859	
	Charles Tucker	6 Nov 1860	
	Charles John Roper Tyler	16 Sept 1860	
	Alfred Rob. Ord	22 Apr 1862	
	Fred. Brown Numa Craufurd	26 Apr 1865	
Lieutenants	William Picton Mortimer	11 Aug 1854	
	William Gordon Trevor	27 Nov 1857	
	Frederick FitzClarence Goddard	5 Mar 1858	
	William Beaver B. Christie	30 Mar 1858	
	Samuel George Huskisson	1 Jan 1859	Adjutant
	Dudley Beaumont	4 May 1859	
	Valentine O'Connor	26 Aug 1859	
	Walter Howard	26 Aug 1859	
	Joseph Bramley Ridout	18 Oct 1859	Inst. of Musketry
	Henry James Brown	6 June 1860	
	Charles George Norris	22 Oct 1861	
	Charles Stuart Wms. Furlong	7 Apr 1862	
	Paul Swinburne	21 Nov 1862	
	William Kelly Westropp	14 June 1864	
	Wm. H. B. Peters	12 Apr 1864	
Ensigns	Thomas Bernard Michell	19 Feb 1858	
	John Hall Green	1 July 1860	
	Allan Saunders	23 Aug 1861	
	James McMillan	4 Mar 1862	
	Basil Henry S. Gower	7 Nov 1862	
	Arnold S. Wilson	3 Jan 1865	
	James Harmer Alston	18 Feb 1865	
	Wilfred Turner Anderson	4 Aug 1865	
	Newport White	1 June 1864	
	Melville T. Neale	9 Mar 1866	
Paymaster	Wellington Browne	1 July 1855	Q-Mr 22 Apr 1853
Instructor of Musketry	Joseph Bramley Ridout	28 Jan 1861	
Adjutant	Samuel George Huskisson	8 Feb 1862	

Rank	Name		
Quarter-Master	Patrick Sheeran	10 May 1860	22 July 1855
Surgeon	Thomas Wright	20 June 1865	
Asst Surgeon	James Inkson, M.D.	19 Oct 1857	
Agent, Messrs. Alex. F. Ridgeway and Sons.	Irish Agent Messrs Cane and Sons.		

1869

Rank	Name	Regiment	Army
Colonel	Henry John French	3 Sept 1867	
Lieut. Colonel	Robert Prescott Harrison	9 Nov 1866	
Majors	Hamilton Charles Smith	18 Oct 1859	
	William George Maresson	16 Oct 1866	
Captains	James Loftus Winniett Nunn	27 Nov 1857	
	Charles Frederick Amiel	5 Mar 1858	
	Robert James Maxwell	18 Oct 1859	
	Henry Rowland	26 Mar 1858	
	John Wilkinson	13 Dec 1859	
	Charles Tucker	6 Nov 1860	
	Charles John Roper Tyler	16 Sept 1860	
	Fred. Brown Numa Craufurd	26 Apr 1865	
	Fredk. N. Dew	21 Aug 1866	
	Edmund Kerrich	20 Jan 1867	
Lieutenants	William Beaver B. Christie	30 Mar 1858	
	Samuel George Huskisson	1 Jan 1859	Adjutant
	Dudley Beaumont	4 May 1859	
	Valentine O'Connor	26 Aug 1859	
	Walter Howard	26 Aug 1859	
	Joseph Bramley Ridout	18 Oct 1859	Inst. of Musketry
	Henry James Brown	6 June 1860	
	Paul Swinburne	21 Nov 1862	
	Wm. H. B. Peters	12 Apr 1864	
	Allan Saunders	9 Mar 1867	
	L. R. Iltid Thomas	11 Jan 1867	
	James Harmer Alston	14 Oct 1868	
	Wilfred Turner Anderson	14 Oct 1868	
Ensigns	Philip A. M. Pearson	11 Jan 1867	
	John Edward Hale Prior	21 Mar 1868	
	Henry James Johnson	8 July 1868	
	Jas. Fra. Wemys Cox	9 July 1867	
	Edward Gillman	16 Sept 1868	
	Bernard J. P. O'N. Power	17 Sept 1868	
	Richard Cliffe Owen	14 Oct 1868	
	James Ormsby Sherrard	15 Oct 1868	
Paymaster	Henry Dickonson Nightingale	27 June 1868	26 July 1864 Capt. 6 May 1861
Instructor of Musketry	Joseph Bramley Ridout	28 Jan 1861	
Adjutant	Samuel George Huskisson	8 Feb 1862	
Quarter-Master	John Belts	25 Sept 1867	
Surgeon	Ralph Robert Scott	9 Mar 1867	
Asst Surgeon	Jonas Richard Leake	1 Oct 1867	
Agent, Messrs. Cox and Co.	Irish Agent Messrs Cane and Sons.		

1870

Rank	Name	Regiment	Army
Colonel	Henry John French	3 Sept 1867	
Lieut. Colonel	Robert Prescott Harrison	9 Nov 1866	
Majors	Hamilton Charles Smith	18 Oct 1859	
	William George Maresson	16 Oct 1866	
Captains	James Loftus Winniett Nunn	27 Nov 1857	
	Charles Frederick Amiel	5 Mar 1858	
	Robert James Maxwell	18 Oct 1859	
	Henry Rowland	26 Mar 1858	
	John Wilkinson	13 Dec 1859	
	Charles Tucker	6 Nov 1860	
	Charles John Roper Tyler	16 Sept 1860	
	Fred. Brown Numa Craufurd	26 Apr 1865	
	Frederick Napleton Dew	21 Aug 1866	
	Edmund Kerrich	20 Jan 1867	
Lieutenants	William Beaver B. Christie	30 Mar 1858	
	Samuel George Huskisson	1 Jan 1859	Adjutant
	Dudley Beaumont	4 May 1859	
	Valentine O'Connor	26 Aug 1859	
	Walter Howard	26 Aug 1859	
	Joseph Bramley Ridout	18 Oct 1859	Inst. of Musketry
	Henry James Brown	6 June 1860	
	Paul Swinburne	21 Nov 1862	
	Allan Saunders	9 Mar 1867	
	James Harmer Alston	14 Oct 1868	
	Wilfred Turner Anderson	14 Oct 1868	
	Philip Ashby Mettam Pearson	10 Feb 1869	
	William Rowland McKay	3 Apr 1869	
Ensigns	John Edward Hale Prior	21 Mar 1868	
	Henry James Johnson	8 July 1868	
	Jas. Fra. Wemys Cox	9 July 1867	
	Edward Gillman	16 Sept 1868	
	Bernard J. P. O'N. Power	17 Sept 1868	
	Richard Cliffe Owen	14 Oct 1868	
	James Ormsby Sherrard	15 Oct 1868	
	Lipton Cumming Potts	17 Mar 1869	
Paymaster	Henry Dickonson Nightingale	27 June 1868	26 July 1864 Capt. 6 May 1861
Instructor of Musketry	Joseph Bramley Ridout	28 Jan 1861	
Adjutant	Samuel George Huskisson	8 Feb 1862	
Quarter-Master	John Belt	25 Sept 1867	
Surgeon	Ralph Robert Scott	9 Mar 1867	
Asst Surgeon	Jonas Richard Leake	1 Oct 1867	
Agent, Messrs. Cox and Co.	Irish Agent Messrs Cane and Sons.		

1871

Rank	Name	Regiment	Army
Colonel	Henry John French	3 Sept 1867	
Lieut. Colonel	Robert Prescott Harrison	9 Nov 1866	
Majors	Hamilton Charles Smith	18 Oct 1859	
	James Loftus Winniett Nunn	27 Apr 1870	

Captains	Charles Frederick Amiel	5 Mar 1858	
	Robert James Maxwell	18 Oct 1859	
	Henry Rowland	26 Mar 1858	
	John Wilkinson	13 Dec 1859	
	Charles Tucker	6 Nov 1860	
	Charles John Roper Tyler	16 Sept 1860	
	Fred. Brown Numa Craufurd	26 Apr 1865	
	Frederick Napleton Dew	21 Aug 1866	
	Edmund Kerrich	20 Jan 1867	
	James Birney	22 June 1870	
Lieutenants	Samuel George Huskisson	1 Jan 1859	Adjutant
	Walter Howard	26 Aug 1859	
	Joseph Bramley Ridout	18 Oct 1859	Inst. of Musketry
	Henry James Brown	6 June 1860	
	Paul Swinburne	21 Nov 1862	
	Allan Saunders	9 Mar 1867	
	James Harmer Alston	14 Oct 1868	
	Wilfred Turner Anderson	14 Oct 1868	
	Henry William Rudkin	16 Oct 1867	
	Philip Ashby Mettam Pearson	10 Feb 1869	
	John George Kirkpatrick Young	22 June 1870	
Ensigns	John Edward Hale Prior	21 Mar 1868	
	Henry James Johnson	8 July 1868	
	Edward Gillman	16 Sept 1868	
	Bernard J. P. O'N. Power	17 Sept 1868	
	Richard Cliffe Owen	14 Oct 1868	
	James Ormsby Sherrard	15 Oct 1868	
	Lipton Cumming Potts	17 Mar 1869	
Paymaster	Henry Dickonson Nightingale	27 June 1868	26 July 1864 Capt. 6 May 1861
Instructor of Musketry	Joseph Bramley Ridout	28 Jan 1861	
Adjutant	Samuel George Huskisson	8 Feb 1862	
Quarter-Master	John Belt	25 Sept 1867	
Surgeon	Ralph Robert Scott	9 Mar 1867	
Asst Surgeon	Jonas Richard Leake	1 Oct 1867	
Agent, Messrs. Cox and Co.	Irish Agent Messrs Cane and Sons.		

1872

Rank	Name	Regiment	Army
Colonel	Henry John French	3 Sept 1867	
Lieut. Colonel	Robert Prescott Harrison	9 Nov 1866	
Majors	Hamilton Charles Smith	18 Oct 1859	
	George Henry Twemlow	10 May 1871	
Captains	Charles Frederick Amiel	5 Mar 1858	
	Robert James Maxwell	18 Oct 1859	
	Henry Rowland	26 Mar 1858	
	John Wilkinson	13 Dec 1859	
	Charles Tucker	6 Nov 1860	
	Charles John Roper Tyler	16 Sept 1860	
	Fred. Brown Numa Craufurd	26 Apr 1865	
	James Birney	22 June 1870	
	Charles Augustus FItzGerald Creagh	14 Jan 1871	
	James Lewis Bradshaw	28 Oct 1868	
Lieutenants	Samuel George Huskisson	1 Jan 1859	Adjutant
	Walter Howard	26 Aug 1859	
	Joseph Bramley Ridout	18 Oct 1859	
	Henry James Brown	6 June 1860	
	Paul Swinburne	21 Nov 1862	
	Allan Saunders	9 Mar 1867	Inst. of Musketry
	James Harmer Alston	14 Oct 1868	
	Wilfred Turner Anderson	14 Oct 1868	
	Henry William Rudkin	16 Oct 1867	
	John George Kirkpatrick Young	22 June 1870	
	John Edward Hale Prior	30 Aug 1871	
	Charles Christopher Cole	22 Mar 1871	
Ensigns	Henry James Johnson	8 July 1868	
	Edward Gillman	16 Sept 1868	
	James Ormsby Sherrard	15 Oct 1868	
	Lipton Cumming Potts	17 Mar 1869	
Paymaster	Hillier Givins	10 May 1871	Lieut. 11 June 1861
Instructor of Musketry	Allan Saunders	30 Aug 1871	
Adjutant	Samuel George Huskisson	8 Feb 1862	
Quarter-Master	John Belt	25 Sept 1867	
Surgeon	D. C. McFall	23 Dec 1871	
Asst Surgeon	Jonas Richard Leake	1 Oct 1867	
Agent, Messrs. Cox and Co.	Irish Agent Messrs Cane and Sons		

1873

Rank	Name	Regiment	Army
Colonel	Henry John French	3 Sept 1867	
Lieut. Colonel	Hamilton Charles Smith	10 Jan 1872	
Majors	George Henry Twemlow	10 May 1871	
	Charles Frederick Amiel	10 Jan 1872	
Captains	Robert James Maxwell	18 Oct 1859	
	Henry Rowland	26 Mar 1858	
	John Wilkinson	13 Dec 1859	
	Charles Tucker	6 Nov 1860	
	Charles John Roper Tyler	16 Sept 1860	
	Fred. Brown Numa Craufurd	26 Apr 1865	
	Charles Augustus FitzGerald Creagh	14 Jan 1871	
	James Lewis Bradshaw	28 Oct 1868	
	Samuel George Huskisson	10 Jan 1872	
	Robert Warner Stone	17 Nov 1863	
Lieutenants	Walter Howard	26 Aug 1859	
	Joseph Bramley Ridout	18 Oct 1859	
	Henry James Brown		
	Paul Swinburne	21 Nov 1862	
	Allan Saunders	9 Mar 1867	Adjutant
	Wilfred Turner Anderson	14 Oct 1868	
	John George Kirkpatrick Young	22 June 1870	Inst. of Musketry
	John Edward Hale Prior	30 Aug 1871	

	Charles Christopher Cole	22 Mar 1871
	Henry James Johnson	28 Oct 1871
	James Ormsby Sherrard	28 Oct 1871
	Lipton Cumming Potts	28 Oct 1871
	Edward H. B. O'Geran	12 July 1867
	Samuel Lang	4 Dec 1866
Ensigns	Saumarez William Cameron	17 Jan 1872
	George Blakemore Robbins	3 Feb 1872
	Godfrey Fox Webster	3 Feb 1872
	Legh Hoskins Master	14 Feb 1872
	C. G.Mackellar	26 June 1872
Instructor of Musketry	John George Kirkpatrick Young	19 Mar 1872
Adjutant	Allan Saunders	19 Mar 1872
Quarter-Master	John Belt	25 Sept 1867
Med. Off. Surgeon-Major	D. C. McFall	23 Dec 1871
Asst Surgeon }	J. Murray, M.B.	30 Sept 1864
	B. Cruickshank, M.B.	1 Apr 1871
Agent, Messrs. Cox and Co.	Irish Agent Messrs Cane and Sons.	

1874 - 1875

Rank	Name	Regiment	Army
Colonel	Charles Crutchley	26 Jan 1874	
Lieut. Colonel	Hamilton Charles Smith	10 Jan 1872	
Majors	George Henry Twemlow	10 May 1871	
	Charles Frederick Amiel	10 Jan 1872	
Captains	Henry Rowland	26 Mar 1858	
	Charles Tucker	6 Nov 1860	
	Charles John Roper Tyler	16 Sept 1860	
	Fred. Brown Numa Craufurd	26 Apr 1865	
	Charles Augustus FitzGerald Creagh	14 Jan 1871	
	James Lewis Bradshaw	28 Oct 1868	
	Samuel George Huskisson	10 Jan 1872	
	Robert Warner Stone	17 Nov 1863	
	Walter Howard	10 Dec 1873	
	Fredk. Blair Staples	26 July 1866	
Lieutenants	Henry James Brown	6 June 1860	
	Paul Swinburne	21 Nov 1862	
	Allan Saunders	9 Mar 1867	Adjutant
	Wilfred Turner Anderson	14 Oct 1868	
	John George Kirkpatrick Young	22 June 1870	Inst. of Musketry
	John Edward Hale Prior	30 Aug 1871	
	Charles Christopher Cole	22 Mar 1871	
	Henry James Johnson	28 Oct 1871	
	James Ormsby Sherrard	28 Oct 1871	
	Lipton Cumming Potts	28 Oct 1871	
	Edward H. B. O'Geran	12 July 1867	
	William H. Walmisley	28 Oct 1871	
	Tankerville James Chamberlain	18 Oct 1873	
	Henry Hollingworth Harward	13 May 1874	
Ensigns	Saumarez William Cameron	17 Jan 1872	
	Otway Mayne	28 Feb 1874	
	Arthur Wellesley Hast	28 Feb 1874	
	Archibald Borthwick Horsbrugh	28 Feb 1874	
	Legh Hoskins Master	14 Feb 1872	
	William Moore	28 Feb 1874	
Instructor of Musketry	John George Kirkpatrick Young	19 Mar 1872	
Adjutant	Allan Saunders	19 Mar 1872	
Quarter-Master	John Belt	25 Sept 1867	
Med. Off. Surgeon-Major	D. C. McFall	23 Dec 1871	
Agent, Messrs. Cox and Co.	Irish Agent Messrs Cane and Sons.		

1876

Rank	Name	Regiment	Army
Colonel	Sir Richard Wilbraham, KC.B	16 Mar 1875	
Lieut. Colonel	Hamilton Charles Smith	10 Jan 1872	
Majors	George Henry Twemlow	10 May 1871	
	Charles Frederick Amiel	10 Jan 1872	
Captains	Henry Rowland	26 Mar 1858	
	Charles Tucker	6 Nov 1860	
	Charles John Roper Tyler	16 Sept 1860	
	Fred. Brown Numa Craufurd	26 Apr 1865	
	Charles Augustus FitzGerald Creagh	14 Jan 1871	
	James Lewis Bradshaw	28 Oct 1868	
	Samuel George Huskisson	10 Jan 1872	
	Robert Warner Stone	17 Nov 1863	
	Walter Howard	10 Dec 1873	
	Henry James Brown	23 June 1875	
Lieutenants	Paul Swinburne	21 Nov 1862	
	Allan Saunders	9 Mar 1867	Adjutant
	Wilfred Turner Anderson	14 Oct 1868	
	John Edward Hale Prior	30 Aug 1871	
	Charles Christopher Cole	22 Mar 1871	
	Henry James Johnson	28 Oct 1871	Inst. of Musketry
	James Ormsby Sherrard	28 Oct 1871	
	Lipton Cumming Potts	28 Oct 1871	
	William H. Walmisley	28 Oct 1871	
	Tankerville James Chamberlain	18 Oct 1873	
	Saumarez William Cameron	17 Jan 1874	
	Henry Hollingworth Harward	13 May 1874	
Ensigns	Otway Mayne	28 Feb 1874	
	Arthur Wellesley Hast	28 Feb 1874	
	Archibald Borthwick Horsbrugh	28 Feb 1874	
	William Moore	28 Feb 1874	
	Henry Charles Savage	13 June 1874	
Instructor of Musketry	Henry James Johnson	5 Nov 1874	
Adjutant	Allan Saunders	19 Mar 1872	
Quarter-Master	John Belt	25 Sept 1867	
Med. Off. Surgeon-Major	D. C. McFall	23 Dec 1871	
Agent, Messrs. Cox and Co.	Irish Agent Messrs. Sir. E. R. Borough, Bt.		

1877

Rank	Name	Regiment	Army
Colonel	Sir Richard Wilbraham, KC.B	16 Mar 1875	
Lieut. Colonel	Hamilton Charles Smith	10 Jan 1872	
Majors	George Henry Twemlow	10 May 1871	
	Charles Frederick Amiel	10 Jan 1872	
Captains	Henry Rowland	26 Mar 1858	
	Charles Tucker	6 Nov 1860	
	Charles John Roper Tyler	16 Sept 1860	
	Fred. Brown Numa Craufurd	26 Apr 1865	
	Charles Augustus FitzGerald Creagh	14 Jan 1871	
	James Lewis Bradshaw	28 Oct 1868	
	Samuel George Huskisson	10 Jan 1872	
	Robert Warner Stone	17 Nov 1863	
	Walter Howard	10 Dec 1873	
	David Barry Moriarty	6 Jan 1876	
	Charles Edward Whitaker Roworth	17 Dec 1875	
Lieutenants	Paul Swinburne	21 Nov 1862	
	Allan Saunders	9 Mar 1867	Adjutant
	Wilfred Turner Anderson	14 Oct 1868	
	John Edward Hale Prior	30 Aug 1871	
	Charles Christopher Cole	22 Mar 1871	
	Henry James Johnson	28 Oct 1871	Inst. of Musketry
	James Ormsby Sherrard	28 Oct 1871	
	Lipton Cumming Potts	28 Oct 1871	
	Tankerville James Chamberlain	18 Oct 1873	
	Saumarez William Cameron	17 Jan 1874	
	Arthur Wellesley Hast	28 Feb 1874	
	Henry Hollingworth Harward	13 May 1874	
	Henry Charles Savage	13 June 1874	
Ensigns	Otway Mayne	28 Feb 1874	
	Archibald Borthwick Horsbrugh	28 Feb 1874	
	William Moore	28 Feb 1874	
	Thomas Edward Griffin	31 May 1876	
Instructor of Musketry	Henry James Johnson	5 Nov 1874	
Adjutant	Allan Saunders	19 Mar 1872	
Quarter-Master	John Belt	25 Sept 1867	
Agent, Messrs. Cox and Co.	Irish Agent Messrs. Sir E. R. Borough, Bt.		

1878

Rank	Name	Regiment	Army
Colonel	Sir Richard Wilbraham, KC.B	16 Mar 1875	
Lieut. Colonel			
Majors	Charles Frederick Amiel	10 Jan 1872	
	Henry Rowland	5 May 1877	
Captains	Charles Tucker	6 Nov 1860	
	Charles John Roper Tyler	16 Sept 1860	
	Fred. Brown Numa Craufurd	26 Apr 1865	
	Charles Augustus FitzGerald Creagh	14 Jan 1871	
	James Lewis Bradshaw	28 Oct 1868	
	Samuel George Huskisson	10 Jan 1872	
	Robert Warner Stone	17 Nov 1863	
	Walter Howard	10 Dec 1873	
	David Barry Moriarty	6 Jan 1876	
	Charles Edward Whitaker Roworth	17 Dec 1875	
	Paul Swinburne	5 May 1877	
	Allan Saunders	5 May 1877	
Lieutenants	Wilfred Turner Anderson	14 Oct 1868	
	John Edward Hale Prior	30 Aug 1871	
	Henry James Johnson	28 Oct 1871	Inst. of Musketry
	James Ormsby Sherrard	28 Oct 1871	
	Charles Christopher Cole	22 Mar 1871	
	Lipton Cumming Potts	28 Oct 1871	
	Tankerville James Chamberlain	18 Oct 1873	
	Saumarez William Cameron	17 Jan 1874	
	Arthur Wellesley Hast	28 Feb 1874	
	Archibald Borthwick Horsbrugh	28 Feb 1874	
	William Moore	28 Feb 1874	
	Henry Hollingworth Harward	13 May 1874	
	Henry Charles Savage	13 June 1874	
	Thomas Edward Griffin	31 May 1876	
Instructor of Musketry	Henry James Johnson	5 Nov 1874	
Quarter-Master	John Belt	25 Sept 1867	
Agent, Messrs. Cox and Co.	Irish Agent Messrs. Sir E. R. Borough, Bt.		

1879

Rank	Name	Regiment	Army
Colonel	Sir Richard Wilbraham, KC.B	16 Mar 1875	
Lieut. Colonel	Charles Frederick Amiel	9 Nov 1877	
Majors	Charles Tucker	9 Nov 1877	
	Charles John Roper Tyler	18 Nov 1877	
Captains	Fred. Brown Numa Craufurd	26 Apr 1865	
	Charles Augustus FitzGerald Creagh	14 Jan 1876	
	James Lewis Bradshaw	28 Oct 1868	
	Samuel George Huskisson	10 Jan 1872	
	Robert Warner Stone	17 Nov 1863	
	Walter Howard	10 Dec 1873	
	David Barry Moriarty	6 Jan 1876	
	Charles Edward Whitaker Roworth	17 Dec 1875	
	Paul Swinburne	5 May 1877	
	Allan Saunders	5 May 1877	
	Wilfred Turner Anderson	9 Nov 1877	
	John Edward Hale Prior	18 Nov 1877	
Lieutenants	Henry James Johnson	28 Oct 1871	Inst. of Musketry
	James Ormsby Sherrard	28 Oct 1871	
	Charles Christopher Cole	22 Mar 1871	
	Lipton Cumming Potts	28 Oct 1871	
	Tankerville James Chamberlain	18 Oct 1873	
	Saumarez William Cameron	17 Jan 1874	
	Arthur Wellesley Hast	28 Feb 1874	

Colours, Battle Honours and Medals of a Staffordshire Regiment

	Archibald Borthwick Horsbrugh	28 Feb 1874	
	William Moore	28 Feb 1874	
	Henry Hollingworth Harward	13 May 1874	
	Henry Charles Savage	13 June 1874	
	Thomas Edward Griffin	31 May 1876	Adjutant
Ensigns	Alfred Henry Lindop	2 Feb 1878	
	Frederick William Lyons	16 Feb 1878	
	Herbert Aveling Raitt	27 Mar 1878	
	Edward Kaye Daubeney	11 May 1878	
	Beverley William Reid Ussher	12 June 1878	
	Francis Macleod Hastings Marshall	11 May 1878	
Paymaster			
Instructor of Musketry	Henry James Johnson	5 Nov 1874	
Adjutant	Thomas Edward Griffin	10 May 1878	
Quarter-Master	James Pendery	30 Oct 1878	
Agent, Messrs. Cox and Co.	Irish Agent Messrs. Sir E. R. Borough, Bt.		

1880

Rank	Name	Regiment	Army
Colonel	Sir Richard Wilbraham, KC.B	16 Mar 1875	
Lieut. Colonel	Charles Tucker, C.B.	9 July 1879	
Majors	Charles Augustus FitzGerald Creagh	9 July 1879	
	James Lewis Bradshaw	15 Nov 1879	
Captains	Fred. Brown Numa Craufurd	26 Apr 1865	
	Robert Warner Stone	17 Nov 1863	
	Walter Howard	10 Dec 1873	
	Charles Edward Whitaker Roworth	17 Dec 1875	
	Paul Swinburne	5 May 1877	
	Allan Saunders	5 May 1877	
	Wilfred Turner Anderson	9 Nov 1877	
	John Edward Hale Prior	18 Nov 1877	
	Henry James Johnson	13 Mar 1879	
	James Ormsby Sherrard	28 Mar 1879	
	Charles Christopher Cole	13 May 1879	
	Lipton Cumming Potts	9 July 1879	
Lieutenants	Tankerville James Chamberlain	18 Oct 1873	
	Saumarez William Cameron	17 Jan 1874	
	Arthur Wellesley Hast	28 Feb 1874	
	Archibald Borthwick Horsbrugh	28 Feb 1874	
	William Moore	28 Feb 1874	
	Henry Hollingworth Harward	13 May 1874	
	Henry Charles Savage	13 June 1874	
	Thomas Edward Griffin	31 May 1876	Adjutant
	Alfred Henry Lindop	28 Mar 1879	
	Frederick William Lyons	17 May 1879	
	Herbert Aveling Raitt	9 July 1879	
2nd Lieutenants	Edward Kaye Daubeney	11 May 1878	
	Beverley William Reid Ussher	12 June 1878	
	Francis Macleod Hastings Marshall	11 May 1878	
	George Albanus Williams	22 Jan 1879	
	Richard P. Columb	23 July 1879	
	Randal W. Johnston	13 Aug 1879	
Instructor of Musketry			
Adjutant	Thomas Edward Griffin	10 May 1878	
Quarter-Master	James Pendery	30 Oct 1878	
Agent, Messrs. Cox and Co.			

1881

Rank	Name	Regiment	Army
Colonel	Sir Richard Wilbraham, KC.B	16 Mar 1875	
Lieut. Colonel	Charles Tucker, C.B.	9 July 1879	
Majors	Charles Augustus Fitzgerald Creagh	9 July 1879	
	James Lewis Bradshaw	15 Nov 1879	
Captains	Fred. Brown Numa Craufurd	26 Apr 1865	
	Robert Warner Stone	17 Nov 1863	
	Charles Edward Whitaker Roworth	17 Dec 1875	
	Allan Saunders	5 May 1877	
	Wilfred Turner Anderson	9 Nov 1877	
	John Edward Hale Prior	18 Nov 1877	
	Henry James Johnson	13 Mar 1879	
	James Ormsby Sherrard	28 Mar 1879	
	Charles Christopher Cole	13 May 1879	
	Lipton Cumming Potts	9 July 1879	
Lieutenants	Tankerville James Chamberlain	18 Oct 1873	
	Saumarez William Cameron	17 Jan 1874	
	Arthur Wellesley Hast	28 Feb 1874	
	Archibald Borthwick Horsbrugh	28 Feb 1874	
	William Moore	28 Feb 1874	
	Henry Charles Savage	13 June 1874	Inst. of Musketry
	Frederick William Lyons	17 May 1879	
	Herbert Aveling Raitt	9 July 1879	
	John Fane Charles Hamilton	24 Jan 1880	
	Claude Grenville Way	10 Oct 1878	
2nd Lieutenants	Edward Kaye Daubeney	11 May 1878	
	Beverley William Reid Ussher	12 June 1878	
	Francis Macleod Hastings Marshall	11 May 1878	
	George Albanus Williams	22 Jan 1879	
	Harry Warry Steward	23 Oct 1880	
Paymaster	William Howard		Hon Capt. (Paym. A. Pay Dep.)
Instructor of Musketry	Henry Charles Savage	5 Oct 1880	
Quarter-Master	James Pendery	30 Oct 1878	
Agent, Messrs. Cox and Co.			

APPENDIX B
BATTLE HONOURS OF THE STAFFORDSHIRE REGIMENT AND ITS ANTECEDENTS

The history of the Staffordshire Regiment goes back nearly 300 years. The first two of the Regiment's two hundred and five battle honours were awarded to both the 38th and 64th Regiments of Foot for their actions at Guadaloupe in 1759. The latest two were awarded to The Staffordshire Regiment (The Prince of Wales's) for taking part in the Gulf War, the battle honours 'Gulf 1991' and 'Wadi al Batin'.

The following numbers of battle honours were awarded to each of the regiments.

38th Regiment of Foot	18
80th Regiment of Foot	7
The South Staffordshire Regiment	82
64th Regiment of Foot	9
98th Regiment of Foot	2
The North Staffordshire Regiment	85
The Staffordshire Regiment -	2

38th REGIMENT OF FOOT 1751 - 1781

GUADELOUPE 1759
MARTINIQUE 1762

38th REGIMENT OF FOOT (1st STAFFORDSHIRE) 1782 -1880

MONTE VIDEO	SALAMANCA	INKERMAN
ROLICA	VITTORIA	SEVASTOPOL
VIMIERA	ST. SEBASTIAN	AVA
CORRUNNA	NIVE	LUCKNOW
BUSACO	PENNINSULA	
BADAJOZ	ALMA	

80th REGIMENT OF FOOT (STAFFORDSHIRE VOLUNTEERS) 1793 - 1880

EGYPT	FEROZESHAH	CENTRAL INDIA
(The sphinx superscribed 'Egypt')	SOBRAON	SOUTH AFRICA 1878/79
MOODKEE	PEGU	

THE SOUTH STAFFORDSHIRE REGIMENT 1881 - 1959

EGYPT 1882	ARRAS 1917	HINDENBURG LINE
KIRBEKAN	SCARPE 1917	HAVRINCOURT
NILE 1884-85	ARLEUX	CANAL DU NORD
SOUTH AFRICA 1900-02	BULLECOURT	ST. QUENTIN CANAL
MONS	HILL 70	BEAUREVOIR
RETREAT FROM MONS	MESSINES 1917	CAMBRAI 1918
MARNE 1914	YPRES 1917	SELLE
AISNE 1914	LANGEMARCH 1917	SAMBRE
YPRES 1914	MENIN ROAD	EGYPT 1916
LANGEMARCK 1914	POLYGON WOOD	SULVA
GHELUVELT	BROODSEINDE	LANDING AT SULVA
NONNE BOSSCHEN	POELCAPPELLE	SCIMITAR HILL
FRANCE & FLANDERS 1914-18	PASSCHENDAELE	GALLIPOLI 1915
NEUVE CHAPELLE	CAMBRAI 1917	PIAVE
AUBERS	SOMME 1918	VITTORIO VENETO
FESTUBERT 1915	ST. QUENTIN	ITALY 1917-18
LOOS	BAPAUME 1918	NORTH WEST EUROPE 1940, '45
SOMME 1916	LYS	CAEN
ALBERT 1916	MESSINES 1918	NOYERS
BAZENTIN	BAILLEUL	FALAISE
DELVILLE WOOD	KEMMEL	ARNHEM 1944
POZEIERS	SCHERPENBERG	SIDI BARRANI
FLERS-COURCELETTE	AISNE 1918	NORTH AFRICA 1940
MORVAL	ALBERT 1918	LANDING IN SICILY
THIEPVAL	ARRAS 1918	SICILY 1943
ANCRE 1916	SCARPE 1918	ITALY 1943
BAPAUME 1917	DROCOURT-QUEANT	CHINDITS 1944
		BURMA 1944

64th REGIMENT OF FOOT (2nd STAFFORDSHIRE) 1758-1880

GUADALOUPE 1759	SURINAM	KOOSH-AB
MARTINIQUE 1794	RESHIRE	PERSIA
ST LUCIA 1803	BUSHIRE	LUCKNOW

98th REGIMENT OF FOOT 1824-1875

CHINA (The Dragon superscribed 'China')
PUNJAUB

THE NORTH STAFFORDSHIRE REGIMENT 1881-1919

HAFIR	MENIN ROAD	BEAUREVOIR
SOUTH AFRICA 1901-02	POLYGON WOOD	CAMBRAI 1918
AISNE	BROODSEINDE	YPRES 1918
ARMENTIERES 1914	POELCAPPELLE	COURTRAI
FRANCE & FLANDERS 1914-18	PASSCHENDAELE	SELLE
LOOS	CAMBRAI 1917	VALENCIENNES
SOMME 1916	SOMME 1918	SAMBRE
ALBERT 1916	ST. QUENTIN	EGYPT 1916
BAZENTIN	BAPAUME 1918	TIGIS 1916
DELVILLE WOOD	ROSIERES	KUT AL AMARA 1917
POZIERES	AVRE	BAGHDAD
GUILLEMONT	LYS	MESOPOTAMIA 1916-18
ANCRE HEIGHTS	MESSINES 1918	BAKU
ANCRE 1916	BAILLEUL	PERSIA 1918
ARRAS 1917	KEMMEL	SULVA
SCARPE 1917	AISNE 1918	SARI BAIR
ARLEUX	ALBERT 1918	GALLIPOLI 1915-16
MESSINES 1917	HINDENBURG LINE	N W FRONTIER, INDIA 1915
YPRES 1917	HAVINCOURT	AFGHANISTAN 1919
PILCKEM	CANAL DU NORT	
LANGEMARCK 1917	ST. QUENTIN CANAL	

THE NORTH STAFFORDSHIRE REGIMENT (THE PRINCE OF WALES'S) 1920-1959

DYLE	MONT PINCON	ANZIO
DEFENCE OF ESCAUT	BRIEUX BRIDGEHEAD	ROME
YPRES-COMINES CANAL	DJEBEL KESSKISS	ADVANCE TO TIBER
NORTH WEST EUROPE 1940'44	MEDJEZ PLAIN	GOTHIC LINE
CAEN	GUERIAT EL ATACH RIDGE	MARRADI
NOYERS	NORTH AFRICA 1943	ITALY 1944-45
		BURMA 1943

NB The following Battle Honours were also awarded to the North Staffordshire Regiment as well as to other Regiments during the Second World War 1939-1945, they do not appear on any 'Colours' :-

NORTH WEST EUROPE 1944-1945	GAB GAB GAP	ITALY 1943-45
ORNE	CARROCETTO	

THE STAFFORDSHIRE REGIMENT (THE PRINCE OF WALES'S) 1959 -

GULF 1991	WADI AL BATIN